We dedicate this book to our brothers who lost their lives in the earthquake that affected 10 provinces in Turkey in February 2023, their relatives, their immortal memories, and the heroes who struggled to get our people out of the rubble.

We will never forget you, we will not make you forget...

Editorial Advisory Board

Bankruptcy and Reorganization in the Digital Business Era

Fahri Özsungur
Mersin University, Turkey

Nevzat Tetik
Inonu University, Turkey

Ersin Kanat
Zonguldak Bulent Ecevit University, Turkey

IGI Global
PUBLISHER of TIMELY KNOWLEDGE

A volume in the Advances in Business Strategy and Competitive Advantage (ABSCA) Book Series

Published in the United States of America by
IGI Global
Business Science Reference (an imprint of IGI Global)
701 E. Chocolate Avenue
Hershey PA, USA 17033
Tel: 717-533-8845
Fax: 717-533-8661
E-mail: cust@igi-global.com
Web site: http://www.igi-global.com

Library of Congress Cataloging-in-Publication Data

Names: Özsungur, Fahri, 1981- editor. | Tetik, Nevzat, 1970- editor. | Kanat, Ersin, 1982- editor.
Title: Bankruptcy and reorganization in the digital business era / Fahri Özsungur, Nevzat Tetik, and Ersin Kanat, editor.
Description: Hershey, PA : Business Science Reference, [2023] | Includes bibliographical references and index. | Summary: "With businesses all over the world being affected to varying degrees by the negative economic effects of the COVID-19 pandemic and the financial crises, this book offers an examination of the basic structure of the arrangement of bankruptcy in various countries and the evaluation of the financial results on the enterprises that have declared the arrangement of bankruptcy"-- Provided by publisher.
Identifiers: LCCN 2022027244 (print) | LCCN 2022027245 (ebook) | ISBN 9781668451816 (hardcover) | ISBN 9781668451823 (ebook)
Subjects: LCSH: Bankruptcy--Case studies. | Corporate reorganizations--Case studies. | Risk management--Case studies.
Classification: LCC HG3761 .H36 2023 (print) | LCC HG3761 (ebook) | DDC 332.7/5--dc23/eng/20220803
LC record available at https://lccn.loc.gov/2022027244
LC ebook record available at https://lccn.loc.gov/2022027245

This book is published in the IGI Global book series Advances in Business Strategy and Competitive Advantage (ABSCA) (ISSN: 2327-3429; eISSN: 2327-3437)

British Cataloguing in Publication Data
A Cataloguing in Publication record for this book is available from the British Library.

For electronic access to this publication, please contact: eresources@igi-global.com.

Advances in Business Strategy and Competitive Advantage (ABSCA) Book Series

Patricia Ordóñez de Pablos
Universidad de Oviedo, Spain

ISSN:2327-3429
EISSN:2327-3437

Mission

Business entities are constantly seeking new ways through which to gain advantage over their competitors and strengthen their position within the business environment. With competition at an all-time high due to technological advancements allowing for competition on a global scale, firms continue to seek new ways through which to improve and strengthen their business processes, procedures, and profitability.

The **Advances in Business Strategy and Competitive Advantage (ABSCA) Book Series** is a timely series responding to the high demand for state-of-the-art research on how business strategies are created, implemented and re-designed to meet the demands of globalized competitive markets. With a focus on local and global challenges, business opportunities and the needs of society, the **ABSCA** encourages scientific discourse on doing business and managing information technologies for the creation of sustainable competitive advantage.

Coverage

- Balanced Scorecard
- Small and Medium Enterprises
- Ethics and Business Strategy
- Tacit Knowledge
- Value Chain
- Co-operative Strategies
- International Business Strategy
- Resource-Based Competition
- Innovation Strategy
- Entrepreneurship & Innovation

IGI Global is currently accepting manuscripts for publication within this series. To submit a proposal for a volume in this series, please contact our Acquisition Editors at Acquisitions@igi-global.com or visit: http://www.igi-global.com/publish/.

The Advances in Business Strategy and Competitive Advantage (ABSCA) Book Series (ISSN 2327-3429) is published by IGI Global, 701 E. Chocolate Avenue, Hershey, PA 17033-1240, USA, www.igi-global.com. This series is composed of titles available for purchase individually; each title is edited to be contextually exclusive from any other title within the series. For pricing and ordering information please visit http://www.igi-global.com/book-series/advances-business-strategy-competitive-advantage/73672. Postmaster: Send all address changes to above address.

Titles in this Series

For a list of additional titles in this series, please visit: http://www.igi-global.com/book-series/advances-business-strategy-competitive-advantage/73672

Handbook of Research on Business Model Innovation Through Disruption and Digitalization
Erik Stavnsager Rasmussen (University of Southern Denmark, Denmark) and Nicolaj Hannesbo Petersen (UCL University College, Denmark)
Business Science Reference • © 2023 • 425pp • H/C (ISBN: 9781668448953) • US $325.00

Strategic Management and International Business Policies for Maintaining Competitive Advantage
Ailson J. De Moraes (Royal Holloway University of London, UK)
Business Science Reference • © 2023 • 340pp • H/C (ISBN: 9781668468456) • US $250.00

Challenges and Opportunities for Aviation Stakeholders in a Post-Pandemic World
Salim Kurnaz (Suleyman Demirel University, Turkey & Kazimiero Simonaviciaus University, Lithuania) Antonio Rodrigues (Instituto Superior de Gestão, Portugal) and Dorothea Bowyer (Western Sydney University, Australia)
Business Science Reference • © 2023 • 315pp • H/C (ISBN: 9781668468357) • US $260.00

Opportunities and Challenges of Business 5.0 in Emerging Markets
Sumesh Dadwal (Northumbria University, UK) Pawan Kumar (Lovely Professional University, India) Rajesh Verma (Lovely Professional University, India) and Gursimranjit Singh (Lovely Professional University, India)
Business Science Reference • © 2023 • 315pp • H/C (ISBN: 9781668464038) • US $250.00

Rapid Innovation and Development in the Global Cannabis Market
Pfano Mashau (University of KwaZulu-Natal, South Africa) and Jabulani Nyawo (University of KwaZulu-Natal, South Africa)
Business Science Reference • © 2023 • 352pp • H/C (ISBN: 9781668463468) • US $250.00

Analyzing International Business Operations in the Post-Pandemic Era
Bryan Christiansen (The Christiansen Foundation, USA) and John D. Branch (University of Michigan, USA)
Business Science Reference • © 2023 • 309pp • H/C (ISBN: 9781668437490) • US $250.00

Intellectual Capital as a Precursor to Sustainable Corporate Social Responsibility
Bartolomé Marco-Lajara (University of Alicante, Spain) Patrocinio Zaragoza-Sáez (University of Alicante, Spain) and Javier Martínez-Falcó (University of Alicante, Spain & Stellenbosch University, South Africa)
Business Science Reference • © 2023 • 291pp • H/C (ISBN: 9781668468159) • US $250.00

IGI Global
PUBLISHER of TIMELY KNOWLEDGE

701 East Chocolate Avenue, Hershey, PA 17033, USA
Tel: 717-533-8845 x100 • Fax: 717-533-8661
E-Mail: cust@igi-global.com • www.igi-global.com

Table of Contents

Detailed Table of Contents

In today's rapidly globalizing and digitalizing world, many factors may cause businesses to fail. Financial crises and corporate scandals experienced in the developed financial markets have resulted in the bankruptcies of many companies like Lehman Brothers, Enron, Parmalat, Wirecard, etc. Financial failure can be defined as the business's inability to meet its obligations to lenders. When financial failure is unmanageable, some companies may become bankrupt. The purpose of this study is to figure out the causes of business failure. The factors that may lead to business failure have been separately revealed in this context. Mismanagement is one of the main reasons for financial failure. A company can also fail if it cannot generate more returns than its fixed costs. In addition, the wrong merger and acquisition decision of a firm that has reached a certain maturity may be the reason for failure. Failure to comply with corporate governance principles, which aim to increase the efficiency of businesses, is also a probable reason for failure.

Financial failure has various hidden reasons in corporate firms' life cycles, and finding the symptoms of financial sickness is becoming crucial in worldwide economies. There are many studies and models used in the literature conducted on different variables, sectors, and economies. The most common methods and models used in the bankruptcy area come out to be the logistic regression (LOGIT) and neural network. Altman model is preferably used in most of the bankruptcy prediction studies conducted with different financial indicators. Among important indicators are solvency, profitability, and liquidity. Multiple discriminant analysis (MDA) model and MDA and Z-score and support vector machine are used as alternatives. Artificial intelligence and machine learning models are becoming popular. Literature shows that Altman model is preferably used in most of the bankruptcy prediction studies.

Financial distress is a multidimensional and complex subject. Financial distress has physical and physiological effects and harmful consequences for individuals and families, ranging from unpaid debts and deteriorating health to suicide. For this reason, it has been a widely researched subject by different branches of science such as finance, psychology, and sociology. In this study, financial distress was examined from a subjective point of view. The effect of financial distress on physical and psychological health, its effect on families and children, and the effect of social support and socio-economic status on financial distress were investigated. The role of financial capability and financial resilience in reducing financial distress was emphasized. This study aimes to consolidate and expand knowledge about financial distress. The issue of financial distress has been extensively researched under the behavioral finance framework.

This study explains bankruptcy by talking about risk, risk types, and risk management and bankruptcy forecasting models. The studies in the literature are examined and explained as risk, danger, possibility of bad consequences, loss, or misfortune. Types of risks, purchasing power, interest rate, market, political, exchange rate, financial, industry, corporate bond, liquidity, taxation, reinvestment, country, dynamic, structural, conditional, customer, financial/regulatory, reputation/loss, corporate and interpretation risks are identified in the literature. The study explains bankruptcy as the situation that occurs when a business cannot obtain sufficient value to cover the costs of doing business. Finally, it is stated in this study that bankruptcy estimation methods, which are constructed with historical observations and evaluated with historical observations, are used to predict firms without failing. The findings, which are obtained by examining the literature, offer important contributions to company managers.

The ratio analyses are used to evaluate firms in the sector. Similarities and the differences between the DAP calculated ratios and the investment firm calculated ratios are shown. Companies are compared among each other and with the sector. Automated calculations and potential robo advisory directions are proposed. Auto calculations and comparisons are found to be reliable after 2018. Suggestions for the improvement of computer-assisted calculations are given. There are alternative ways to avoid bankruptcy and concordat. Also, there are choices between bankruptcy procedures, liquidation, and restructuring. The DAP is a useful tool to investigate a sector as a whole, but it is not enough to decide whether a firm failure is close or not. The given 35 equations on the financials of companies are powerful tools but not enough to decide. Policies play a key role in the agri-food industry worldwide. The effects of these policies cannot be observed by just looking at the financial statements.

The aim of this study is to examine the causality relationship between external factors and financial risk situations of companies experiencing financial distress among companies traded on Borsa Istanbul. In the study covering the periods of 2016-2021, financial ratios measuring liquidity risk and capital structure risk were used from the financial statements for 20 periods. In addition, 20-period data in quarterly periods were utilized for inflation, interest rates, and exchange rates as external factors. In the study where Toda Yamamoto causality test was used as a method, the relationship between the financial risks of the companies subject to the application and the situations affected by external factors was analyzed. As a result of the study, it has been determined that the most encountered causal relationship is from foreign exchange to liquidity and CPI to leverage, while the least encountered causal relationship is from CPI to liquidity and interest to leverage.

The novel coronavirus (COVID-19) poses unprecedented challenges to global economy and international development and has become a humanitarian crisis affecting millions of lives and livelihoods throughout the world. It affects almost every economic activity and operation and at the same time poses a threat to every sector of the economy, people, places, and businesses. COVID-19 brought not only crisis, disruptions, and challenges but also bred fertile ground for opportunities, innovations, and digitalization of economic sectors. In this context, this chapter focuses keenly on the economic impacts of the COVID-19 crisis, including the economic challenges and opportunities it creates, and accordingly, recommendations have been presented.

Any debtor who cannot pay his debts even though they are due or is in danger of not being able to pay on time can request a concordat. In the concordat process, tax-related practices and results concern more than one area. Therefore, it would be useful to consider the tax consequences of the concordat application as a whole. In addition, the concordat process will be discussed in terms of debtor and creditor. The consequences of the concordat by the creditor are in some cases "doubtful debt" and generally "worthless credit" being accepted and written off as an expense. In terms of the debtor, the resulting amount of "withdrawal receivable" must be followed in a provision account for three years and amortized with the losses incurred in these years. In addition, according to Article 308/g of the Execution and Bankruptcy Law, it also provides privileges in terms of fees, stamp duty, and BITT. However, the concordat decision accepted by the court is not obligatory for public receivables within the scope of Law No. 6183.

The aim of this study is to investigate the effects of firm bankruptcy risk and auditing factors on the market value of firms and to investigate the effect of auditing on firm bankruptcy risk. The period of the research is 2011-2021. In the study on BIST Sustainability-25 Index, in the first model, the dependent variable is the market value/book value; the independent variables are Springate S Score, Fulmer H Score, Altman Z Score, Çolakoğlu MFA Score; the ratio of the number of independent auditor members to the total number of members; the number of members in the supervisory board; and the number of early risk detection committee members.

This study develops the Turkey banking sector stress index for the period of 2012-2021. For this, sector beta, volatility, return on assets, capital adequacy ratio, and asset quality variables were used. The variables were combined with the variance equal-weight method, and a single index was constructed. The reliability of the index was evaluated in terms of whether it detects the years shown as the economic crisis years by the experts. As a result, it has been determined that the index detects the exchange rate crisis that broke out in Turkey in 2018 and the global economic crisis caused by COVID-19, the effects of which began to appear in 2020. In addition, it is predicted that there may be an increase in the number of concordats and bankruptcies in years when the stress index is high. It has been determined that the Turkish banking sector is resistant to crises.

This chapter's objectives are two-fold: first, to technically modify Altman's model and formulate Altman's index (AIN) in such a manner that only two out of five stipulated financial ratios would suffice the major purpose of projection of soundness of any business organization's financial health; and second, to formulate a financial performance index (FPI) consisting of five financial ratios treated as independent variables that would help to provide a holistic overview of a firm's performance regardless of its functional domain. Since the much-discussed and strongly valid issue of non-normality is closely associated with the financial ratios in the macroeconomic perspective (group of industries), in order to avoid the underlying controversy, the microeconomic approach is followed considering a single firm, Wal-Mart, primarily for two reasons: first, for its financial soundness and, second, it can be used for a comparative study with a financially bankrupt firm by using the financial ratios as common variables to derive the "specific" condition for bankruptcy.

Preface

Businesses around the world are affected to varying degrees by the negative economic impacts of the COVID-19 pandemic, financial crises, and changing technologies. The economic administrations of the countries apply to various legal regulations in order to reintegrate the businesses that have deteriorated financial structures and gone into bankruptcy. One of these arrangements is the arrangement of bankruptcy (concordat).

Arrangement of bankruptcy aims to improve the payment of debts of enterprises and to protect the rights of creditors. Arrangement of bankruptcy, which is an important issue especially for the debtors whose financial structure has deteriorated, protects the debtors from bankruptcy and at the same time enables the creditors to collect their receivables, albeit partially. Although the concordat is intended to protect bona fide debtors and creditors, it can be said that payments not made during the concordat deadlines put the creditors in financial distress and have a negative impact on the economy at the macro level. In this context, it is necessary to examine the subject in depth in order to prevent abuse of concordat requests and to obtain better results both legally and financially.

It is observed that the practices and results of the arrangement of bankruptcy in the world are different. It is foreseen that it will be beneficial for all economic units to take successful studies in this field as an exemplary model and to learn from wrong or incomplete practices. The main theme of this study is the examination of the basic structure of the arrangement of bankruptcy of the countries and the evaluation of the financial results on the enterprises that have declared the arrangement of bankruptcy. In this context, the book aims to provide significant contributions to both the law and finance literature with theoretical and empirical original studies conducted by researchers in different countries. The book consists of 14 chapters.

ORGANIZATION OF THE BOOK

A brief description of each of the chapters follows:

Chapter 1 presents the concepts of financial success and financial failure in detail. These concepts are related to the ability of businesses to maintain their economic life in line with the desired targets. In addition, financial failure can be characterized as a pre-bankruptcy warning system.

Chapter 2 aims to investigate bankruptcy prediction models according to their accuracy depending on different variables and indicators.

Chapter 3 focuses on Blockchain applications and examines their impact in this digital era. In this chapter, applications of hyper ledgers in B2B transactions are analyzed and a case study is conducted with a real-time dataset to better understand the applications of blockchain in finance.

Chapter 4 discusses the Slovenian normative regulation and practice of commercial bankruptcy.

Chapter 5 presents the reasons and solution proposals that lead businesses to concordat. The concept and purpose of the concordat, the types of concordat, the documents to be attached to the concordat request, the concordat process, the approval of the concordat and the results of the approval decision were examined. In addition, in the study, the reasons that lead businesses to concordat were evaluated and tried to be explained with solution suggestions.

Chapter 6 discusses financial distress from a different perspective. The effect of financial distress on physical and psychological health, its effect on families and children, and the effect of social support and socio-economic status on financial distress were investigated. The role of financial capability and financial resilience in reducing financial distress was emphasized. This study aims to consolidate and expand knowledge about financial distress. The issue of financial distress has been extensively researched under the behavioral finance framework.

Chapter 7 explains bankruptcy by addressing risk, risk types, and risk management and considers bankruptcy forecasting models.

Chapter 8 is on the financial examination of the agriculture, forestry, and fishing sector of Turkey.

Chapter 9 aims to examine the relationship between firm-specific micro factors (financial risk situations) and macroeconomic factors (namely interest rates, inflation rates, and exchange rates), which are the main indicators of the economy, in the context of companies experiencing financial distress.

Chapter 10 discusses the impact of COVID-19 in terms of challenges and opportunities.

In Chapter 11, the arrangement of bankruptcy process in Turkey is evaluated in terms of tax applications.

Chapter 12 investigates the effects of firms' bankruptcy risk and auditing factors on the market value of firms and to investigate the effect of auditing on firms' bankruptcy risks.

In Chapter 13, a stress index was developed to detect financial disruptions in the Turkish banking sector.

In Chapter 14, an attempt has been made to simplify the existing Altman's model by keeping its basic foundation intact while dealing with the same 5 independent variables simultaneously. Although this study has been done on a single business firm (micro perspective) (i.e., Wal-Mart), the regressionary relationships could be replicated in macro perspective also (for a group of firms).

Fahri Özsungur
Mersin University, Turkey

Nevzat Tetik
İnönü University, Turkey

Ersin Kanat
Zonguldak Bülent Ecevit University, Turkey

Acknowledgment

We are experiencing incredible pain as I write these lines. Therefore, these lines are not specific to the book. Because we are faced with an indescribable disaster. In February, we experienced very severe earthquakes for two consecutive days in Kahramanmaraş, Adana, Adıyaman, Diyarbakır, Gaziantep, Hatay, Kilis, Malatya, Osmaniye and Şanlıurfa. What a pain!!!

Our hearts hurt, we hurt. We lost our brothers and sisters. Our brothers, sisters, mothers, fathers, sons and daughters, and their hopes... Their dreams were full of hope for the future.

We are all in mourning. We are in mourning because tens of thousands of lives have vanished.

The memories of each became immortal. Our brothers and sisters who were pulled out from under the rubble, had been tightly hugged each other. A mother and a child, a man and a wife, all had hugged each other.

We continue to learn a lot every day. What a painful experience it is to lose one's relatives.

We are all one in this unforgettable pain. We bonded with each other.

Each disaster tells us very well the fine line between life and death. You know, sometimes we get angry with each other, we hurt each other. Let's not hurt each other while there is a disaster close to us like an earthquake. Let's live in peace, brotherly, as if we were going to die tomorrow. Let's hug each other tightly. Let's love each other for we are human. Death is a painful reality for all of us. Let's never forget this.

As I finish my words, I invite all countries to peace and brotherhood for a hopeful future. Finally, I would like to thank the countries that have made great efforts to save our people due to the earthquake in our country, our state, all our people, and the secret heroes who have reached out for help.

If we are breathing, there is hope...

Chapter 1
The Reasons for Financial Failure and Bankruptcy

Yeşim Şendur
https://orcid.org/0000-0003-4695-2181
Izmir Kâtip Çelebi, Turkey

ABSTRACT

In today's rapidly globalizing and digitalizing world, many factors may cause businesses to fail. Financial crises and corporate scandals experienced in the developed financial markets have resulted in the bankruptcies of many companies like Lehman Brothers, Enron, Parmalat, Wirecard, etc. Financial failure can be defined as the business's inability to meet its obligations to lenders. When financial failure is unmanageable, some companies may become bankrupt. The purpose of this study is to figure out the causes of business failure. The factors that may lead to business failure have been separately revealed in this context. Mismanagement is one of the main reasons for financial failure. A company can also fail if it cannot generate more returns than its fixed costs. In addition, the wrong merger and acquisition decision of a firm that has reached a certain maturity may be the reason for failure. Failure to comply with corporate governance principles, which aim to increase the efficiency of businesses, is also a probable reason for failure.

INTRODUCTION

Globalization and digitalization, which are the main trends of today, have severe consequences for businesses. Due to the increasing integration of national economies, companies operate in a more challenging competitive environment. Businesses need to generate enough cash flow to pay off their obligations and partner return expectations to stay in business. In an ever-increasing competitive environment, some companies may be successful while others may fail. While business success can be defined as the ability of firms to retain their economic lives aligned with their goals, business failure can be expressed as the inability of businesses to continue their existence. The failure of a company is not a condition that happens immediately; instead, it is a situation that results from a series of occurrences that cascade like dominoes. In the process of failure, some businesses may face a financially difficult situation. Due to

DOI: 10.4018/978-1-6684-5181-6.ch001

various internal and external reasons, firms experience efficiency loss during this negative process. The financial failure of the business occurs when it cannot meet its obligations to creditors. Companies that cannot develop adequate solutions to prevent their financial failure may face bankruptcy, a further stage of financial failure. In other words, financial failure is a warning before bankruptcy. An official declaration of financial failure is bankruptcy. Even though it's widely acknowledged that bankruptcy is the clearest sign that a company has failed, it just means that its operations have been formally ended. When monetary issues such as a lack of cash or the inability to meet obligations persist and cannot be fixed, businesses must stop operating. Business bankruptcy is the term used to describe this situation. The company is only considered bankrupt if a court has made a formal bankruptcy ruling.

The appearance of a negative difference between income and expenses, in other words, the loss of the business for a period, does not mean bankruptcy. However, this loss may indicate that the firm needs to develop a few new strategies to correct its internal difficulties and adverse environmental conditions. Companies will only survive if they can identify the causes of financial failure fully and accurately and take sufficient precautions to prevent it. It is also very important that these measures are taken quickly enough. If the required steps are implemented on time, the business can resume its regular operations (Çavuş&Başar, 2020, p.294). In such a circumstance, firms turn to various recovery strategies (merger, sale of subsidiaries, etc.) to carry on with their operations. For instance, businesses that are deeply indebted while also experiencing a steady decline in business may merge with other companies or sell off their assets to survive because bankruptcy is the worst and final option. A company must have regular, large losses to discuss about the risk of going bankrupt. Companies that can no longer operate can go into liquidation. Another option for a company that has filed for bankruptcy is restructuring. This study investigates the reasons for a firm's financial failures and bankruptcy. Various indicators can be used to determine whether a business is insolvent. According to Aktaş et al. (2003), losing half the capital, losing 10% of the company's assets, losing three years in a row, having trouble paying off debts, ceasing production, and having more outstanding obligations than total assets are some of these signs.

BACKGROUND

Business failure encompasses a long process, from the company's temporary inability to meet its financial obligations to its bankruptcy. If the measures taken are insufficient to prolong a company's life in distress, the company's liquidation will be inevitable. A business with a high level of risk is more likely to go bankrupt. The risk of a business may be financial risk arising from its debts and operational risk arising from fixed investments (Sayılgan,2011, p.424). According to some point of view, firm size positively affects the survival of a firm that is in distress. Large firms with strong asset structures are expected to cope better with distress than smaller firms. Start-ups generally have more difficulty in managing distress. Therefore, many start-ups often come to the brink of financial failure (Brealey, Myers, and Marcus, 2020, p.444). The definition of failure patterns is as follows;1. Distress, 2. Insolvency,3. Bankruptcy. A firm that has trouble meeting its debt obligations is in financial distress. Financial distress occurs when a firm's financial position weakens because of difficulty in meeting its obligations to creditors. In addition, the possibility of not being able to meet the fixed costs caused by fixed asset investments causes economic distress. An organization is deemed insolvent if it cannot pay its debts when they become due. Even if an insolvent business still has more assets than liabilities, it faces a liquidity crisis. It is generally accepted that the more net working capital a company has, the more liquid it is and the smaller its insolvency risk (Gitman&Zutter,2015, p.792). Bankruptcy is the last phase of business failure. The legal process of liquidating a company's or person's assets to pay off creditors' claims entirely or partly while shielding the debtor(s) from further legal action is known as bankruptcy (Helfert, 2000, p.434). A firm that has filed for bankruptcy may be decided to either restructure or liquidate. As a preliminary stage of bankruptcy, the stated value of a firm's liabilities falls below the fair market value of its assets. As a result, a bankrupt firm's net asset value, calculated by subtracting its liabilities from its total assets, is negative; in other words, it has a negative stockholders' equity. The costs associated with finding and fixing the failure rise as the company gets closer to bankruptcy. The lengthy and difficult bankruptcy procedure has expenses for the company and its investors in both direct and indirect ways (Berk, DeMarzo, and Harford, 2012, p.479). Direct costs are the legal, managerial, and financial consultancy costs required by the bankruptcy process. It may also be necessary to pay investment bankers for a potential financial restructuring. Indirect costs are caused by a decrease in the efficiency of the firm's operations due to the possibility of bankruptcy. These expenses are hard to estimate precisely and frequently exceed the direct costs of bankruptcy. For example, many of these indirect costs might be incurred even if the company is not now in financial difficulties but faces a high likelihood of bankruptcy in the future. Companies with more intricate business models and more debtors are likely to incur more expenditures. Since the probability of bankruptcy increases with an increasing debt ratio, the more the firm borrows, the higher the expected costs of bankruptcy and the lower the firm's market value (Gitman & Zutter, 2015). Dr. Edward Altman created the Z-score bankruptcy predictor to decide the probability that a company will go bankrupt. Lenders can also use this score to determine a company's solvency. The company scandals that started in the 2000s and the global financial crisis in 2008 led to an increase in companies' financial failures and bankruptcies. This situation has led researchers to examine the causes of financial failure and bankruptcy. In addition, the covid-19 pandemic crisis has also increased this trend worldwide. Financial failure has various hidden reasons in corporate firms' life cycle, so improving diagnosis to discover symptoms has become crucial to prevent it. For example, net worth erosion, bad operating results, manufacturing layoffs, dividend cutbacks, and falling stock prices are all accepted signs of financial failure in the literature (Ghosh, 2017, p.54). In addition, if all the bank credit limits are being used, all credit accounts are inactive, and bank deposits are at an all-time low, and this condition takes a long time are other signs of financial hardship. Finally, payment delays are the clearest indication that the company is experiencing financial difficulties (Akguc, 2008, p.949). Banerjee et al. (2020) mentioned that expected default frequencies (EDFs) and real GDP, prospective measures of default risk derived from equity prices, give essential information regarding company bankruptcies in developed economies historically. These two variables indicate that the Covid-19 pandemic will cause a 20 percent increase business bankruptcy by 2021 across their advanced sample economies. The anticipated probability of bankruptcies calls for aid to firms that are likely to be saved. In this context, the reasons for financial failure and bankruptcy will be examined within the scope of the above definitions.

REASONS FOR FINANCIAL FAILURE AND BANKRUPTCY

Mismanagement is one of the leading causes of financial failure. Business management is expected to make decisions that increase the company's market value and shareholders' well-being. Sometimes business managers can put their interests ahead of business partners. The conflict between the interests of the managers and shareholders may cause agency problems in the business. Agency problems are one of the factors that may result in business failure. One of the main reasons underlying the global financial crisis that broke out in the USA in 2008 was the agency problem. As a result of this financial crisis, which caused serious economic problems, many giant companies worldwide filed for bankruptcy. Other companies took over some companies at risk of bankruptcy. States have provided support to many companies. Investors who fund companies may not have the level of knowledge and experience required by business activities. For this reason, they leave the critical decisions to the business managers. As a result, company executives may pursue their self-interest as they direct the company's activities. According to a study conducted in the USA, managers of 25 companies whose stock prices fell more than 75% in the stock market between January 1999 and May 2002 made significant gains simultaneously. While the companies they manage are making losses, they have increased their wealth considerably. As can be seen, the interests of other stakeholders in businesses are not always considered by the managers (Kayacan, 2006, p. 1-26). The delegator can overcome this problem by controlling the agent and signing a contract to compensate for damages if he acts against his interests. Another way for the delegator to align his interests is by providing the agent with appropriate incentives (Sendur & Doğukanlı, 2019, p.58). These incentives may prompt managers to make riskier investment choices, similar to the global financial crisis of 2008. As a result of the substantial incentives provided to managers in the American economy, many of them chose to act contrary to the interests of the owners of the businesses they represent and made risky investments.

The unethical behaviour of managers can also be a reason for firm failure. For example, managers' lack of social responsibility awareness and ethical values have resulted in corporate scandals in developed financial markets like Europe and U.S. (Enron, Parmalat, Wells Fargo, Wirecard). A company's failure can also result from a lack of coordination between managers of different departments, including those in charge of production, planning, marketing, and sales. Another factor is the management's lack of technical expertise and experience. Setting unrealistic goals for managers and employees is another misapplication of businesses. Wells Fargo Bank, for example, had set an unrealistic daily product quota system for employees. Employees were expected to sell eight products daily, which was an unlikely number; thus, they started to open accounts even with acquaintances to fill this quota (www.academia.edu,2023).

The ownership structure and the board of directors impact the firm's success or failure. Separating ownership and control in businesses is crucial. The fact that the company's power is concentrated under one manager or family members rather than qualified executives may result in the company's failure. A good illustration of this scenario is the Italian food giant Parmalat corporation. Parmalat's thirteen-member board of directors was mostly family members. As one of the three independent members on the board of directors was the former president of one of the banks that Parmalat got a loan from in Parma, he was not considered independent. There was a relationship between the company and the bank based on mutual interests. Moreover, Castilo Tanzi, who created the Parmalat, ran the business alone until the corporate scandal broke out, and Tanzi's behavior was typical of many family businesses (Sendur&Doğukanlı,2019, p.27).

Failure of a business could also stem from overexpanding. If management is unaware of this scenario and does not attempt to control it, rapid growth might severely restrict the firm's resources, resulting in its impending insolvency. The number of firms that rapid growth leads to bankruptcy is not less than the number of firms whose slow growth leads to bankruptcy. Many of these companies, even if they launch a product with high demand in the market, may face bankruptcy because they do not have enough financial strength to control their growth (Higgins, 2012, p.123). Some businesses have reached a size that states cannot allow bankruptcy. Financial managers of these companies are more inclined to make risky investments because they know that the state will support them in any adverse condition. One of the businesses that were adversely impacted by the global financial crisis of 2008 was General Motors. It was once one of the largest companies in America in terms of market value. Because GM is crucial to both the U.S. and Canadian economies, the governments have purchased GM stock to avoid bankrupting the business (Gitman, 2015, p.793).

Inconsistencies in accounting transactions and fraudulent financial reporting have been the underlying causes of corporate scandals in recent years. In addition, firms' manipulation of earnings by transferring their liabilities and low-value assets to off-balance sheet partnerships has led to their failure. The deliberate misrepresentation of firm losses by accountants has made firms appear more valuable than they should have been. It was determined that 4 billion Euros, which should be in the records of the Italian Parmalat company, were transferred to the Cayman Islands to hide it. These transactions were made through the Epicurum Company of Parmalat, established in Cayman. In short, Parmalat collected cash with bonds and used this money for investment purposes in subsidiary investments and money transfers to offshore companies. Therefore, it employed more loans to fill the liquidity gap. All of these transactions were made to affect stock prices (Sendur, 2019, p.27). Failure to strictly enforce penalties due to inconsistency in accounting documents and fraudulent reporting is an important factor that will increase firm failure. The sanctions against those who cheat in the accounting records were insufficient until the adoption of SOX in the USA. The chairman of the board of directors (CEO) and the chief financial officer (CFO) of the enterprises are obliged to give assurance to the users of the financial statements that the financial reports produced regularly and sent to the relevant government institutions accurately reflect the issues related to the activities of the companies in all respects.

Failure to comply with changing laws and regulations can result in short-lived firms. In the company scandals, it has been observed that the relevant companies have carried out commercial transactions in markets that do not have legal regulations and regulatory authorities. The business management acts against the legislation to keep the business's reputation high. Businesses should operate by the spirit of the law, not by hiding behind legislative loopholes. Company management should take strict measures regarding business activities that involve strict controls and require constant market adaptation.

Excessive debt can also lead to bankruptcy. The main problems of the companies affected by the 2007-2009 financial crises are debt dependency and excessive debt financing. Because they were financed predominantly by debt, Merrill Lynch, Lehman, Bear Stearns, and other bankrupt companies were highly vulnerable. In addition, most of these loans are short-term loans that require frequent refinancing. Lehman and other investment banks were frequently financed with more than 95% debt and less than 5% equity. Therefore, a 5% decline in the value of their assets might eliminate their equity "shielding" and render the banks insolvent (Brealy et al., 2020, p.49-51).

In order to avoid financial difficulties, businesses must have an efficient internal control system. Internal control refers to an organization's strategy and all connected actions taken to protect assets, assure accurate and trustworthy accounting records, and enhance operational efficiency among personnel. Internal and external auditors monitor internal controls (Nobles et al., 2016, p. 399). Rating agencies, which have easier access to companies' data than ordinary investors, sometimes delay downgrading risky companies. Before the bankruptcies of some companies, such as Enron, Parmalat, and Wirecard, these organizations showed reluctance to downgrade. The fact that Arthur Andersen, an independent audit firm, did not adequately fulfill his duties at Enron and did not give the necessary warnings on time also contributed to the bankruptcy process (Sagner, 2012, p.12). The apparent goal of its top financial managers was to increase Enron's share prices. While these managers were trying to achieve their goals, they needed to maintain control and create a corporate structure in which the financial transactions of the company could be monitored.

The company's low operating efficiency and high fixed expenses are also reasons for failure. Economic distress arises from the inability of a firm to continue its activities efficiently, which invests more than necessary fixed capital. Financial failure is often caused by high fixed costs and a lack of operating income to offset them.

There need to be viable contingency plans to avoid the failure of companies. As experienced in the Covid-19 crisis, companies with contingency plans are less likely to be affected by the crisis. In today's highly dynamic business environment, a good risk management is essential. Success or failure in risk management is decisive for the survival of businesses. In times of crisis, companies' use of all kinds of methods to get out of the crisis may also fail. The important thing is to apply the most correct and most suitable solution for the business to solve the crisis.

The economic cycle seriously impacts the financial failure and bankruptcy of a firm. Due to fluctuations (volatilities) in the economic conjuncture, companies or investors are exposed to market risk, which may result in financial losses. If there is a slowdown in economic activities, companies may be unable to meet their fixed costs, as operating incomes will decrease. In addition, increasing inflation, exchange rate, and interest rate risks because of the deteriorating economic stability of the countries cause cash flow problems and make it difficult for companies to access finance.

The delusion that a company's primary goal is profitability might result in its demise. Although some businesses are profitable according to their accounting records, they may not have the cash they need to continue their daily activities. Therefore, good cash management is essential for companies to continue their operations. The view that the current assets to current liabilities ratio should be as high as possible is incorrect. Such mismanagement of working capital can lead to idle assets in businesses, leading to long-term failure of the company. Therefore, for businesses to continue their activities for a long time, they need to have an ideal working capital.

The company's reliance on a limited number of customers and vendors and inadequate control over inventory and receivables can cause it to fail. Credit sales have some advantages and disadvantages for companies. The advantage is the potential revenue and increased profitability from selling to a broader customer base. However, selling on credit also has a cost for businesses. Some customers fail to make payments on time, resulting in uncollectible receivables. The high amount of uncollectible receivables may increase the expenses and cause the company to enter into financial distress. For example, the optimism of WorldCom, a US telecommunications company, when calculating its uncollectible receivables is one of the reasons behind its failure (Sendur & Doğukanlı, 2019). Similarly, a sudden decrease in the sales of businesses can cause liquidity problems.

The firm's erroneous merger and acquisition decisions may lead to business failure. When companies reach a certain maturity in their life cycle or start a decline stage, they may choose to buy a company or merge with another company. As seen in some company scandals such as Enron, company executives' wrong merger and acquisition decisions accelerated the company's bankruptcy processes. Enron's acquisition of Wessex Water in England and Dabhol Energy Factory in India are samples of wrong choices. By removing its losses from the balance sheet through these entities, Enron hid its risk (Sagner,2002, p.11). These partnerships were created to conceal Enron's debt and fake earnings and reward its senior executives. Due to the significant financial losses from these deals in late 2001, the company filed for bankruptcy (Gitman & Zutter, 2015, p.792).

Investment banks have been a major contributor to previous corporate bankruptcies. It has been observed that they lend to businesses without adequate consideration of their debt repayment capabilities and mislead investors. The primary task of investment banks is to offer professional assistance in improving businesses' capital and debt levels. However, sometimes investment banks violate the fundamental rules of financial management and transfer billions of dollars to insolvent firms. In recent years, business scandals have regularly involved this scenario. For example, the Bank of New York ($2 billion) and J.P. Morgan ($2.6 billion) pour billions of dollars into Enron, etc. (Sagner,2002, p.11). In addition, analysts and investment companies behaved unethically and encouraged investors to buy risky companies' shares. The underlying reason for this behavior of investment companies may be the concern about maintaining their existing agreements with firms.

One of the factors affecting the failure of businesses is their inability to adequately implement corporate governance principles that aim to increase their efficiency and protect the interests of business stakeholders (shareholders, investors, creditors, employees, customers, suppliers, and others) by ensuring that businesses operate within certain rules. High corporate governance quality in companies means low capital costs, increased financing opportunities and liquidity, and easier recovery from crises. Noncompliance with corporate governance principles such as transparency, fairness, accountability, and responsibility and poor functioning of corporate governance mechanisms are among the main reasons for bankruptcies after company scandals in the last thirty years. The bankruptcy of the Germany-based Wirecard company demonstrates the importance of corporate governance. Wirecard was a financial technology company providing contactless and cashless payment services worldwide. The company employee reported to the Financial Times and claimed that the Singapore subsidiary's accounting officer was laundering money and manipulating the accounts. In October 2019, the Financial Times claimed that profits in Dubai and Ireland were fraudulently high, and the customer list given to Ernst&Young was not genuine. Wirecard then hired KPMG from outside to clean itself on the media. The audit lasted for six months. The report published by the audit firm stated, "The profits shown in the accounting records that make up the income of the Wirecard company have not been equivalent to any income." It is shaped. KPMG couldn't figure out where the missing 1.9 million euros were after looking into the subsidiary companies (McCrum,2020).

SOLUTIONS AND RECOMMENDATIONS

This section will discuss some measures that can be taken to prevent business failure. The establishment of audit committees and the independence of committee members should be guaranteed by law. In addition, auditors should be prohibited from performing non-audit services and penalized for misdirection. Heavy penalties should be given for auditors' misconduct. A "notice" mechanism, which requires workers to report irregularities in companies and protects those who do, should be legally adopted by countries. For example, the Enron and Wirecard scandals resulted from reports from middle managers in the accounting department. Strict enforcement of penalties for inconsistency in accounting documents and fraudulent reporting is a factor that will reduce firm failure. The company's board of directors should be held responsible for the misconduct in the company accounts, and it should be accepted that their rights and interests could be seized. Company CEOs and CFOs should be held responsible for the accuracy of financial reports and other company-related information. Directors of the company should not be allowed to take out personal loans from the business. High premiums promised to business managers lead them to make risky investments for business profitability. A standardized and reliable mechanism for determining executive salaries and rewards is essential. Firms' commercial transactions in markets that do not have legal regulations and regulatory authorities should be prohibited (www.spl.com.tr,2022). Companies must protect the value of their intellectual assets, including qualified human resources, brand value, know-how, software, license and copyright fees, information technologies, and corporate reputation.

FUTURE RESEARCH DIRECTIONS

Global financial crises have increased the motivation for research on business bankruptcies. Future research can be conducted on the prevention of financial failure and bankruptcy.

CONCLUSION

In this chapter, the following issues have been identified as the causes of financial failure and bankruptcy. One of the primary causes is mistakes in corporate management. Ownership and board structure of the companies (ownership composition, foreign ownership, manager's ownership) have an impact on success or failure. There is always a conflict of interest between the company's owners and managers. Executives may operate in their self-interest when managing the company's operations. Plenty of corporate scandals generally stem from the manager of some large international companies hiding their risky investment decisions from the public and investors with incomplete and false notifications. Moreover, all over the world, it is common to include family members rather than professional managers in the management of businesses. Often a single family member runs the firm for many years. As a result, these companies went bankrupt, and economies suffered significant losses. Furthermore, inadequate internal control may be one of the reasons for financial failure. Rating agencies must provide unbiased assessments for the parties to financial transactions (lenders, borrowers, and investors). However, in practice, they can prepare reports that are not impartial. In this case, the public is misinformed and biased about the company. Problems arising from the external environment of the businesses, such as the sudden outbreak of the Covid-19 pandemic, are among the reasons for failure. The wrong merger and acquisition decisions also increase the risk of insolvency. Finally, the enterprise's inadequate corporate governance policies may raise the risk of failure.

REFERENCES

Aktaş, R., Doğanay, M., & Yıldız, B. (2003). Financial Failure Prediction: Comparison of Statistical Techniques with the Neural Networks. Ankara University Faculty of Political Sciences Journal, 58(4), 1-24.

Banerjee, R., Cornelli, G., & Zakrajsek, E. (2020). The outlook for business bankruptcies. *BIS Working Papers, 30*, 1-6.

Berk, J., DeMarzo, P., & Harford, J. (2012). *Fundamentals of Corporate Finance*. Pearson Education.

Bragg, S. M. (2002). *Business Ratios and Formulas*. John Wiley and Sons.

Brealey, R., Myers, S. C., & Marcus, A. J. (2020). *Fundamentals of Corporate Finance* (10th ed.).

Çakır, G. (2023). *The Wells Fargo Scandal: The Ordinary Situations of Capitalism*. Retrived from: https://www.academia.edu/28957463/Wells_Fargo_Skandal%C4%B1_Kapitalizmin_Ola%C4%9Fan_Halleri

Çavuş, G., & Başar, A. B. (2020). The Role of Cash Flow Information in Forecasting Financial Failure. *The World of Accounting Science, Special Issue of MODAV's 16. International Conference on Accounting*, 292-318. 10.31460/mbdd.647542

Corporate Governance. (2022). Retrieved from: https://www.spl.com.tr/icerik/sinav-calisma-notlari

Ghosh, P., Khatun, M., & Tarafdar, P. (2018). Bankruptcy via Learning Volatility: Does it integrate in Financial Institutions? *Asian Economic and Financial Review*, *8*(1), 52–62. doi:10.18488/journal.aefr.2018.81.52.62

Gitman, L. J., & Zutter, C. J. (2015). *Principles of Managerial Finance*. Pearson Education Limited.

Helfert, E. A. (2000). *Financial Analysis: Tools and Techniques*. McGraw-Hill.

Kayacan, M. (2006). *New company agenda in our globalizing world: corporate governance (Publication No: 1)*. Ethical Values Foundation of Turkey.

McCrum, D. (2020). *Wirecard: The timeline*. https://www.ft.com/content/284fb1ad-ddc0-45df-a075-0709b3686 8db

Sagner, J. (2002). *The Real World of Finance*. John Wiley and Sons.

Sendur, Y., & Doğukanlı, H. (2019). *The Effect of Corporate Governance on Dividend Policy: Theories and Literature*. Gazi Publishing.

KEY TERMS AND DEFINITIONS

Insolvency: It is the inability of businesses to meet their obligations to creditors.

Liquidation: Sale of a bankrupt firm's assets via auction under the supervision of a trustee.

Restructuring: Reorganizing financial claims on a failing company to enable it to continue running.

Sarbanes-Oxley Act: Act passed in 2002 to safeguard shareholders from deceptive accounting and unethical behavior.

Chapter 2
Predicting Financial Failure and Bankruptcy:
Predictive Analytics Models on Financial Failure and Bankruptcy

Abdullah Cevdet Bayhan
https://orcid.org/0000-0002-0749-1151
Istanbul Stock Exchange, Turkey

ABSTRACT

Financial failure has various hidden reasons in corporate firms' life cycles, and finding the symptoms of financial sickness is becoming crucial in worldwide economies. There are many studies and models used in the literature conducted on different variables, sectors, and economies. The most common methods and models used in the bankruptcy area come out to be the logistic regression (LOGIT) and neural network. Altman model is preferably used in most of the bankruptcy prediction studies conducted with different financial indicators. Among important indicators are solvency, profitability, and liquidity. Multiple discriminant analysis (MDA) model and MDA and Z-score and support vector machine are used as alternatives. Artificial intelligence and machine learning models are becoming popular. Literature shows that Altman model is preferably used in most of the bankruptcy prediction studies.

INTRODUCTION

Financial failure and bankruptcy refer to various dependent and independent reasons in corporate life cycle which reflect improving diagnosis to find out those symptoms of financial sickness to be very crucial over decades in worldwide economies. There are many studies and models used in the literature conducted on different variables, sectors, and economies. Studies differ mostly within countries, sectors, period, and several factors on determinants. This chapter aims to investigate existing bankruptcy prediction models used in literature and show their accuracy while using different variables and indicators. The chapter firstly consider the factors behind financial bankruptcy and distress. There are solid

DOI: 10.4018/978-1-6684-5181-6.ch002

reasons determined in many studies focused on different events and models. The chapter continue with analyzing prediction models mostly preferred in the literature. Before conclusion, a short assessment on lately pandemic facts and financial risks are given. The chapter lasts with future research opportunities and motivation for researchers.

FACTORS BEHIND FINANCIAL BANKRUPTCY AND DISTRESS

Economies suffered from huge economic crises in recent decades. Every crisis reflects its own unique structural causes in deep analysis. While integrity and economic exposure increased highly among economic units in global environment, factors causing severe effects of crisis spreads easily among those units, even affecting the stable and solid economies. A big cause of economic corrosion is high corporate debt levels. Firms suffer from sharp increase in debt obligations and duration of recovery increases during financial distress conditions. One another important cause of financial bankruptcy of firms is unprofessional business management. In this case, particularly family-oriented businesses suffer from unreliable methods creating conflict within self-concern economic conditions acting faints rules and legislations. Expansion of business and growth concerns can be considered as a leverage factor of financial bankruptcy under severe economic crisis. Another important cause is deterioration in financial assets due to economic recessions. During low economic activity, lack of sales, pure market demand, loss in production levels reveal firm's adequate cash flow issues in order to cover fixed expenses. This situation makes financial indicators even more important to be monitored.

As mentioned above, there are various factors defined in financial bankruptcy studies in literature. In order to analyze financial bankruptcy and distress conditions, several factors, parameters and indicators are used in many studies. Ghosh (2017, p.54) studied on financially sick company case of Hindustan Motors Ltd between 2004 to 2013 with the National Council of Applied Economic Research (NCAER) distress prediction model to define the financial health of the firm. Trend analysis and $\chi 2$ test are used to indicate a relationship between observed and trend variables defining financial distress. When the company starts experiencing cash losses and have a loss in its funds, financial stability is threatened. When prediction of financial difficulty becomes harder there may be an outstanding trigger of financial distress. The study shows different stages of sickness defined as the tendency to become sick, incipient sickness, and fully sick according to three parameters in the model. These parameters are profitability measured reflected by cash profit position, liquidity measured by net working capital position, and a solvency measure of net worth position. They find out that the cash profit position of Hindustan Motor has suffered, cash profit earnings decreased, and fluctuating nature of the cash profit position is being noticed. Sales declined and standard cash profit through sales caused the actual value of working capital lower than the estimated values of working capital. Liabilities like salaries, tax positions, and bills caused high costs in working capital also causing a fall down in the net worth of the company. According to diagnostics, the company provides an easy signal to possible sickness according to low productivity, lack of funds, and demands over time. Incremental cash flow loss over the year caused the stop of operations.

Achima et. al. (2012), developed a statistical model to predict the financial indicators on the risk of bankruptcy for two groups of companies in the Romanian manufacturing sector, between 2000 and 2011. They used Principal Component Analysis, a multivariate analysis technique. They predict company's financial conditions with formulas based on profitability, leverage, activity, liquidity, and solvency ratios for a determined period. Their sample comprises 53 companies divided into two categories depending on their level of financial difficulties and analyzed increasing financial stability until companies enjialad up with an unlisted situation on Bucharest Stock Exchange. The reason behind this is to define financial indicators to assess bankruptcy probability accurately. Results show that variables provide accuracy explaining more than 85% of the total variance during analysis by using variable components. Return on assets, working capital ratio, flexibility ratio, current liquidity, return on equity, financial leverage ratio, total assets turnover, current assets turnover, and financial expenses ratio affect solvency in the long term.

Some studies show that the size of firms is one of the most important factors in a bankruptcy situation. The number of bankruptcy filings increased since 1990 in Japan. Tsuruta, Marea, and Xu (2007, p.2) studied Japanese small firms with a huge amount of data with 176,104 samples that had a problem increase in debt over assets for consecutive two years. The study has high accuracy with a large number of small firms. They analyzed samples of small firms going bankrupt and between 1996 to 2002 at the time of bankruptcy they conducted Credit Risk Database (CRD) large panel data. Timing of bankruptcy is accepted when the company either has a court case filing for bankruptcy procedures having a problem with debt obligations or the court's bankruptcy decision and approval.

Defining the factors behind bankruptcy provides us with meaning about finding out early warnings of starting a bad financial health cycle. An example from an emerging market is studied by Van, Şehribanoğlu, and Hanifi (2021, pp.63-75) on 139 manufacturing companies listed on Borsa İstanbul in 2017. They grouped companies into three different categories which consist of distress, grey and safe zone and they used Altman-Z score values for the early warning system with a generalized ordered logit model. Due to outcomes, they found out, that operating margin, asset turnover, net profit margin, and acid-test support companies in a safe zone likewise a high financial leverage ratio has negative effects on bankruptcy probability causing it to remove from the safe zone. Economic problems under increasing inflation cause countries to raise interest rates which affect young companies the most. According to the coefficients obtained from the logit model liquidity ratios shows companies' power to oblige short-term debts with a greater amount of net sales. High-profit margin and acid-test ratios increase the probability of companies staying in the safe zone. Financial leverage becomes highly important whether it is provided by foreign sources or internal capital.

Distressed firms generally suffer from a huge increase in trade payables which makes them more vulnerable to bankruptcy situations. In smaller companies' cases, suppliers are easily able to define bankruptcy risk situations faster than the banking industry and stop sending trade credits which are usually unsecured. Distressed firms have more problems with trade credits and bankruptcy is becoming faster showing that there is a decrease in their trade payable power.

Bankruptcy regulations are observed to change according to economies and may differ according to industries. Lubben (2011, p.1263) examined American bankruptcy law dated 1898 which excludes banks and insurance companies from bankruptcy processes in line with big companies compared to several ones from different industries. Defining companies in the financial industry becomes the main concern of this study. To be defined in the financial industry according to American acts, 85% of the total consolidated revenues of companies must be derived from financial activities, or more than 85% of the firm's consolidated assets may be placed financial nature. Acts show uncertainty in defining the %85 rule for traditional banks expanding to different areas like market funds, securitization, and private funds. Volatile and small markets can suffer from a big manipulation over this ratio rule in case of crisis which priors the government's response and the most important action to be taken. What makes the situation more difficult is also that companies running different funds over parent companies. Such blur areas show that there is still a need for improvement in regulation that would lead to removing manipulation over the rule and also over the resolution procedures for excluded corporations. The key players are turned out to be government authorities for making blur areas into clear judgments, especially in the case of the financial crisis.

In the literature, some special words can be used for financially distressed firms. Banerjee and Hofmann (2021, p.1) defined zombie firms in their study depending on listed non-financial firms through 14 advanced economies between 1980 and 2017. Zombie firms are defined to be smaller ones with poor production, and facing a significant loss of market valuation, investing less in the capital which causes to reduce their assets, obligations, and employment. Their financial condition gives signs many years before the status of zombification and compared to other healthy firms there are easily recognizable in the market. Zombie firms with a percentage of 25% have no other option other than exiting from the market besides 60% of them recover but still have lower performance compared to never zombie firms with the solid status of not converting into zombies.

Zombie firms are defined as firms with both an interest coverage ratio less than 1 and Tobin's q below the median firms over 2 years and business cycle changes according to this ratio observed. In the study, some other factors were observed to have significant effects like listing procedures, and tax and insolvency regimes. Sector trends also differ in zombification status. In 2017 commodities sectors have more likely with 40% zombie firms depending on the commodity cycle over two years. Likewise, it changed to a positive trend in the Covid-19 period which maximize their stock valuations. SMEs tend to be more zombie firms and if it is considered from the overall economy unlisted zombie firms have a great impact on poor production.

Zombie firms can remain on the market for a long time without a takeover by other firms or realizing bankruptcy procedures which leads them into a different life cycle than other firms. They occupy huge necessity in overall economies. In Ryan Banerjee and Boris Hofmann (2021, p.1)'s study factors of zombification are found to be profitability, interest payment power on debts, and growth potential besides low market values regarding Tobin's q ratios. Financial company statements are used from listed companies. The number of zombie firms increase significantly from 4% in the 1980s across 14 advanced economies to 15% in 2017. The ratio of assets and capital debt is found to be around 6-7%. Poor performance rises at most two years before zombification which can be understood easily. Zombie firms with decreasing financial performance are likely to increase assets and equities and borrowing. A lower rate interest rate environment has a valuable impact on zombie firms holding them for many years in operation.

High leveraged zombie firms with huge borrowings pay less dividends and get more subsidized credits. Zombie firms faced a 17% probability of exiting the market compared to on-zombie firms with a level of 9%. Leverage and interest payments are crucial facts pushing them into an exit. Median zombie firms exit the market in 12 years compared to on-zombie firms after 15 years. Zombification also increases hazard problems. Over 12,727 zombie cases 60% have recovered while 2.955 firms exit the market and others remained stable. After the mid-1980s a 10% decrease in nominal interest rates across advanced economies cause a 17% increase in zombie firms depending on the financial dependency ratio. The study covers large data but only for listed companies considering also unlisted SMEs. They play a great role in economies. Recovered zombies, 34% of them is weaker and tend to slow growth and poor financial health and certainly weak during business cycles, financial crises which in some cases government should take precautions for their longer zombification and exit decisions.

FINANCIAL FAILURE PREDICTION MODELS

Literature shows that they are many studies on financial failure prediction models. Prediction models are preferred according to the improvement in the results through decades of financial predictions. Global crises have huge effects on study motivation and model formation. Other motivation themes are found to be emerging economies and differentiated sectorial firms. There are many other authors emphasizing signal indicators before bankruptcy. With the development of information technology and statistical tools, different prediction models on bankruptcy with better results tend to increase over decades.

Shi and Li (2014, s.114) examined the literature in their financially not supported systematic study about company's bankruptcy prediction models comparing methods used in the period between 1968 and 2017. Firstly, to say that bankruptcy has become an outstanding field globally, especially after the global financial crisis in 2008 which had serious effects on corporate firms. The most common methods and models used in this area come out to be the Logistic Regression (Logit) and Neural Network. Other methods also rise nowadays mostly depending on the improving technology, especially in computer science and artificial intelligence.

Altman Model is preferably used in most of the bankruptcy prediction studies conducted with financial indicators. During the time of improving prediction models, comparisons between the studies also increased. Hillegeist (2004) compared Altman's (1968) Z-score and Ohlson's (1980) O-score models to a model based on Black-Scholes-Merton option pricing and refers to the last model that provides more accuracy than the two others. According to Shi and Li's (2014, pp.120-123) research, there are few articles on bankruptcy between 1968 and 1999. After 2000 there seems to be a great trend and numbers of studies conducted increased. The global financial crisis in 2008 is also a turning point in the growing trends motivating researchers to focus on this topic.

According to 496 studies searched between 1968 and 1999, 175 of them is not directly depending on their titles, subjects, or keywords and mentioned models. According to the remaining rest totaling 321 studies, the most used and conducted model in this topic comes out to be the classical statistical Logistic Regression, also known as the logit model.

The most second used model is the artificial intelligence Neural Network model with 56 studies. 52 studies used the Discriminant analysis model as a third alternative. The other remaining models include MDA & Z-score and Support Vector Machine. Artificial intelligence &machine learning models are becoming popular lately. Even though there is no exact definition of corporate or business failure studies show interest in the keywords like default, insolvency, and bankruptcy.

Altman's study in 1968 had the highest total number of citations. Among the most cited 10 papers, 6 of them used a neural network model for their primary research. The studies show that there is a small collaboration between authors depending on their self-work or in small groups with serious connections. The Logistic Regression (Logit) and Neural Network come out to be the most preferred ones of statistical models. Comparing different models used formerly and their accuracies with nowadays techniques will likely be popular in this bankruptcy field and verifying prediction models with empirical data.

In the last five decades bankruptcy prediction effectiveness is becoming more and more important for financial institutions in the scope of accurate lending and funding corporate actions. In this field, the most important ways for effective prediction come out to be financial ratio indicators and techniques designed by statistical and machine learning. Besides financial ratio indicators, corporate governance indicators inclusion become very important as input selection in the models. Liang, Lu, Tsai, and Shih (2016, p.561) examines prediction performance in their study by using seven different financial ratios and five other corporate governance indicators based on the Taiwan market dataset. Selected financial ratios are solvency, profitability, cash flow ratios, turnover ratios, capital structures, growth, and others. Corporate governance indicator selections are board structure, ownership structure, cash flow rights, and personnel continuity. Five techniques and selection methods are applied to develop effective prediction models by combining financial ratios and corporate governance indicators. Both two increase the model's accuracy compared to ones that are used alone. The most accurate analysis comes out to be stepwise discriminant analysis and support vector machine analysis.

Solvency and profitability are the most critical ones in financial ratios. From the corporate governance side, board structure and ownership are very important. Corporate governance indicators improve the prediction model but they are also dependent on the market. In the scope of this companies under financial stress definitions and companies' corporate characteristics are affecting the prediction results. When the definitions of companies under unhealthy situation is not certain, prediction models tend to be ineffective. From the corporate governance side, some of them become unimportant in the Chinese market most of the companies are under public or government ownership which board structure tends to be different. Shortly, inputs are market-driven factors affecting the prediction. To have more accuracy, researchers have to be certain about the definitions of companies under financial stress and their characteristics.

Many models are used for describing the failure. Altman and Hotchikiss (2006) describe bankruptcy in two ways. The first one is a condition of the net worth situation of the enterprise. The second one is more about legal actions taken by the court which mostly ends up with liquidating the assets of the firms or a restructuring program on the way. Altman and Hotchikiss (2006) describe failure upon the realized rate of return which results in lower ratios compared to risks of alternative reasonable and similar investments. In the situation of a firm's liabilities becoming more than its assets, insolvency issues start to become a part. When the corporate firms are not capable of meeting their debts and obligations, the situation shows itself to be a financial problem and an indicator of lack of liquidity. Firms face in a law court because of not paying their loans or in broader sense debts, default issues reasonably come out in case of legal actions.

While Ross, Westerfield, and Jaffe (1999) describe bankruptcy in three ways. One of these is legal bankruptcy which the company is subject to a court case and moves into the bankruptcy process. The second is described as technical bankruptcy. In this one, the company cannot pay its obligations like not meeting obligations of its business contracts on time or cannot pay back loans or other financial obligations subject to loans like partial payments. The last one is accounting bankruptcy. This one points out to net asset value which becomes negative under hard circumstances.

Besides Yin Shi and Xiaoni Li (2014, p.114)'s study on the Taiwan market and their referrals missing Chinese corporate governance issues, WANG Luzhuang, ZHANG Simeng, and HE Jia's (2011, 1009-1012) study on Chinese listed companies in 2009 under factor analysis and logistic regression methods and they also use non-financial indicators for financial failure prediction. They compared the probability of bankruptcy levels P ratios based on 2006'a published data. They used 21 financial indicators and also added two non-financial indicators including shareholder and listed years to represent the actions of corporate firms. According to prediction results, 80.77% of non-financials increased to 86.54% ending with a higher ratio. They concluded that with non-financial indicators financial failure prediction statistically increases. The study is important by being based on Chinese companies and gives more concrete results on non-financial items and corporate governance issues.

BANKRUPTCY AMONG DIFFERENT SECTORS, SMEs AND ALTERNATIVE PREDICTION MODELS

Corporate bankruptcy differs and every sector has its unique circumstances. Darmawan and Supriyanto (2018, p.110) studied 119 mining companies listed on Indonesia Stock Exchange between 2011-2014 and used the Altman Z-score method. They focused on four ratios consisting of net working capital, retained earnings, earnings before interest and tax to total assets, and market value of equity to book value of debt. They find out that all the ratios have a positive effect on financial distress. The study is limited to the mining sector and the number of samples is small. The companies under investigation mostly are similar ones and they just used one method also the annual reports of many companies are not fully completed. Nevertheless, the outcomes are case for investors looking for opportunities in mining sector companies.

Bankruptcy prediction also has significantly different impacts among different industries in emerging markets. Navitha Singh Sewpersadh (2020, pp.1-16) conducted a study on 673 Johannesburg Stock Exchange listed firms between 2011 to 2016 and used De la Rey K-score model, a risk-based model with early warnings. Statistical methods of one-way ANOVA and OLS findings are used in the study. Results show that the mean K-score shows a healthy range for consumer and consumer good sectors for each year in the study. An inconsistent healthy range is described as grey zones in health care and telecommunications and the financially distressed sectors were industrial and technology sectors which can lead to hard times in the economic stability of emerging markets' production lines. K-score model is a good method for early warning signal for financial distress which policymakers and regulators can benefit from in emerging economies. The study also proves financial instability in South Africa by a downward trend over declining averages K-scores in the mentioned period. Outcomes also refer to solution strategies that should be conducted on profitability and growth in distressed and grey areas. The current ratio, inventory efficiency, and cash flows do not have consistent significant importance thus they are suggested to be replaced in a new failure prediction model for emerging market sectors.

Alaa Al Saedi and Basrah Suhail (2018, pp.1-20) examine seven industry companies listed on the Qatar Stock Exchange for ten years between 2008 and 2017 and examine them for giving a sign of financial failure. Qatar market is described as a growth market and Qatari companies are different from regional companies in sense of modernity of technology and standards. Their study indicates the relationship between failure and the market value of companies. Altman Z-score calculation model is used for financial ratios consisting of the most operational and financial activities. The study has an outcome of Qatari companies showing that they are not weak to financial failure by the means of a strong emerging growth economy and there is a positive relationship between failure score and market value of the industrial companies in Qatar. The lack of this study is a small sample and the market size is also small on Qatar Stock Exchange.

The methods chosen for bankruptcy prediction are very important and can have different outcomes. Lonneke Mous (2005, p.31) compared two models of Multiple discriminant analysis (MDA) and decision tree for two years and find out correctly prediction %81 and %89 ratios ending with higher accuracy for decision tree analysis. One powerful side of this model is that using samples with missing values compared to MDA loses entire information. The decision tree can also process qualitative variables like financial ratios. Besides MDA, the decision tree supports less strict assumptions which makes it more flexible. Even though they use different variables, both methods use probability and a ratio for liquidity or leverage which makes these ratios the most necessary aspects of corporates under bankruptcy prediction. The calculation method of these aspects according to different countries and sectors becomes important. The study included varied countries and sectors which makes further research may focus on specific kinds of businesses.

While taking into consideration bankruptcy analysis that changes depending on the variables, González, Fernández-Rodríguez, and Ganga (2017, p.228) focus on the Spanish construction sector between 1995 and 2011. The study selected econometric models not just with corporate firms' financial ratios and also with macroeconomic variables of the overall economy. They focused on five optimal econometric models for 5 years and achieve high rates of predictive success. Economic cycle and sector trends in regulatory policies have serious impacts on predictions. For 4 years, their models demonstrate failure with a %80 success rate which tends to be higher than Altman's Z score model. They discover that the Spanish construction sector is more fragile to different conditions in the negative macroeconomic factors. The most important variables of macroeconomics are found to be credit and land price volatilities in the sector. The study is reasonable for 4 years for more time failure prediction accuracy declines.

Tong (2021, p.9) compared expressions of bankruptcy and financial distress as generally used for the same meaning but refer to different conditions. There is certainly a distinction between the two aspects. Bankruptcy is the cycle of experiencing financial distress and in the end resulting in bankruptcy. Corporate firms can have financial problems like not meeting their obligations but that does not mean that they are in bankruptcy. At this point, they may suffer from financial distress which can lead to bankruptcy in the end. These two different aspects are also different in the prediction processes. There is a variety of solutions for corporates experiencing financial distress. These include restructuring financial conditions, analyzing debts and taking precautions with creditors, and cashing out some assets to repay debts in short term. Smaller firms generally have greater problems since they do have not adequate assets to repay debts. Financial unhealthy conditions damage small and mid-sized enterprises (SMEs) more.

SMEs have great value in overall economies actually in Europe 99% percent of total enterprises are driven by them. According to Tong (2021, p.9)'s study, Portugal is ranked third in Europe by the number of SMEs. Under Portugal's technology sectors, high and medium-high firms produce one-fourth of total sales in 2016 in the manufacturing industry. Yehui Tong examines the differences between business failure and financial distress in Portugal's technology manufacturing sectors. In this study logistic regression method is used with financial indicators to predict both aspects of mentioned firms in Portugal.

According to the study, the difference between failed firms compared to distressed firms is certainly analyzed. Another fact is the decrease of failure prediction accuracy over time with lower stable financial distress levels. The third fact is similar to all the studies in prediction research. Profitability is the most important indicator and is negatively related to failure and distress. Liquidity and debt issues behind profitability are the most common important factors in predicting failure and distress.

There is a significant difference between distress group firms and failure groups. This should be easily understood since the distress situation is a prior stage of bankruptcy. Firms generating high profitability tend to have more internal capital which prevents high borrowings and financial expenditures that may cause distress. There is also a positive significance between profitability and the probability of failure. Longer time decreases the ability of indebtedness to predict failure. General liquidity ratios are more significant than indebtedness or leverage in the long term which both are positively related to failure prediction. The total liabilities to total assets ratio can be negatively related to bankruptcy. Since higher leverage means being more financially distressed, it may be easier to trigger financial problems and failure in a broader sense. The source of leverage either utilizing internal capital or borrowings become a real issue in the distressing period. Short-term distress may cause more bankruptcy risk than long-term debt so SMEs can benefit from professionally organized longer time-based liabilities.

Since the research and development activities are highly important for technology firms, those activities become an inevitable issue to discuss upon. Powerful total assets make bigger firms stronger to cope with failure compared to SMEs. Firm size comes out to be a positive effect on survival from distress times. One of the weak points of Tong's study is small data niched in Portuguese technology SMEs. Larger data sets with different countries over the same sector may be considered as a development of this study.

Since the Altman model is one of the traditional models used in bankruptcy prediction some authors study different alternatives for better accuracy prediction rates. Horváthová and Mokrišová (2018, pp.1-22) used Data Envelopment Analysis (DEA) on competitiveness in addition to bankruptcy prediction for non-manufacturing Slovak companies. According to the research, the DEA method is an appropriate alternative to the Altman model using not only outputs but also inputs. Prediction models generally do not involve input indicators. Certain inputs should also be used to provide more accuracy in the model. The cost ratio becomes one of the most important factors affecting Slovak companies' financial situation as significant as profitability indicators. Cost of ratio calculation is also advised in this model for Slovak companies. DEA model is a more complex model with input analyses. When liquidity and cost ratio is analyzed, some of the hotels in the Slovak tourism industry come to be in the grey distressed zone comparing Altman's safe zone outcome. DEA model is a proven model for analyzing also operational indicators in the process. This model shows input and output selection calculations for financial stability. The disadvantage of the model is that all inputs and output are not processed at the same level and also the data set is considerably small.

COVID-19 PANDEMIC FACTS ON FINANCIAL RISKS

Bankruptcy evaluation become even more popular with the worldwide COVID-19 pandemic situation. Companies shut down and stop their business worldwide and many countries especially emerging ones suffer from unstable economic and healthcare industries more than ever in history. The pandemic situation made bankruptcy issues being considered by investors, managers, and policymakers even more affected under the pandemic situation in most countries worldwide.

Yousaf and Bris (2021, p.45-53) studied on financial risks of Czech companies by conducting a regression technique with selected 15 financial ratios. According to statistical numbers, 16.111 companies closed their operations in 2020 the highest number in Czech Republic history. The study is valuable for evaluating financial ratios from varied sectors simultaneously for an overall prediction. Outcomes show that ratios including return on capital, current ratio, net working capital turnover rate, and current assets turnover rate create a positive influence on corporates' financial stability. On the other side, return on capital employed, asset turnover rate, inventory turnover rate, fixed assets turnover rate, and debt to equity ratio have negative impacts in this period. An overall outcome is that liquidity, activity, profitability, and indebtedness ratios are considered as these ratios affecting the company's financial situation.

Covid-19 and the pandemic create a huge chaos in worldwide economies and increased the number of bankruptcies among different sectors. One of the most affected countries by the pandemic is the United States. Jialan Wang, Jeyul Yang, Benjamin Iverson, and Raymond Kluende (2020, p.1-28) searched the effects of the Covid-19 economic crisis on bankruptcies in the US by conducting analyze with real-time data. They reversely find out that bankruptcy total filings dropped in some parts of the pandemic period and start to increase again but remained at 20% below 2019 levels. Compared to the 2007-2009 global recession, 2019's pandemic recession had high unemployment but there were huge drops in bankruptcy filings. Bankruptcies by big scale firms increased since 2019. This situation shows bankruptcy filings differ from the size of firms in the US. One of the great facts about this is the regulations behind which do not allow small businesses to benefit from the bankruptcy system, especially during the time of high unemployment.

FUTURE RESEARCH DIRECTIONS

Under several severe financial crisis over last decades, financial control mechanism is becoming inevitably more important nowadays. In order to prevent financial distress and to be more proactive under control mechanism, predicting financial failure and bankruptcy is becoming utmost necessary field in new world of digital business era. Meanwhile, accurate and reliable financial data is a key input for prediction models used for control mechanisms which signals critical levels of stress, instable outcomes and supply relevant signals in particular parameters under precaution otherwise entities deeply suffer from hidden causes. Artificial intelligence (AI) and robots are becoming substantially powerful in analyzing financial data. These tools are improving in a non-linear way that will be also dominant in corporate financial management which should every corporate adopt in near future. These tools analyze not only reliable data also process non-financial or non-numerical social events and their outcomes. Extended analyze over an integrated financial data with economic events probably improve the accuracy of existing formerly experienced used models. AI models give opportunity to process more input variables and produce alternative outcomes faster than existing tools. Therefore, rapid development in artificial intelligence and robotic studies on financial economics will motivate researchers to improve models depending on AI and robotic tools.

CONCLUSION

There are many studies conducted on financial bankruptcy and prediction models in the literature. Literature shows that studies and models are analyzed on this topic according to the results through decades and improved nowadays. Crisis provides big motivation for those studies with increasing bankruptcy cases and prediction models. There are also studies emphasizing signal indicators before bankruptcy. After 2000 there seems to be a great trend and the global financial crisis in 2008 is also a turning point in the growing trends motivating researchers to focus on this topic. With the development of information technology and statistical tools, different models increase over the decades. Studies differ mostly from the selected topics over countries, sectors, timing, and other factors on determinants.

There are many definitions of bankruptcy in the literature. There is distinction between financial distress and bankruptcy. Bankruptcy is the cycle of experiencing financial distress and in the end resulting in bankruptcy. Most of the studies define bankruptcy as a situation of not meeting obligations and a condition of poor financial health which mostly show itself in a court case and certain legal actions taken by the court. This situation mostly ends up with liquidating assets or a restructuring program for the firm. One other definition considers the condition of net worth situation of the enterprise. This one points out to net asset value which becomes negative under hard circumstances.

Bankruptcy become a major topic worldwide, especially after the global financial crisis in 2008 that created big devastation on corporate firms. In the scope of finding factors, determinants of devastation prediction models are created regarding different data selections. The most common methods and models used in the bankruptcy area come out to be the Logistic Regression (Logit) and Neural Network. Other methods also rise nowadays mostly depending on the improving technology, especially in computer science and artificial intelligence. Altman Model is preferably used in most of the bankruptcy prediction studies conducted with financial indicators. Discriminant analysis model used as an alternative. The other remaining models include MDA & Z-score and Support Vector Machine models. DEA model is a more complex model with input analyses. DEA model is a proven model for analyzing also input indicators in the process. Artificial intelligence & machine learning models are becoming popular lately.

Defining the factors behind bankruptcy provides how to get bad causes of early warnings. Some of the results show that certain indicators have high accuracy and a great impact on analyzing bankruptcy situation. Before a bankruptcy situation according to diagnostics studied, companies provide a signal to possible sickness according to low productivity, lack of funds, demands, and incremental cash flow loss over years causing operation failure. Solvency and profitability are the most critical in financial ratios. One of the most important issues is liquidity. If corporate firms cannot meet their debt obligations, they are mostly accepted to be in a financial problem and suffer from a lack of liquidity. Those companies come out in law court because of not paying their loans, debts, and default issues reasonably come out in case of legal actions. Growth, internal and also working capital, and earnings have a positive effect on financial health.

Some studies show that size of firms is one of the most important factors in a bankruptcy situation. Companies in distress generally have huge trade payables which makes them more vulnerable and their situation is becoming riskier as lenders stop sending trade credits.

In addition to financial ratio input indicators like operating margin, asset turnover, net profit margin, and acid-test; corporate governance indicators are becoming very important as alternative input selection. These are most likely board and ownership structure, cash flow rights and personnel continuity. Inclusion of these indicators increases the accuracy of prediction models.

Global financial crises increase motivation for bankruptcy studies since economic cycle have serious impacts on predictions but finding solutions to bankruptcy situation is less assessed in the literature. There is a variety of solutions for corporates experiencing financial distress before bankruptcy. These include restructuring financial conditions, analyzing debts and taking precautions with creditors, and cashing out some assets to repay debts in short term. Profitability as the most important indicator is negatively related to failure and distress. Studies shows powerful total assets make bigger firms stronger to cope with failure compared to SMEs. Firm size comes out to be a positive effect on survival from distress times. Economic problems under increasing inflation cause countries to raise interest rates and this condition affect young companies the most. Financial leverage becomes highly important whether for it is provided by foreign sources or internal capital.

Covid-19 created big economic consequences on global economies and bankruptcy studies are consider to be enhanced. Futures studies are more likely to focus on situations over post pandemic high-inflationary period under increasing cost variables. Meanwhile investors, managers, and policymakers move into hard times for predicting and finding solutions to prevent economic downturn. Blur areas in financial distress and bankruptcy regulations need to be fulfilled in order to remove manipulation. Government authorities are key responsible players by being proactive taking solid economic and legal precautions before bankruptcy crisis for a more sustainable financial environment.

REFERENCES

Achima, M. V., Marea, C., & Borleab, S. N. (2012). A statistical model of financial risk bankruptcy applied for the Romanian manufacturing industry. *Procedia Economics and Finance*, *3*, 132–137. doi:10.1016/S2212-5671(12)00131-1

Altman, E. & Hotchkiss, E. (2006). *Corporate financial distress and bankruptcy*. Wiley. doi:10.1002/9781118267806

Banerjee, R., & Hofmann, B. (2021). Corporate zombies: Anatomy and life cycle. *BIS Working Papers*, *882*, 1-14.

Darmawan, A., & Supriyanto, J. (2018). The Effect of Financial Ratio on Financial Distress in Predicting Bankruptcy. *Journal of Applied Managerial Accounting*, *2*(1), 110–120. doi:10.30871/jama.v2i1.727

Ghosh, P. (2011). Financial Failure: The Case of Hindustan Motors Limited. *Anvesha, 10*(1), 54.

Gonzalez, E. A. (2017). *Predicting Corporate Financial Failure Using Macroeconomic Variables and Accounting Data.* Springer Science and Business Media.

Hillegeist, S. & Keating, E. & Cram, D., & Lundstedt, K. (2004). *Assessing the Probability of Bankruptcy*. doi:10.1023/B:RAST.0000013627.90884.b7

Horvathova, J., & Mokrisova, M. (2018). *Risk of Bankruptcy, Its Determinants, and Models*. MDPI. doi:10.3390/risks6040117

Liang, D., Lu, C., Tsai, C., & Shih, G. (2016). Financial ratios and corporate governance indicators in bankruptcy prediction: A comprehensive study. *European Journal of Operational Research*, *252*(2), 561–572. doi:10.1016/j.ejor.2016.01.012

Lubben, S. J. (2011). Financial Institutions in Bankruptcy. *Seattle University Law Review*, *34*(1259), 1263.

Mous, L. (2005). *Predicting bankruptcy with discriminant analysis and decision tree using financial ratios*. University Rotterdam.

Ross, S. & Westerfield, R. & Jaffe, J. (1999). *Corporate finance*. Irwin.

Saedi, A. & Timimi, B. S. A. (2018). The Relationship Between Financial Failure and Market Value: An Empirical Study Using A Sample of Industrial Firms Listed At Qatar Stock Exchange. *Academy of Accounting and Financial Studies Journal, 22*(5), 1-10.

Sewpersadh, N. S. (2020). K-score categorization of JSE listed sectors under the financial distress continuum theory. *Cogent Economics & Finance*, *8*(1748969), 1–16.

Shi, Y. & Li, X. (2019). 1354 An overview of bankruptcy prediction models for corporate firms: A systematic literature review. *Intangible Capital, 15*(2), 114-127.

Tong, Y. (2021). Predicting Predictions of failure and financial distress: A study on Portuguese high and medium-high technology small and midsized enterprise. Foundation of International Studies, 9.

Tsuruta, D., Marea, C., & Xu, P. (2007). *Debt Structure and Bankruptcy of Financially Distressed Small Businesses.* RIETI Discussion Paper Series (No:07-E -032 pp.1).

Van, M.V.,, & Şehribanoğlu, S. (2021). Analysis of Factors Which Affect Financial Failure and Bankruptcy with Generalized Ordered Logit Model. *International Journal of Management Economics and Business, 17*(1), 63. doi:10.17130/ijmeb.803957

Wang, J., Yang, J., Iverson, B., & Kluende, R. (2020). *Bankruptcy and the COVID-19.* Harvard Business School. (Working Paper 21-041)

Wang, L., Zhang, S., Tsai, C., & He, G. (2011). Financial Failure Analysis Based on Both Financial and Non-financial Indicators with Financial Materilas. *Applied Mechanics and Materials, 63-64*, 1009–1012. doi:10.4028/www.scientific.net/AMM.63-64.1009

Yousaf, M., & Bris, P. (2021). Assessment of bankruptcy risks in Czech companies using regression analysis. *Problems and Perspectives in Management, 19*(3), 45–53. doi:10.21511/ppm.19(3).2021.05

Chapter 3
Analysis of B2B Blockchain Apps Using Hyperledgers and Their Implications in This Digital Era

Jeya Mala D.
https://orcid.org/0000-0002-2100-8218
Vellore Institute of Technology, Chennai, India

Priya N.
https://orcid.org/0000-0003-2247-9078
Sri Ramachandra College of Engineering and Technology, India

Pradeep Reynold A.
ASET College of Science and Technology, India

ABSTRACT

In this digital era, at most 80-90% of business transactions are digitized using different mechanisms. In the case of businesses and financial institutions, such digitization poses both merits as well as challenges. Nowadays, the IT industries are focusing on providing a trustworthy solution, namely blockchain-based applications, to provide secured online transactions. This blockchain technology provides a comprehensive solution to B2B applications by providing support to process information across organizations in a highly secured manner. In blockchain, these kinds of secured online transactions are achieved using hyperledgers. In particular, the hyperledger is decentralized as it is replicated across the entire network for all the participants to collaborate in a secured manner. In this chapter, an analysis of the application of hyperledgers in B2B blockchain apps to and their implications in this digital era is provided.

DOI: 10.4018/978-1-6684-5181-6.ch003

INTRODUCTION

Generally, a Blockchain is a distributed data structure that can be considered as a decentralized ledger that contains all the transactions performed over a communication network. Each transaction is recoded as encrypted data and is stored in blocks based on time of transaction. These blocks are organized as chains with back-links. As the transactions are transparent over the network, anyone doing his/her transaction on the network can see the others transaction details.

If an organization wants its B2B or B2C operations to be secured over the network, they will build their own with fully customized or partially customized private Blockchain based on their needs. This will help enhance the security aspects of using Blockchain in secured online transactions.

Especially, in the finance sector, the most important characteristics such as transaction transparency and data immutability are the primary concerns. Some of the banking sectors use Blockchain and they apply cryptography with zero-knowledge proof or zero-knowledge protocol (Morais et al., 2019) to give an authentication to both the parties that the given statement is true. Hence, the parties need not send any additional information apart from the actual fact that, the statement is true. Several online banking transactions are applying Blockchain with machine learning to ensure data protection.

Organizations are nowadays offering smart contracts to allow automatic execution of agreements among the parties when all the conditions mentioned in them are fulfilled. Some of the examples are pledge agreements and agreements on deposits (Westerkamp, Victor, and Kupper, 2018).

Current real-estate businesses are applying Blockchain to solve major tasks of ensuring data storage and validation of property ownership and fund transfer. In these B2B or B2C applications, the transactions are immutable and help the owners to preserve the payment history. Some globally reputed real estate businesses are using this Blockchain technology to simplify the data management process.

Due to the advantages of Blockchain such as reliability and automation, the real estate businesses reap the successful business operations. The smart contracts between the real estate providers and consumers are very fast and secure and are fully automatic.

The global business organizations such as BMW, Walmart, and FedEx have deployed Blockchain for improved data security and operational transparency. By applying Blockchain in business operations, the organizations are getting the benefits of tamper-proof records on all their operations and transactions can simplify the analysis of efficiency of their operations.

Several B2B organizations are using Blockchain to authenticate the assets. Now, organizations are applying trust model based algorithms instead of centralized organizations providing authorities. For them, Blockchain becomes the boon to establish secured operations.

Based on several existing research works discussed in the literature review, it is understood that, several security mechanisms have been introduced by researchers to protect financial transactions from intruders and hackers. Also, it is observed that, the Blockchain technique based on Hyperledger fabric is applied by researchers to protect B2B transactions.

Hence, the objective of this chapter is going to analyze the application of hyper ledgers in B2B transactions and the analysis of existing works in this crucial area of research so that, researchers can work on higher level security mechanisms while dealing with B2B transactions. Further, a case study with real time data set is also demonstrated to better understand the application of Blockchain in finance in this chapter.

BACKGROUND ON BLOCKCHAIN AND ITS FRAMEWORKS

Blockchain technology provides a decentralized, distributed ledger system that can provide a complete record of transactions between multiple parties in a B2B or B2C environment. Even though the Blockchain technology was started up as a means for Bitcoin based transactions, due to its security aspects, it is now expanded its operations in other mitigation technologies. This reduces the human errors involved in data storage when secured storage of data becomes essential.

The Blockchain technology can be applied in any industry or business as it handles everything as digital assets and transactions. As it applies encryption based mechanism, it provides secured online transactions and the integrity preservation in transactions.

While applying Blockchain technology in secured online transactions, it is essential to understand which type of platform to be used to implement Blockchain. There are two most popular platforms are available: namely Hyperledger and Ethereum. Each of them has their applications in real time domains. In the next sections, the detailed view of these frameworks are provided with their advantages and disadvantages in real time problem domains and which framework will be suitable for which kind of applications are provided.

Ethereum Platform for Real-time Applications

It is a public, decentralized, distributed and community-built platform to carry out smart contracts. A smart contract is basically a script that contains parameters that can do some actions or computations when some events happened.

In Etherium Blockchain platform, there is a virtual machine called as Etherium Virtual Machine (EVM) that has a single, canonical state of computer system in which it is working. It is a decentralized, public platform, each node in the network agrees with the state of EVM and also keeps a copy of the state of the system. Whenever a transaction occurs, a new block is added to the Blockchain and it is also added to the global copy of the network which exists in all the nodes of the network.

It is generally a permission-less public network, and the transactions are visible to anyone on the network to access to view the transactions. It is governed by the Ethereum developers. It starts with smart contracts. A smart contract is a software code or condition written in that code that gets executed when the conditions are met.

It provides the control in transfer of digital assets among the parties in that contract. The transactions are immutable, and cannot be altered by anyone. To develop applications using Ethereum, high-level languages such as JavaScript, Python and Golang are used. As Ethereum has a POW mechanism, number of transactions is limited to 20 per second. It has its own cryptocurrency called Ethereum(ETH) and any one can mine ETH by paying for it.

As this provides a decentralized network, a Proof-Of-Work (POW) is running throughout the Blockchain. It helps the participants of a transaction to ensure that, the transaction is a correct one and not the fake.

Typical applications of Ethereum include, Public or B2C applications that help the organizations to create decentralized applications for customer use and they can use Ethereum smart contracts. Using Ethereum, anyone can join the network and can create a node. Each node possesses a copy of the entire Blockchain.

Hyperledger Platform for Real-time Applications

It is an open source, private and confidential platform to build distributed ledger-based solutions. It has modular architecture that can ensure high level of flexibility, scalability, resiliency and confidentiality. This has made it to be the most popular one for several B2B, B2C and other industrial applications. It is managed by Linux.

Generally, Hyperledger is used to create B2B business applications that can have multiple industrial clients. It is used as a platform through which the developers can work with Distributed Ledger Technology(DLT). The B2B Blockchain apps are developed with customized features related to the specific business purpose.

Hyperledger platform provides secured and confidential access with limited access rights across the Blockchain network. Like, SSL certificates, here the Authorization certificates are provided to individuals by which only the businesses that have the authorization rights can only view all the transactions on the network (Li et.al 2019).

This platform which is also called as Hyperledger Fabric is governed by the Linux foundation for which the major contributor is IBM (2018). As this is a product of IBM and Linux, it has achieved huge success.

As the Hyperledger platform provides authorized access, only the members and the peers can access the tools in the platform. This helps to hide and prevent any malicious access to the confidential information from external people who are not having the authorization rights. This platform allows some code to be executed to create transactions when some specific conditions are met. This code is called as chaincode which helps to create dynamic transactions on the go. Some of the programming languages used to write chaincode are Google's Go and advanced Java Script language.

As this platform is a private and authorization based network, there is no need for Proof of Work (POW) to validate the transactions. As the participating organizations agree on a particular transaction, the access by third party organizations cannot view or interfere that transaction. This helps to improve the scalability, transaction rate and performance of the entire network.

Application of Hyperledger in Business Domain

Mainly the Hyperledger focuses on the enterprise solutions. Many business applications preferred Hyperledger for its working mechanism towards the improvement of their business. Lots of research works were done in the business field using Blockchain.

The businesses which use Hyperledger platform need not keep their confidential data on the public Blockchain. It provides the ability to maintain the privacy of organization information when creating a Blockchain application.

Hyperledger fabric has the own network which consists of two or more organizations, peers, fabric code, orderer and channels. It's core components are nodes, peers, ordering service ledger and channels. Each organization is called a member and each member in turn can set up one or more peers as authorized ones to participate in the network using fabric certificate authority. To access the network and to get involved in the transaction, a client side application will be developed and this is written using SDK written in any programming language such as Java Script, Go language, etc.

Workflow of Hyperledger Fabric

In Hyperledger Fabric, the process starts with the client application sending transaction proposals: Each client application proposes transactions to endorse peers for the simulation and endorsement process. Each endorsing peer simulates the proposed transaction and stores sets of read and written data named RW sets. These sets are signed by endorsing peers and are returned to the client application.

Once a client application receives the RW set and endorsed transactions, it has to submit these to the ordering service. This method keeps working, regardless of the transaction endorsement and RW set submitted by other client applications. The ordering service accepts both RW sets and endorsed transactions and arranges them into blocks, then forwards them to committing peers.

The committing peer validates the transactions to ensure the RW set matches the current world state. Once the committing peer validates the transaction, the transaction is updated to the ledger and the world state is automatically updated with write data from the RW set.At each step of the transaction flow, from endorsement to version check, identity verification remains a continuous process.

Hyperledger Fabric is an open-source platform for building distributed ledger solutions, with a modular architecture that delivers high degrees of confidentiality, flexibility, resiliency, and scalability. This enables solutions developed with fabric to be adapted for any industry. This is a private and confidential Blockchain framework managed by the Linux Foundation.

Steps Involved in Business Transaction Management Using Hyperledger Fabric

Step 1: Proposal Creation

Consider a scenario that, a Laptop manufacturing company and its dealership firm. The transaction will be started when a member industry proposes or accesses a transaction request through a client website or portal. The client application then sends this request to the members or peers in the network for endorsement.

Step 2: Transaction Endorsement

Once the peers receive the transaction request, the peers who are in the organization as endorser peers check the Hyperledger fabric certificate authority along with the details required for authentication. Then, the chain of code is getting executed which may be written in 'Go' or 'Java' programming language. Upon execution, the code returns a response. It represents either acceptance or rejection of the transaction itself. This response is sent to the client.

Step 3: Ordering Service Submission

The peers, on receiving the transaction endorsement output, classifies the accepted and rejected transactions. Only the accepted transactions are sent to the ordering service using the client-side application. Then, the peer which is responsible for the ordering service includes the details of the transaction into its specific block and then it sends this request to the other peer nodes which are the members different from them on the network.

Step 4: Ledger Updation

The peer nodes or the organizations which have received this service request shall then update their local ledger in that block. Once it is done, the transactions are committed.

LITERATURE SURVEY

Analysis of Existing Works

Le et al. (2022) discussed the details of blood bank chain a Blockchain-based system called BloodChain, an improved system to support blood information management, providing more detailed information about blood, such as blood consumption and disposal. Blood Chain exploits private Blockchain techniques with a limited number of relatively fast and reliable participants, making them suitable for B2B (Business to Business) transactions. Blood-Chain prevents forgery and information tampering, making the blood management operation more transparent by solving problems in traditional medical institutions, such as missing entry inputs, exit, and band errors. Moreover, the Blood Chain system supports blood transactions among medical institutions and can easily manage blood quality.

In an industry whitepaper released by IBM corporation and GTD solution (2021), gave a detailed report on a Hyper Ledger based supply chain platform proposed by TradeLens. This platform provides real time access to the tracking data and documents related to shipping. This report also indicates that, the platform also handles shipping milestones and exceptions. But it lacks in providing the details on how this task is implemented.

Mohamed (2021) has proposed an architecture that was implemented using Hyperledger Fabric or simply Fabric. It is a permissioned Blockchain implementation that helps to establish a trust model for enterprise context and supports programming languages such as Java, Javascript and Go. However, it has some issues related to sequential execution of transaction and confidentiality of smart contract execution. The fabric proposed here has an execute-order-validate architecture to overcome these kinds of issues. Transactions are executed in parallel which thus increases the overall throughput and also it proposes an isolated environment to install and execute smart contracts. Apart from that, the Blockchain state is shared among all the peers in the network. This has improved the contract confidentiality by having the secured data ledger.

Hammoud H.et al.(2021) analyzed the problem of distributed storage of electronic documents (both metadata and files) in decentralized Blockchain-based B2B systems (DApps).The proposed work solves the main challenges of distributed data storage by grouping data into clusters and managing them with a load balancer, while preventing data tempering using a block- chain network. The considered DApps storage methodology easily scales horizontally in terms of distributed file storage and can be deployed on cloud computing technologies, while minimizing the required storage space. access control implementation, as well as testing and debugging the horizontal scaling algorithm of the described architecture are not implemented and further not considered for future work.

Kassab et al. (2021) discussed the progress and opportunities of remote patient monitoring using futuristic Blockchain technologies and its two primary frameworks: Ethereum and Hyperledger Fabric. An Ethereum-based system is introduced that has competency in storing Electronic Health Data within a secure and immutable Blockchain network. System demonstration indicates that the prototype allows the permissioned stake-holders to add, update, and retrieve EHR data on a RESTful API environment.

Kuhle, Arroyo, and Schuster (2021), demonstrated that asset management in commercial aircraft leasing can realistically be handled by a Blockchain solution. The decentralized aircraft leasing system integrates well with other decentralized applications (identity management, payments, supply chains, insurance, etc.) and will deliver more value in a more developed ecosystem. More and more companies in the aviation industry have included decentralized solutions IoT strategy. Hyperledger sawtooth architecture is applied in the in their implementation stage.

Mueen (2021) proposed a new and novel track and trace Blockchain-enabled Medledger system that leverages the Hyperledger Fabric Blockchain platform using chaincodes (smart contracts).It helps to efficiently and securely execute drug supply chain transactions in a fabric enabled private permissioned distributed network of different pharmaceutical stakeholders. It introduces a non-repudiation process with provenance and traceability for the fast tenacity of any conflicts in the pharma supply chain. The scalability, governance, identity registration, privacy, standards, and regulations have issues with existing implementation.

Demichev, Alexander, and Prikhod'ko (2021) suggested a novel approach to designing totally decentralized data management systems in distributed environments with administratively unrelated or loosely related user groups and in conditions of partial or complete lack of trust between them. the operating principles, structure and algorithms were developed for a system entitled ProvHL (Provenance Hyperledger),which provides provenance metadata management, control of operations with data files, as well as resource access management in the CDCS environment. The results obtained provide the basis for creating a reliable and secure system for managing provenance metadata, access rights and operations with data in collaborative distributed computing environment with partial or complete lack of trust between user groups as well as with a variable number of attached resources and with practically unlimited possibility of increasing the volume of stored data and metadata.

Khan et al. (2021) proposed a MF-Ledger a Blockchain Hyperledger sawtooth-enabled novel, secure and efficient digital forensic investigation architecture where participating stakeholders create a private network to exchange and agree on different investigation activities before being stored on the Blockchain ledger, using Hyperledger Sawtooth. They created the smart contracts to enable the business logic and accomplish the consensus based on the PBFT consensus policy for core systems fault tolerance and PoET engine to simulate a trust execution environment for attaining the evidence chain of custody

Desai et al. (2020) provided an implementation of integrating IoT based product tracking with Blockchain in an open-source multi-sided B2B platform to address integration challenges. It focuses on product-tracking events and sensor data from the factory environment. With this solution, monitoring product information and their production environment are possible for quality control as well as the users within a supply chain. Saving a large amount of sensor data to Blockchain is substituted by creating structured data and its cryptographic hash between two events of the product. Through the immutability feature of Blockchain, the product's information is secured and through the registration method via specific APIs, and the end-users can register if the data integrity is maintained throughout all production locations. The performance scalability has some limitations with this work. In future they planned implementation for automated environment.

Zhang et al. (2020) proposed new system architecture in the entire grain supply chain based on Blockchain technology and designed a multimode storage mechanism that combines chain storage. This prototype system was tested and verified using actual cases and application scenarios. To achieve business data interaction in the industrial chain as well as hazard information supervision in the whole supply chain, customized smart contracts were designed, and a prototype system was instantiated based on Hyperledger Fabric. It can also provide reliable industrial chain information sources for participants, consumers, and third-party supervision departments as well as hazard-related assessment, prediction, and early warning. They planned to combine Internet of Things technology and Blockchain to achieve credible data collection to avoid the flaws in data base collection.

Zang and Lee (2020) have investigated some protocols of Blockchain and provided an analysis of their performance and various application scenarios. They have analyzed the various protocols applied for business applications. The protocols analyzed are: PoW (Proof of Work), PoS (Proof of Stake), DPoS (Deligated Proof of Stake), PBFT (Practical Byzantine Fault Tolerance) and Ripple. Their comparison results indicate that, the PoW, PoS and DPoS are probabilistic finality protocols. This indicates, the attackers have to create a private chain with large amount of computational power to replace the valid chain. For infiltrating into the Bitcoin based transaction network, if the fraction of computational power is greater than or equal to 50%, the network can be easily hacked. Whereas, in the case of PBFT, the fault tolerance is 1/3 that is the number of normal nodes must be greater than 2f+1 and the number of malicious or crashed nodes must be less than f. In the case of Ripple Protocol, the fault tolerance is only 20%. That means, in a Blockchain network with Ripple protocol, can tolerate the Byzantine problem in 20% of nodes in the entire network without any problem in consensus result.

Yong et al. (2020) have given a solution that can handle the major processes of vaccine supply chain. The Ethereum based solution proposed by them can handle virtual payment using virtual coins. It also has some intelligent recommendation models to forecast vaccines demand, production evaluation and assisting the identification of vaccine recipient.

Chang et al. (2020) have proposed a model to re-engineer the business process using Blockchain. In their work, some of the advantages such as real-time tracking, cost reduction and payment time reduction are achieved. They have also proposed some control points for B2B supply chain by some modification in the data structure. The authors included concepts of on-chain and off-chain as the mechanisms for data management. In the B2B environment, the entire data must be present in the Blockchain ledger for audit and traceability purposes. According to their work, in B2B environment the application of permissioned Blockchain with limited number of stakeholders help improve the throughput and completely eliminates the fees required for transactions.

Bumblauskas et al. (2020) have proposed a novel architecture based on Hyperledger Sawtooth block chain. Their architecture helps to capture the data at every step of the supply chain using IoT. It has a proxy server for authentication to handle the access rights of stakeholders and ensures that, the users access only the authorized data. They have also focused on the implementation of B2B logistic chain traceability using smart contracts.

Cui et al. (2019) proposed a framework that uses Electronic Chip ID(ECID) to identify the devices uniquely. This unique id is used to register the devices on the Blockchain. The framework has used the Hyperledger Fabric framework's smart contract. This proposed framework is used to track the IoT objects that are helped to collect the data used for traceability.

Wen et al. (2019) proposed a mechanism based on Attribute Based Encryption (ABE) as a traceability solution with privacy compliance. It helps to provide the facility to decrypt the encrypted data based on their access privileges. Their work was proposed on Ethereum with permissionless Blockchain without compromising data privacy. However, for B2B applications, these kinds of permissionless Blockchain are not suitable.

Hasan et al. (2019) proposed a traceability solution using Ethereum smart contracts and Raspberry PI. But there are some conditions that could not cover all the contexts with specific needs such as limited status reporting and transport conditions. Also, non-compliance notifications of this approach leads to efficiency issues for the management of smart contracts. To avoid several physical contracts signed by shipper, consigner and consignee, a single digital smart contract is created. This is specifically applied for B2B based shipment management system with smart contracts that have specific needs.

Imeri and Khadraoui (2018) proposed a smart contract based Blockchain solution for shipment emergency case management. It is used for instant notifications and a portal for data access management. In their proposed solution, thru this portal, a stakeholder can decide the specific stakeholder to share the information so that, others cannot see the shared data.

Westerkamp, Victor, and Kupper (2018) proposed a mechanism to preserve the product transformations traceability by focusing on the issue of physical goods projection in digital representation. Here, a smart contract is created to generate non-tangible tokens and then an input that has transformation recipe with these tokens and a token corresponding to the new product as output. Their work has also introduced different roles such as producers, logistic and retail firms and suppliers.

Caro et al. (2018) have proposed an IoT enabled solution for traceability of agriculture food supply management. They have introduced a novel concept of integrating edge devices such as gateways as nodes in the Blockchain. According to their findings, the Hyperledger Fabric gave better latency, network performance and CPU load performance. However, the results of their findings does not show any advanced usage of smart contracts to control business logic.

Vovchenko et al. (2017) analyzed that the Blockchain technology contributes to financial security of the modernization operations of business processes and high organized centralized structures of the Blockchain technology. The Blockchain application for financial transactions allows providing high quality of the contracts implementation between the digital economy's economic agents.

This extensive literature survey indicated the application of Blockchain with Hyperledger platform which helps in providing secured B2B transactions. As this chapter's objective is to showcase the various existing approaches, to strengthen the readers' understanding on this specific area, a case study is also taken and explained below.

CASE STUDY: APPLICATION OF BLOCKCHAIN IN B2B TRANSACTIONS FOR FINANCE APPLICATIONS

Here, the case study is taken from Solana Dataset. The Solana is a Blockchain platform available publicly which is a decentralized and open source one with proof of stake and proof of history as its consensus achievement. It can be used by anyone who wants to do their research. Solana is a Hyperledger based platform and can interact with smart contracts. It is very easy to use and will be an effective DeFi platform. It can handle approximately about 50000 transactions per second and is much faster than Ethereum.

As this chapter focuses on the application of Hyperledger platform in Finance applications, it is taken for this case study analysis.

The data set contains the daily prices of the products and the study helps to predict the price based on the history.

Python Code for Data Analysis

```
import gc
from tqdm import tqdm
import numpy as np
import pandas as pd
from pylab import rcParams
import matplotlib.pyplot as plt
from sklearn.metrics import mean_squared_error
from scipy.stats import probplot
import datetime as dt
from datetime import date
from datetime import timedelta
from fbprophet import Prophet
```

Code to Display the Input Dataset

```
%matplotlib inline
import os
import warnings
warnings.filterwarnings("ignore")
In [2]:
data0 = pd.read_csv("../input/solana-data/SOL1-USD.csv")
data0[-5:]
Out[2]:
```

The input data for analysis is given in table 1.

Table 1. The input dataset for analysis

	Date	Open	High	Low	Close	Adj Close	Volume
546	2021-10-08	154.256546	168.846375	152.755768	158.949203	158.949203	2.781849e+09
547	2021-10-09	158.704697	161.407318	154.869797	156.825836	156.825836	1.522024e+09
548	2021-10-10	156.751923	158.361572	146.898239	148.048706	148.048706	1.556965e+09
549	2021-10-11	147.800446	153.921143	140.363968	144.858139	144.858139	1.851795e+09
550	2021-10-12	145.002853	145.574509	141.153732	144.095398	144.095398	1.856836e+09

Code to Display Price Details

```
data1=data0
data1['date']=pd.to_datetime(data1['Date'])
data1=data1.drop(['Date'],axis=1).reset_index(drop=True)
```

Now, the data based on date-wise price particulars is given in table 2.

Table 2. Price data representation with date

S.No.	Open	High	Low	Close	Adj Close	Volume	Date
0	0.832005	1.313487	0.694187	0.951054	0.951054	8.736428e+07	2020-04-10
1	0.951054	1.049073	0.765020	0.776819	0.776819	4.386244e+07	2020-04-11
2	0.785448	0.956670	0.762426	0.882507	0.882507	3.873690e+07	2020-04-12
3	0.890760	0.891603	0.773976	0.777832	0.777832	1.821128e+07	2020-04-13
4	0.777832	0.796472	0.628169	0.661925	0.661925	1.674761e+07	2020-04-14
...	...	...	...	...	...	...	...
546	154.256546	168.846375	152.755768	158.949203	158.949203	2.781849e+09	2021-10-08
547	158.704697	161.407318	154.869797	156.825836	156.825836	1.522024e+09	2021-10-09
548	156.751923	158.361572	146.898239	148.048706	148.048706	1.556965e+09	2021-10-10
549	147.800446	153.921143	140.363968	144.858139	144.858139	1.851795e+09	2021-10-11
550	145.002853	145.574509	141.153732	144.095398	144.095398	1.856836e+09	2021-10-12

```
import mplfinance as mpf
mpf.plot(data1a[-60:], type='candle',mav=(3,6))
```

Figure 1. Finance data analysis with date Vs. price

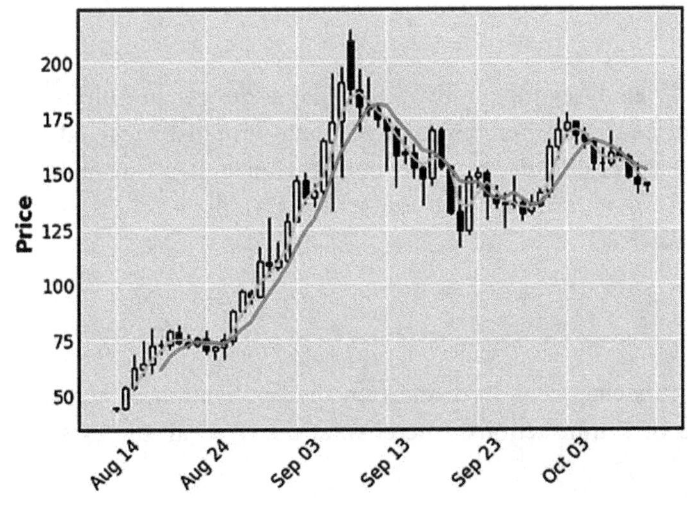

Fit Past and Predict Past

In [9]:

```
ph = Prophet()
ph.fit(item1)
forecast1=ph.predict(item1)
figure = ph.plot(forecast1)
figure.show()
```

Figure 2. Price Prediction Plot

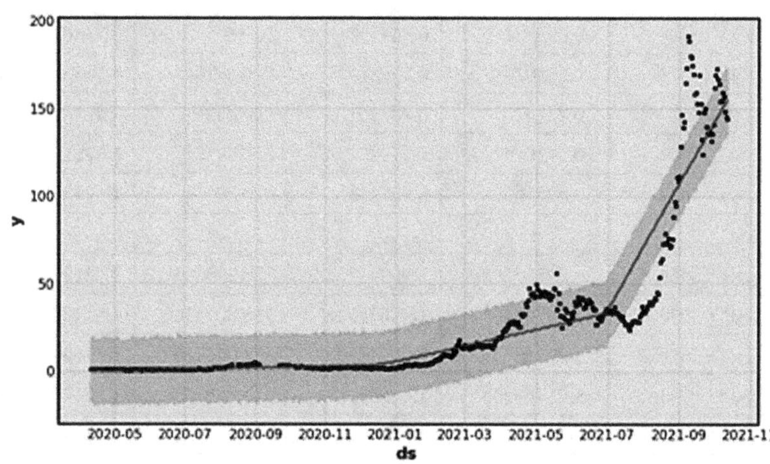

In figure 2, the price prediction is done based on the historical data analysis.
The dataset is found in:

https://www.kaggle.com/datasets/varpit94/solana-data
https://www.kaggle.com/datasets/sapere0/bitcoinheist-ransomw
are-dataset/code

The above case study analyses the application of Hyperledger in Solona dataset for a business application in which the price is predicted based on the data-wise historical data. This helps the customers to buy a share based on the predicted price particulars. Hence, it is especially useful for B2B and B2C transactions.

CONCLUSION

The major purpose of this chapter is to discuss on the application of Hyperledger based Blockchain technology for secured B2B transactions. The chapter analyzes all the existing works done by the researchers on the Hyperledger platform which provides insights to the researchers to conduct further research works in this area.

As per the analysis, it is summarized that, the key component of Blockchain technology is it is decentralized and can be utilized on any network. As it is distributed, there will be several target points instead of a single target. In the case of Hyperledger fabric implementation of Blockchain, because of the authenticated access of the transactions over the network, the infiltration into the systems or websites is prevented. Because of its decentralized nature, the network traffic and storage overloading will be avoided. Hence, the application of Hyperledger based Blockchain implementation helps in mitigating B2B transactions with high throughput without cyber threats on their implementation. Also, by using the Hyperledger based implementation, the fraudulent transactions and Anti-money laundering crimes are prevented. Finally, this chapter discusses a case study on the application of Hyperledger in B2B transactions using an existing dataset. Thus, this chapter analyzes the existing works and discusses on how it can be extended for future research works to enable secured B2B transactions using Hyperledger fabric framework.

REFERENCES

Bumblauskas, D., Mann, A., Dugan, B., & Rittmer, J. (2020), A Blockchain use case in food distribution: Do you know where your food has been? *International Journal of Information Management, 52*. doi: .2019.09.004 doi:10.1016/j.ijinfomgt

Caro, M. P., Ali, M. S., Vecchio, M., & Giaffreda, R. (2018), Blockchain-based traceability in agri-food supply chain management: A practical implementation. *Proceedings of 2018 IoT Vertical and Topical Summit on Agriculture - Tuscany (IOT Tuscany),* 1–4. doi:10.1109/IOT-TUSCANY.2018.8373021

Chang, S.E., Chen, Y.C., & Lu, M.F. (2019). Supply chain re engineering using Blockchain technology: A case of smart contract based tracking process. *Technological Forecasting and Social Change, 144*, 1 – 11. doi: .techfore.2019.03.015 doi:10.1016/j

Cui, P., Dixon, J., Guin, U., & Dimase, D. (2019). A Blockchain-based framework for supply chain provenance. *IEEE Access: Practical Innovations, Open Solutions*, *7*, 157113–157125. doi:10.1109/ACCESS.2019.2949951

Demichev, A., & Alexander, K. (2021). Business Process Engineering for Data Storing and Processing in a Collaborative Distributed Environment Based on Provenance Metadata, Smart Contracts and Blockchain Technology. *Journal of Grid Computing*, *19*(3), 2021. doi:10.100710723-021-09544-4

Desai, S., Deng, Q., Wellsandt, S., & Thoben, K. (2020). An Implementation of IoT-Based Product Tracking with Blockchain Integration for a B2B Platform. *Proceedings of the 2020 IEEE International Conference on Engineering, Technology and Innovation (ICE/ITMC)*. 10.1109/ICE/ITMC49519.2020.9198639

Hammoud, O., Tarkanov, I., & Kosmarski, A. (2021). An Architecture for Distributed Electronic Documents Storage in Decentralized Blockchain B2B Applications. *Computers*, *2021*(10), 142. doi:10.3390/computers10110142

Hasan, H., AlHadhrami, E., AlDhaheri, A., Salah, K., & Jayaraman, R. (2019). Smart contract based approach for efficient shipment management. *Computers & Industrial Engineering*, *136*, 149–159. doi:10.1016/j.cie.2019.07.022

IBM. (2018). *The Linux Foundation's Hyperledger Fabric enables confidentiality in blockchain for business*. https://www.ibm.com/blogs/blockchain/2018/04/hyperledger-fabric-enables-confidentiality-in-blockchain-for-business/

Imeri & Khadraoui, D. (2018). *The security and traceability of shared information in the process of transportation of dangerous goods*. doi:10.1109/NTMS.2018.8328751

Kassab, M., Destefanis, G., DeFranco, J., & Pranav, P. (2021, May). Blockchain-Engineers Wanted: an Empirical Analysis on Required Skills, Education and Experience. In *2021 IEEE/ACM 4th International Workshop on Emerging Trends in Software Engineering for Blockchain (WETSEB)* (pp. 49-55). IEEE.

Khan, A., Uddin, M., Shaikh, A., Laghari, A., & Rajput, A. (2021). MF-Ledger:Blockchain Hyperledger Sawtooth-Enabled Novel and Secure Multimedia Chain of Custody Forensic Investigation Architecture. *IEEE Access: Practical Innovations, Open Solutions*, *9*, 103637–103650. doi:10.1109/ACCESS.2021.3099037

Kuhle, P., Arroyo, D., & Schuster, E. (2021). Building A blockchain-based decentralized digital asset management system for commercial aircraft leasing. *Computers in Industry*, *126*, 103393.

Le, T., Tran, T., Tuan, A., Xuan, S., & Nghia, D. (2022). BloodChain: A Blood Donation Network Managed by Blockchain Technologies. *Network (Bristol, England)*, *2*(1), 21–35. doi:10.3390/network2010002

Li, D., Wong, W. E., & Guo, J. (2019). A Survey on Blockchain for Enterprise Using Hyperledger Fabric and Composer. *Proceedings of the 2019 6th International Conference on Dependable Systems and Their Applications (DSA)*, 71-80. 10.1109/DSA.2019.00017

Mohamed, M. A. (2021). *Enhancing the traceability of B2B logistic chains using Blockchain, IoT and Deep Learning. Software Engineering*. Institut Polytechnique de Paris.

Morais, B., Peydró, J. L., Roldán-Peña, J., & Ruiz-Ortega, C. (2019). The international bank lending channel of monetary policy rates and QE: Credit supply, reach-for-yield, and real effects. *The Journal of Finance*, *74*(1), 55–90. doi:10.1111/jofi.12735

Mueen, U. (2021). Blockchain Medledger: Hyperledger fabric enabled drug traceability system for counterfeit drugs in pharmaceutical industry. *International Journal of Pharmaceutics*, *597*, 120235. doi:10.1016/j.ijpharm.2021.120235 PMID:33549813

Vovchenko, N. G., Andreeva, A. V., Orobinskiy, A. S., & Filippov, Y. M. (2017). Competitive Advantages of Financial Transactions on the Basis of the Blockchain Technology in Digital Economy. *European Research Studies*, *20*(3B), 193–212.

Wen, Q., Gao, Y., Chen, Z., & Wu, D. (2019). A Blockchain-based data sharing scheme in the supply chain by iiot. *2019 IEEE International Conference on Industrial Cyber Physical Systems (ICPS 2019)*, 695–700. doi: 10.1109/ICPHYS.2019.8780161

Westerkamp, M., Victor, F., & Küpper, A. (2018). Blockchain-based supply chain traceability: Token recipes model manufacturing processes. *2018 IEEE International Conference on Internet of Things (iThings) and IEEE Green Computing and Communications (GreenCom) and IEEE Cyber, Physical and Social Computing (CPSCom) and IEEE Smart Data (SmartData)*, 1595–1602.

Yong, J. (2020). An intelligent Blockchain-based,system for safe vaccine supply and supervision. *International Journal of Information Management*, 52.

Zhang, X., Sun, P., Xu, J., Wang, X., Yu, J., Zhao, Z., & Dong, Y. (2020). Blockchain-Based Safety Management System for the Grain Supply Chain. *IEEE Access: Practical Innovations, Open Solutions*, *8*, 36398–36410.

KEY TERMS AND DEFINITIONS

B2B Transactions: These transactions refer to business transactions between two business entities. It includes subscriptions, product purchases, contract agreements, investments etc. They typically mean wholesale transactions.

B2C Transactions: B2C transactions are related to the relationship between Business and Customers. These transactions typically mean the individual customers' purchases of products from an organization.

Blockchain: Blockchain is a distributed data structure that can be considered as a decentralized ledger that contains all the transactions performed over a communication network. Each transaction is recoded as encrypted data and is stored in blocks based on time of transaction.

Chain Code: The hyperledger platform allows some code to be executed to create transactions between two business entities when some specific conditions are met. This code is called as chain code which helps to create dynamic transactions on the go. Some of the programming languages used to write chain code are Google's Go and advanced Java Script language.

Ethereum: It is a technology that focuses on digital money transactions including global fund transactions, payments via internet.

Ethereum Platform: It is one of the Blockchain platform that establishes a decentralized, peer to peer network which executes smart contracts between the business transactions.

Hyperledger Fabric: It is developed by IBM with Linux as a flexible Blockchain framework which acts as a standard for enterprise Blockchain platforms. It has a wide range of customer base.

Proof of Work: It is a technique applied to verify the transactions' accuracy when the transactions are made using cryptocurrencies. As there is no centralized control authority in cryptocurrency-based transactions, they use Proof of Work (POW) to ensure the transaction integrity.

RW Sets: In Hyperledger Fabric, the process starts with the client application sending transaction proposals: Each client application proposes transactions to endorse peers for the simulation and endorsement process. Each endorsing peer simulates the proposed transaction and stores sets of read and written data named RW sets. These sets are signed by endorsing peers and are returned to the client application.

Smart Contracts: They allow the participants of a business transaction to do their transactions without any intermediary or any centralized trusted authority.

Chapter 4
Crisis Resolution Through Insolvency Proceedings in Modern Times:
The Perspective of Slovenian Practice

Drago Dubrovski
https://orcid.org/0000-0001-9753-9552
International School for Social and Business Studies, Slovenia

ABSTRACT

Crises in business occur at different levels and in different dimensions, and often cannot be managed without the help of insolvency proceedings and insolvency law. Crisis management in these cases is extremely challenging and risky, although often the last way out of an acute crisis situation. The Slovenian normative regulation and the business and insolvency practices in place give companies that find themselves in an acute crisis and require the protection of the court a limited formal and practical opportunity to successfully manage (remedy) the resulting crisis and thus ensure their survival and further development, but the insolvency procedure alone cannot be successful if the other business conditions are not ensured to be fulfilled. Taking into account the theoretical findings and research results, the chapter additionally concludes that insolvency law in companies (creditors and debtors) is insufficiently known to managers, thus making it practically less useful in crisis resolution procedures.

INTRODUCTION

In daily communication, various more or less expert studies, and institutional, entrepreneurial and other organisational materials, one often finds references to natural disasters, various conflicts, epidemics, major or minor difficulties of institutions and companies or even their forced changes and dissolutions, the worrying decline in the performance of individual industries or services and even countries, and overt or covert problems of individuals and large or small communities, which are in some way or another associated with the concept of crisis. Namely, the word crisis is a rather frequently used description for

DOI: 10.4018/978-1-6684-5181-6.ch004

uncertain, difficult, dangerous and future-defining situations, as it relates to an extremely wide range of natural, social, economic, health and mental processes and conditions (e.g. political crisis, economic crisis, financial crisis, oil crisis, environmental crisis, moral crisis, art crisis, crisis of values, health or epidemiological crisis, midlife crisis etc.). In everyday language, the crisis mostly has a prevalent negative connotation, as it is associated with a wide variety of inconveniences, difficulties, stressful situations, and threats. Particularly in recent times, this term and concept has become "popular" in daily communication since the second half of 2008, when practically the whole world was hit first by the financial crisis (financial sector problems and drastic fall in the value of investments), followed by the economic crisis (problems of the real economy), and then, in the first half of 2020, when the Covid-19 pandemic crisis occurred. Crises occur at different levels and in different dimensions, and corporate crises often cannot be managed without the help of insolvency proceedings and insolvency law, which must be well understood not only by the active participants in the insolvency process, but also by the managers of the distressed company on the one hand and the managers of the creditor company on the other.

In this chapter the focus is on the Slovenian normative regulation and the business and insolvency practice, and the authors address the questions (a) whether companies in acute crisis that require the protection of a court have sufficient formal and practical options under the current insolvency law to successfully manage (remedy) the crisis and thus ensure their survival and future development, (b) whether the opening of insolvency proceedings is sufficient to ensure that the causes of the crisis are addressed, and (c) whether corporate insolvency law is sufficiently familiar to managers to be of practical use in crisis resolution procedures.

Contemporary Experience With Crises and Insolvency Law

A crisis is a short-lived, undesirable and critical situation in a company (organisation), which directly threatens the achievement of the objectives of the participants of this company and its continued existence and development, which is due to the intertwined and simultaneous operation of both external and internal causes (Crandall et al., 2014, p. 3; Dubrovski, 2022, p. 64; James & Wooten, 2010, p. 17; Roux-Dufort, 2003; Saleh, 2016, p. 21).

The potential crises that virtually every organisation faces in its life cycle cannot be prevented, as any business in a competitive environment is associated with risk (strategic, financial, implementational, commercial, or technical). However, it is possible to use strategic management methods to prevent a situation from escalating to the point of an acute crisis. In this way, companies develop the resilience to survive in the event of a crisis and to operate under uncertainty. Continuous adaptation of company structures, systems and processes will help to maintain or sustain the acquired level of competitiveness of the offer or operation, while at the same time anticipating potential critical (crisis) points in the company's development in order to prepare for them and either eliminate them or limit their negative impact. In this way, strategic management can be an important tool in the fight against potential crises.

If changes in the global or local environment are becoming more frequent, more rapid and less predictable, what rules or prescriptions should management follow in order to prevent the emergence of a latent or acute crisis in the company and to continue to ensure its (competitive) existence and (accelerated) development? In fact, due to the specificities of each individual case (company), there is no common, universally valid recipe. Therefore, in the light of current developments in the environment, business practice is constantly developing new approaches to survive and succeed in such a turbulent, complex, and chaotic global environment, all of which are more or less based on the necessity and continuity of the so-called three-step approach:

- monitoring developments and changes in the company's environment;
- translating current and future environmental characteristics into the company's strategies, models, processes, and structures; and
- implementing changes in the operation of the company based on the observed and included changes in the environment.

This is the only way for a company to respond to the turbulence of an environment that today may be friendly to the company in terms of business conditions, but tomorrow may be completely hostile, and the three-step approach should not be a temporary or intermittent task, but an ongoing management approach.

However, the crisis can also occur due to sudden external causes that could not be foreseen and prepared for. The more volatile, competitive, sensitive, and unpredictable the environment of an industry or market area, the greater the impact of these unpredictable and sudden external causes of crises. The increasing intensity and dynamism of unpredictable events and developments both in a company (or other for-profit or non-profit, private or multinational, production or service, individual and independent or related and dependent, smaller or larger, or newly created or traditional organisation) as well as in its environment – e.g. the global financial crisis in 2008–2013 and the epidemiological crisis in 2020–2021 – have an impact on the increased difficulty and complexity of ensuring sufficient competitiveness and consequently the existence and development of companies (organisations). It is therefore not surprising that such or different crises are already an inseparable part of modern business. In such a turbulent environment, as companies are increasingly exposed to risks that could jeopardise their existence or further development, modern insolvency law is becoming an increasingly important factor in crisis management.

The legal aspect of the scale of the entrepreneurial crisis puts the knowledge of insolvency law at the forefront. In fact, if an acute crisis situation, the consequences of which are strongly reflected in the finance field, cannot be eliminated through radical changes in operation of an enterprise and out-of-court settlements with creditors on write-off, deferral, or reduction of liabilities (out-of-court restructuring, consensual restructuring), the company still has the option of legal remedy or to use the provisions of judicial insolvency proceedings (in-court restructuring), which, pursuant to Slovenian regulations, include (a) bankruptcy procedure, (b) compulsory settlement (classic, simplified, preventive) and (c) compulsory winding-up (liquidation) procedure.

INSOLVENCY PROCEEDINGS, INSOLVENCY LAW, AND CRISES SOLVING

The characteristic of insolvency proceedings, often the last resort from an acute crisis involving competent national courts, is the presence of a special insolvency law, which must be well known and duly taken into account by the participants. Three basic principles are common to insolvency proceedings: the principle of equal treatment of creditors, the principle of ensuring optimum conditions for payment of creditors, and the principle of the promptness of proceedings.

As a result of the increasing internationalisation of companies and globalisation in general, the international uniform regulation of insolvency proceedings is subject to constant debate and further reform, especially in the EU, where there is intertwining or even a conflict between mandated or optional effects and suspensive effects of uniform rules on national insolvency law (Virgós & Garcimartín, 2004, p. 5-6). In general, the EU insolvency law reforms, which are being vigorously pursued by individual countries, have the following priorities: (a) incentives for timely reorganisation, (b) incentives for out-of-court restructuring, (c) the possibility to raise fresh money, and (d) incentives for the debtor to play a role in impending, expected illiquidity.

Wood (2013, p. 96) meaningfully classified global insolvency jurisdictions into three groups: pro-creditor, pro-debtor, and disinterested (not interested, countries without a business tradition). Research shows that the survival rate of companies after restructuring is highest where insolvency law allows effective solutions to be found between the debtor and creditors, and restructuring is therefore the most common insolvency procedure. A well-functioning insolvency framework that includes measures from early intervention before the company gets into serious difficulties, to timely restructuring to ensure the preservation of viable parts of the company that are able to survive (ger. "neue Sanierungskultur"; Brosent, 2018, pp. 53), the realisation of assets when businesses cannot be saved in any other way, and, last but not least, second chances for honest entrepreneurs on the basis of debt relief (breathing space), is an essential part of a good business environment, as it supports trade and investment, helps to create and preserve jobs, and helps economies to better withstand the economic shocks that cause high levels of non-performing loans (NPLs) and unemployment (EU Directive). In countries characterised by modern insolvency law and the developed business practice of restructuring procedures, according to one of the benchmarks, the average rate of repayment is 83 cents per dollar, while in countries dominated by corporate winding-up (bankruptcy, liquidation), only 57 cents per dollar were repaid (European Commission, 2016).

By reviewing the regulation of judicial rehabilitation procedures, generally from the aspect of crises solving the following can be summarised (Dubrovski, 2006):

- practically in all areas, more recent insolvency law provides a wide range of rehabilitation options for companies in deepest crises where considerable creativity and negotiation skills are needed or possible (e.g. the amount of write-offs and repayment deadlines are not exhaustively specified), and bankruptcy as the closure or dissolution of the debtor by selling its assets is the last resort if the procedures fail (the point of no return);
- since it is a combination of business and legal (judicial) aspects of insolvency proceedings, the management and supervision of the respective proceedings is an extremely difficult task, often extended to the monitoring of the debtor until the first deadline for fulfilling obligations, and which requires continuous training not only of managers but also of insolvency judges;
- management (old or new) and managers who are actively involved in designing the insolvency plan proposal in insolvency proceedings, and who in any case must follow the principles of crisis management, have a key role; consequently, they must have the knowledge, skills and experience (competences) appropriate for solving the most demanding business problems by following mandatory legal framework, which is also reflected in their remuneration;
- despite the flexibility, creativity, and innovation in preparing rehabilitation programmes, the supervision of creditors is not reduced and by voting arrangements for each class of creditors and the achievement of a double majority in each class (in terms of amount of claims and number of creditors) the possibility of various adjustments and speculations at the expense of (small) creditors is minimised; and

- since it is almost always the case of more recent legal provisions that allow the debtor greater flexibility in preparing substantive rehabilitation measures, while the supervision of the authorities and the right of decision of creditors is not reduced, not all possibilities have been verified in practice, whereby the insolvency law, which includes the tendency to unify procedures, is being continuously improved.

It was mentioned earlier that the success rate (business rescue rate) of major transformations or restructuring and rehabilitation of companies in crisis is less than 30%, and it is even lower when it comes to rehabilitation projects through court insolvency proceedings. Data show that formal insolvency proceedings as a way of restructuring are largely unsuccessful (only 10% or less than 30%; Moore, 2016, p. 1; http://www.r3.org.uk; Wood, 2013, p. 113). Various surveys have thus consistently pointed to the low survival rate of companies through insolvency proceedings. Regardless of the criteria used, the success rate of transformations or rehabilitations of companies is low when four conditions for successful crisis management are not met, especially if the company does not have a "prioritised, viable business core" (Beale & Keddie, 2018, p. 246). These four conditions are:

- there must be a healthy business core (core activity, core business programme), which is able to provide a positive cash flow and a positive operating result based on added value, also in terms of development or the future;
- a capable, competent management team with the necessary powers (without which even the best projects will be doomed to failure);
- available financial resources (possibly long-term) to bridge the liquidity gap (including payment of rehabilitation costs) and to secure the development step (revitalisation); and
- positive attitude of employees towards the recovery process with sufficient participation and motivation.

If those conditions are not met, then no insolvency law or insolvency procedure will be able to remedy the crisis in such a company, and modern, efficient, understandable, and business-oriented insolvency legislation must provide a framework and assistance for the realisation of these factors (conditions). A modern insolvency law is therefore crucial for an efficient market economy (Lowitzsch, 2007, p. 23). There have been debates in professional circles in the EU for some time now (The Economist, 2002; The Economist, 2009) about the need for Europe to have somewhat more flexible insolvency legislation (softish law approach), and some advocate a version of the US compulsory settlement (Chapter 11), although it is also (Financial Times, 2008) harshly criticised (prolongs the agony of companies that do not generate sufficient added value, allows the retention of incompetent managers, requires high costs of litigation, is too soft or lenient).

Insolvency and Causes of Crisis

Business bankruptcies in developed economies have long been a purely natural and developmentally legitimate phenomenon, which arises when companies, with all other measures, have not been able to defend themselves against the effects of an acute crisis. Bankruptcy procedures are designed to maximize the value of consumer or business debtor's assets and to divide them equitably among creditors (Ferriell & Janger, 2019, p. 7). In the EU, there are around 200,000 bankruptcies per year (or 500 per day), resulting in 1.7 million direct job losses each year (Jourova, 2019), and in the US, with a peak in the 2008 financial crisis, 1.5 million bankruptcies, and an average of 780,000 cases per year thereafter (Ferriell & Janger, 2019, p. 110). It can be estimated that 2,000 companies go bankrupt in the world on a daily basis, but at least that is how many are created, which leads to the exchange of market participants. In Slovenia, the number of bankruptcy proceedings opened against legal persons in the period 2009-2021 ranged from a minimum of 332 (2009) to a maximum of 1384 (2018), with 1016 bankruptcies and 38 compulsory settlements opened in 2021. Bankruptcy generally occurs for three groups of reasons: (a) personal factors related to the personality or characteristics of the entrepreneur or management, (b) factors specific to each individual company and missing resources, or (c) external or environmental conditions (Kücher et al., 2018).

In line with the recommendations of the European Guidelines, the most important objectives of the regulation in the Slovenian Financial Operations, Insolvency Proceedings, and Compulsory Dissolution Act (ZFPPIPP – Zakon o finančnem poslovanju, postopkih zaradi insolventnosti in prisilnem prenehanju [Law on financial operations, insolvency proceedings and compulsory winding-up]) are as follows:

- facilitate legal certainty in the market and promote economic stability and growth;
- maximise the value of the debtor's assets;
- ensure an appropriate balance between the sale of assets to pay creditors and the financial restructuring of the debtor;
- ensure equal treatment of creditors who are in the same position vis-à-vis the debtor;
- enable a timely, effective and impartial assessment of the insolvency situation;
- preserve the value of the bankruptcy estate for equal (proportional) distribution among creditors;
- ensure a transparent and predictable legal regulation for insolvency proceedings, which includes an incentive for the collection and dissemination of information; and
- recognise existing rights of creditors and establish clear rules to determine the order in which claims are paid.

Bankruptcy and insolvency are not interchangeable terms. Bankruptcy is an insolvency procedure in which the debtor's assets are identified and realised and distributed to creditors in the order of priority, determined by law, due to the inability to pay debts. Insolvency proceedings are opened against an insolvent company. Insolvency is a prerequisite (reason) for opening both bankruptcy proceedings and compulsory administration proceedings. In general, insolvency is most often defined as a financial and economic situation in which an entity is unable to repay its debts in time, such as (Curry & Schorer, 2016; Smithson, 2016) long-term insolvency when an entity does not have sufficient funds to pay its debts (balance-sheet insolvency, technical insolvency), or a more persistent insolvency when an entity has sufficient assets, but these are not in a suitable liquid form in order to settle liabilities upon maturity (cash-flow insolvency, actual insolvency). "Insolvency is probably the most commonly spoken, but the least understood word in the vocabulary of corporate renewal" (Platt, 1998, p. 21). The same author cites four related but conflicting definitions of insolvency. In "bankruptcy terms," it means that the company has negative capital (the amount of liabilities exceeds the value of assets). Technical insolvency occurs when a company breaches a contractual obligation, usually in connection with a bank loan. A technically insolvent company is not necessarily insolvent in the sense of bankruptcy. Economic insolvency is a situation where a company's liabilities exceed the present value of its future cash flows; the company will never earn enough to repay all its creditors. Capital insolvency, on the other hand, means insufficient capital to carry on with the business (Platt, 1998, p. 31). In other literature (Knecht, 2006, p. 744), the authors find a division of solvency into actual (the company's ability to settle its liabilities in the event of liquidation by transforming its assets and property into cash necessary for the payment of all liabilities) and technical (the ability of the company to have the necessary liquid assets to cover the due liabilities on the due date), which can also be considered as liquidity. Solvency can also be divided into technical (current, day-to-day) and actual (long-term).

Article 14 of the Slovenian ZFPPIPP defines insolvency in a reasonably analogue way as a situation that arises when the debtor (a) within an extended period of time is not able to settle all their liabilities falling due within such period of time (hereinafter: continuous insolvency), or (b) becomes insolvent in the long-term because they have insufficient assets to repay all debts; both criteria are defined in detail in the continuation of the text of the respective Article.

Long-term insolvency is a situation that arises if the debtor is unable to pay all of their liabilities that are due during that period. The illiquidity position is the opposite of the liquidity position (short-term solvency). Short-term solvency as the ability to meet due obligations in a timely manner is assessed in certain shorter periods of time and means the ability of an individual to settle all liabilities that are due in that period within a certain period of time. Therefore, the authors use the term liquidity as a synonym for short-term solvency. Insolvency over a shorter period therefore does not in itself constitute a situation of insolvency but must be assessed over a longer period. Liquidity is the ability to convert non-monetary assets into monetary assets, and the degree of liquidity depends on the time and cost required to do so. It is therefore a process aspect of the quality of an asset form, which is studied dynamically, in terms of distance to the most liquid asset form – money. In this context, Knecht (2006, p. 744) distinguished between absolute liquidity, which is a characteristic of assets to be converted into a means of payment over time, and relative liquidity, which is the ratio of available cash to matured liabilities.

Long-term insolvency is the permanent inability of a legal or natural person to fulfil all obligations upon their maturity. In the case of economic organisations, we use the term capital adequacy as a synonym for long-term solvency. Capital inadequacy is a financial situation in which an entity does not hold an adequate amount of capital for the volume and types of business it carries out and the risks to which it is exposed. The amount of actual capital a company has is therefore less than the amount of capital it needs. Insolvency therefore arises, in this context, if the debtor is unable to pay the outstanding debts over a longer period (= a more permanent illiquidity) or becomes insolvent in the long term, and is permanently insolvent if they are more than 2 months late in fulfilling one or more obligations in a total amount exceeding 20% of their declared liabilities. A debtor is insolvent if the value of its assets is less than the sum of its liabilities (= over-indebtedness) and if the loss for the current year, together with the losses carried forward from previous years, has reached half of the share capital and that loss cannot be covered by the profits or reserves carried forward.

Although the notion and content of insolvency are sufficiently defined in the insolvency law, from the point of view of the processes of resolving and preventing the crisis situation in the company, it should be emphasised that insolvency (either as a more permanent insolvency or as a long-term insolvency) is not the cause of the crisis, but the consequence. This means that the crisis is addressed in a company not by focusing on how to resolve the insolvency, but by focusing on the areas of the business that caused the crisis in the first place. If a company in difficulty successfully completes a comprehensive recovery in the areas that led to the crisis, the insolvency will resolve itself; but if the primary focus is on the insolvency, then financial recovery measures can only temporarily resolve the situation, which will reoccur if other areas of the business have not been intervened in (e.g. the problem of compulsory settlements with which creditors agreed, but the company ended up in bankruptcy in a few months' time because the causes that led to the insolvency were not addressed). Instead of the insolvency itself, one therefore primarily examines and then addresses the correct, real causes that led to the crisis, which could be:

- direct and indirect causes or
- external and internal causes.

It is the direct causes that are most inextricably linked to the crisis, and their impact on the emergence of the crisis is decisive. Indirect causes do not act directly on crises, but influence other (direct) causes to intensify and bring them closer to crisis. The decline in market share may be a direct cause of the crisis, but it has previously been influenced by other, indirect causes of the first order (such as quality problems), indirect second-order causes (such as outdated technology not allowing for quality production), third-order causes (such as inadequate maintenance of key hardware), etc. External causes of crises are usually those that have arisen in the company's environment and over which it has had no significant influence. This is why they are often referred to as objective and exogenous. The internal causes of crises are those that arose in the company, so they are also characterized as subjective and endogenous.

Figure 1 should therefore first identify the causes of business failure, which would then be eliminated, or their impact reduced in the recovery process, resulting in the elimination of insolvency.

Figure 1. Example of the Sequence of Causes, Symptoms and Consequences of a Crisis

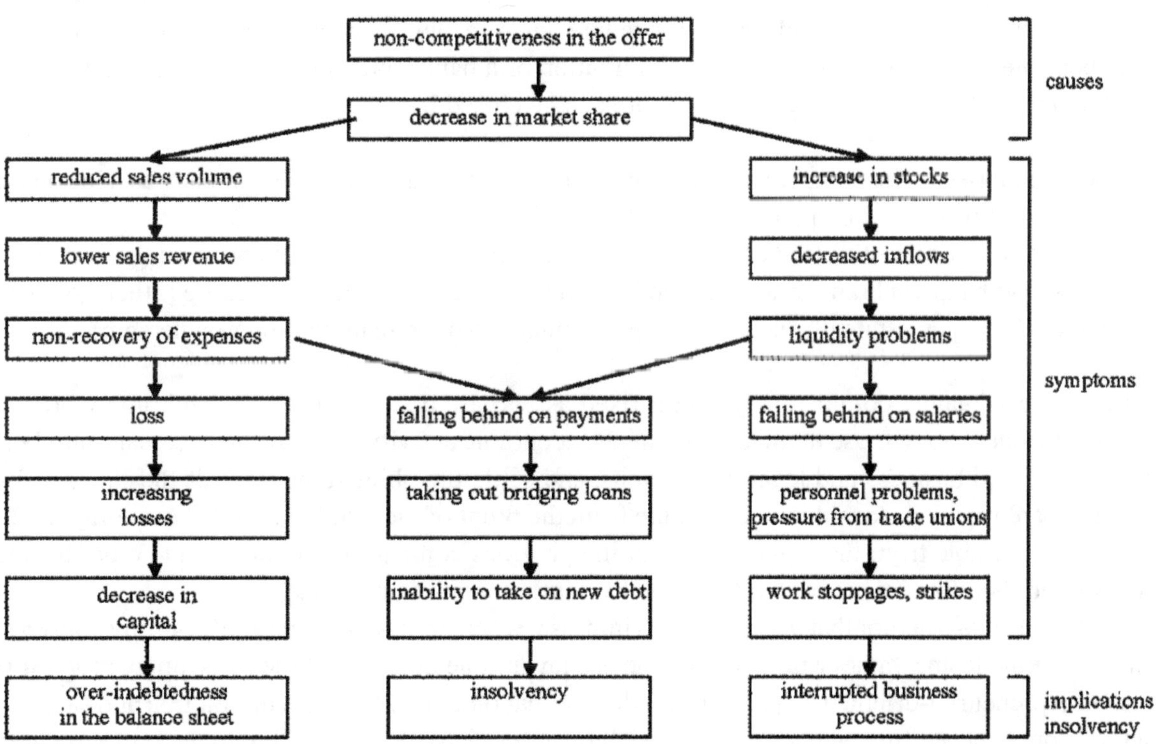

Bankruptcy is the result of a loss of legitimacy of the company, which causes a break in its links with the environment (exit from the business ecosystem). Since bankruptcy is a form of exit from a crisis, and bankruptcy is therefore directly linked to the crisis, the causes of bankruptcy are those that led the company into the crisis situation. To these should be added those that have taken effect in the last phase of the process from the onset of the crisis to bankruptcy, which are most often classified: unsolvable or unresolved conflicts between the interests of the participants of the company; unwillingness or inability of creditors or owners to financially support the needs of the debtor; inability of the creditor and the debtor to resolve their relationship on their own; limited and tightened conditions for the provision of the necessary funds (material, energy, services, ðnancial assets, personnel, equipment, guarantees, etc.); inability to recover payment or sell surplus stocks; departure of key individuals; strikes and other forms of termination of work; termination of long-term contracts by the most important buyers, negative views expressed by the lay and professional public in the media, etc.

Insolvency Proceedings in Slovenia in Theory and Practice

The legal consequence of the bankruptcy procedure is that the company (bankruptcy procedure may also be opened for a sole trader carrying out a commercial activity or for a natural person) is dissolved and the insolvency estate obtained from the sale of its assets is distributed among the creditors in proportion to the amount and position of their claims. Since a company is deleted from the Companies Register (www.ajpes.si) after it has gone bankrupt, it is an unfavourable resolution of the crisis from the point of view of the company. However, if a basic and promising activity or a production and sales programme can be preserved as part of a bankruptcy procedure, such resolution of a crisis, when it comes to the lowest possible point of (poor) performance (initiation of a bankruptcy procedure), is indeed a favourable outcome. Indeed, the bankruptcy procedure can be closed by:

- the sale of assets (the company ceases to exist, its assets are sold out, the company as a legal entity is removed from the Companies Register); or
- the sale of a legal entity (the entity is sold without liabilities as a legal entity on the active side, usually with known brand, references and certificates, the bankruptcy procedure is then conducted to the insolvency estate, the sold company continues to operate under other ownership).

If the assets (mainly commercially useful fixed assets) are bought out of the bankruptcy proceedings by someone who will use them to continue the economic activity, employ the necessary number of people, enter into business and legal transactions, and settle the obligations towards the state, such an end to the bankruptcy is considered favourable from the point of view of the national economy (and, of course, unfavourable from the point of view of the previous company). Productive and other business assets should therefore be put back into productive use as soon as possible.

An asset-deal of a debtor that has reached an impasse, where its assets are partially or fully unused and at the same time losing value, while in principle is a favourable outcome of the bankruptcy proceedings for an entrepreneurial-oriented acquirer, is not the optimal outcome. With the dissolution and sale of the assets of a once successful company, exceptional human (professional) and technological cores (centers), years of accumulated knowledge and experience, brand, industrial property, references, standards, etc. are lost, which once represented the so-called intangible assets of the company and the relative value (structural connection of individual parts and network market connection).

A peculiarity of Slovenian law is that a company that has been placed in bankruptcy proceedings can no longer enter any other type of proceedings that would allow the insolvent company to continue to operate (e.g. comparatively to US law, the transition from Chapter 7 to Chapter 11; cf. https://thismatter.com/money/credit/bankruptcy/chapter-conversion.htm), so that the bankruptcy that has been commenced is also the final form of insolvency up to the time of the company's winding-up (of course, in the opposite direction, a company can move from compulsory settlement to bankruptcy). A single insolvency procedure, e.g. under the German regulation, can be directed in four directions: (a) the continuation of the debtor's business through the implementation of a resolution programme (ger. Sanierung), (b) transfer of the company or activity in whole or in part to an interested acquirer with a transfer of the rights and obligations towards the creditors of the bankruptcy estate (uberträgende Sanierung), (c) sale of the company as a legal person without assumption of the obligations towards the bankruptcy estate (Liquidation), or (d) winding-up (liquidation) of the debtor, liquidation of the bankruptcy estate (sale of the debtor's assets) and distribution of the estate to the creditors (Liquidation).

Apart from the fact that an insolvent company that has been the subject of bankruptcy proceedings can no longer enter other forms of rehabilitation (compulsory settlement), Slovenian practice with regard to attempts to manage the crisis through insolvency proceedings is characterised by the following:

- creditors see bankruptcy as the quickest and most effective means of repayment which does not require their specific engagement;
- regulatory regime and case-law do not encourage rehabilitation procedures in bankrupt companies; and
- pre-bankruptcy depletion of the company.

Although it is in the interest of creditors to be repaid as much as possible and as quickly as possible from the debtor's bankruptcy estate, there is rarely a balancing act between the estimated share of repayment in the event of an asset sale and the possibility of a higher repayment in the event of a rehabilitation operation in the context of bankruptcy proceedings. Therefore, creditors, which are predominantly banks and other ðnancial institutions, as well as the State, do not participate in bankruptcy proceedings other than by passively monitoring the process of dividing the proceeds of the sale of the assets of the bankrupt debtor. Slovenian practice in this area has shown the following reasons:

- lack of professional staff with creditors, as bankruptcies are handled by their lawyers or legal departments, who have little managerial or entrepreneurial skills or a comprehensive view;
- active participation in crisis management, while being an unglamorous job, carries additional risks and requires additional commitments, which in most cases, given the prevailing creditors mentioned above, are not accepted by the staff;
- lack of knowledge of the legal frameworks that allow for the treatment of bankrupt companies;
- the conviction of workers as creditors that they will receive higher repayments in a short period of time;
- concealment of personal liability of individuals with creditors (bankruptcy comes in handy as an objective excuse);
- the different actions of competitors in order to promote their interests; and
- the insufficiently active and coordinated role of state institutions.

In insolvency proceedings, creditors are classified into four basic categories, which have different positions with regard to the order in which they are paid out of the bankruptcy estate: separation creditors are those whose claims are secured by a pledge of certain assets, excluded creditors have the right to have certain assets excluded from the bankruptcy estate, preferred creditors have a preference for payment out of the available bankruptcy estate that does not "belong" to the separation creditors, and everyone else is an ordinary (unsecured) creditor.

The position of the creditor's claim in the bankruptcy proceedings is of the utmost importance when it comes to assessing the possibility of repayment from the bankruptcy estate. Although it is estimated that the average payout from the bankruptcy estate in Slovenia is around 45%, the payout ratios vary considerably from one class of claim to another. While secured creditors are paid very high (sometimes as much as 100%) and preferred creditors around half of that, ordinary (unsecured) creditors rarely receive a payout exceeding 10% of the value of their claim. According to some other studies, which also included proceedings against sole proprietors and natural persons (Cepec, 2021), the average repayment of creditors in bankruptcy proceedings in Slovenia was only 4%, while the average repayment of ordinary creditors was only 2%; for secured creditors it was 28% and preferred creditors 22%.

Secured creditors are therefore in principle in the best position in bankruptcy proceedings, but this is not always the case. Despite established mortgages and other insurance, the amount of their repayment will depend on:

- the market value of the assets for which separate repayment is claimed (assets sold in bankruptcy that are not operational rarely reach the values they had at the time of the evaluation and the collateral arrangement),
- the order of rights to separate repayment on the same assets,
- a legally uncontested and substantially accurate entry (record) of the separation right,
- determining whether that part of the property is part of the bankruptcy estate at all (the debtor does not have to be the pledgee of the property),
- time of sale and payment of the purchase price (interval between sale and acquisition of the purchase price), and
- costs of bankruptcy proceedings (separation creditors assume a proportionate share of the costs).

These facts are often ignored by separation creditors, who assume that their claims are well secured, which may be true de jure but not de facto. This inconsistent assumption then leads them not to take an active part in the proceedings, as this is the "task of the administrator." The different positions of creditors' claims and the possibilities of actual repayment described above are important in three respects:

- in the event of bankruptcy, the creditor (on average) cannot count on a high percentage of the repayment of their claim,
- the creditor loses a business partner (the buyer) for good, which can be an even more unfavourable business event, and
- the creditor must pay more attention to securing its claims and to monitoring its client's situation on an ongoing basis (pre-bankruptcy prevention).

The different positions of creditors in insolvency proceedings often lead to major or minor conflicts of interest and disputes, which have a decisive impact on the course of the insolvency proceedings, often bypassing the interests of the survival of the company in difficulty.

Neither the regulatory framework nor the case law favours crisis resolution in the context of bankruptcy proceedings or compulsory settlement. Because of the disruption of established business relationships, bankruptcy can be the worst form of repayment for creditors, as they only get paid a fraction of their claims. However, since bankruptcy also means the end of a legal entity – a company, within the economic system, its collapse has other harmful consequences for the state (workers as a new social burden, loss of budget revenue, loss of users of current services of various state institutions, etc.), for workers (termination of employment relationships, some permanently) and for business partners (loss of turnover). This is why bankruptcy proceedings must also be professionally managed on the economic and not merely legal side. Extending the power of the court to insolvency restructurings does not have the expected effects; the involvement of creditors and other stakeholders is more important (Doing Business in 2004, 2004, p. 74).

Another particular problem is often the so-called pre-bankruptcy exhaustion of a company, when bankruptcy proceedings are introduced relatively late. In a large number of cases, the company has been out of business for some time, there are no active employees in the company anymore, fixed assets are sold out, there are only uncollectible receivables, the transaction account has been blocked continuously for some time, the business is no longer in operation, the business documentation is deficient or even destroyed, and the company is therefore "clinically dead." In Slovenia, too, insolvency proceedings begin too late, which is the responsibility of managers who, despite the progressing crisis, still hope for a miracle that will solve it (Seidl & Voss, 2006, p. 173).

The relatively late introduction of insolvency proceedings is also due to the lack of accountability and sanctioning of management for insolvency and over-indebtedness, in addition to the lengthy court process. The statutory provisions on the necessity to take certain measures in the event of insolvency were intended to protect the company (to prevent the aforementioned exhaustion) as well as to protect creditors and owners. However, there are only a few judicial epilogues on the subject. Thus, there were possibilities of doing business without paying obligations and with continuous account blockage (insolvency), by setting up bypass companies, transferring business to other companies, "tailor-made" state interventions, entering into management contracts, hiding assets, etc. Failure to comply with the provisions on the duties of management in the event of insolvency is elsewhere a direct criminal offence (cf. Faulhaber & Landwehr, 1996, pp. 44-45; Fenger, 2005, p. 130; Ivanjko, 1997; Selinšek, 2006, p. 57), therefore, there is a better chance of avoiding company exhaustion and bankruptcy treatment.

Contrary to what most of the public believes, bankruptcy proceedings do not take so long because of deliberate delays of the bankruptcy trustee. The remuneration system for bankruptcy trustees is designed to encourage them to conclude proceedings as quickly as possible, as their remuneration depends on the amount realised and not on the duration of the proceedings. The often incomprehensibly long duration of proceedings is mainly due to the well-known and lengthy proceedings in the courts, as the bankruptcy trustee is in fact forced to settle many relationships through the courts (payment recoveries, lawsuits for unrecognised claims or disputed actions, land registry matters, the duration of bankruptcy proceedings, etc.).

In terms of legal consequences, bankruptcy is very similar to a liquidation procedure under Slovenian law. In the case of liquidation, a distinction is made between a compulsory (judicial) liquidation procedure, which is carried out over a company that still has sufficient assets to pay its creditors in full but the legal conditions for it to exist have ceased, and a voluntary (out-of-court) liquidation procedure, as defined in the Companies Act. Liquidation proceedings shall be conducted by the administrative receiver. The purpose of the liquidation procedure is to regulate all substantive legal relations internally (employees, management) and externally (company with the environment). The legal consequences of the winding-up procedure are the same as in the case of bankruptcy, with some assets remaining for the owners after the repayment of creditors. Liquidating a company that sees no way out of its difficulties can also be an important and useful rehabilitation process, as it preserves value for the owners. Just as the creation of a company is a natural stage in its life cycle, so is its dissolution (bankruptcy, liquidation, merger). If a company does not have the core capabilities to ensure a minimum competitive capacity to operate without loss (without reducing its own sources of financing), then liquidation as soon as possible is the appropriate measure to ensure that creditors are paid in full, employees can exercise the same rights as in the event of bankruptcy, and the owners are paid a liquidation proceeds which they can use to set up another company with better prospects or to make an investment with more added-value.

Crisis Management Through Compulsory Settlement Procedure

In conjunction with the above-mentioned modern legal frameworks for insolvency proceedings, which aim at preserving business and jobs, leading to more favourable outcomes for all participants, the compulsory settlement procedure is the most important when it comes to avoiding bankruptcy and continuing a company's prospective activity. Judicial compulsory settlement is one of the insolvency proceedings that are conducted with the aim of enabling an insolvent debtor to undergo a financial restructuring that makes it solvent in the short and long term, and to provide creditors with more favourable terms for the payment of their claims than would be the case if the debtor were to be placed in insolvency proceedings, while "preserving their going concern value" (Ferriell & Janger, 2019, p. 693). Compulsory settlement is the process by which a company in difficulty negotiates with its creditors, within the framework and with the help of insolvency law, a different maturity and amount for the settlement of its overdue and unpaid debts. The formal and legal conditions for initiating a compulsory settlement procedure are the same as for bankruptcy, i.e. state of insolvency (permanent insolvency, long-term insolvency).

Compulsory settlement (in-court restructuring) differs from the voluntary settlement (out-of-court procedure, consensual restructuring, voluntary compositions, corporate rehabilitation procedures), which can be carried out when the company has only a few largely unsecured major creditors, among whom there are no conflicting interests, and the structure of debts is relatively simple.

Insolvency proceedings involving a court of competent jurisdiction are characterised by the fact that they usually always involve, in one way or another, the financial sector, which has been most affected by the crisis. The key document to be submitted by the insolvent debtor is the ðnancial restructuring plan (pre-packed bankruptcy plan). The pre-packed bankruptcy plan must contain: (a) a description of the facts and circumstances which indicate that the debtor is insolvent, (b) a proposal for compulsory settlement with predefined content, (c) an estimate of the proportion of unsecured creditors' claims to be paid and the deadlines for payment of such claims if the debtor were to be placed in bankruptcy proceedings, (d) a description of other financial restructuring measures to be implemented by the debtor, and for each of these measures a timetable for implementation, an estimate of the costs of implementation and an assessment of the effects of the implementation of the measure on the remedying of the causes of the insolvency and on the debtor's short-term and long-term solvency, and (e) a description of the facts and circumstances from which it appears that the debtor will be able to meet all of its obligations under the proposed compulsory settlement. The class of exclusion (request for the exclusion of assets from the bankruptcy estate), separation (receivables secured by pledges), and preferred rights (part of employees' receivables) are not affected by the classic compulsory settlement, therefore the company cannot propose a write-off or extend the maturity for them without the consent of such creditors. At the beginning of the procedure, legal consequences arise, which, however, practically mean that on that date the old liabilities that the company temporarily does not have to pay are frozen, while the current liabilities have to be settled on an ongoing basis. By postponing old burdens, a company in difficulty can get some breathing space. The competent court appoints a receiver of compulsory settlement, who, unlike the bankruptcy trustee, has no managerial or administrative powers but is limited to a supervisory function. If the creditors do not approve the compulsory settlement, the law itself immediately triggers the opening of bankruptcy proceedings.

The proportion of compulsory settlements initiated in all insolvency proceedings is very low (Society of Practitioners of Insolvency, 1996, p. 9). The first reason is that it is, as mentioned, an extremely complex project, where both business and legal (and other) skills need to be combined. The second reason is that managers are largely unfamiliar with the field (as long as a company is doing well, recovery and insolvency skills are not a priority) and are not aware of the exceptional opportunities that insolvency law offers. The third reason is that compulsory settlements start too late, which is again the responsibility of managers who, despite the ongoing crisis, are still hoping for a miracle that will save them from their problems (Seidl & Voss, 2006, p. 173), and therefore such a process of revolutionary change will not be necessary.

If bankruptcy is a way of resolving an unmanageable crisis, compulsory settlement is a way of treating a company in which creditors play a decisive role. Successfully prepared and implemented compulsory settlement is often a necessary but also insufficient condition for achieving a turnaround and ensuring redevelopment. The insolvency procedure is a process, not a solution (Miller, 2008, p. 202), under which an entity obtains time and access to new ways of financing the reorganisation (last option of keeping the entity afloat). Compulsory settlement is therefore only one of the stages in treating a company that does not yet guarantee its future positive operation, but in order to be able to carry out other stages of crisis resolution, it must be performed (risk of bankruptcy).

Taking into account the legal aspect of the compulsory settlement procedure, management must, of course, also take care of the day-to-day running of the business, without which even a well-prepared compulsory settlement procedure has no real effect. Leadership is thus faced with a challenging task, as it must operate in three directions:

- arrange a settlement with creditors for liabilities from the previous period,
- ensure the smooth running of the business, and
- adopt accelerated development measures in the medium term.

The problem encountered when attempting to rehabilitate a company through an insolvency procedure of compulsory settlement is therefore the extremely low success rate (in the UK, the success rate of compulsory settlements, which include the Company Voluntary Arrangement (CVA), similar to the Slovenian compulsory settlement but with greater flexibility in the treatment of creditors, the otherwise formal insolvency procedure with an administrator, or the Scheme of Arrangement without an administrator, which is not a formalised procedure, does not exceed 30%; Moore, 2016, p. 1.), which is measured by the continued survival and development of the previous company in crisis with at least industry-average profit rate, growth in shareholder value and adequate competitive market positioning. However, if the success rate is not even close to 30%, then it should probably be (a) formally and substantively amended or radically improved, or (b) abolished in the current domestic regulation. The latter conclusion is based on the fact that, after the opening of a compulsory settlement, for which the company only has to fulfil the formal conditions (submission of the prescribed documents and payment of the advance), it brings further negative effects for the participants (delay of maturity, creation of new creditors, increase in liabilities at default interest rates, no longer having any control over what is happening, limited enforcement procedures, interruption of business projects undertaken and carried out to the detriment of the clients, non-payment of obligations up to maturity, disruption of the market due to the acceptance of business at any price, etc.).

One of the author's studies (Dubrovski, 2020) analysed all 23 cases of companies in Slovenia for which the commencement of classical compulsory insolvency proceedings was announced on the Ajpes website in 2013 (www.ajpes.si/eobjave), and the period of deferred and reduced repayment of liabilities and the restoration of long-term solvency was expected to last until 2018 at the most or, exceptionally, until the first half of 2019, when one can conclude on the success of the implementation of insolvency proceedings with rehabilitation. These are companies that have attempted to resolve the acute crisis through an insolvency procedure of compulsory settlement, an inseparable part of which, in addition to financial restructuring, is a comprehensive business restructuring in all other areas. Of all the companies in crisis that were examined in 2013 and sought to remedy their difficult situation through a traditional compulsory settlement procedure (the survey did not include cases of simplified and preventive compulsory settlement, as well as proceedings against sole proprietors), only two companies (8.7% of the total) were still in business in 2019, but only in one case successfully (with a profit), which is the only way to consider the rehabilitation process successfully completed. In four cases, the compulsory settlement procedure was discontinued, and bankruptcy proceedings were opened, in one case the debtor was merged into the acquiring company after the confirmed compulsory settlement, which ended up in bankruptcy in 2017, and in the remaining 16 cases, bankruptcy proceedings had already been opened for the debtors in 2013 (seven cases), 2014 (eight cases), and 2015 (one case). The mere 4.3% success rate of the compulsory settlements initiated in 2013 points to major shortcomings in (a) the legal framework, (b) the preparation, and (c) the implementation of the financial and business rehabilitation.

A financial restructuring measure is any measure whose implementation, in accordance with the rules of the business and financial profession, makes it possible to eliminate the causes of the debtor's insolvency and ensures that the debtor becomes solvent again in the short and long term, but a financial restructuring by itself will not ensure the recovery of the company unless it is accompanied by restructuring in other areas, in particular in the strategic sales and marketing area within the framework of a competitive business model, which is the starting point for all other restructurings, including financial restructurings.

Empirical Findings on Crisis Resolution Through Insolvency Proceedings in Slovenia

An acute crisis in a company can be manageable or unmanageable. In the event of an unmanageable crisis, the solution is to wind up the company, which can take several forms:

- bankruptcy (the liabilities to be paid to creditors exceed the realisable liquidation value of the assets, so creditors' claims will not be paid in full);
- voluntary or judicial liquidation (the value of the assets still exceeds the liabilities, so creditors will be paid in full, but there are no conditions for the company's continued existence);
- a non-operating business (no value is created, management or owners have not decided to formally wind it up, even though it is not in business);
- an acquisition by another company (the acquired company ceases to exist as a separate legal entity and its assets, liabilities and employees are transferred to another legal entity – the acquirer); or
- merger with another company (two or more companies merge to form a new company, which takes over the assets, liabilities, and employees, while the previous two companies cease to exist).

In the latter two cases, although the company ceases to exist as a separate company, it "acts" with its assets as part of the new company, so it is not dissolved in the classical sense (it is a transfer of activities or assets to another legal entity). It should also be borne in mind that, due to the chain reaction effect of the crisis on the acquiring company, such capital transactions would normally take place after a prior "clean-up" of the company in crisis ("ugly duckling"). As previously mentioned, a specific feature of the bankruptcy procedure in Slovenia is that it is no longer possible to move from bankruptcy to any other form, i.e. the rehabilitation of a company in difficulty is no longer possible once bankruptcy proceedings have been initiated (it is possible to sell assets or a legal entity as a whole). The key type of rehabilitation procedure, which is carried out with the involvement of the competent court, should therefore be compulsory settlement. However, the above-mentioned success rate of only 4.3% for such procedures points to serious shortcomings.

Based on the previous theoretical discourse, several concise analyses of cases from Slovenian business and insolvency practices and the author's long-standing experience in the respective field, it can be established that the judicial compulsory settlement in the current legal framework and business practice has failed to fulfil its purpose, as it does not principally take the rehabilitation function of the company in crisis, and some of the following deficiencies have been detected as well:

- in a vast majority of cases, it means only a short-term resolution of the company's liquidity situation, and not a comprehensive rehabilitation and management of the crisis (which is why the authors witnessed multiple successive compulsory settlements and bankruptcies in the same company few months after the otherwise confirmed compulsory settlement), which was supposed to be the primary purpose of this rehabilitation process, but this way all the parties involved are at a loss;
- There are many instances of abuse of this instrument solely with the purpose of preventing the bankruptcy procedure proposed by the creditor for the debtor, since the compulsory settlement procedure takes precedence over bankruptcy, without a credible and realistic rehabilitation plan being the focus of attention.
- Compulsory settlement is decisively affected by individual groups or even by a single creditor with the largest claims, allowing for many speculative "adjustments" or even abuses to the detriment of small (minority) creditors.
- Financial restructuring measures are often not agreed with the parties involved and they are ineffective, imaginary, and merely formally included, since after the confirmed compulsory settlement it turns out that debtors do not have realistic possibilities to obtain liquid assets from the divest-

ment of commercially unnecessary assets (disinvestments) in a relatively short period of time, the financial restructuring methods do not result in write-off of a significant part of the liabilities or their conversion into equity (recapitalisation). The debtors do not conclude an agreement on a longer repayment of preferential creditors, who have the legal option to require the debtor to repay their claims in full immediately after the settlement is approved.

- Following the finality of the decision to confirm the compulsory settlement in the financial restructuring plan, the agreed fulfilment of the debtor's liabilities is no longer monitored (the court proceedings are closed, the asset manager and the committee of creditors are dismissed), and creditors have to wait with possible measures (enforcement) until the deadline for fulfilling the liabilities (usually between 1 and 5 years), and by then the debtor may already be in an impossible situation or has personally proposed the initiation of bankruptcy procedure in the meantime.
- Compulsory settlement is a rather expensive, complex, and therefore demanding process, which is hampered by unclear legal provisions in terms of detail and implementation, and it is not surprising that there is no completely unified practice on individual issues, which unnecessarily complicates the preparation and implementation of this procedure, which is remedial in principle.
- Compulsory settlement procedure and crisis resolution are not managed by sufficiently qualified management, and the manager has only a supervisory function and does not prepare or propose the financial restructuring plan (this falls under the exclusive competence of the debtor).
- Financial restructuring plans as a central document in the compulsory settlement procedure are most often prepared by some (the same) consultancy, evaluation, and audit firms and persons entering typical and abstract content, irrespective of the specificities of each individual case, while mandatory reports from authorised business assessors, who, of course, (otherwise the proposal for the initiation of compulsory settlement procedure cannot be lodged) in all cases provide favourable opinion that there is at least 50% likelihood for the crisis to be eliminated, the operation successful and the plan achieved, are vague, and the management does not even identify with the content of the plan, which in turn is also not a result of the actually changed vision, strategy and business model. Written measures are not based on the real business practice and are not even implemented after the judicial confirmation of the compulsory settlement.
- The companies in crisis, which are subject to the compulsory settlement procedure, often do not even meet the four basic substantive conditions for a successful rehabilitation, so a real rehabilitation is predestined to fail in advance.

It can be established that, due to a number of legal and business deficiencies, compulsory settlement as a judicial insolvency procedure and often the final option before bankruptcy in domestic economic practice has not actually proved to be a rehabilitation process that would allow companies in crisis to continue to exist and develop in line with the objectives of modern insolvency law, and the respective deficiencies addressed here may therefore be a possible starting point for further analysis and guidance at national or corporate level.

For the purposes of this paper, an additional study on the familiarity of the Slovenian Insolvency Act (ZFPPIPP) was carried out in the summer of 2022 and the perception of its usefulness and practicality was used as a research sample by companies from the metal industry according to the list of the Chamber of Commerce and Industry of Slovenia. The Slovenian metal industry comprises 3,600 companies with a total of 65,000 employees and ranks among the top manufacturing industries in terms of both turnover and export. Metal industries account for 29% of turnover, 30% of export, 34% of employment, and 30% of added value of all manufacturing activities in Slovenia (data for 2020).

In relation to the topic addressed here, this study found that:

- the formal regulation of insolvency procedures in Slovenia is adequate (45% satisfied and 24% dissatisfied), but the current regulation of insolvency procedures offers only limited possibilities for troubled companies to resolve acute crises;
- the law is less understandable and therefore less useful for practicing managers in many segments;
- the amount of repayment of claims, according to the managers, depends mainly on the statutory preferential treatment of secured and preferred creditors, which leaves very little of the bankruptcy estate for ordinary creditors, and in compulsory settlement procedures the latter assume the main and disproportionate burden of rehabilitation;
- while the sanctions provided for the conduct of management that fails to take measures to remedy insolvency and thereby protect creditors are sufficient, they are rarely actually enforced (71% of responses);
- whereas insolvency proceedings with the sale of the debtor's assets prevail, creditors have very little chance of influencing the course of such proceedings (83% of the responses), but at the same time, they do not seek to play a more active role;
- while creditors' managers would prefer debtors' rehabilitation proceedings (compulsory settlement) over liquidation proceedings, such proceedings should be supervised to completion by qualified trustees or crisis managers, otherwise they too will end up in bankruptcy sooner or later;
- the compulsory settlement procedure as a last resort out of the current crisis situation is not adequately regulated in the current legal framework, as it is dominated by either secured or speculative creditors, so that a company that successfully completes a compulsory settlement has little chance of survival, at least in the medium term, which would also be to the benefit of ordinary creditors;
- modern, efficient, understandable, and business-oriented insolvency legislation will not be enough to resolve a company's crisis, as it only provides a legal framework for the design and implementation of other solutions that are part of a company's business rehabilitation.

It follows (among other things) that while insolvency law allows debtor companies to rehabilitate successfully, the awareness about these possibilities among managers who are supposed to deal with rehabilitation is less than desired, which is also due to the complexity of the law, which, in the part that does not deal with the sale of the debtor's assets and its winding up, should be more oriented towards business practice and the business problems that prevail in rehabilitation proceedings. In the light of the previous theoretical/normative discussion and the research carried out, it is therefore possible to answer the research questions posed in the introduction by stating that:

- the Slovenian regulatory framework and the business and insolvency practices in place give companies that find themselves in an acute crisis and require the protection of a court limited formal and practical options to successfully manage (remedy) the resulting crisis and thus ensure their survival and further development;
- an insolvency rehabilitation procedure alone cannot be successful, at least in the medium term, if the other business conditions (a healthy business core, a capable management team, available

financial resources, and a positive attitude of employees) are not met, and the focus should be on the underlying causes rather than on the insolvency, as the insolvency will itself be resolved as a consequence (reversing this sequence leads to a purely temporary and very short-term stabilisation of the business); and
- insolvency law is often not well known to managers in creditor and debtor companies, which makes it practically less useful in crisis resolution procedures.

SOLUTIONS AND RECOMMENDATIONS

Crisis resolution through insolvency procedures and insolvency law, which must be well understood by the actors involved and properly taken into account in their actions, is an extremely challenging and risky, although in many cases the only way out of an acute crisis situation. However, as the most important rehabilitation procedure for a debt-ridden company, the compulsory settlement procedure should be reorganised, dominated by the joint or combined business motives of the debtor and the creditors to continue the business, from which the old liabilities would be gradually repaid. The process should be monitored by highly qualified administrators or competent crisis managers until the final repayment, and the impact of secured and speculative creditors should be appropriately balanced against the risks of ordinary creditors (changes in the treatment of secured creditors are an old controversy for which no best general rule has yet been found; White, 2020, p. 232). In the bankruptcy procedure, it seems, the possibility of switching to another rehabilitation type of insolvency procedure would be restored.

If these business conditions (a healthy business core, a capable management team, available financial resources, and positive employee attitudes) are not met (= the task of managers), then no insolvency law or insolvency procedure will be able to resolve the crisis in such a company, and modern, effective, understandable and softish law approach-oriented insolvency legislation (= the task of legislators) needs to provide a framework and support for the realisation of the aforementioned factors (conditions).

Although the transition from bankruptcy proceedings to the rehabilitation of an insolvent company is not possible under Slovenian law, the involvement of individual companies in the global environment or in a network of internationally connected companies creates the need for qualified administrators who are also familiar with the characteristics of crisis management particularly accentuated in Slovenia. The development of international insolvency law requires highly qualified administrators who must specialise in "corporate crisis resolution, rehabilitation and insolvency" (Seagon, 2004, p. 112).

CONCLUSION

In an increasingly uncertain economic and business environment, crises in organisations are becoming more frequent, especially on the basis of external unpredictable events, and the dimensions, causes and actions in each individual crisis are different, which is why there is a growing interest in modern insolvency law among all actors, both in the managers at the debtor or creditor company, and on the national, regional, and international level.

Although the concept and content of insolvency are satisfactorily defined in the Slovenian Insolvency Act, from the perspective of the processes of resolving and preventing a crisis situation in a company, it should be emphasised that insolvency (either as a more permanent illiquidity or long-term insolvency) is not a cause of the crisis, but rather a consequence, and that the prevailing legal approach should therefore be more firmly linked to the necessary business principles and the practice of crisis management. As research has shown, the Slovenian regulatory framework gives companies in acute crisis only limited formal and practical options for rehabilitation, where, however, measures in other business areas must prevail, thus fulfilling the four unavoidable conditions (a healthy business core, a capable management team, available financial resources, and a positive attitude of employees).

REFERENCES

Beale, S., & Keddie, P. (2018). *Insolvency and restructuring manual*. Bloomsbury Professional.

Brosent, N. (2018). *Strategische Insolvenzen – Grenzen der Instrumentalisierung des Insolvenzplanverfahrens zur Lösung von Gesellschafterkonflikten* [Strategic insolvencies – limits of the instrumentalisation of the insolvency plan procedure to resolve shareholder conflicts]. Peter Lang.

Cepec, J. (2021, Sept. 23). Opomnik ob pričakovanju novele ZFPPIPP-H [A reminder of the anticipation of the ZFPPIPP-H novella]. *Pravna praksa*.

Crandall, W. R., Parnell, J. A., & Spillan, J. E. (2014). Crisis management. *Sage (Atlanta, Ga.)*.

Curry, D. S., & Schorer, J. U. (2016). The effects of business insolvency on the duties and liabilities of directors and officers – A comparative analysis with recommendations to promote good decision-making. In T. M. Hajjiri & A. Cohen (Eds.), *Global insolvency and bankruptcy practice for sustainable economic development* (p. 2). Palgrave Macmillan. doi:10.1007/978-1-137-56175-6_5

Doing Business in 2004. (2004). *Understanding regulation*. The International Bank for Reconstruction and Development / The World Bank.

Dubrovski, D. (2006). Insolvenčni postopki kot oblika uspešnega ali neuspešnega razreševanja kriz v podjetjih [Insolvency proceedings as a form of successful or unsuccessful resolution of corporate crises]. *Podjetje in delo, 32*(8), 1795-1829.

Dubrovski, D. (2020). Ali so sodni postopki prisilne poravnave resnično sanacijski postopki [Are compulsory settlement proceedings really remedial proceedings?]. *Podjetje in delo, 46*(2), 294-319.

Dubrovski, D. (2022). *Razsežnosti kriznega managementa* [The dimensions of crisis management]. International School for Social and Business Studies.

European Commission. (2016). *Predlog Direktive evropskega parlamenta in sveta o okvirih preventivnega prestrukutiranja, drugi priložnosti ter ukrepih za povečanje učinkovitosti postopkov prestrukturiranja, postopkov v primeru insolventnosti in postopkov za odpust dolgov ter spremembi Direktive 2012/30/ EU* [Proposal for a Directive of the European Parliament and of the Council on preventive restructuring frameworks, second chance and measures to increase the efficiency of restructuring, insolvency and discharge procedures and amending Directive 2012/30/EU].

Faulhaber, P., & Landwehr, N. (1996). *Turnaround-management in der praxis*. Campus.

Fenger, H. (2005). *Insolvenzrecht. Schnell erfasst* [Insolvency law. Quickly captured]. Springer.

Ferriell, J., & Janger, E. J. (2019). *Understanding bankruptcy.* Carolina Academic Press.

Financial Times. (2008, September 15). *Insolvencies debate rages but there's no silver bullet.* Author.

Ivanjko, Š. (1997). Kriza podjetja [It's a corporate crisis]. *Podjetje in delo, 23*(6-7), 961-978.

James, E. H., & Wooten, L. P. (2010). *Leading under pressure.* Routledge.

Jourova, V. (2019). Early restructuring and a second chance for entrepreneurs. Fact Sheet. European Commission.

Knecht, T. C. (2006). Steuerung von Zahlungsfähigkeit und Unternehmensliquidität [Management of solvency and corporate liquidity]. In U. Homel, T. C. Knecht, & H. Wohlenberg (Eds.), *Handbuch Unternehmensrestrukturierung.* Dr. T. Gabler/GWV. doi:10.1007/978-3-8349-9149-2_27

Kücher, A., Mayr, S., Mitter, C., Duller, C., & Feldbauer-Durstmüller, B. (2018). Firm age dynamics and causes of corporate bankruptcy: Age dependent explanations for business failure. *Review of Managerial Science, 14*(3), 633–661. doi:10.100711846-018-0303-2

Lowitzsch, J. (2007). *The insolvency law of Central and Eastern Europe.* INSOL Europe.

Miller, S. (2008). *The turnaround kid.* HarperCollins.

Moore, H. (2016). *Business turnaround. How to do it.* Longhirst Publishing.

Platt, H. D. (1998). *Principles of corporate renewal.* The University of Michigan Press.

Roux-Dufort, C. (2003). *Gérer et decider en situation de crise* [Manage and decide in crisis situations]. Dunod.

Saleh, Y. D. (2016). *Crisis management.* Mill City Press.

Seagon, C. (2004). Grundlagen der insolvenzordnung [Fundamentals of the Insolvency Code]. In A. K. Buth & M. Hermanns (Eds.), *Restrukturierung, sanierung, insolvenz.* Verlag C. H. Beck.

Seidl, A., & Voss, T. (2006). *Die zweite Chance* [The second chance]. Campus Verlag.

Selinšek, L. (2006). Insolvenčna kazniva dejanja. [Insolvency offences]. *Revizor,* (2), 56–68.

Smithson, H. (2016). Role of insolvency practitioners in restructuring and bankruptcy in the UK. In T. M. Hajjiri & A. Cohen (Eds.), *Global insolvency and bankruptcy practice for sustainable economic development* (Vol. 2). Palgrave Macmillan. doi:10.1007/978-1-137-56175-6_2

Society of Practitioners of Insolvency. (1996). *Company insolvency in the United Kingdom.* Jardine Insolvency Insurance.

The Economist. (2002, March 23). Fear of failure. *The Economist,* 15.

The Economist. (2009, January 3). European bankruptcy law. *The Economist,* 45-46.

Virgós, M., & Garcimartín, F. (2004). *The European insolvency regulation: law and practice.* Kluwer Law International.

White, M. J. (2020). The treatment of secured credit in bankruptcy: A unified model. In B. E. Adler (Ed.), *Research handbook on corporate bankruptcy law* (pp. 210–236). Edward Elgar. doi:10.4337/9781781007884.00017

Wood, P. R. (2013). Principles of international insolvency. In I. F. Fletcher (Ed.), *A special collection celebrating 21 years*. INSOL International & John Wiley & Sons. https://thismatter.com/money/credit/bankruptcy/chapter-conversion.htm

KEY TERMS AND DEFINITIONS

Business Rescue Rate: The proportion of companies that, through insolvency proceedings, ensure their continued survival and development with at least industry-average profit margins, growth in shareholder value and adequate competitive market positioning.

Conditions for Successful Recovery: In addition to the insolvency procedure, a healthy business core, a capable crisis management, available financial resources, and a positive attitude of the employees.

Crisis: A short-lived, undesirable, and critical situation in a company (organisation), which directly threatens the achievement of the objectives of the participants of this company and its continued existence and development, which is due to the intertwined and simultaneous operation of both external and internal causes.

Insolvency (According to the Slovenian Law): In a reasonably analogue way is a situation that arises when the debtor (a) within an extended period of time is not able to settle all their liabilities falling due within such period of time (continuous insolvency), or (b) becomes insolvent in the long-term because they have insufficient assets to repay all debts.

Insolvency Law: In addition to regulating bankruptcy proceedings, it also includes provisions to prevent the debtor from being wound up, to prevent the sale of the company's assets, to relieve debts, and to provide the possibility of a fresh start.

Insolvency Proceedings: Often the last resort from an acute crisis involving competent national courts, is the presence of a special insolvency law.

Reorganisation: The process of healing a company and managing a crisis, the purpose of which is to remedy an unfavourable and future-threatening crisis situation by preventing further deterioration of the business and restoring conditions that will ensure the company's continued existence and development.

ZFPPIPP: Slovenian Financial Operations, Insolvency Proceedings, and Compulsory Dissolution Act.

Chapter 5
The Reasons Leading Businesses to Concordat and Solution Suggestions

Halime Karaca
İnönü Üniversitesi, Turkey

ABSTRACT

There are many factors that lead businesses to bankruptcy. The risk environment created as a result of changes in some macroeconomic indicators such as exchange rates, interest rates, inflation, and financial instability as a result of the inability to manage risk properly cause businesses to go bankrupt or an economic crisis. The bankruptcy of a business imposes a cost not only on stakeholders, but on society as a whole. In this context, in order to ensure economic welfare and maintain the economic existence of enterprises, the function of the institution of concordat in the execution and bankruptcy law has been increased; the way of restructuring their debts in accordance with the final decision of the court in line with the consent of their creditors has been opened for the debtors. In the study, the institution of concordat was examined in outline, the reasons leading businesses to concordat were evaluated, and solution suggestions were developed.

INTRODUCTION

Concordat institution has existed in Turkish law since 1929.At the beginning of the 2000s, its application decreased considerably as the conditions were heavy for the debtors (Kurt Konca, 2018: 9). However, it was transformed into a new structure with the Law No. 7101 enacted in 2018, and the concordat was brought into effect with the changes made.With the concordat, it is aimed to ensure that the debtors who intend to pay their debts, but have difficulty in payment due to the deterioration of the income-expense balance, repay their debts and continue their economic activities (Pekcanıtez and Erdönmez, 2018, p.112).

It has been determined that the results envisaged in the regulation could not be achieved during the implementation of the concordat.In addition, there have been criticisms from the public aboutthe concordat is abused by the debtor companies, some debtors use this method only to save time, with the

DOI: 10.4018/978-1-6684-5181-6.ch005

mentioned regulations the benefits of the creditors and the debtor aren't properly balanced and kept, and the courts have different practices on the subject (Bilen and Güler, 2019, p. 82).

In order to eliminate malicious uses, by aggravating application conditions all companies requesting concordat were obliged to submit the audit reportproviding more assurance than the financial analysis report to the court (Yavuz, 2019, p. 239). With the said change; it is aimed that the court has correct information about the debtors requesting concordat and to make relationship of interest between the parties is more balanced (Kurt Konca, 2018, p. 12). There are various internal and external factors that lead businesses to financial failure.External factors are generally the crises in the global economy, economic contractions, rapid changes in technology, international competition, contractions in the country's economy and the informal economy. In addition to external factors, internal factors are also effective in the failure of businesses. Although these factors differ in terms of businesses, there are common reasons as well. Failure in risk management, poor reliability of financial statements, confusion between family relations and business relations in family businesses, failure to manage cash successfullyby the mangement, insufficient profits can be countedethical reasons for business owners and managers. The bankruptcy of a business imposes a cost not only on its partners and employees, but also on the whole-society as in different ways. The businesses in question with the domino effect put the businesses with which they have a debt-credit relationship into economic difficulties, causea vicious circle by rendering their commercial activities inoperable.In this context, in order to ensure economic welfare and maintain the economic existence of enterprises, the function of the institution of concordat in the Execution and Bankruptcy Law has been increased;the way of restructuring their debts in accordance with the final decision of the court in line with the consent of their creditors has been opened for the debtors.

In this context, the aim of the study is to examine the reasons and solution proposals that lead businesses to concordat. For this purpose, first of all, the concept and purpose of the concordat, the types of concordat, the documents to be attached to the concordat request, the concordat process, the approval of the concordat and the results of the approval decision will be examined.In addition, in the study, the reasons that lead businesses to concordat will be evaluated and tried to be explained with solution suggestions.

CONCEPT OF CONCORDAT AND PURPOSE OF CONCORDAT

Concordat means agreement, which is the equivalent of the Italian word "concordat". TDK defines 'concordat ' as Collateral bankruptcy as the term of law and economy and as an agreement between the papal authority and other provisions as the term of history.

This definition falls short of explaining the concordat in terms of quality. Because the concordat does not meet the meaning of bankruptcy. On the contrary, it is an opportunity for debtors to maintain their economic assets before bankruptcy (Akyürek, 2019, pp.23-24).

Concordat is a forced agreement made by a debtor with a certain majority of his creditors and valid with the approval of the commercial court. In this way, creditors give up some of their debts from the debtor or give the debtor a certain time to pay their debts.It is a legal institution that allows the debtor to get rid of all his debts by paying the accepted part of his debt during this time (Uyar, 2018, p.3).The economic crisis, market conditions, may put non-malicious borrowers in a position to be unable to pay their debts.If the debtors who cannot pay all their debts on time due to their financial situation are subject to bankruptcy, they are on the verge of bankruptcy.If they are not subject to bankruptcy, the debtors who are due or act first may receive their receivables in full, while others may not be able to receive their receivables.The legislator by makinga regulation in this regard gave the debtors the opportunity to pay their debts by negotiating with the debtor's creditors under the supervision of the court (Bilen and Güler, 2019, p. 82).Concordat application can be made by the debtor or by any person who is a creditor from the debtor in question (İİK Madde 285).

Concordat is for the benefit of the creditors as well as the debtors. With the concordat, if the debtors are subject to bankruptcy, they are freed from bankruptcy and all legal and penal obligations of bankruptcy.However, if the debtor is not subject to bankruptcy, he gets rid of his creditors partially through the sale of all his assets by seizure by his creditors and tries to continue his activities with the threat of forced execution of the creditors who cannot receive some or all of his debt.Concordat is also for the benefit of the creditors. Because, through concordat, creditors obtain their receivables without making the necessary expenses for foreclosure and bankruptcy (Uyar, 2018, p. 7).

- The philosophy that forms the basis of the formation of the concordat (Çukacı, 2019, p. 7): Creditors' ability to reach financial results in more favorable conditions than bankruptcy,
- Damage to national capital and entrepreneurial spirit due to the fact that enterprises, which are economic units, go out of the economy due to bankruptcy,
- Businesses can maintain their employment capabilities (even if it decreases compared to their normal economic life),
- Ensuring the economic sustainability of the enterprises (even by becoming smaller),
- It is based on the principles of ensuring the public interest.

With the concordat, it is aimed to reintegrate the enterprises into the economy, in other words, to ensure the continuation of the existence of the enterprises.The bankruptcy of a business will impose an indirect cost that will affect not only its partners and employees, but also the whole society in different ways.Because the bankruptcy of a large-scale enterprise will causedamage by creating a "domino" effect to third parties, especially credit institutions, banks, suppliers and customers, which are associated with the business in question, and will have a negative impact on the economy as a result.

TYPES OF CONCORDAT

Concordat by Official Authorities

The concordat process is taking advantage of restructuring function by debtors and creditors under the supervision of official authorities.The reason for the distinction here is that it is possible to make the structuring only between debtors and creditors, apart from official authorities.In this context, the structuring process can be done in two ways, in-court and out-of-court.

Official Concord

The official title of the concordat is given since the applications are made to the judicial authorities and the agreement can become valid and effective as a result of the approval of the agreement by the judicial authorities.Provisions regulated in Enforcement and Bankruptcy Law are related to official concordat (Aydemir, 2018, p. 21).This type of concordat also binds creditors who have not ratified the contract.

Special Concordat

In this type of concordat, the restructuring agreement is not made through the mediation and approval of the judicial authorities.Here, the debtors can make agreements regarding the liquidation of their debts within the scope of the freedom of contract in the Turkish Code of Obligations.However, the agreement will be binding only for the creditor who is a party, it will not be an obligation for other creditors.The provisions of the Turkish Code of Obligations are applied in the agreements made between the debtor and each of the creditors (Toroslu, 2018, pp.28-29).

Concordat According to How It Is Made

It is the evaluation of the debt restructuring agreement according to the content of the concordat.The structuring of debts, in other words, the preparation of payment plans, is defined in three ways as maturity, percentage and a combination of the two.

Maturity Concordat

In the maturity concordat, the amounts receivables of the creditors are preserved and an additional period is given to the debtors to pay their debts without any change in the said amounts.According to the maturity concordat, debts can be paid in a certain maturity or in installments.In concordat applications, debtors are generally unable to pay all their debts at once.For this reason, it is important for the debtor to pay his debts in a certain time, in terms of paying the debt in the promised amount.

Discount (Percent) Concordat

It is called a deduction concordat whcnborrowers undertake to repay their debts at a certain percentage; however, creditors waive a certain percentage of the amount they will receive.According to the discount concordat, the debtors can get rid of all their debts by paying a certain amount of their debts.

Mixed Concordat

Mixed concordatfrequently used in practice, is formed by the combination of maturity and discount concordat.In this type of concordat, a certain percentage of the receivable is waived and the maturity is extended by changing the payment date (Eroğlu, 2018, pp.23-24).

Concordat According to the Time of Completion

In the doctrine, concordat is divided into two as in bankruptcy and non-bankruptcy.Here, one of the distinguishing features is the initiation of the concordat process at the request of the debtor or one of the creditors before the bankruptcy process begins, and the other is that the debtor initiates the concordat process after the bankruptcy process begins (Çıtak and Güneş, 2020, p.503).

Non-Bankrupt Ordinary Concordat

The main purpose here is to save the debtors from bankruptcy. It is a type of concordat made by debtors to get rid of bankruptcy before going bankrupt.For this reason, this type of concordat is also called bankruptcy preventive concordat (Uyar, 2018, p. 28).

Ordinary Concordat in Bankruptcy

According to the bankruptcy concordat, even if the debtors go bankrupt, they can reach an agreement with the bankruptcy creditors to avoid bankruptcy and regain their lost reputation.In case the proposal of the bankrupt who applied to the commercial court for concordat is accepted and approved by the court, the bankruptcy will cease to exist together with the provisions of the bankruptcy and its consequences (Bilen and Güler, 2019, p. 84).

Concordat According to the Purpose

According to its purpose, it can be done in two ways: concordat for the purpose of liquidation of debts and concordat by abandonment of assets.

Concordat for the Liquidation of Debts

In the concordat regarding the liquidation of debts, the debtors want to terminate their debts. For this reason, it offers to creditors in order to pay their debts.This type of concordat; All types of concordat are included except concordat by abandonment of property.All types of bankruptcy and non-bankruptcy concordat, maturity, percentage and mixed concordat also form concordat by liquidating debts.

Concordat with Abandonment of Assets

According to the concordat by abandoning the assets, the debtors propose not to pay their debts under certain conditions, but to transfer the powers of disposition on their assets to the creditors.Concordat with the abandonment of assets is made in two ways.Here, the first method is the transfer of the powers of disposition regarding the assets of the debtors to the creditors, and the collection of the receivables of the creditors by selling the said assets.A second method in concordat is the transfer of some or all of the debtor's assets to third parties by paying the debt to the creditors with certain maturities.With the income obtained as a result of this transfer, the creditors collect their receivables (Pekcanıtez and Erdönmez, 2018, p.111). Debtors cannot continue their commercial activities in concordat by abandoning their assets (Eroğlu, 2018, pp. 24-26).

REASONS LEADING BUSINESSES TO CONCORDAT AND SUGGESTIONS FOR SOLUTIONS

The risk environment created as a result of changes in some macroeconomic indicators such as exchange rates, interest rates, inflation; It causes financial instability in businesses, an increase in borrowing costs, a decrease in debt solvency, and as a result, the bankruptcy of businesses or an economic crisis. The bankruptcy of a business imposes a cost not only on its partners and employees, but also on the whole society in different ways. The businesses in questionput the companies with which they are in a debt-credit relationship into economic difficulties with the domino effect, causing a vicious circle by rendering their commercial activities ineffective.Similarly, the bankruptcy of a large-scale enterprise harms third parties, especially credit institutions, banks, suppliers and customers associated with the enterprise, and as a resulthasa negative impact on the economy.In order to prevent the bankruptcy of the enterprises that are in bad financial situation but hope to be saved, arrangements were made in the concordat institution in order to bring them into the economy.

There may be internal as well as external reasons for the financial failure of the enterprises and their coming to the concordat stage. While the reasons that lead businesses to concordat differ in terms of businesses, there are common reasons as well.Failure in risk management, poor reliability of financial statements, confusion between family relations and business relations in family businesses, failure to manage cash successfullyby the mangement, insufficient profits can be countedethical reasons for business owners and managers (Uzay, 2019, pp. 174-175).

Failed Risk Management

Businessesare exposed to various risks such as disaster, war and financial collapses. Not taking the necessary precautions bringsabout disasters. Massive and sometimes unexpected institutional failures draw attention to the importance of risk management (Kızılboğa, 2012: 303).Unsuccessful or weak risk management practices are shown as reasons for company collapses, scandals and corruption (Manab et al., 2010: 242).Businesses can make new investments, company acquisitions, share transfers, etc. can make wrong decisions on strategic issues. Operational risks may not be carried out correctly (Uzay, 2018, p.174). Similarly, it may be unprepared for the crises in the global economy and the economic contractions in the country's economy. The inability to adapt to rapidly changing technology, the shift of competition from national to international areas, and their inability to enter the said markets are important factors in the financial failure of businesses.

Risk Concept and Management

The dictionary meaning of the word risk is "the probability of an event that may cause a loss, a loss or a danger (Emhan, 2009, p. 210). Due to its versatility, the concept of risk expresses different meanings in different situations and is mostly shaped by perceptions and attitudes (Fone and Young, 2005, pp. 11-12). The most widely accepted definition of risk has been made by the COSO (The Committee of Sponsoring Organizations of The Treadway Commission), and according to this definition, risk is "the probability that an event will occur and adversely affect the success of the organization in achieving its goals". (Reding et al., 2009, pp. 3-4).

Risk; It is the uncertainty in the results of plans and decisions, it is inevitable, it is a function of strategic goals (Burnaby and Hass, 2009, p. 540). In summary, the risk is; It can be defined as the threats and negativities that may be encountered in the future and may prevent the realization of the objectives, or the opportunities that may facilitate the achievement of the objectives (Derici et al., 2007, p. 152).In this context, the risk arising from unexpected events; the uncertainty of the risk arising from change; It can be said that the risk that can be used in favor of the enterprise includes opportunities (Uzay and

Özşahin Koç, 2015, p. 206). It is necessary to manage risks well in order to ensure the formation of positive situations or events or to prevent the occurrence of negative situations or events (Reding et all, 2009, pp. 3-4).

The risks that a company may face can be classified in many different ways. Structural and sectoral characteristics of the business significantly affect this classification. In this context, although there are many ways to classify risks, it is possible to group risks under four main headings, according to the most widely used classification (Bozkurt, 2010, p. 20).These are classified under various names as strategic, institutional or operational, financial and disaster-related risks (Walker-Shenkir et al. 2002, p. 3).

Regardless of the institutions operating as public, private or non-governmental organizations, every institution that has a purpose and carries out activities for this purpose continues its activities in a certain risk environment (Pehlivanlı, 2014, p. 59). Businesses try to stay away from these risks in order to increase their profits, but they need to evaluate the risks correctly in order to catch the opportunities (Göğüş, 2012, p. 17).

Businesses should analyze the reliability of processes for identifying, prioritizing, managing and monitoring risks that are important to the organization. Integrating risks with the strategy formation process and business plans makes risks an element in the decision-making process. Not only strategy and business planning, but also the coordination of all processes with risks will make it easier for the institution to make the right decisions (Kızılboğa Özaslan and Özşahin Koç, 2016, p. 281).However, risks should be kept within acceptable limits.This limit is influenced by the organization's willingness to take risks and other factors.The most basic way of reducing the risks arising from the uncertainty of the future and keeping them within acceptable limits is to perform risk management (Pehlivanlı, 2014, p.59).

Risk management is expressed as a process consisting of pre-defining, evaluating, managing and controlling possible events and situations in order to provide reasonable assurance for the organization to achieve its objectives (Nielsen, 2010, p. 17). The purpose of risk management is to control the deviations that may occur in the possible results by reducing the events that may harm the institution and the negativities that may occur in the event of these events (Griffiths, 2005, p. 21).

The economic and financial collapses experienced by large-scale institutions had a great impact on the importance of risk management. Institutions have realized the fact that in order to get rid of the negativities and reach their goals, the risks and opportunities that may arise in the future should be managed by being aware of in advance. Risk management process includes country, sector, location, priorities of partners, domestic and foreign conjuncture, product lifetime etc. may vary depending on many different factors (Yarız, 2009, p.23).

Suggestions for Success in Risk Management

The problem for businesses is not the risk, but the failure to understand, misjudge, manage and ignore the risk.A good risk management helps corporate managers in making and managing prospective decisions and not only preventing or reducing losses, but also realizing value-adding opportunities (Kızılboğa, 2012, p. 302).Businesses should develop some methods to manage risks and turn them into opportunities.In this context, in order to control the unexpected losses that may occur in the enterprise at the lowest cost and to protect the earning power of the enterprise, enterprises should create a risk portfolio and benefit from internal auditing to evaluate the risk management process of the institution and to give assurance that the risks are fully and accurately determined.The internal control system in enterprises should be arranged on a risk-based basis.In addition, as long as businesses use risk management techniques effectively, they will have the opportunity to be warned early against the factors that lead to concordat and even to bankruptcy.In addition, in possible crisis situations, businesses will survive the crises more easily as they will have the necessary capital adequacy in return for the risks they undertake.

Businesses Should Create a General Risk Portfolio to Perform Risk Management

Businesses should integrate their risk profiles and the strategic, institutional or operational, financial and disaster-related risks they may encounter.This risk profile determines the earnings and earnings elasticity of the business in general.The company that wants to manage risks effectively has to reveal not only the risks, but also the relationship between the risks.In order to deal with risks systematically, the businesses need to create a risk management framework suitable for their organizational structure. The stages of the said risk management framework are as follows (Gönen, 2017: 295);

- **Determination of Risk Management Framework:** It starts with the evaluation of the events related to the risks that businesses should focus on and ends with the creation of strategic targets based on the availability and financeability of the risks. At this stage, senior management is responsible for directing and determining risk controls, as well as continuously monitoring operations in order to mitigate risks and prioritize strategic risks.
- **Risk Requirements:** The main purpose of this step is to determine the objectives and strategies of the organizations regarding the risks.In order to evaluate risk requirements, risk models must first be defined and analyzed.
- **Description of Information Flow:** Identifying threats and opportunities provides accurate and detailed reporting of information flow.
- **Feasibility Analysis:** Requirements for risk management should be determined.The workload should be calculated by considering the cost of the proposed system, the purpose of the system and the competence of the people using the system.
- **Decision Phase:** As a result of the analysis, a customized risk management framework is determined to include strategic, corporate or operational, financial and disaster-related risks.

Internal Audit Function Should Be Involved in Risk Management to Assure and Advise the Process

Among the duties of the internal audit function; Evaluating the risk management process of the institution, providing assurance that the risks are fully and correctly identified and prioritized, testing the effectiveness of the control activities applied for the risks, evaluating the adequacy of the risk monitoring and reporting processes, and providing consultancy to the institution on the management of risks (Ilgar and Erdoğdu, 2018, p. 73).

Internal audit provides management with objective assurance that significant risks in an organization are properly managed and the internal control system is functioning effectively. Risk management is one of the main responsibilities of corporate management (Bozkurt, 2010: 24).In this context, corporate management is responsible for developing various risk responses, processes and structures. The function of internal audit is to review internal controls to determine whether they are adequate and effective.

Internal Audit must proactively identify emerging business issues and trends to maintain effectiveness within the organization. Emerging business trends bring new risks. The internal auditor needs to continually monitor these risks and their potential impact on the organization. To provide the greatest added value, the internal auditor must act quickly when faced with emerging risks and seize opportunities to challenge the status quo to reduce risk, improve controls, and realize efficiency and cost benefits across the organization(Can and Cetin, 2019: 162).

The Internal Control System in Businesses Should Be Arranged on a Risk-based Basis

According to the COSO model, one of the elements of internal control is risk assessment. Risk assessment is the process of identifying and analyzing significant risks that prevent the business from achieving its objectives and determining appropriate responses to them.Therefore, the internal control activity should be organized on a risk-based basis.

There are constantly changing risk factors in the field of operation of the enterprise.Accordingly, analysis should be made regarding the strengths and weaknesses of the business system, risk areas should be determined and control activities should be concentrated on these areas.Risk assessment aims to make continuous changes in internal control in order to identify and analyze opportunities, risks by constantly monitoring changing conditions, and to cope with the risks that arise due to changes in conditions (Bayrak, 2018, p. 981).

Weak Reliability of Financial Statements

Businesses; Prepares financial statements such as balance sheet, income statement, profit distribution statement, summary of accounting policies and footnotes. Financial statements can also be expressed as the most important tool by which companies present information to the public and inform the public (Karaca, 2018, pp. 3-4). The reliability, transparency and uniformity of financial statements, informationenableusers to make the right decisions (Rezaee, 2005: 278).Reliable financial statements are those that contain financial information prepared in accordance with GAAP (Generally Accepted Accounting Principles) and standards and presented in a fair way (Doyrangöl, 2007, p. 53). However, the financial statements prepared and presented within the body of the enterprises are not always reliable and may deviate from reality and accuracy due to the fact that they may contain errors and frauds (Sarıkale and İlter, 2018, pp. 168-169).

Accounting errors are causedbymistakes made in accounting transactions due to ignorance, inexperience, carelessness or forgetfulness; accounting frauds are caused by corruption, irregularity, fraud and deliberate mistakes.In general, two types of accounting fraud can be mentioned in accounting records and in the preparation of financial statements.While it is aimed to reduce public liabilities by showing expenses higher than they are and revenues lower than they are, it is aimed to increase the value of the enterprise by showing expenses and liabilities lower than they are, and incomes and assets higher than they are (Demir, 2014, p.169). Such cheating includes violation of generally accepted accounting principles (Whiting et al., 2012, pp. 507-508).

The general characteristic of capital companies is that the people forming the company cannot be held responsible for the debts of the company with their personal assets.Accordingly, partners who have fulfilled their commitment to put in capital are not responsible for the debts of the company (Organ and Sevinç, 2017, p. 43). Due to the limited liability of the partners, the banks require the personal guarantees of the partners in the company management for the loan agreements in order to guarantee themselves, and even not content with this, they demand personal guarantees for the debt securities issued up to the loan amount.However, the main reason behind this evaluation is that the financial statements and information given to banks for loan requests are not reliable enough.There are many reasons for this practice, which is not encountered in developed countries such as the USA and Germany.These; It is the fact that the financial statements do not reflect the truth due to reasons such as informality or conflict of interest, the capital-poor shareholders of the companies are rich, the public offering is not developed enough, the wrong practice has become established over time, the increase in the value of the enterprise and the stock prices by showing the incomes and assets higher than they are (Uzay, 2018, p. 174).

Recommendations for Increasing the Reliability of Financial Statements

Because the purpose of financial statements is providing useful information tothe users, enabling them to make better decisions, financial statements should be structured to reflect user needs (Aydın and Tuğay, 2018, p. 280). The preparation of reliable financial statements is a prerequisite for the increase in the demand of the investors for the stocks of the enterprises and for them to find suitable loans, and it is very important for the enterprise to be able to make some contracts in the market and to work with certain intermediaries.

Financial statements appeal to a wide range of financial information users. For this reason, an external audit is needed to determine whether the information in these tables reflects the situation of the business in a realistic way and whether it is prepared accurately and honestly. This function is fulfilled by independent auditing (Memiş, 2016. p. 39). Independent external audits play an important role in improving the quality of financial reports. However, ensuring quality in auditing increases the reliability of audit results; It ensures that the audit opinions, recommendations and improvement suggestions produced to meet the needs of the audited institutions and organizations are taken more seriously (Akçay and Bilen, 2018, p. 230).

International financial reporting standards arc the standards prepared with the aim of presenting the information appropriate to the needs of financial information users in a truthful manner.

The independent audit process, by expressing an opinion on whether the financial statements prepared by the business management are prepared in accordance with these standards, will serve to some extent for the stakeholders to have an idea about the accuracy and honesty of the information in the financial statements and whether it reflects the financial position of the business in a realistic way. Today, from the audit process; In addition to the function of increasing the reliability of the financial statements; Additional value-creating functions are also expected in business activities, such as detecting and reporting irregularities within the business, identifying risks, and providing consultancy services to the management on malfunctions and corrective suggestions in internal control systems (Memiş, 2016, p. 42).

While expressing an opinion on the reliability of financial information with independent audit; Today, the audit area related to the reliability of information other than financial information is provided by assurance auditing. Assurance audit services are becoming increasingly widespread due to the fact that technological developments bring countries, economies, financial markets and businesses closer to each other (Coşkun Aslan and Demirkan, 2017, p.127).

Mixing Family and Business Relationships in Family Businesses

Family businessesis expressed as businesses that carry out their activities under the control of family members, and where the determined value judgments and profit making methods are determined by the members of the family in question (Barry, 1975, p. 42). The main factors that distinguish the family business from other companies are; the ratio of family members in the company is whether the ownership and operating rights of the company are controlled by family members (Lin, 2018, pp. 1093-1094). Contrary to the general opinion in society, family businesses are not considered as small businesses, they are not defined by scale, but only as businesses under the control of the family. Although business types are generally defined with industry, sector, structure, strategy, etc the family business, it is an alternative type of organization that includes all these segments (Craig and Moores, 2006, p. 2). Emotional bond, love and desire to work constitute the basis of family businesses, which form the basis of the country's economies and act as a lever in the development of countries.

The most important problem of family businesses is that they cannot be institutionalized.The most important problems in the failure of family businesses are that the organizational culture is not settled, the negative situations that occur as a result of the reflection of family relations to the business, the lack of competent personnel at the management levels due to favoring the family from the close circle (nepotism), the inability to carry out emotional relations correctly due to blood ties (Sorgun and Türk, 2008, p. 57).In addition, mistakes such as generational change in family businesses, poor preparation of the next generations for work, upbringing, and lack of education can be encountered (Uzay, 2018, pp. 174-175).

Suggestions for Family Businesses to Succeed

Family businesses need to realize certain elements in order to be successful.These elements are; making long-term investments, establishing appropriate partnerships and being in strong communication with the partners, not being under the influence of the partners when making decisions, keeping the connections tight in partnership relations, establishing a balance between family members and the business, and making the business independent from family members (Sorgun and Türk, 2008, p. 57). However, it is important to strengthen rational behavior among family members and to establish and implement a "family constitution" in which the rights, responsibilities and obligations of family members are defined. In addition, some written agreements such as partnership agreement and inheritance planning should also be made (Uzay, 2017, p.23).

Failed Cash Management

Cashis the basic input that businesses use while carrying out their work, and it gives power and life to businesses by providing profit and payment power. For this reason, cash management and control is very important in the success of businesses and is one of the vital functions that management is responsible for (Walker and Baughn, 1961, p. 151). From here, cash management can be defined as accelerating cash inflows, slowing down cash outflows and determining the distribution of available cash among safes, banks and securities. Businesses that are successful in cash management can make timely payments related to their daily activities, act prudently against risks, benefit from economies of scale more effectively, and have the opportunity to take their relations with banks and financial institutions to an advanced level.On the other hand, cash management causes businesses to incur a significant opportunity cost.The existence of excess liquidity raises the issue of evaluating alternative investment opportunities (Yıldız and Demireli, 2019, p. 417).

With cash management, it is aimed to provide a balance between cash inflows and outflows, and this balance directly affects the profitability of the enterprises. However, failure to provide the optimal cash amount can reduce the effectiveness of operational and financial practices in businesses, along with the opportunity cost (Yıldız and Demireli, 2019, p. 425).

Suggestions for Success in Cash Management

In order to ensure a balanced cash flow management in enterprises, it is necessary to develop and implement an effective estimation system and to create cash budgets for a certain time period (Uzay, 2018, p. 175). However, in cash management; cash should be kept to a minimum and the cash cycle should be accelerated. In providing this; inventory, credit and debt management must be effective (Uzay, 2017, pp. 23-24).

Unprofitability

Businesses are established to make a profit. Therefore, profit is a very important concept for businesses. Profit is the positive difference between the income and expenses of a business at the end of a certain period. While businesses aim to make a high amount of profit in the short term, it is aimed to make the profit sustainable in the long term. The extreme competitive environment in the global business world encourages businesses to compete with their competitors and to develop with new investments by strengthening their financial structures in order to emerge as a winner from the said competition. Making the right investment decisions and obtaining a high level of profit from the investments to be made are very important for the continuity of the enterprises (Turaboğlu and Timur, 2018, pp. 137-138).

It is unlikely that businesses that make permanent losses will continue to exist. Therefore, even if the bad situation is delayed for a while with capital increase or debt restructuring in these businesses, the underlying causes of the loss should be determined and solutions should be found.

Causes of Unprofitability and Solution Suggestions

There can be many reasons for unemployment. However, among the main reasons; reasons such as wrong investment decisions, mismanagement of the company's operations, excessive indebtedness, inability to collect its receivables (Uzay, 2018, p. 175).With the increase in debts, businesses face the problem of repayment. For this reason, it would be more beneficial to accelerate cash inflow and make debt restructurings rather than using new debt.In investment financing; The objectives should be clear and unambiguous, and there should be no lack of feasibility.In addition, the resources used in the investment should be selected in accordance with the investment and financial structure (Uzay, 2017, pp. 23-24).

Compliance With the Code of Ethics for Business Owners and Managers

Business ethics, in general, means "knowing what is right and wrong in the business environment and doing the right thing". Businesses are economic entities established to meet human needs and to generate profit. However, this economic life cannot be considered separately from social or communal life.

Businesses are affected by the habits, customs and morals of the society in which they operate.In this context, business ethics brings judgment and judgment based on both principles and beliefs in order to make choices that will balance the economic interests of the business with its social and welfare demands (Doğan, 2009, pp. 179-181).

Ethical collapses revealed by bribery, corruption, embezzlement and fraud scandals in businesses make it difficult for businesses to continue their existence. Similarly, the most common cause of bankruptcy risk in cooperatives; It is the fact that the elected managers leave the cooperative in a difficult situation as a result of corruption (Uzay, 2018, p. 175).With the globalizing world economy, business ethics has now become an indispensable requirement for businesses. The fact that businesses carry out their activities in accordance with business ethics affects their long-term success positively, and adverse behaviors affect them negatively.

CONCLUSION AND RECOMMENDATIONS

Businesses are faced with many financial problems in order to continue their activities in the challenging competitive environment of today's economic conditions. Financial failures as a result of these problems, which are also due to the inability to act in advance against the dizzying change in the market, can bring businesses to the brink of bankruptcy.With the concordat, it is aimed to reintegrate the enterprises into the economy, in other words, to continue the existence of the enterprises.The bankruptcy of a business imposes a cost not only on its partners and employees, but also on the wholesociety in different ways.The businesses in question; It also puts the companies with which they have a debt-credit relationship into economic difficulties with the butterfly effect, causing a vicious circle by rendering their commercial activities ineffective.Similarly, the bankruptcy of a large-scale enterprise harms third parties, especially credit institutions, banks, suppliers and customers, which are associated with the enterprise, and as a result, it has a negative impact on the economy.

Concordat is an institution established to ensure that debtors who intend to pay their debts, but have difficulty in paying their debts due to the deterioration of their income-expense balance, repay their debts and continue their economic activities. With the concordat, natural or legal person debtors who cannot pay their debts in due time or who have the risk of not paying their debts in due time, have been provided with the opportunity to pay their debts within the scope of a payment plan, within the framework of a mixed concordat formed by giving maturity or deduction or by combining the maturity and reduction concordat.

There may be external and internal reasons for the financial failure of the enterprises and the fact that they come to the concordat stage. External causes are generally the crises in the global economy, economic contractions, rapid change in technology, international competition, contractions in the country's economy and the informal economy.Although the internal causes of financial failures of enterprises differ in terms of enterprises, there are common causes as well.Failure in risk management, poor reliability of financial statements, confusion between family and business relationships, failure in cash management, unprofitability, and failure to comply with ethical rules regarding business owners and managers can be counted.

It is important for the continuity of the enterprises to make a healthy diagnosis of the causes of financial failure of the enterprises and to develop solutions without going to the concordat.In this context, a general risk portfolio should be created in order for businesses to be successful in risk management.

However, in risk management, the internal audit function should be involved in providing assurance and consulting to the process.In addition, the internal control system should be arranged on a risk-based basis.

Financial statements prepared by businesses appeal to a wide range of financial information users.An independent audit is needed to determine whether the information in these tables reflects the situation of the business in a realistic way.Independent audits play an important role in improving the quality of financial statements.The preparation of quality, reliable financial statements is very important in terms of increasing the demand of investors for stocks and finding suitable loans, making certain contracts in the sector and working with certain intermediaries.

In order for family businesses to be successful, it is important to establish a balance between family members and the business and to make the business independent from family members. However, by creatingthe family constitution the rights, responsibilities and obligations of family members should be defined.

In order for businesses to be successful in cash management, a balance should be maintained between cash inflows and outflows, cash should be kept at a minimum and cash cycle should be accelerated. In providing this; Stock, receivable and debt management must be effective.

It will be more beneficial for businesses to accelerate cash inflows and debt restructurings rather than using new debt in order to earn sufficient profits. In investment financing, the objectives should be clear and unambiguous. In addition, the resources used in investment financing should be selected in accordance with the investment and financial structure.

As a result, businesses should have an effective corporate governance and risk management approach, and necessary importance should be givento accounting and auditing. Therefore, it is very important for businesses to consider the aforementioned issuesseriously in terms of the continuity of their activitiesand not to face possible negative consequences. Otherwise, bankruptcy is inevitable for businesses in the event of the concordat process and the failure of the process.

REFERENCES

Akçay, A., & Bilen, A. (2018). Denetim Kalitesi ve Göstergeleri [Audit Quality and Indicators]. *Yüzüncü Yıl Üniversitesi Sosyal Bilimler Enstitüsü Dergisi*, (40), 227–256.

Akyürek, A. (2019). *Konkordato Hukuku* [Concordat Law]. Yetkin Yayınları.

Aslanoğlu, S., Cengiz, S., Dinç, Y., & Dilsiz, M. (2016). Yaratıcı Muhasebe Uygulamalarının Bağımsız Denetim Kalitesi Üzerine Etkisi: BİST'de Bir Uygulama [The Impact of Creative Accounting Practices on Independent Audit Quality: An Application in BIST]. *Muhasebe ve Finansman Dergisi*, (69), 1–24. doi:10.25095/mufad.396655

Aslanoğlu, S., Özalp, A. D., & Özalp, A. R. (2018). Bir Yeniden Yapılandırma Kurumu Olarak Konkordato Başvurusu, Geçici Mühlet Ve Gerekçeleri [Application for the concordat as a restructuring institution, temporary deadline and its justifications]. *Ekonomi İşletme Siyaset ve Uluslararası İlişkiler Dergisi*, (3), 63–68.

Aydemir, E. (2018). Konkordato ve Yeniden Yapılandırma [Concordat and Restructuring]. Seçkin Yayınları.

Aydın, Ü., & Tuğay, O. (2018). Hileli Finansal Raporlama: Bağımsız Denetçilerin Meslek Etiği ve Hileli Finansal Raporlamaya Bakış Açılarına Yönelik Bir Araştırma [Fraudulent Financial Reporting: A Study of the Professional Ethics of Independent Auditors and Their Perspectives on Fraudulent Financial Reporting]. *Süleyman Demirel Üniversitesi İktisadi ve İdari Bilimler Fakültesi Dergisi*, *23*(1), 279–30.

Barry, B. (1975). The Development Organization Structure in the Family Firm. *Journal of General Management*, *3*(1), 42–60. doi:10.1177/030630707500300105

Bayrak, T. (2018). İç Denetim Felsefesi [Internal Audit Philosophy]. *Muhasebe Bilim Dünyası Dergisi, 15*, 977-990.

Bilen, C. İ., & Güler, S. (2019). Konkordato ve Alacakların Akıbeti [Concordat and Fate of Receivables]. *Vergi Dünyası*, *449*, 81–97.

Bozkurt, C. (2016). Risk, Kurumsal Risk Yönetimi ve İç Denetim. *Denetişim*, (4), 17–30.

Burnaby, P., & Hass, S. (2009). Ten steps to enterprise-wide risk management. *Corporate Governance*, *9*(5), 539–550. doi:10.1108/14720700910998111

Can, E. N., & Çetin, C. (2019). COSO ERM 2017 Çerçevesinde Kurumsal Risk Yönetiminde İç Denetimin Rolü [The Role of Internal Audit in Corporate Risk Management in the Framework]. *Akademik Sosyal Araştırmalar Dergisi*, *6*(41), 153–166.

Çıtak, N., & Güneş, M. A. (2020). Bir Yeniden Yapılandırma Müessesesi Olarak Konkordato ve Bir Üretim İşletmesi Uygulaması [The Concordat as a Restructuring Institution and the Application of a Production Enterprise]. *Finans Ekonomi ve Sosyal Araştırmalar Dergisi*, *5*(3), 501–517.

Coşkun Aslan, M., & Demirkan, S. (2017). *Denetim ve Güvence Hizmetleri* [Audit and Assurance Services]. Muhasebe ve Finansman Dergisi. doi:10.25095/mufad.402669

Craigh, B. L., & Moores, K. (2006). A 10-Year Longitudinal Investigation of Strategy, Systems and Environment on Innovation in Family Firms. *Family Business Review*, *19*(1), 1–10. doi:10.1111/j.1741-6248.2006.00056.x

Çukacı, Y. C. (2019). *Konkordato* [Concordat]. Ekin Yayınları.

Demir, Ş. (2014). Muhasebe Hataları ve Hileleri ile Bunlara Dair Yaptırımların Yasal Mevzuat Kapsamında Değerlendirilmesi [Evaluation of Accounting Errors and Cheats and Related Sanctions within the Scope of Legal Legislation]. *Muhasebe Bilim Dünyası Dergisi*, *1*, 169–193.

Derici, O., Tüysüz, Z., & Sarı, A. (2007). Kurumsal Risk Yönetimi ve Sayıştay: Uygulaması [Enterprise Risk Management and the Court of Auditors: Its Implementation]. *Sayıştay Dergisi*, *65*, 151–172.

Doğan, N. (2009). İş Etiği ve İşletmelerde Etik Çöküş [Business Ethics and Ethical Collapse in Businesses]. *Sosyal Ekonomik Araştırmalar Dergisi*, *8*(16), 179–200.

Emhan, A. (2009). Risk Yönetim Süreci ve Risk Yönetmekte Kullanılan Teknikler [Risk Management Process and Techniques Used to Manage Risk]. *Atatürk Üniversitesi İktisadi ve İdari Bilimler Dergisi*, *23*(3), 209–220.

Eroğlu, O. (2018). *Uygulamada Konkordato* [Concordat in practice]. Seçkin Yayıncılık.

Fone, M., & Young, P. C. (2005). *Managing Risks in Public Organisations*. Perpetuity Press.

Göğüş, E. H. S. (2012). *Risk Odaklı İç denetimde Risklerin Saptanması ve Değerlendirilmesi* [Determination and Evaluation of Risks in Risk-Oriented Internal Audit]. Türkmen Kitapevi.

Gönen, S. (2017). Risk Raporlamasına İlişkin Kuramsal Yaklaşım [Theoretical Approach to Risk Reporting]. *İnsan ve Toplum Bilimleri Araştırmaları Dergisi, 6*(6), 293-301.

Griffiths, P. (2005). *Risk- Based Auditing*. Gower Publishing Limited.

Ilgar, T., & Erdoğdu, G. (2018). Kurumsal Risk Yönetimi Türk Kamu Yönetimine Nasıl Entegre Edilebilir? [How Can Corporate Risk Management Be Integrated into Turkish Public Administration?]. *Denetişim, 8*, 63–76.

Karaca, H. (2018). *Büyük ve Orta Boy İşletmelerin Sahipleri ve Yöneticilerinin Bağımsız Denetçi Algısı ve Bağımsız Denetimden Beklentilerine Yönelik Bir Araştırma* [A Study on the Independent Auditor Perception and Expectations of Owners and Managers of Large and Medium-sized Enterprises from Independent Auditing]. İnönü Üniversitesi Sosyal Bilimler Enstitüsü, Yüksek Lisans Tezi.

Kızılboğa, R. (2012). Geleneksel Risk Yönetiminden Kurumsal Risk Yönetim Sistemine Geçiş [Transition from Traditional Risk Management to Enterprise Risk Management System]. *Atatürk Üniversitesi Sosyal Bilimler Enstitüsü Dergisi, 16*(3), 297–316.

Kızılboğa Özaslan, R., & Özşahin Koç, F. (2016). Kurumun Sürdürülebilirliğinde "İtibar Riski" Yönetiminin Yeri ve Önemi. [The Place and Importance of "Reputation Risk" Management in the Sustainability of the Organization]. *Niğde Üniversitesi İİBF Dergisi, 1*, 273–283.

Kocamış, T. U. (2019). Konkordato Sürecinde Bağımsız Denetim Raporu GDS 3400- İleriye Yönelik Finansal Bilgilerin İncelenmesi Standardı Açısından Değerlendirme [Independent Audit Report in the Concordat Process GDS 3400- Evaluation in terms of the Standard for the Examination of Prospective Financial Information]. *Turkish Studies - Economics, Finance, Politics, 14*, 1093–1105.

Konca, K. N. (2018). Konkordato Uygulamalarına İlişkin Beklentiler ve Riskler [Expectations and Risks for Concordat Implementation]. *Analiz, 263*, 7–18.

Konkordato Talebine Eklenecek Belgeler Hakkında Yönetmelik. https://www.resmigazete.gov.tr/eskiler/2019/01/20190130-2.htm

Lin, Q. (2018). A Survey of Internal Governance in Family Business. *American Journal of Industrial and Business Management, 8*(4), 1093–1100. doi:10.4236/ajibm.2018.84075

Manab, N. A., Hussin, M. R., & Kassim, I. (2010). Enterprise-wide Risk Management Practices: Between Corporate Governance Compliance and Value Creation. International Review of Business Research Papers. *Temmuz., 6*(2), 239–252.

Memiş, M. Ü. (2016). Kurumsal İşletme Yönetiminde Denetimin Önemi [Expectations and Risks for Concordat Implementation]. *Ekonomi Bilimleri Dergisi, 8*(1), 34–49.

Nielsen, D. B. (2010). *Risk Management Reporting and Value Creation in Danish Companies* [Unpublished Master Thesis]. Copenhagen Business School, Finance and Accounting, Denmark.

Organ, İ., & Sevinç, C. (2017). Ticaret Şirketlerinde Ortakların İflas ve İflas Erteleme Döneminde Kamu Alacaklarından Sorumlulukları [Responsibilities of Partners in Trading Companies from Public Receivables during the Bankruptcy and Bankruptcy Postponement Period]. *Gümrük ve Ticaret Dergisi*, (10), 41–48.

Özşahin Koç, F., & Uzay, Ş. (2015). Risk Raporlaması: Gelişmiş Ülke Uygulamalarından Çıkarılacak Dersler. *Erciyes Üniversitesi İktisadi ve İdari Bilimler Fakültesi Dergisi*, *0*(45), 205–230. doi:10.18070/euiibfd.74619

Pehlivanlı, D. (2014). *Modern İç Denetim* [Modern Internal Auditing]. Beta Yayınları.

Pekcanıtez, H., & Erdönmez, G. (2018). 7101 Sayılı Kanunla Yürürlüğe Giren Konkordato Hükümlerinin Değerlendirilmesi [Evaluation of the Concordat Provisions Enacted by Law No. 7101]. *Bankacılar Dergisi*, *105*, 108–156.

Redıng, K. F., Sobel, P. J., Anderson, U. L., Head, M. J., Ramamoortı, S., Salamasıck, M., & Rıddle, C. (2009). *Internal Auditing: Assurance & Consulting Services* (2nd ed.). The Institute of Internal Auditors Research Foundation.

Rezaee, Z. (2005). Causes, consequences, and deterence of financial statement fraud. *Critical Perspectives on Accounting*, *16*(3), 277–298. doi:10.1016/S1045-2354(03)00072-8

Sarıkale, H., & İlter, B. (2018). Finansal Analiz Sürecindeki Temel Mali Tablo Düzeltmelerinin Oran Analizine Etkisi [The Effect of Key Financial Statement Adjustments in the Financial Analysis Process on Ratio Analysis]. *Afyon Kocatepe Üniversitesi Sosyal Bilimler Dergisi*, *20*(1), 165–184.

Sayılı Abonelik Sözleşmesinden Kaynaklanan Para Alacaklarına İlişkin Takibin BaşlatılmasıUsulü Hakkında Kanun Http. Www.Resmigazete.Gov.Tr/Eskiler/2018/12/20181219-1.Htm

Sayılı İcra Ve İflâs Kanunu Ve Bazı Kanunlarda Değişiklik Yapılması Hakkında Kanun. www.resmigazete.gov.tr/eskiler/2018/03/20180315-28.htm

Sayılı İcra ve İflas Kanunu www.mevzuat.gov.tr/MevzuatMetin/1.3.2004.pdf

Sorgun, C. & Türk, M. (2008). Aile Şirketlerinde Yönetim Sorunları: Adana İlinde Bir Araştırma [Management Problems in Family Companies: A Study in Adana Province]. *Çukurova Üniversitesi İktisadi ve İdari Bilimler Fakültesi Dergisi*, *12*(1), 56-72.

Toroslu, M. V. (2019). *Hukuksal ve Finansal Açıdan Konkordato* [Concordat from a Legal and Financial Perspective]. Adalet Yayınevi.

Turaboğlu, T. T., & Timur, E. (2018). İşletmelerde Kârlılığı Etkileyen Faktörler: BİST Kurumsal Yönetim Endeksindeki Firmalara İlişkin Bir Uygulama [Factors Affecting Profitability in Enterprises: An Application for Companies in the BIST Corporate Governance Index]. *Bulletin of Economic Theory and Analysis*, *3*(2), 135–157.

Uyar, T. (2018). Yeni Konkordato Hukukumuzun Temel İlkeleri [Basic Principles of Our New Concordat Law]. *İstanbul Barosu Dergisi*. 4,15-102.

Uzay, Ş. (2017). *Bağımsız Denetimin İşletmenin Sürekliliğine Katkısı, Kamu Gözetimi Kurumu, Muhasebe ve Denetim Sempozyumu* [The Contribution of Independent Auditing to the Continuity of the Enterprise, Public Oversight Authority, Accounting and Auditing Symposium]. İktisadi Gelişmede Muhasebe ve Denetimin Önemi, İstanbul, Turkey.

Uzay, Ş. (2019). İflasın Ertelenmesi Kurumunun Türkiye Uygulamasının Değerlendirilmesi [Evaluation of the Turkish Practice of the Bankruptcy Postponement Institution]. *Uluslararası İktisadi ve İdari İncelemeler Dergisi*, *23*, 169–178.

Walker, E. W., & Baughn, W. H. (1961). *Financial Planning and Policy*. Harper-Row.

Walker, P. L., Shenkir, W. G., & Barton, T. L. (2002). *Enterprise Risk Management: Pulling it all Together*. The Institute of Internal Auditors Research Foundation.

Whiting, D. G., Hansen, J. V., Mcdonald, J. B., Albrecht, C., Steve, W., & Albrecht, W. S. (2012). Machıne Learnıng Methods For Detectıng Patterns Of Management Fraud. *Computational Intelligence*, *28*(4), 505–527. doi:10.1111/j.1467-8640.2012.00425.x

Yarız, A. (2012). *Bankacılıkta Risk Yönetimi Risk Matrisi Uygulaması* [Risk Management Risk Matrix Application in Banking]. Nobel Akademik Yayıncılık.

Yavuz, M. (2019). Son Düzenlemeler Işığında Konkordato Talep Eden Şirketlerce Mahkemeye Sunulması Gereken Belgeler [Documents to be Submitted to the Court by Companies Requesting Concordat in the Light of Recent Regulations]. *Mali Çözüm.*, *153*, 239–248.

Yıldız, B., & Demireli, E. (2019). Nakit Yönetimini Etkileyen Değişkenler Üzerine BİST Perakende Sektöründe Panel Veri Analizi [Panel Data Analysis in BIST Retail Sector on Variables Affecting Cash Management]. *Hitit Üniversitesi Sosyal Bilimler Enstitüsü Dergisi*, *12*(2), 416–429. doi:10.17218/hititsosbil.589396

KEY TERMS AND DEFINITIONS

Business Ethics: It is in general, means knowing what is right and wrong in the business environment and doing the right thing.

Cashis: It is the basic input that businesses use while carrying out their work, and it gives power and life to businesses by providing profit and payment power.

Concordat: It is a forced agreement made by a debtor with a certain majority of his creditors and valid with the approval of the commercial court.

Family Businesses: It is expressed as businesses that carry out their activities under the control of family members, and where the determined value judgments and profit-making methods are determined by the members of the family in question.

Profit: It is the positive difference between the income and expenses of a business at the end of a certain period.

Risk: It is the probability that an event will occur and adversely affect the success of the organization in achieving its goals.

Risk Management: It is expressed as a process consisting of pre-defining, evaluating, managing and controlling possible events and situations in order to provide reasonable assurance for the organization to achieve its objectives.

Chapter 6
A Multi-Dimensional View of Financial Distress

Bilgehan Kübilay
Zonguldak Bülent Ecevit University, Turkey

ABSTRACT

Financial distress is a multidimensional and complex subject. Financial distress has physical and physiological effects and harmful consequences for individuals and families, ranging from unpaid debts and deteriorating health to suicide. For this reason, it has been a widely researched subject by different branches of science such as finance, psychology, and sociology. In this study, financial distress was examined from a subjective point of view. The effect of financial distress on physical and psychological health, its effect on families and children, and the effect of social support and socio-economic status on financial distress were investigated. The role of financial capability and financial resilience in reducing financial distress was emphasized. This study aimes to consolidate and expand knowledge about financial distress. The issue of financial distress has been extensively researched under the behavioral finance framework.

INTRODUCTION

Stress is an unpleasant feeling experienced when something valuable is lost or when the person feels threatened. This loss or threat can be financial (for example, loss of home), social (for example, the breakup of a relationship), symbolic (for example, loss of status), economic (for example, job insecurity). People experience stress when they believe they don't have the coping skills or resources needed to face perceived threat or loss. Factors that cause stress are called stressors. This stressor can be something that comes from the outside world (economic recession, layoff) or inner world and cannot be observed by the outside world (like fear of failure). Stressors can be acute or chronic, predictable or unpredictable, controllable or uncontrollable (Davis & Mantler, 2004, p. 3). It can be assumed that stress from one or more stressors is not just an emotion, but also a physiological response (Heo, et al., 2020, p. 3).

People are happier when they are healthy, are married or in a committed relationship, have a job, work, and feel financially secure (Xio & Garman, 2005, p. 73). An important part of general psychological

DOI: 10.4018/978-1-6684-5181-6.ch006

well-being is contentment in various areas of life. One of these areas is related to the financial situation of the person. The terms used to name constructs that describe one's feelings about one's financial situation vary. In the literature, while positive expressions such as financial well-being, financial wellness, financial satisfaction, financial resilience, financial health, perceived income adequacy are used to describe the financial situation of the person, negative expressions such as financial distress, financial stress, financial strain, debt stress, economic distress and economic strain are also used. In the literature, either objective or subjective measures are used to describe the financial status of individuals. Objective and subjective measures evaluate different aspects of a person's financial situation and provide different sources of information. There is no consensus on which is the best measure. Both measures are useful for providing information about the financial situation of individuals. The ease of access to objective measurements also makes it easy to measure numbers, assuming accurate and appropriate data are provided. But it can be said that knowing one's feelings and judgments about one's financial situation will be more helpful. Because, while objective evaluations express verifiable, calculable, fact-based items (such as total savings, household income); it does not measure the depth of one's feelings and reactions to one's financial situation. Differences in perception, cognition and experience are included in subjective evaluations. Thus, subjective measure provides a richness that objective measure cannot provide. Because it helps to examine not only how people perceive their financial situation, but also how it affects individuals and families, physical and psychological health (Wuth & Cismaru, 2021, pp. 1-3; Prawitz et al., 2006, pp. 34-35). On the other hand, there is not always a strong link between economic hardship and financial (di)stress. People without financial difficulties may also feel financial (di) stress, or some with financial difficulties may not experience as much financial distress (Davis and Mantler, 2004, p. 23).

Due to its impact on individuals and society, financial distress has been a widely researched topic by different disciplines such as finance, psychology, sociology, marketing with different terms and different meanings. Although approached in different fields, some of these terms are similar, have overlapping aspects but not the same. When referring to negative financial health behaviors in the literature, it is seen that subjective measures are used more frequently than objective measures. According to the literature review, the terms economic hardship, financial distress, financial strain and economic deprivation are the most common negative financial terms in the databases, respectively (Wuth & Cismaru, 2021, p. 1-2).

In this study, the term of financial distress, which expresses a negative financial situation, will be evaluated subjectively. Because objective measures are not enough to evaluate a person's financial situation. Two people with the same income may have different perceptions of their consumption, spending habits and financial situation. A person subjectively evaluates her/his financial situation by looking at the extent to which she can meet her/his own desire and needs in response to the financial demands of life (Prawitz et al., 2006, p. 35). For example, the level of financial distress varies according to the perspective of the person towards money. Those who associate money with generosity, freedom, and power experience more financial distress, while those who associate money with security experience less financial distress (Fenton O'Creevy & Furnham, 2021). In addition, the perception of financial distress changes according to demographic characteristics. According to the researchers, those with higher education levels (undergraduate, graduate), those who are employed and those with disposable income experience less financial distress (Wrosch et al., 2000, p. 388; Koomson et al., 2022). According to Ryan's (2012) study, the level of financial distress is especially higher in people between the ages of 20 and 30, and the level of financial distress decreases with age.

People, who are experience financial distress, have difficulties in fulfilling their financial obligations and seek financial assistance from others and cannot cope with financial issues (Marks, 2007, p.

1). Financial distress is a subjective, unpleasant feeling that one cannot meet the financial demands, the necessities of life, and not have enough money to make a living. It includes feelings of fear, anxiety, anger and frustration in the person. Financial distress is associated with low self-esteem, a pessimistic viewpoint on life, decreased mental health, and increased depression and hostility (Davis & Mantler, 2004). Therefore, financial distress has emotional, relational and physiological aspects (Heo, et al., 2020).

Bray (2001) defined three different sources of stress related to the financial situation. The first type of stress cause from being deprived. Deprivation refers to the extent to which households make concessions on what they can or cannot do within their budget. For example, not being able to take a vacation away from home, not being able to participate in activities such as hobbies, and not being able to eat special meals outside with family or friends can cause deprivation. The second is the type of stress caused by cash flow problems. Borrowing money from family or friends, just as not being able to pay bills (electronics, telephone, gas bills and so on) on time. The third is the type of stress caused by financial difficulties. It refers to the situations of not being able to meet the need for heating and food, getting help from social institutions, pawning or selling goods. Bray argues that the situations in which financial distress occurs most often are related to deprivation, followed by cash flow problems and financial difficulties due to lack of income.

Three sources of financial distress identified by Joo & Grable (2004) are related to personal, family and financial situations. Sources of personal stress include investment losses, injuries, disability, accidents, illnesses, and wage cuts. Family stressors include life-cycle events such as death-birth, marriage-divorce, retirement, and job loss. Resolving such events requires a significant amount of money, which leads to serious financial problems. Financial stressors also include personal consumer preference situations such as moving, paying for home, vehicle repairs, foreclosure, bankruptcy, medical bills, and excessive consumer debt (Freeman et al., 1993; Joo, 1998).

Aldana & Liljenquist (1998, p. 12) stated the conditions that may cause financial distress as follows: Inability to meet basic needs and desires for oneself or family, little money left after paying bills, high debt level, financial dissatisfaction, low self-esteem, negative financial changes such as bankruptcy, expulsion, dismissal, retirement cause financial strain.

Kim et al., (2013) argue that not every negative financial event cause financial distress. They explored which negative financial events cause the most distress in people. Accordingly, the participants in the research stated that they were more stressed when they received a notice of delay from the creditor, when they received a call from the creditor about the overdue invoice, when their homes were foreclosed, when their wages and belongings were confiscated. In addition, the financial well-being levels of people who were more exposed to events that cause negative financial distress were found to be lower in the research. Davis & Mantler (2004, p. 3) also stated that triggering stress factors (such as job loss, loss of investment) that cause financial distress in general were chronic, unpredictable and uncontrollable, and therefore more wearisome than acute, predictable and controllable stressors.

RESEARCH METHODOLOGY

In this study, it was decided to deal with financial distress under the framework of behavioral finance. A detailed, extensive and systematic literature review on financial distress was conducted. The literature review provides the theoretical framework for the research while determining the subject and narrowing the subject (Demirci, 2014).

As a result of the comprehensive literature review, the boundaries of the subject were drawn and the subject headings were determined by considering the redundancy of the studies on the effect of financial distress. In the study, it was tried to create a meaningful integrity by summarizing the different results of independent studies on financial distress.

THEORETICAL FRAMEWORK

In this study, financial distress is investigated over five dimensions. The effect of financial distress caused by negative financial events/situations on physical health and psychological health, as well as on the effect on family and their children who are their extensions, has been wondered. Since financial distress is thought to be related to social factors, research topics on the effect of social support and socio-economic status on financial distress are also included. Finally, the role of financial capacity and financial resilience in overcoming financial distress is investigated.

The Effect of Financial Distress on Physical Health

Financial distress is not the only factor that causes health problems. But medical research suggests that such symptoms represent chronic stress. The body has a fight-or-flight response to stress. When stressed, the body releases hormones such as adrenaline and cortisol. In case of constant stress, the body tries to establish a new balance and adapt to adverse conditions. High levels of chemicals in the body can cause vital damage to body systems such as blood pressure, heart rate, memory, mood and immunity (Choi, 2009, p.121). According to the researchers, financial distress caused by socio-economic situation, excessive debt and negative financial events cause many physiological disorders (Heo et al., 2020).

In Finland, study of adults with excessive debt for at least 15 years found a higher incidence of chronic disease and diabetes risk, especially in women (Blomgren, et al., 2016). Research by Advani et al., (2014) reveals the relationship between financial strain and cancer risk. According to the research of Sturgeon et al., (2016) negative financial events affect inflammation in the body. Ochsmann et al., (2009) suggest that excessive debt exacerbates back pain and it may make sense to consider the financial burden when taking a medical history of back pain.

Münster et al., (2009) conducted a study on adults in Germany, and it was observed that individuals with excessive debt had a higher risk of obesity compared to the general population. According to researchers, there is a link between an individual's financial situation and the diversity of their access to healthy food. The inverse relationship between the energy intensity of food and its costs, couple with the risk of failure to pay, may be a cause of obesity risk among heavily indebted subjects.

In addition to an unhealthy diet, the use of addictive substances such as cigarettes, alcohol and drugs, accompany financial distress and impair health (French & McKillop, 2017). In the study of Widome et al., (2015) it was revealed that those with nicotine addiction and those who smoked a lot of cigarettes during the day experienced financial difficulties, and therefore they were more financially worried about both food and shelter. Low-income smokers experience greater financial distress as tobacco expenditures displace other expenditures.

Drentea & Lavrakas (2000) argues that high debt will deprive people of quality goods and services and accordingly, will negatively affect their financial health. According to the researchers, having to provide basic needs such as food, medicine and clothing from credit cards and having too many credit cards may be an indicator of the financial crisis. Being in debt and paying high interest rates lead to increase financial distress and deterioration of one's health.

In the study of Kosminsky et al., (2020) in which they compiled published research on financial distress and painful situations, they found results showing a consistent relationship between socioeconomic status and pain. While people with high financial distress felt pain more strongly, those with moderate financial distress stated that they experienced the effect of daily financial anxiety on pain more moderately, and those with low financial distress stated that pain had no effect. These findings indicated that there is evidence of significant interindividual variation in the relationship between daily financial worry and pain. Rantakeisu et al., (1999) determined that besides the psychological effects of financial distress, it physically causes an increase in headaches and stomachaches and causes insomnia.

In fact, there is a mutual interaction between debt and health. Health problems can also cause people to be unable to pay their debts (Pollack & Lynch, 2009). When the health of people with high debt and low income deteriorates, these people will have difficulty in finding a stable job or continuing their work. As a result of this, the poverty trap will become more serious, and it will be more difficult for those who fall into the debt trap to get out of this situation (Lenton & Mosley, 2008).

Psychological Effects of Financial Distress

Sources of financial distress are complex and multidimensional (Guan et al., 2022). Although financial distress is a subjective feeling, objective conditions cause economic difficulties. Economic difficulties can result from poor income, poverty, unemployment, excessive debt, foreclosure, bankruptcy, unexpected medical or legal expenses, recession, loss of investment, bad habits such as gambling (Davis & Mantler, 2004, p. 3). These financial difficulties have serious and long-lasting effects on people's lives (Turunen & Hiilamo, 2014). It is inevitable for people to experience financial distress under these conditions, and their psychological reflections differ in each person, and financial distress causes many mental health problems. Financial distress can cause problems with self-care, problems performing normal daily activities, suffering and feeling anxious and depressed (French & McKillop, 2017).

On the other hand, for some, a worsening financial situation may cause psychological stress, while for others, psychological stress may contribute to worsening financial situation (Beauchaine et al., 2020, p. 1). Sad and sometimes dysfunctional thought patterns are set in motion by major life crises such as economic hardships. Guilt, anger, irritability are common emotional responses in people struggling with important life issues (Tedeshi & Calhoun, 2004, pp. 2-8). This is actually inherent in neoliberalism. Because in neoliberalism, being in debt makes one feel responsible, guilty and frustrated (Charbonneau & Hanse, 2014, p. 1042). So, money is more than just cash and coins. It is understandable that those who have been laid off, witness their retirement savings disappear, or watch helplessly as their homes devalue, associate money with security, power, independence and freedom (Choi, 2009, p. 121).

Honor and reputation are associated with financial success, while failing financially is considered embarrassing. Shame manifests itself in the form of feelings of worthlessness, humiliation, feeling under pressure and being criticized. People with financial difficulties experience more embarrassing situations and have lower self-esteem. Especially unemployed men experience more psychological problems than women and experience more intense feelings of embarrassment. For some people, therefore, suicide has been the most dramatic way to save their dignity and that of their families (Rantakeisu et al., 1999, p. 879). Turunen & Hiilamo (2014) found that unpaid financial obligations were perceived as shame and failure, especially among wealthier countries, that people with financial distress experienced more depression and thought more about committing suicide.

Research by Catalano et al., (2011) shows that negative financial experiences and financial distress increase substance use along with violence and suicide events. Jenkins et al., (2008) investigated the relationship between both debt and income level and their mental health. They found that the more debt people have, the higher the probability of experiencing mental disorder, neurosis, psychosis, and alcohol and drug addiction. In a study conducted by Rojas (2021) on persons aged 18 to 64 with a debt record in the Swedish Enforcement Office, it was determined that people with financial debts were more likely to commit suicide than those who did not have this experience. In another study investigating the relationship between financial distress and suicide, it was found that adults with attention deficit/hyperactivity disorder had a four times higher risk of committing suicide due to financial distress (Beauchaine et al., 2020).

According to Meltzer et al.,'s (2011) research, the number of debts, the source of debt and the causes of debt are the main correlates of suicidal ideation. Those who have a lot of debt and are also hopeless are more likely to report suicidal thoughts. The results of the same research conducted in England revealed that while men over 55 years of age had less suicidal ideation, it was higher in women aged 35-54 years. In particular, a strong relationship was found between housing-related debts (such as rent-mortgage debts), difficulty paying credit card debt, and suicidal ideation. According to research by McLaughlin et al., (2011) people who experience a foreclosure experience more depressive symptoms than people who do not. In the study of Jenkins et al., (2008) it was determined that the most frequently reported debts in people with mental disorders were telephone, rent, gas, water, electricity, municipal taxes. Certain types of debt have been found to be more common in people with certain conditions. For example, credit card debts were more likely to be associated with neurotic disorders, and rent debt was more likely to be associated with alcohol addiction. Although substance abuse was not associated with low income, it was found that people with substance addiction had twice the risk of debt than those without substance abuse.

Haw et al., (2014) found that economic recession causes unemployment, financial loss and debt growth, leading to mental health problems such as depression, anxiety and excessive alcohol consumption and then suicide. In the study by Warth et al., (2020) in which they investigated the relationship between excessive debt and antidepressant use, they found that the use of antidepressants in Germany was significantly higher than the general population.

Lund et al., (2010) investigated the relationship between poverty and common mental disorders (depression, anxiety) in low-and middle- income countries. For this, they conducted a systematic review of the findings of 115 studies from 33 countries with different methods, working environments and populations published in the literature between 1990 and 2008. 79% of studies showed a positive relationship between poverty and generalized mental disorder.

Another factor causing financial difficulties is the psychological distress associated with gambling, which leads to loss of money and property. Oksanen et al., (2018) argue that consumer loans provide gamblers with resources to continue these habits and consumer loans make financial problems worse because of this.

Financial distress also affects work efficiency (Delafrooz & Paim, 2013). Financial distress affects organizational commitment and absenteeism. Employees with high financial distress have lower levels of organizational commitment and higher absenteeism. Employees with a high-income level are more absent than those with a lower income level (Kim & Garman, 2003). Employees with high levels of financial distress are less satisfied with life (Joo & Grable, 2004).

There are also studies on the effect of financial distress on students' psychological health. Lange & Byrd (1998) investigated how students' estimates of both current and future debt levels affected their perceptions of financial distress. As a result of the research, it has been determined that a high perceived current debt level increases the amount of anxiety associated with meeting daily living expenses, and a higher level of expected debt in the future causes chronic financial distress. Researchers examined financial distress from two aspects: the daily financial distress of meeting daily financial needs; chronic financial distress caused by the long-term impact of debt. In the study, it was determined that chronic financial distress had a negative effect on students' self-esteem. Similarly, in Joo et al.'s (2008) study, it was found that students with financial distress had lower self-esteem. In the study of Archuleta et al., (2013) on university students, it was stated that all debts including student loans, credit cards, auto loans, installment debts were important factors in estimating financial anxiety. According to the research, the higher the financial satisfaction of the person, the lower of the financial anxiety. Drentea (2000) found that young people's credit card debts were high, and the level of anxiety increased as their credit card debt increased.

In fact, debt is not inherently problematic when it can be repaid or managed. The first sign of debt problems is delayed payments. These delays can lead to penalties and deterioration of mental health. Psychiatrists, although they are not financial advisors, may have roles to play in this regard. It is important for psychiatrists to determine whether the person can cope with repayments, whether they need support and whether they fully understand the financial implications of the person's delayed payments. Psychiatrists can assess whether people have sufficient mental capacity to manage their financial situations and can help patients develop self-confidence and skills. For this, psychiatrists working with financial advisors and directing individuals to financial advisors who are experts in debt may produce more effective results (Fitch et al., 2007, pp. 194-199).

The Effect of Financial Distress on Family Relationships

Boss (2001, p. 3) defines family stress as follows, by set off medical, sociological, engineering and psychological disciplines. A disturbance in the stagnant state of the family system. He says that this discomfort may be caused by external factors (unemployment, war, etc.), internal factors (divorce, death, etc.) or the emergence of both at the same time. In any case, the balance of the family system is threatened by the changes. However, family stress does not always have to result in problems. Some high tensions can make families more robust and functional. The flexibility of such families in family rules, roles, problem-solving and adapting abilities to changing conditions can save them from disintegration (Yakymchuk et al., 2021, p. 138).

The subject of financial distress has been an important study in the field of family studies, marriage and family therapy as well as in the field of finance. Because money problems lie at the root of most marital problems. There is a relationship between the spouses' decision to stay married to the same person or leave the relationship and financial distress. As financial distress increases, marriages are less likely to work out. On the other hand, how married couples handle financial distress is also important. If the married couples can develop methods of coping with financial distress among themselves and are willing to work and cooperate together, these couples can reduce the level of anxiety in the relationship (Archulate et al., 2011, p. 12).

Therefore, the interaction of married couples plays a key role in overcoming financial distress. For this, it is necessary to look at the frequency and severity of the discussions on financial matters of the spouses. According to the research conducted by Yakymchuk et al., (2021), the most stressful and frequently discussed issue among married couples is the lack of funds needed by the spouses for their current needs. In the study, it was determined that spouses mostly criticized each other's financial behavior differences (such as stinginess or wastefulness) and these behavior differences caused negative feelings in the married couples. An interesting result of the research is that wifes are more inclined to begin a discussion on economic issues and have economic anxiety, while men are more optimistic about economic issues. It has been stated that while the woman is relieved when the husband takes on the solution of the problems, when the woman undertakes to solve the financial problems, on the contrary, this situation increases the financial distress of the husband. This situation has been attributed to the fact that the equalization of gender differences in modern societies causes confusion in marriage roles. Accordingly, the married couples do not understand what economic roles they should play in the household.

According to Poduska (1992, p. 756) married couples who can manage their financial affairs well have been able to establish a budget like a wall, which not only maintains their lives, but also increase their quality of life. For most couples, it's not enough to stop foreclosure, get out of debt, or have enough food on the table. Poduska suggests that married couples should formulate a financial management plan that goes beyond survivability and helps give meaning to life. According to Turunen & Hiilamo (2014, p. 1) household debt is not always a sign of financial problems. Rather, most households borrow to finance their housing purchases and other forms of private consumption, in some cases using loans for private investments or trade. Loans are given according to the borrower's ability to repay. Researchers suggest that financial problems arise only when households are unable to manage their debts when debts pile up due to unemployment, serious illness, or rising interest rates.

For this reason, most of the time in families experiencing financial difficulties, stressful events do not occur for a single reason, they are cumulative (O' Neill et al., 2006b, p. 489). According to Davis & Mantler (2004, p. 3), as financial distress increases, the process that leads to increase discord and separation in marriages works as follows. As financial pressure increases, couples become more preoccupied with financial matters, leading to mutual blame, frustration, and arguments about money. As individuals become depressed, they withdraw from their partners and give each other less emotional support.

Financial distress varies according to the demographic and socio-economic status of the family. Worthington's (2006) study in Australia found that financial distress was associated with the demographic and socioeconomic characteristics of the household, and that households with high disposable income had low financial distress, it was determined that financial distress was higher in families with more children and in ethnic minorities.

According to the research conducted by O' Neill et al., (2006b) married people experience more stress than unmarried people. Yakymchuk et al., (2021, p. 138) stated that gender roles played an important role in the partners' strategies for coping with financial distress. Due to the overall role of "breadwinner", husbands feel that they should take on more stress. Women, on the other hand, tend to cooperate with their partners in order to be connected to each other. On the otherhand in the study of Mills et al., (1992) on married adults, it was found that financial distress did not differ between wives and husbands and husband and wife were equally affected by economic stress in terms of psychological well-being.

Patrica (1990, p. 1108) stated that the economic welfare of a family depended on the number of income earners, the amount of income brought to the family, the non-income contributions to the family economy (such as childcare, household chores) and the needs of the family and the size of the family. In a two-person family, the financial distress level is lower in these households than in single-adult households, as couples can be interchangeable and complementary in the labor market, home and childcare.

Having money and time management skills and a wider support network can help families cope with financial distress.

According to the study of Aydıner Boylu (2014) as the financial difficulties of single-parent families increase, the functions of fulfilling family functions (such as meeting economic needs, planning the education of children, protecting each other, providing status) become unhealthy. Kempson et al., (2004) found that single parents had higher levels of arrears, including delays in both household bills and loan commitments, than two-parent families.

Housing loans and consumer loans in debt type bring a significant burden to families and this situation adversely affects the psychological health of families (Gathergood, 2012). Kempson et al., (2004) investigated the characteristics of indebted families and the nature of debt, and it was determined that while the level of consumer loan debt was especially high among families in their twenties, it decreased sharply among those aged 30 and over. A strong correlation was found between those aged 16-59 who had overdue debts and those with psychological problems. Delays in household bills, as well as consumer loan debts, tended to decrease with age. Researchers argue that the more a family's income goes towards loan payments, the higher the probability that the family will not be able to pay its debts. According to the research, loss of income is one of the main reasons for families to borrow at a high rate. Causes of loss of income are job loss, illness, disability, death of a spouse, less commonly a drop in wages, and the majority of financial problems faced by families are long-term rather than short-term.

The financial distress level of families with and without children also differs. Families with children are more likely to experience financial difficulties and stress than families without children. Childless families are more successful in making a living, while lone parents are the worst in making a living. In addition, this difficulty level changes according to the age levels of the children. Especially in families which small children (between 0-4 years old) are added, the high cost of childcare puts more strain on families and causes them to need more additional income (Breuning & Clark, 2006; Atkinson et al., 2007, p. 64). According to a study by Reading & Reynolds (2001), depression is more common among women with financial difficulties and with small children. In particular, debt and debt-related concerns, which are a cause of socio-economic distress, have a central place on mothers' depression.

In another study, the relationship between the place of residence of households and bankruptcy, which causes significant financial distress, was investigated. In the research found that if households lived in areas (districts) with higher rates of filing for bankruptcy, these households were also more likely to file for bankruptcy. This situation is interpreted as helping the households to decide on bankruptcy more easily, as it reduces the pain of those who receive bankruptcy news from their friends or relatives. This shows that the social environment also affects the financial situation and financial distress of families.

The Effect of Financial Distress on Children

Financial distress affects not only parents but also children. Financial distresses of parents and financial difficulties in childhood affect both the psychology, health and quality of life of children. Studies show that the effects of socioeconomic status begin before birth and continue into adulthood and are associated with a wide range of health, cognitive, and socio-emotional outcomes in children (Bradley & Corwyn, 2002).

Financial distress can cause parents to become less sensitive to their children's needs. The behavior of parents experiencing financial distress can lead to children having low self-esteem, impulsive behavior and depression, health problems, poor academic performance, and drug and alcohol use (Davis & Mantler,

2004, p. 3). The study of Joo et al., (2008) shows that financial distress affects academic performance, and financial problems cause university students to drop out of school.

The longer and more severe the impact of financial distress, the more contagious and permanent than it is thought to be. In the study conducted by Kim et al., (2016) it was determined that people with poor economic status during childhood had negative and permanent effects of long-term poverty on their mental health, and these people were more likely to show symptoms of depression. Those with good economic status in childhood showed lower depression symptoms. Similar results were obtained in the research of Bolger et al., (1995). According to the research, psychiatric disorders are more common in children from low socio-economic families who experience economic distress than in children from more affluent conditions. These children also have lower self-esteem and have problems of adaptation in social relations.

Research by Boe et al., (2017) shows that financial difficulties in childhood lead to depression at different stages of a person's life. In the study conducted in 19 European countries, it was found that in 10 of 19 countries, financial difficulties in childhood were associated with depression, especially in young adults aged 25-40. Kahn & Pearlin (2006) investigated when and at what age level (pre-18, 18-35, 35-50, 50-65 years old) financial difficulties occured and whether these financial difficulties would damage health and well-being in the future. The research revealed that most people experience financial difficulties in childhood and before the young age of 35. Previous financial difficulties exacerbate the impact of later financial conditions. Financial difficulties experienced before age 35 only have an impact on health problems in later life when additional difficulties follow after age 35. Recent experiences with financial difficulties do not appear to have deleterious effects if they occur after a period of relative financial comfort.

Poverty has negative consequences on quality of life. The poor are more likely to be exposed to stressful life events such as unemployment, economic hardship, being a victim of crime and illness. Considering that poverty is associated with stress, chronic tensions, low levels of social support and problematic family relationships, it is almost inevitable that children growing up in these conditions are relatively unhealthy from a psychological point of view. In addition, financial distress differs between women and men with and without children in urban and rural areas. Amato & Zuo (1992) investigated the effects of poverty in both rural and urban areas on depression, happiness and health. While the rate of happiness is low and depression is high among single men without children in poor rural areas, the rate of happiness is high among married women with children in poor cities, and the level of depression is low among married women without children.

The Relationship Between Financial Distress and Social Support and Socio-Economic Status

It is known that people experience various levels of stressful or traumatic events throughout their lives. Still, some can cope with negative experiences, financial difficulties with great resilience. One reason for this resilience is access to social support (Park et al., 2017). There is an important interaction between financial distress and social support. Interactions with others can reduce an individual's distress or increase their well-being. On the other hand, existing psychological conditions can also affect interpersonal relationships (Sturgeon et al., 2016). Strengthening social networks has the potential to improve quality of life. People with high social support have less effect of financial distress (Aslund et al., 2014). Among the main types of support, there are instrumental aids such as money, goods and services, and moral support such as emotional accompaniment, advice and feedback. Support can come from a variety of sources, from friends, family, relatives, colleagues, various charitable or service organisations. However, using social supports to cope with financial difficulties is a complex process involving many important dimensions. Is there any support available, can the existing supports be used, is the support provided to meet the needs? (Patrica, 1990, p. 1108). Because only when these conditions are met, social support can reach its goal.

Many people believe that economic hardship is a private matter and withdraw from social relationships and may not use or miss an opportunity to seek help and support (Davis & Mantler, 2004, p. 3). For example, men with financial difficulties have less communication with their families and relatives and tend to reduce their leisure activities (Rantakeisu et al., 1999). Some people, when faced with life-threatening stressful situations, turn off their minds and bodies and show inactivity, helplessness and freezing behavior against the stressors instead of fighting or fleeing. This reaction is a common feature of animals and humans. Especially those who face several serious financial stresorss (such as job loss, illness, foreclosure, divorce) at the same time are more likely to be exposed to this situation. However, people who are willing to get financial help experience less financial distress (Grable et al., 2015).

For this reason, the importance of social networks such as family, colleagues and peers who provide emotional and practical support should be emphasized. People will feel better when they integrate into a strong social network that supports them (Viseu et al., 2018). Social support creates a safety net that protects against the negative effects on mental health, especially in times of economic recession (Fernandez et al., 2015). According to the research of Sturgeon et al., (2016) having a high social status in the community makes individuals more resistant to financial distress. The study found that higher perceived social status served as a protective factor for psychological health in the absence of major financial stressor. In another study, it was determined that people living in places with high debt problems were less affected psychologically by the effect of social norms (Gathergood, 2012). On the other hand, according to a study conducted in Turkey, the depth of socio-economic and socio-psychological depression experienced by people with high economic income, quality of life and social status in case of commercial failure is greater than that of other social groups. The social network and support weaken around individuals who commit suicide as a result of commercial failure, and it is difficult for them to participate in society and return to normal life in their next life (Sezer, 2011).

Sometimes, the effect of debt on individuals' social relations manifests itself in the form of social isolation, social exclusion and difficulties in close relationships (Fitch et al., 2007, p. 196). In addition to social exclusion, people with excessive debt are also financially excluded. There are also cause and effect relationships between excessive borrowing and financial exclusion. Over-indebted persons are seen as less reliable because of their track record and their claims are denied by the bank. If the person has not come out of a situation of financial distress, presents too many elements of financial weakness (such as low income, excessive debt, unstable job, poor financial management ability), banks do not care much about people in this segment and do not want to serve them. As a result, such a customer has to use loans at high interest rates. This feeds the vicious circle found in the order of over-indebtedness, insolvency, bankruptcy and financial exclusion (Anderloni & Vandone, 2008, p. 17).

The lack of access of the low-income or poor to a bank account, consumer loan, financial products such as savings or insurance indicates financial exclusion. Those most at risk of financial exclusion are single parents, people unable to work due to long-term illness or disability, low-income and very elderly people. This situation also contributes significantly to social exclusion. In addition, the concentration of financially excluded people in poor geographical areas may cause feelings such as resentment and anger towards financial institutions (Kempson et al., 2000). Marks (2007, p. 1) stated that even low-income people could only meet the basic necessities of life, and they were excluded from even normal lifestyles for modern life and could not cope with financial issues.

Financial Capability and Resilience Against Financial Distress

Two people with the same income and expenses are likely to react very differently to the same debt problem. One may mobilize their resources to deal with the debt problem, for example, change their spending habits, seek other sources of income, while the other may think that they cannot manage the same situation and are beyond their abilities (Davis & Mantler, 2004, p. 3). The person may not consider himself/herself financially capable. On the other hand, no matter how financially talented some people may be, planning for the future financially may be an unrealizable desire for them. In other words, even if some people want, they may not have enough resources and savings (Atkinson et al., 2007, p. 64). In addition, people's financial capabilities or resilience may change over time, depending on the context, circumstances and supports that surround them (Salignac et al., 2019).

Financial capability refers to people's knowledge of financial matters, their ability to manage their money and take control of their financial situation. In other words, financial capability covers a set of skills, behaviors and knowledge related to a person's ability to manage their income (Taylor, 2011, p. 298). According to Atkinson et al., (2007) financial capability is not an absolute but a relative concept. There is no single indicator of financial capability. Financial capability covers four different areas. Managing money: abilities related to making a living, attitude towards credit, spending habits.

- Planning ahead: abilities related to retirement, preparation for unexpected events.
- Choosing: includes the ability to choose suitable financial products, attitude towards risk, level of knowledge about financial products, participation in the financial services market.
- Keeping up with current economic developments covers the skills related to the level of knowledge and follow-up in financial matters.

However, there is no guarantee that those who are successful in one of these areas will be successful in the others. Also, those with high enough incomes can make a living without having many money management skills. One thing to consider for this group is how well they monitor their financial situation. Therefore, it is necessary to evaluate each individual according to their own financial conditions.

According to Taylor (2011, p. 298) low financial capability is conceptually different from being low-income or suffering from deprivation. Financially capability people may have low incomes, while those with high incomes and high living standards may have low financial capability. However, having insufficient or low income makes the money management process does not easier, it makes it harder. In general, it is foreseen that people, no matter how good they are in planning ahead, choosing financial products or having financial knowledge, cannot be considered financially sufficient if they cannot make a living (Atkinson et al., 2007). On the other hand, economic difficulties and financial distress can also open the door to positive results. Such as finding a new job or improving one's ability to manage one's finances. When such obstacles are overcome, one can feel better and more successful (Davis & Mantler, 2004, p. 1). Obstacles overcome can make the person feel capable.

Many people experience adverse financial events or hurdles, including bankruptcy, mortgage, car or home repurchase, loan refusal, difficulties meeting loan repayments. To understand why some people, suffer bad financial results and others do not, it is necessary to consider the financial conditions that people create and live in, as well as differences in financial capabilities and attitudes towards money (Fenton O'Creevy & Furnham, 2013). People often find themselves in financial distress because they cannot distinguish between their physiological and psychological needs. They choose to meet their psychological needs before meeting their physiological needs, and they are short of money for their basic physiological needs (Aldana & Liljenquist, 1998, p. 11; Poduska, 1992). These are the people most at risk for financial shocks, and they are also the ones most in need of developing their capability to cope with financial difficulties.

Money management is an important and necessary component of financial capability. Money management practices differ according to age groups. According to the research conducted by Atkinson et al., (2007, p. 41) it has been determined that the people who use credit cards for daily expenses and cannot pay and have the highest probability of experiencing financial difficulties are between the ages of 29 and 40. People aged 60 and over are the least likely to have and use a credit card, and it has been determined that this age group has less financial difficulties and they follow their financial situation very closely. The group with the lowest level of awareness about their financial situation is people between the ages of 30-59. Therefore, it can be said that people in this age range are also at financial risk.

Financial capability requires financial literacy. Financial literacy is also a prerequisite for financial resilience (Lyons et al., 2020). An important component of financial literacy is debt literacy. Individuals with low debt literacy tend to make high-cost transactions and excessive borrow money. In addition, these people are not able to evaluate their debt situation, overestimate them, and therefore they are under an excessive debt burden. According to Lusardi & Tufano's (2009) research, the lowest level of debt literacy is among the elderly, young people and women. On the other hand, debt literacy increases in parallel with income.

According to Taylor's (2011) research, employment and education can increase people's capability to manage their financial situations efficiently by increasing their access to financial institutions and resources. In the study investigating the relationship between demographic characteristics and financial capability, single and unemployed adults had lower financial capabilities, while older men and women who worked full-time with a working spouse had more financial capability. The level of financial capability was higher among men working in the financial sector who were heads of families. On the other hand, according to the research, the financial capabilities of women who had a non-working spouse decreased.

Those who can plan their future retirement, have a comfortable retirement period and have savings can also be considered financially capable. According to the research of Kim et al., (2005) those who receive training on retirement, those who calculate their retirement fund needs and those who plan their retirement have more savings. People with better health and financial education feel more ready and secure about retirement.

Financial resilience and vulnerability are two sides of the same coin and are about how a person/household accesses, builds and protects financial assets and how they can reduce their financial liabilities (Jacobsen et al., 2009). According to Sanchez et al., (2021, p. 3) financial resilience is one's ability to maintain a livelihood by preventing or reducing the impact of financial shocks on income and spending. People need to have appropriate skills and access to tools for money management (to deal with foreseeable shocks) and risk management (to deal with unforeseen shocks). Therefore, financial resilience is also necessary for financial capability. Because financial resilience can increase one's ability to recover from financial difficulties and stressors as a result of unplanned life events (Donaldson et al., 2021). According to the research conducted by Hussain et al., (2018) those who receive financial education and are engaged in financial activities are more financially resilient. For example, those who have a financial account are more financially resilient than those who do not. In the research, it has been determined that there is a difference between men and women in terms of financial resilience, and that men are more financially resilient than women. It has been stated that while the financial resilience increases as the income level rises, it is more difficult for those with lower incomes to easily cope with unexpected situations such as illness, unwanted death or job loss, and therefore they are more vulnerable financially. It has also been found that people who save are more likely to be financially resilient than those who do not save.

Fenton O'Creevy & Furnham (2013) investigated the factors that contribute to the likelihood of experiencing adverse financial events. Researchers hypothesized that the likelihood of experiencing negative financial experiences was linked to variables including financial capability, attitudes towards money, and socioeconomic factors. In the research, it has been determined that financial capability has the riskiest and strongest effect on the probability of experiencing negative financial events. It is stated that those most at risk for adverse financial events are generally the poorest in society because they are the most vulnerable to the consequences of the economic downturn. In the research, it has been determined that the risk of experiencing negative financial events decreases as the education level and income level increase.

SOLUTIONS AND RECOMMENDATIONS

People need to develop their financial capabilities and financial resilience so that they do not fall into situations that creat financial stressors or cope with financial stressors and create financial conditions in their favor. For this, psychological supports that increase financial resilience should be provided, financial training should be organized to improve financial ability, and policies should be created to increase the level of financial literacy. Psychology and finance professionals should identify those most exposed to financial distress, the mechanisms underlying financial distress, and collaborate to reduce financial distress.

Research on the causes, negative effects, and degree of financial distress can provide a better understanding of those experiencing financial distress. Thus, measures can be taken to reduce financial distress, policies can be developed, treatments, financial trainings and programs can be arranged accordingly. Increases in assets, decreases in liabilities and progress on a financially successful retirement are indicators of improvements in financial position and improvement in financial ability (Prawitz et al., 2006, p. 46; O'Neill et al., 2006b, p. 489). According to the research conducted by O'Neill et al. (2006a) it was determined that the financial problems of the people who participated in the debt management program decreased after two years, their financial well-being increased, they were faced with less negative financial events, and as a result, their health improved. While it takes time for financial difficulties to subside, progress is being made with participation in debt management.

Faced with major life crises, the person may attempt to re-establish some useful, basic cognitive guides for life, adapting to adverse conditions. Thus, people who experience stress can establish more meaningful interpersonal relationships, change their priorities, acquire a richer existential and spiritual life, and become more resilient. Traumas can develop people, grow, increase their abilities (Tedeshi & Calhoun, 2004, pp. 2-8). Therefore, changes in the living conditions of individuals affect their financial difficulties. People whose financial situation improves over time experience lower levels of financial distress. The incidence of stress events is lower in those who change jobs, are promoted, or retire (Ryan, 2012). Individuals experience more financial distress as they try to develop and maintain careers during their teenage and adult years. For this reason, individuals need to receive financial education at an earlier age in order to improve their financial capabilities. On the other hand, it may become more difficult to manage financial distress during retirement. Because in this period, people have less opportunity to manage their financial problems (Wrosch et al., 2000, p. 388).

FUTURE RESEARCH DIRECTIONS

This study is limited to a comprehensive literature review on the physiological, psychological and sociological effects of financial distress. Empirical studies of each of these key issues can be carried out in future studies. Investigating the cultural and intergenerational differences in financial distress may shed light on other studies. If the trainings for the development of financial ability and financial resilience specified in the solutions and suggestions section of this study are carried out, it can be revealed through research whether the results provide improvement or not. In the study, it is determined that there are very few studies on the effect of financial distress on suicide and on the subject of financial resistance. This issue should be supported by the joint work of psychology and finance experts.

CONCLUSION

Financial distress is a subjective and unpleasant feeling experienced by people with or without financial difficulties. In this study, financial distress is examined from a subjective point of view, since the person's feelings, perceptions and reactions to financial distress are different. When the studies on financial distress are compiled, the following results are encountered.

Studies on physical health of financial distress show that financial distress, although not the only factor, is an important factor in the deterioration of health. According to studies, financial distress leads to many diseases: Diabetes (Blomgren et al., 2016), obesity (Münster et al., 2009), inflammation in the body (Sturgeon et al., 2016), chronic pain conditions (Kosminsky et al., 2020), back pain (Ochsmann et al., 2009), cause headaches and abdominal pain, insomnia (Rantakeisu et al., 1999), and cancer (Advani et al., 2014).

In addition to the physical effects of financial distress, there are also psychological effects. There are many studies in the literature proving that economic difficulties (poverty, insufficient income, unemployment, excessive debt, foreclosure, bankruptcy, economic recession, etc.) impair psychological health (Warth et al., 2020; Haw et al., 2014; McLaughlin et al., 2011; Lund et al., 2010; Jenkins et al., 2008; Rantakeisu et al., 1999). These economic difficulties evoke feelings such as shame, guilt, disappointment, anger, and hostility in people (Turunen & Hiilamo, 2014; Charbonneau & Hanse, 2014; Tedeshi & Calhoun, 2004; Davis & Mantler, 2004). Psychological disorders such as anxiety, depression, psychosis, and neurosis are common problems faced by those experiencing financial distress. In addition, bad habits such as alcohol and gambling accompany financial distress, making the situation worse both psychologically and financially. Moreover, there are many studies showing that people whose psychological health deteriorates due to financial difficulties are at high risk of suicide (Rojas, 2021; Beauchaine et al., 2020; Catalano et al., 2011; Meltzer et al., 2011).

Financial distress differs according to the demographic characteristics of the family. Accordingly, in families with/without children (Breuning & Clark, 2006; Atkinson et al., 2007), in families with one/two parents (Aydiner Boylu, 2014; Kempson et al., 2004), according to the number of children (Worthington, 2006), the level of financial distress differs according to the socio-economic status of the region where the family lives (Fay et al., 2002). Studies show that financial distress causes disagreements between spouses, but the stronger the relationship between spouses in a family, the less separation / divorce experienced, and even spouses can come out of financial difficulties stronger, and the family is less affected by financial distress (Yakymchuk et al., 2021; Archulate et al. al., 2011; Poduska, 1992).

The effect of financial distress on children starts before they are born and continues until adulthood and has lasting effects. Financial difficulties in childhood affect children's physical and psychological health (such as depression, low self-esteem) and cause them to have difficulties in social relations. (Kim et al., 2016; Bradley & Corwyn, 2002; Bolger et al., 1995). Although the financial situation and stress of families affect children, there are roles and duties for families in this regard. Because financial education starts in the family first and children are socialized financially within the family first. Families need to have financial knowledge and ability to educate their children on issues such as using credit cards, borrowing and saving (Kübilay & Tuncel, 2021). Financial distress affects parents, children and society in a chain of ways. This is not a problem that individuals or families are exposed to alone, but it is also an issue that concerns society. Because children are the future of a society, and everyone's lives are in contact with each other in some way.

Studies show that social support from families, relatives and colleagues reduces financial distress (Viseu et al., 2018; Park et al., 2017; Sturgeon et al., 2016; Aslund et al. 2014). In addition, while social status (Sturgeon et al., 2016) and social norms (Gathergood, 2012) make the person more resistant to financial distress, on the other hand, the socio-economic status of the person (such as being poor, low-income or in debt) can cause financial and social exclusion (Sezer, 2011; Kempson et al., 2000).

For financial health, one must be financially resilient. Increasing financial resilience is linked to financial ability and financial literacy.

REFERENCES

Advani, P. S., Reitzel, L. R., Nguyen, T. N., Fisher, F. D., Savoy, E. J., Cuevas, A. G., Wetter, D. W., & McNeil, L. H. (2014). Financial strain and cancer risk behaviors among African Americans. *Cancer Epidemiology, Biomarkers & Prevention*, *23*(6), 967–975. doi:10.1158/1055-9965.EPI-14-0016 PMID:24740200

Aldana, S. G., & Liljenquist, W. (1998). Validity and reliability of a financial strain survey. *Financial Counseling and Planning*, *9*(2), 11–18.

Amato, P. R., & Zuo, J. (1992). Rural poverty, urban poverty and psychological well-being. *The Sociological Quarterly*, *33*(2), 229–240. doi:10.1111/j.1533-8525.1992.tb00373.x

Anderloni, L., & Vandone, D. (2008). *Households over-indeptedness in the economic literature*. Universit'a degli Studi di Milano Working Paper, 46,775.

Archuleta, K., Dale, A., & Spann, S. M. (2013). College students and financial distress: Exploring debt, financial satisfaction, and financial anxiety. *Financial Counseling and Planning*, *24*(2), 50–62.

Archuleta, K. L., Britt, S. L., Tonn, T. J., & Grable, J. E. (2011). Financial satisfaction and financial stressors in marital satisfaction. *Psychological Reports*, *108*(2), 563–576. doi:10.2466/07.21.PR0.108.2.563-576 PMID:21675570

Aslund, C., Larm, P., Starrin, B., & Nilsson, K. (2014). The buffering effect of tangible social support on financial stress: Influence on psychological well-being and psychosomatic symptoms in a large sample of the adult general population. *International for Equity in Health*, *13*(1), 2-9. Doi: doi:10.1186/s12939-01400853

Atkinson, A., Mckay, S., Collard, S., & Kempson, E. (2007). Levels of financial capability in the UK. *Public Money & Management*, *27*(1), 29–36. doi:10.1111/j.1467-9302.2007.00552.x

Beauchaine, T. P., Ben-David, I., & Bos, M. (2020). ADHD, Financial distress, and suicide in adulthood a population study. *Science Advances*, *6*(40), 1–8. doi:10.1126ciadv.aba1551 PMID:32998893

Blomgren, J., Maunula, N., & Hiilamo, H. (2016). Over-indeptedness and chronic disease: A linked register-based study of Finnish men and women during 1995-2010. *International Journal of Public Health*, *61*(5), 535–544. doi:10.100700038-015-0778-4 PMID:26733074

Boe, T., Balaj, M., Eikemo, T. A., McNamara, C. L., & Solheim, E. F. (2017). Financial difficulties in childhood and adult depression in Europe. *European Journal of Public Health*, *27*(1, suppl_1), 96–101. doi:10.1093/eurpub/ckw253 PMID:28355649

Bolger, K. E., Patterson, C. J., Thompson, W. W., & Kupersmidt, J. B. (1995). Psychosocial adjustment among children experiencing persistent and ınternittent family economic hardship. *Child Development*, *66*(4), 1107–1129. doi:10.2307/1131802

Boss, P., Bryant, C., & Mancini, J. A. (2016). *Family stress management: A contextual approach*. Sage Publications. https://books.google.com.tr/books?hl=tr&lr=&id=7U-0DAAAQBAJ&oi=fnd&pg=PP1&dq=Family+stress+management:+a+contextual+approach.+Sage+Publications.&ots=EJgFDQlstp&sig=NARJjhjVFTosUR43aHTzVqdBZo0&redir_esc=y#v=onepage&q=Family%20stress%20management%3A%20a%20contextual%20approach.%20Sage%20Publications.&f=false

Boylu, A. (2014). Tek ebeveynli ailelerde finansal sıkıntı ve fonksiyonlar arasındaki ilişkinin incelenmesi [Examination of the relationship between financial hardship and functions in single-parent families]. *Hacettepe Üniversitesi İktisadi ve İdari Bilimler Fakültesi Dergisi*, *32*(1), 55–72. doi:10.17065/huiibf.34906

Bradley, R. H., & Corwyn, R. (2002). Socioeconomic status and child development. *Annual Review of Psychology*, *53*(1), 371–379. doi:10.1146/annurev.psych.53.100901.135233 PMID:11752490

Bray, J. R., (2001). Hardship in Australia: An analysis of financial stress ındicators in the 1998-99 Australian bureau of statistics household expenditure survey. *Macroeconomics: Consumption*.

Breunig, R. & Cobb-Clark, D. (2006). *Understanding the factors associated with financial stress in Australian households*. Australian Social Policy.

Catalano, R., Goldman-Mellor, S., Szxton, K., Margerison-Zilko, C., Subbaraman, M., Lewinn, K., & Anderson, E. (2011). The health effects of economic decline. *Annu Rev. Public Health*, *32*(10). Retrieved May 5, 2022, from https://www.ncbi.nlm.nih.gov/pmc/articles/PMC3855327/

Charbonneau, M., & Hanse, M. P. (2014). Debt, neolibarislizm and crisis: Interview with maurizio lazzarato on the ındebted condition. *Sociology*, *48*(5), 1039–1047. doi:10.1177/0038038514539207

Choi, L. (2009). Financial stress and its physical effects on individuals and communities. *Community Development Innovation Review*, *3*, 120–122.

Davis, C. G. & Mantler, J. (2004). *The consequences of financial stress for ındividuals, families and society*. Carleton University, Centre for Research on Stress, Coping and Well-Being, Ottoawa Canada.

Delafrooz, N., & Paim, L. H. (2013). Role of financial stress on relationship between financial problem and financial wellness among Malaysia workers. *African Journal of Business Management*, *7*(20), 1966–1972.

Demirci, A. (2014). Literatür taraması [Literature review]. In Y. Arı & İ. Kaya (Eds.), Coğrafya araştırma yöntemleri (pp. 73-106). Balıkesir: Coğrafyacılar Derneği Yayınları.

Donaldson, K., Fonberg, J., Heisz, A., Kaddatz, J., Kaplan, J., Olson, E., & Walker, I. (2021). *The financial resilience and financial well-being of Canadians during the covıd-19 pandemic*. Retrieved May 1, 2022, from https://www150.statcan.gc.ca/n1/en/pub/75f0002m/75f0002m2021008-eng.pdf?st=Bc3GpVCz

Drentea, P. (2000). Age, Debt and anxiety. *Journal of Health and Social Behavior*, *41*(4), 437–450. doi:10.2307/2676296 PMID:11198567

Drentea, P., & Lavrakas, P. J. (2000). Over the limit: The assocation among health, race and debt. *Social Science & Medicine*, *50*(4), 517–529. doi:10.1016/S0277-9536(99)00298-1 PMID:10641804

Fay, S., Hurst, E., & White, M. J. (2002). The household bankruptcy decision. *The American Economic Review*, *93*(3), 706–718. doi:10.1257/00028280260136327

Fenton O'Creevy, M., & Furnham, A. (2013). Financial capability, money attitudes and socioeconomic status: Risks for experiencing adverse financial events. *Personality and Individual Differences*, *54*(3), 344–349. doi:10.1016/j.paid.2012.09.019

Fenton O'creevy, M., & Furnham, A. (2021). Financial distress and money attitudes. *Journal of Neuroscience, Psychology, and Economics*, *14*(3), 138–148. doi:10.1037/npe0000143

Fernandez, A., Garcia-Alonso, J., Royo- Pastor, C., Garrell-Corbera, I., Rengel-Chica, J., Agudo-Ugena, J., Ramos, A., & Manual Mendive, J. (2015). Effects of the economic crisis and social supoort on health-related quality of life. *The British Journal of General Practice*, *65*(632), e198–e203. doi:10.3399/bjgp15X684025 PMID:25733442

Fitch, C., Chaplin, R., Trend, C., & Collard, S. (2007). Debt and mental health: The role of psychiatrists. *Advances in Psychiatric Treatment*, *13*(3), 194–202. doi:10.1192/apt.bp.106.002527

Freeman, C., Carlson, J., & Sperry, L. (1993). Adlerian marital therapy strategies with middle income couples facing financial stress. *The American Journal of Family Therapy*, *21*(4), 324–332. doi:10.1080/01926189308251003

French, D., & McKillop, D. (2017). The impact of debt and financial stress on health in Northern Irish households. *Journal of European Social Policy*, *27*(5), 458–473. doi:10.1177/0958928717717657

Gathergood, J. (2012). Debt and depression: Casual links and social norm effects. *Economic Journal (London)*, *122*(563), 1094–1114. doi:10.1111/j.1468-0297.2012.02519.x

Grable, J., Heo, W., & Rabbani, A. (2015). Financial anxiety, physiological arousal, and planning ıntention. *Journal of Financial Therapy*, *5*(2), 1–18. doi:10.4148/1944-9771.1083

Guan, N., Guargilia, A., Moore, P., & Xu, F. (2022). Financial stress and depression in adults: A systematic review. *PLoS One*, *17*(2), e0264041. doi:10.1371/journal.pone.0264041 PMID:35192652

Haw, C., Hawton, K., Gunnel, D., & Platt, S. (2014). Economic recession and suicidal behaviour: Possible mechanisms and ameliorating factors. *The International Journal of Social Psychiatry*, *61*(1), 1–9. doi:10.1177/0020764014536545 PMID:24903684

Heo, W., Cho, S. H., & Lee, P. (2020). APR financial stress scale: Development and validation of a multidimensional measurement. *Journal of Financial Therapy*, *11*(1), 1–28. doi:10.4148/1944-9771.1216

Hussain, A. H. M. B., Das, S., Chowdhury, M. T. A., Haque, N., Sultana, S., & Ahmed, K. J. (2018). Does financial inclusion increase financial resilience? evidence from Bagladesh. *Development in Practice*, *29*(6), 798–804. doi:10.1080/09614524.2019.1607256

Jacobsen, K., Marshak, A., & Griffith, M. (2009). *Increasing the financial resilience of disaster-affected populations*. Retrieved May 01, 2022, from https://www.semanticscholar.org/paper/Increasing-the-Financial-Resilience-of-Populations-Jacobsen-Marshak/2de16e6ddaba60a084813199822176cf26ce03da

Jenkins, R., Bhugra, D., Bebbington, P., Brugha, T., Farrel, M., Coid, J., Fryers, T., Weich, S., Singleton, N., & Meltzer, H. (2008). Debt, ıncome and mental disorder in the general population. *Psychological Medicine*, *38*(10), 1485–1493. doi:10.1017/S0033291707002516 PMID:18184442

Joo, S. (1998). *Personal financial wellness and worker job productivity* [Unpublished doctoral dissertation]. Virginia Polytechnic Institute and State University.

Joo, S., & Grable, J. E. (2004). An exploratory framework of the determinants of financial satisfaction. *Journal of Family and Economic Issues*, *25*(1), 25–50. doi:10.1023/B:JEEI.0000016722.37994.9f

Joo, S.-H., Durband, D. B., & Grable, J. (2008). The academic impact of financial stress on college students. *Journal of College Student Retention*, *10*(3), 287–305. doi:10.2190/CS.10.3.c

Kahn, J. R., & Pearlin, L. I. (2006). Financial strain over the life course and health among older adults. *Journal of Health and Social Behavior*, *47*(1), 17–31. doi:10.1177/002214650604700102 PMID:16583773

Kempson, E., McKay, S. & Willitts, M. (2004). *Characteristic of families in debt and nature of ındeptedness*. Departmant for Work and Pensions Research Report. No: 211.

Kempson, E., Whiley, C., Caskey, J., & Collard, S. (2000). *In or out? financial exlusion: A literature and research review*. Financial Services Authority.

Kim, J., & Garman, E. T. (2013). Financial stress and absenteeism: An emprically derived model. *JECP Research Journal*, *14*(1), 31–42.

Kim, J., Garman, E. T., & Sorhaindo, B. (2013). Relationships among credit counseling clients' financial wellbeing, financial behaviors, financial stressor events and health. *Financial Counseling and Planning*, *14*(2), 75–87.

Kim, J., Kwon, J., & Anderson, E. A. (2005). Factors related to retirement confidence: Retirement preparation and workplace financial education. *Financial Counseling and Planning*, *16*(2), 77–89.

Kim, W., Kim, T. H., Lee, T.-H., Ju, Y. J., & Park, E.-C. (2016). The effect of childhood and current economic status on depressive symptoms in South Korean ındividuals: A longitudinal study. *International Journal for Equity in Health*, *15*(111), 2–7. doi:10.118612939-016-0402-0 PMID:27430636

Koomson, A. Churchill, S. A., & Munyanyi, M. E. (2022). *Gambling and financial stress, social ındicators research*. doi:10.1007/s11205-022-02898-6

Kosminsky, M., Nasciment, M. G., & de Oliveira, G. N. S. (2020). Financial stress and pain, what follows an economic crisis? *Integrative Review. British Journal of Pain*, *3*(3), 280–284.

Kübilay, B., & Tunçel, Ö. (2021). The effect of family financial socialization levels on money attitudes of university students. *Süleyman Demirel Üniversitesi Vizyoner Dergisi*, *12*(30), 393–416. doi:10.21076/vizyoner.815919

Lange, C., & Byrd, M. (1998). The relationship between perceptions of financial distress and feelings of psychological well-being in New Zealand university students. *International Journal of Adolescence and Youth*, *7*(3), 193–209. doi:10.1080/02673843.1998.9747824

Lenton, P., & Mosley, P. (2008). *Debt and health.* Sheffield Economic Research Paper Series SERP Number: 2008004.

Lund, C., Breen, A., Flisher, A. J., Kakuma, R., Corrigal, J., Joska, J. A., Swartz, L., & Patel, V. (2010). Poverty and common mental disorders in low and middle ıncome countries: A systematic review. *Social Science & Medicine*, *71*(3), 517–528. doi:10.1016/j.socscimed.2010.04.027 PMID:20621748

Lusardi, A., & Tufano, P. (2009). *Debt literacy, financial experiences, and overindebtedness.* National Bureau of Economic Research. Working Paper 14808. doi:10.3386/w14808

Lyons, A. C., Kass-Hanna, J., Liu, F., Greenlee, A. J., & Zeng, L. (2020). *Building financial resilience through financial and digital literacy in South Asia and Sub- Saharan Africa*. ADBI Working Paper Series No: 1098. Retrieved May, 01, 2022, from https://www.adb.org/sites/default/files/publication/574821/adbi-wp1098.pdf

Marks, G. N. (2007). *Income powerty, subjective poverty and financial stress.* Australian Government Social Policy Research Paper No: 29. FaHCSIA. doi:10.2139/ssrn.1728587

McLaughlin, K. A., Nandi, A., Keyes, K. M., Uddin, M., Aiello, A. E., Galea, S., & Koenen, K. C. (2011). Home foreclosure and risk of psychiatric morbidity during the recent financial crisis. *Psychological Medicine*, *42*(7), 1441–1448. doi:10.1017/S0033291711002613 PMID:22099861

Meltzer, H., Bebbington, P., Brugha, T., Jenkins, R., McManus, S., & Dennis, M. S. (2011). Personal debt and suicidal ideation. *Psychological Medicine*, *41*(4), 771–778. doi:10.1017/S0033291710001261 PMID:20550757

Münster, E., Rüger, H., Ochsmann, E., Letzel, S., & Toschke, A. M. (2009). Over-Indebetedness as a marker of socioeconomic status and ıts association with obesity: A cross- sectional study. *BMC Public Health*, *9*(1), 1–6. doi:10.1186/1471-2458-9-286 PMID:19664214

O' Neill, B., Prawitz, A. D., Sorhaindo, B., Kim, J., & Garman, E. Thomas. (2006a). Changes in health, negative financial events, and financial distress/financial well-being for debt management program clients. *Financial Counseling and Planning*, *17*(2), 46–63.

O' Neill, B., Sorhaindo, B., Prawitz, A., Kim, J., & Garman, E. T. (2006b). Financial distress: Definition, effects and measurement. *Consumer Interest Annual, 52*. Retrieved May, 05, 2022, from https://www.consumerinterests.org/assets/docs/CIA/CIA2006/oneill_financialdistressdefinitioneffectsandmeasurement.pdf

O'Neill, B., Sorhaindo, B., Xio, J. J., & Garman, E. T. (2005). Financially distressed consumers: Their financial practices, financial well-being, and health. *Financial Counseling and Planning*, *16*(1), 73–87.

Ochsmann, E. B., Rueger, H., Letzel, S., Drexler, H., & Muenster, E. (2009). Over ındebtedness and ıts association with the prevalence of back pain. *BMC Public Health*, *9*, 451. doi:10.1186/1471-2458-9-451

Oksanen, A., Savolainen, L., Sirola, A., & Kaakinen, M. (2018). Problem gambling and psychological distress: A cross-national perpective on the mediating effect of consumer debt and dept problems among emerging adults. *Harm Reduction Journal*, *15*(45), 1–11. doi:10.118612954-018-0251-9

Park, N., Heo, W., Ruiz-Menjivar, J., & Grable, J. E. (2017). Financial hardship, social support, and perceived stress. *Financial Counseling & Planning Education*, *28*(2), 322–332.

Patrica, V. (1990). Economic distress and family relations: A review of the eighties. *Journal of Marriage and the Family*, *52*(4), 1099–1115.

Poduska, B. (1992). Money, marriage and Maslow's hierarchy of needs. *The American Behavioral Scientist*, *35*(6), 756–770.

Pollack, C., & Lynch, J. (2009). Helath status of people undergoing foreclosure in the Philadelphia region. *American Journal of Public Health*, *99*(10), 1833–1839.

Prawitz, A. D., Garman, E. T., Sorhaindo, B., O'Neill, B., Kim, J., & Drentea, P. (2006). Incharge financial distress/financial well-being scale: Development, administration, and score ınterpretation. *Financial Counseling and Planning*, *17*(1), 34–50. doi:10.1037/t60365-000

Rantakeisu, U., Starrin, B., & Hagquist, C. (1999). Financial hardship and shame: A tentative model to understand the social and health effects of unemployment. *British Journal of Social Work*, *29*(6), 877–901.

Reading, R., & Reynolds, S. (2001). Debt, social disadvantage and maternal depression. *Social Science & Medicine*, *53*(4), 441–453. doi:10.1016/S0277-9536(00)00347-6

Rojas, Y. (2021). Financial ındebtedness and suicide: A1 –year follow-up study of a population registered at the Swedish enforcement authority. *The International Journal of Social Psychiatry*, *61*(1), 1–9. doi:10.1177/0020764014536545

Ryan, C. (2012). *Responses to financial stress at life transition points*. FaHCSIA Occasional Paper No. 41. doi:10.2139/ssrn.2230176

Salignac, F., Marjolin, A., Reeve, R., & Muir, K. (2019). Conceptualizing and measuring financial resilience: A multimensional framework. *Social Indicators Research*, *145*(1), 17–38.

Sanchez, A., Sparreboom, P., & Laufer, H. (2021). *Building financial resilience: How financial service providers can help low-ıncome customers to manage risk*. Oxford Policy Management. Retrieved May, 05, 2022, from https://www.opml.co.uk/files/Publications/a0600-savings-at-the-frontier/satf-building-financial-resilience.pdf?noredirect=1

Sezer, S. (2011). *Ticari başarısızlık sonucu ortaya çıkan intihar ve intihar girişimi olaylarının sosyo - ekonomik nedenleri* [Unpublished doctoral thesis]. İstanbul Üniversitesi Sosyal Bilimler Enstitüsü Sosyoloji Anabilim Dalı, İstanbul, Turkey.

Sturgeon, J. A., Arewasikporn, A., Okun, M. A., Davis, M. C., Ong, A. D., & Zautra, A. J. (2016). The psychological context of financial stress: Implications for ınflammation and *psychological health. Psychosomatic Medicine*, *78*(2), 134–143.

Taylor, M. (2011). Measuring financial capability and ıts determinants using survey data. *Social Indicators Research*, *102*, 297–314. doi:10.100711205-010-9681-9

Tedeshi, R. G., & Calhoun, L. G. (2004). Posttraumatic growth: Conceptual foundations and emprical evidence. *Psychological Inquiry*, *15*, 1–18.

Turunen, E., & Hiilamo, H. (2014). Health effects of ındebtedness: A systematic review. *BMC Public Health*, *14*(1), 489. doi:10.1186/1471-2458-14-489

Viseu, J., Leal, R., Neves de Jesus, S., Pinto, P., Pechorro, P., & Greenglass, E. (2018). Relationship between economic stress factors and stress, anxiety, and depression: Moderating role of social supoort. *Psychiatry Research*, *268*, 102–107. doi:10.1016/j.psychres.2018.07.008

Warth, J., Beckmann, N., Puth, M. T., Tillmann, J., Porz, J., Zier, U., Weckbecker, K., Weltermann, B., & Münster, E. (2020). Association between over-ındebtedness and antidepressant use: Across-sectional analysis. *Plos One*. *Public Library of Science*, *15*(7), 1–11.

Widome, R., Joseph, A. M., Hammett, P., Ryn, M. V., Nelson, D. B., Nyman, J. A., & Fu, S. S. (2015). Associations between smoking behaviors and financial stress among low-ıncome smokers. *Preventive Medicine Reports*, *2*, 911–915. doi:10.1016/j.pmedr.2015.10.011

Worthington, A.C. (2006). Debt as a source of financial stress in Australian households. *International Journal of Consumer Studies*, *30*(1), 2-15. Doi: .1470-6431.2005.00420.x doi:10.1111/j

Wrosch, C., Heckhausen, J., & Lachman, M. E. (2000). Primary and secondary control strategies for managing health and financial stress across adulthood. *Psychology and Aging*, *15*(3), 387–399.

Wuth, A., & Cismaru, M. (2021). A conceptual and operational review of the negative financial health terminology and constructs. *International Business Research*, *14*(4), 1–16.

Yakymchuk, I. P., Olkhovetskyi, S. M., Beyz, A. M., & Martseniuk, M. O. (2021). Experiencing and overcoming financial stress in married couples: A study in covıd 19 pandemic era. *Amazonia Investiga*, *10*(42), 124–140. doi:10.34069/AI/2021.42.06.12

KEY TERMS AND DEFINITONS

Behavioral Finance: Behavioral finance is an interdisciplinary field that tries to explain people's behavior in decision-making processes with psychology, sociology, and anthropology factors along with finance.

Financial Capability: It refers to a set of skills and behaviors related to one's knowledge of financial matters, managing one's financial situation (such as spending habits, financial planning for the future, the ability to choose appropriate financial products) and controlling it.

Financial Distress: Financial stress is related to the anxiety, sadness, and fear that a person feels about her/his financial situation and expresses dysfunctional thought patterns.

Financial Hardship: It refers to the situation that a person faces due to individual or economic conditions such as unemployment, poverty, insufficient income, economic crises, economic recession, foreclosure, bankruptcy, excessive debt.

Financial Health: It refers to a situation in which a person can evaluate and manage her/his financial situation and relationship with money in a psychologically healthy way and obtain healthy results in financial terms (such as income increasing, loss prevention).

Financial Resilience: People's readiness for unexpected financial difficulties and financial stress refers to their ability and capacity to cope with these difficulties.

Mental Health: It is the state of well-being related to the cognitive, emotional, and social well-being of how people think, feel and act in all aspects of their lives, from childhood and adolescence to adulthood. It is related to how people deal with stress.

Social Support: It refers to having a social environment (spouse, family, relatives, friends, etc.) where one can seek help and support in the face of financial difficulties, and a person's security area.

Subjective Financial Distress: Subjective financial stress refers to a person's subjective feelings, judgments, and reactions to their financial situation. It includes assessments of how financial stress affects the person, one's family, social environment, physical and mental health.

Chapter 7
Enterprise Risk Management and Bankruptcy

Pınar Avci
https://orcid.org/0000-0001-9480-8016
Tekirdağ Namık Kemal University, Turkey

Sevgi Sümerli Sarigül
https://orcid.org/0000-0002-3820-6288
Kayseri University, Turkey

ABSTRACT

This study explains bankruptcy by talking about risk, risk types, and risk management and bankruptcy forecasting models. The studies in the literature are examined and explained as risk, danger, possibility of bad consequences, loss, or misfortune. Types of risks, purchasing power, interest rate, market, political, exchange rate, financial, industry, corporate bond, liquidity, taxation, reinvestment, country, dynamic, structural, conditional, customer, financial/regulatory, reputation/loss, corporate and interpretation risks are identified in the literature. The study explains bankruptcy as the situation that occurs when a business cannot obtain sufficient value to cover the costs of doing business. Finally, it is stated in this study that bankruptcy estimation methods, which are constructed with historical observations and evaluated with historical observations, are used to predict firms without failing. The findings, which are obtained by examining the literature, offer important contributions to company managers.

INTRODUCTION

Today, with the increasing rate of change, the increase in customer demands and the globalization of the markets further increase the importance of risk management in enterprises and this situation emphasizes that enterprises must have a comprehensive risk management strategy in order to survive in the market and gain competitive advantage. Therefore, risk management is one of the important phenomena facing businesses and other institutions, and even cases such as Barings and Railtrack in the UK and Enron, Adelphia in the US and Worldcom and Parmalat show the consequences of not managing risk correctly

DOI: 10.4018/978-1-6684-5181-6.ch007

(Merna & Al-Thani, 2008). Hence, the aim of this study is to explain bankruptcy by talking about risk management and to talk about bankruptcy forecasting models. In this study is explained by examining and evaluating the studies in the literature.

The word risk is used synonymously with the word uncertainty. Uncertainty is a state of mind characterized by suspicion or a conscious lack of knowledge about the outcome of an event. In other words, uncertainty involves subjective possibilities. However, risk encompasses objective probabilities (Head, 1967). The word risk is the French origin word ‘risqu’e and the main word is “riziko” (Özbilgin, 2012). The etymological origin of the word risk is based on the Latin word “risicum” (Çıtak, 1999). According to the Oxford English Dictionary Council, risk is explained as danger, the possibility of bad outcomes, loss or exposure to misfortune (McNeil, 2005). The situation in which objective evaluations can be made about what the results of an investment decision may be in an environment of uncertainty (Çıtak, 1999) or the degree of uncertainty in winning or losing is called risk (Aksoy & Tanrıöven, 2014). From a financial perspective, risk is any event or action that can adversely affect an organization’s ability to achieve its goals and implement its strategies (McNeil, 2005). In technical terms, risk is expressed as the distribution of probability values for returns around the average value. In terms of investment analysis, risk is defined as negative deviations in the expected return of financial investment (Çıtak, 1999). At the same time, risk consists of four basic parameters. The first is the varying probability and the probability of occurrence involving low/high frequency, the second is the severity of the impact, which includes the threat potential and continuous variability in terms of cost & time, the third is the sensitivity to change or external influences with opportunities and positive/negative consequences, and the last is the degree of interdependence with other risk factors (Merna & Al-Thani, 2008).

In addition, risks are divided into many varieties. Çıtak (1999) risks; the researcher distinguishes it as systematic risks consisting of purchasing power, interest rate, market and political risks and non-systematic risks consisting of financial, business, management, non-repayment and marketability risks. Similarly, Aksoy and Tanrıöven (2014) describe systematic risks such as purchasing power, interest rate, market, political and exchange rate risks and non-systematic risks financial, industrial and management risks. Merna and Al-Thani (2008) explain financial risks including structural delay, exchange rate, interest rate, equity, corporate bond, liquidity, taxation, reinvestment, country risks and non-financial risks including dynamic, structural, conditional, customer, financial/regulator, reputation/loss, corporate and interpretation risks. Hull (2018) and Guégan and Hassani (2019) also mention that there are types of risk such as credit risk, market risk and operational risk.

Risk management is an increasingly used tool in all organization to increase security and reliability and minimize losses. This includes identifying, assessing and controlling risks (Merna & Al-Thani, 2008). In other words, risk management is expressed as a process that is influenced by the board of directors, management and other personnel of an organization, implemented in strategy setting and throughout the organization and designed to identify possible events that may affect assets, manage risk within risk appetite, and provide reasonable assurance regarding the achievement of corporate goals (Hull, 2018). Risk management focuses on two elements, the first being risk assessment and the second being precautionary measures to avoid them. Risk assessment includes the application of analysis methods, statistical methods and techniques in grading the factors that may pose a risk in order to minimize losses. Precautionary or protective measures involve directing transactions to low-risk areas as much as possible and sometimes abandoning such transactions (Bordeianu et al., 2011). In the implementation phase of risk management; firstly, the sources of risk are clearly revealed, then the risk is measured, that is, it is determined and the effects of the risk in the realization of the objectives of the enterprise are revealed, then it is decided whether to assume the risk or not, and in the final stage, the tools to prevent the risk are selected and applied (Sayılgan, 1995). At the same time, Guégan and Hassani (2019) mentions that there are some models for measuring risks. These are modern portfolio theory, risk management in assets, risk-free asset and capital allocation, risk management with systematic and private risk, capital asset pricing model, arbitrage pricing theory and downside risk measurement. According to the study, when we refer to quantitative risk measurements; value at risk (VAR), expected shortfall (ES), tail value at risk (Tvar) and entropic risk measures (EVaR).

Another issue that is based on this study is bankruptcy. Bankruptcy is explained as the situation that occurs when a business cannot obtain enough value to cover the costs of doing business (Thornhill and Amit, 2003). It also expresses the incompetence of the enterprise, in other words, the inefficiency of the ongoing activities of the enterprise and the inability to meet its mandatory obligations is also called bankruptcy. Although the economic and financial activities of enterprises in recent years have been dynamic, it is necessary to have more precise information about the risk of bankruptcy in the future (Bordeianu et al., 2011). Therefore, with effective risk management, the probability of bankruptcy decreases and the risk decreases, which provides evidence that businesses will have a longer life (Marin & Montréal, 2015).

In risk management, especially for financial institutions, predicting financial distress and bankruptcy is crucial, and getting this forecast right is a critical issue for shareholders, lenders, policymakers, and business managers. In addition, the understandability and transparency of bankruptcy forecasting models is very important (Olson et al., 2012; Kovacova & Kliestikova, 2017). In estimating business bankruptcy, In the study of Kumar and Ravi (2007), they explain artificial intelligence techniques such as fuzzy cluster theory, neural networks, decision trees, rough cluster theory, case-based reasoning, support vector machines, data envelopment analysis and soft computing, and statistical techniques such as linear diskriminant analysis (LDA), multivariate diskriminant analysis (MDA), quadratic diskriminant analysis (QDA), logit and factor analysis. Agarwal and Taffler (2008) explain about market-based and accounting-based forecasting models. Market-based models are recommended by Hillegeist et al. (2004) and Bharath and Shumway (2004), based on the studys of Black and Scholes (1973) and Merton (1974). Accounting-based models are the Z-score model Altman (1968). In the study of Min and Jeong (2009) are divided bankruptcy forecasting models models into artificial intelligence methods and based on statistical methods. Statistical methods; multi-discriminant analysis and stochastic models. Artificial intelligence methods; decision tree, fuzzy cluster theory, case-based reasoning, genetic algorithm, support vector machine, data envelopment analysis, rough cluster theory and back propagation neural network (BPNN), probabilistic neural networks (PNN) and self-organizing map (SOM). As mentioned above, many researchers in the literature are mentioned various bankruptcy prediction models in their studies. However, the performance of bankruptcy prediction models depends only on their characteristics and quantitative methods, but also on the samples selected for the implementation of the models and the time they are applied to these examples (Agarwal & Taffler, 2008; Olson et al., 2012).

Thus, the rest of the study is designed as follows. In the first part, the methodology of the study is mentioned. In the second part, risk, risk types, bankruptcy, bankruptcy prediction methods are explained within the scope of the theoretical framework.

RESEARCH METHODOLOGY

Since this study is a theoretical study, risk, risk management, risk types, bankruptcy and bankruptcy prediction methods for firms are explained by examining and evaluating the studies in the literature. Therefore, it is explored and examined the studies in Turkey and in the world (Mellahi & Wilkinson, 2004; Tapiero, 2004; Merna & Al-Thani, 2008; Bacovia, 2011; Eiser et al., 2012; Wieczorek-Kosmala et al., 2018; Guégan & Hassani, 2019; Kasser, 2020).

THEORETICAL FRAMEWORK

In the study, firstly, risk and risk types are mentioned, then risk management techniques are explained by considering risk management and finally the bankruptcy estimation models of enterprises are summarized by explaining bankruptcy.

Types of Risks and Risks

Risk arises from uncertainty (Eiser et al., 2012). The word risk is quite modern, and this word, which comes from the French word *risqu´e*, entered the English language in the mid-17th century. In the second quarter of the 18th century, English risk writing began to appear in insurance transactions (Flanagan & Norman, 1993). The word risk is defined as the measurement of the probability of an outcome or the size of an outcome, or a combination of both. For many organizations, risk is a four-letter word that they try to isolate themselves from (Merna & Al-Thani, 2008). Risk is also considered as the variability of an activity outcome under environmental pressure (Bacovia, 2011).

Uncertainty about the outcome of an event in which two or more probabilities exist is defined as risk. This shows that some errors related to the definition occur. The reasons for these are; replacing risk with uncertainty that is the same word, causing results contrary to common usage and understanding in concrete situations, and hindering further analysis as it makes it difficult to measure and quantify risk. (Head, 1967, p. 205-206). Risk is also defined as an integrated combination of the probability of occurrence, the magnitude of the incident, and the resulting personal injuries and related costs change (Gratt, 1987), while risk is expressed as the undesirable negative potential consequences of an activity or event (Rowe, 1977). On the other hand, in the study of Eiser et al. (2012), the risk of moving under conditions of uncertainty is also explained as a function of probability and the value of some possible future event or events. Thus, the terms "probability" and "value" are important for risk, but more importantly, risk arises not only from how the future can be defined, but also from actual or perceived uncertainty.

The specificity of the activities that develop the risk factor, the management policy adopted for all hierarchical levels of the organizational and functional structure, the relations of economic units with stakeholders such as suppliers and customers, political, legal and legal framework and other factors constitute (Bacovia, 2011).

At the same time, some factors are the source of the formation of risk, and as a result of these sources, the occurrence of risk and some effects after the risk occurs. The sources of risk are as follows (Flanagan & Norman, 1993):

- Inflation increase above the appropriations in the account,

- Unforeseen adverse ground conditions,
- Exceptionally cold weather,
- Late delivery of critical materials, such as after a fire at a supplier's workplace,
- Incorrect design details,
- The inability of the basic contracting party to pay its debt,
- It is the lack of coordination.

There are also some serious effects of risk and these effects are explained as follows (Flanagan & Norman, 1993);

- Inability to make cost estimation,
- Failure to fulfill the required completion date,
- Failure to make the necessary qualifications,
- Failure to succeed in the project to meet the necessary business needs,
- Lack of safety conditions
- Having defective equipment,
- Damage to property as a result of fire and flooding,
- It is the damage of a worker due to the inadequate system of operation.

Many types of risks are being studied by different researchers (Tapiero, 2004; Merna & Al-Thani, 2008; Hull, 2018). Therefore, the main risks are explained as follows.

- Exchange rate risk measures the risk associated with unexpected changes in exchange rates, and this risk consists of two elements. The first is an internal element that depends on the flow of funds associated with foreign exchange, investment, etc., and the second is an external element that is independent of the activities of a firm. Exchange rate risk management mainly focuses on short-term decisions that involve the accounting exposure components of a firm's working capital. Exchange rate risk is divided into three risks; the transaction risk associated with the flow of funds in the firm; conversion risk associated with ongoing, current and future transactions; and competitive risk associated with the firm's competitive stance following a change in exchange rates (Tapiero, 2004).
- Currency risk is associated with changes in currency markets and exchange rates. A currency is not risky as it is likely to lose value. This risk is associated with a currency and its randomness. In addition, it is seen that exchange rate risks are related to macroeconomic variables such as trade deficit, political stability, fiscal and monetary policy, interest rate differences, inflation and leadership (Tapiero, 2004).
- Credit risk has traditionally been the greatest risk facing a bank, and this risk is the risk of counterparties defaulting in credit transactions and derivatives transactions (Hull, 2018). At the same time, credit risk covers risks arising from raising or decreasing the borrower's creditworthiness. There are basically two sources of uncertainty in credit risk: these are the default of one of the parties to the financial contract and a change in the present value of future cash flows (such as changes in financial market conditions, the economic environment and interest rates). Credit risk assessments form the basis of the necessary capital adequacy requirements arrangements, and

investors, banks and financial institutions continue to reduce this risk with risk management tools. Credit risk issues affect financial markets and global deflationary forces (Tapiero, 2004).

- Interest rate risk is a type of risk that directly affects the borrowing and investing business. This risk is based on the maturity of the funds raised and developments in the financial market where the funds are collected (Merna & Al-Thani, 2008).
- Market risk arises from the bank's trading operations and is the risk associated with the possibility of the depreciation of the instruments in the bank's commercial portfolio (Hull, 2018). This risk is also associated with movements in market indices. For example, it can be caused by stock price change, unpredictable interest rate changes, or market liquidity (Tapiero, 2004).
- Operational risk, which is generally considered to be the greatest risk faced by banks, is the risk that internal systems are not working as they should or that loss will occur due to external events. The time horizon that regulators use to consider losses from operational risks is one year (Hull, 2018).
- The risk of volatility is associated with changes in quadratic times. This risk reduces the ability to predict the future and causes investors to take preventive actions to reduce this risk. Volatility risk is an important factor in the decisions of speculators and investors. This risk is a risk that is becoming increasingly important to assess and value due to increased volatility in stocks, currency and other markets (Tapiero, 2004).
- Industry risk arises from factors affecting the performance of the securities group as a whole. Analysts try to understand the sources of uncertainty in the sector and their relations with other sectors (Tapiero, 2004).
- Liquidity risk is one of the important risks encountered in the banking sector and refers to the bank's lack of liquidity to fulfill its obligations. What reveals liquidity risk is that depositors do not know when and in what number of deposits to withdraw and when and in what amount of money loan requesters will need (Çelik & Akarım, 2012).
- Political risk is uncertainty in changes in political practice. The impact of political risk is more devastating with globalization, especially with hot money (Aksoy & Tanrıöven, 2014).

Risk Management and Risk Management Techniques

Different businesses assume a risk based solely on the profitability they foresee. In this context, the concept of "risk management" needs to be explained (Bacovia, 2011). Risk management is the discipline to live with the possibility of future events having adverse effects (Flanagan & Norman, 1993). At the same time, risk management deals with both insurable and non-insurable risks and is the approach that involves a formal and regular process for systematically identifying, analyzing, and responding to risk events throughout the life of a project to achieve an optimal or acceptable degree of risk elimination or control (Merna & Al-Thani, 2008). In other words, risk is managed in a variety of ways, including 'insurance pricing, controls, risk sharing and bonus loss' (Tapiero, 2004).

Risk identification, followed by measurement and evaluation, is a critical element of the risk management process. Risk assessment is about estimating the frequency of risk (how often it may occur) and the severity of risk (how high the possible risk outcomes may be) (Wieczorek-Kosmala et al., 2018). The risk management system is the exposure accounting system and the control system. The exposure accounting system, on the other hand, gives managers the opportunity to evaluate the effects of changes in economic factors such as interest rate movements, yield curve shifts, currency change and commodity price movements and stock price movements on the economic profit and loss of the enterprise. It is also a dynamic system that determines the capital need of the enterprise to support its positions (Scholes, 2000).

Considering the historical development of risk management, which is considered one of the more exciting and important parts of planning and managing investments, assets and liabilities at the corporate, strategic business and project levels, the birth of risk management dates back to the 20th century. When this development process is mentioned (Merna & Al-Thani, 2008);

- **The birth of risk management** dates back to 2000 years before this period, insurance companies were on the rise in the eighteenth century, Benjamin Franklin founded the first American fire insurance company in the United States in 1752, and in 1771 marine insurance was established by British businessmen to insure the potential losses of customers in shipping. Therefore, the twentieth century witnesses the birth of risk management.
- **In the 1970s, risk management** was either ignored or hided because the effects of risk on businesses and projects were not identified. This process is referred to as project risk management, and this risk management has developed rapidly throughout the 1970s, first in relation to quantitative evaluation, then to methodologies and processes.
- **Risk Management in the 1980s–The dominance of quantitative analysis,** the use of methods based on risk and reaction diagrams began in the 1980s. These methods are based on the idea that it is not possible to realistically model a risk situation without taking into account possible reactions. In the late 1980s, it was also the starting point for the use of effect diagrams combined with probability theory and for the first applications of system dynamics. These techniques are being developed to a higher level, and commercial software is available for both methods.
- **Risk Management in the 1990s-Emphasis on methodology and processes,** many of the risk management techniques used today are based on methods developed in the 1980s. The use of questionnaires and checklists was greatly improved in the 1990s, and this development led to the concept of knowledge-based systems. The important principles on the contractual distribution of risk established in the 1980s continue in the 1990s. The foundations of partnership and "alliance building" strategies are laid to avoid traditional contract competition and encourage a risk and reward sharing.

In addition, in their study, Flanagan and Norman (1993) describe the stages of the risk management process as follows;

- **Identify risk**, identify risks before any response is given, classify them, and indicate the sources and impacts of risks.
- **Classify risk**, taking into account the types of risk and the effects of risk on individuals and organizations.
- **To analyze the risk**, to evaluate the results or combination of risks associated with the types of risk using analytical techniques and to determine the impact of the risk by using various risk measurement methods.
- **Risk attitude**, any decision related to risk will be influenced by the decision-making attitude of the individual or organization.

- **Responding to risk**, responding to risk are in four forms. These include holding risk, reducing risk, transferring risk or avoiding risk. In other words, it considers how the risk should be managed either by transferring it to the other side (side) or by controlling it.

At the same time, Kasser (2020) describes the stages of risk management carried out by adding risk reduction and prevention planning and focusing on the process as much as the product, that is, using the system approach. These:

- ***Risk identification:*** At this stage, first the process step required to determine the risk and then the product produced by the process is realized. In this context, first of all, a risk is defined as anything that can negatively affect the cost of the process and plan. Then, risk is anything that can cause a failure in operation or increase the cost of the product.
- ***Risk analysis consists*** of two parts.
    - The first is ***risk impact analysis***. Risk impact analysis is also carried out with the effect of cause and failure. The reason is to start with a proposed failure, to reveal the symptoms from this failure that lead to the identification of this cause. The impact is to start with a symptom and understand what failure can cause what risk.
    - The second is ***risk impact analysis***. It analyzes each risk to determine the likelihood and effects that will occur with any interdependence.
- ***Risk mitigation and prevention planning*** plans mitigation activities and prevention, and transfers risk information into decisions and activities both today and in the future. This is also done as part of the creation of process steps by incorporating prevention and mitigation activities into the appropriate stage in the planning process.
- ***Risk monitoring***, risks and measures taken against risks are monitored.
- ***Risk control*** carries out the planned corrective action at the appropriate processing steps. If an unforeseen event occurs, which will adversely affect the cost and schedule, the occurrence of the event subsequently identifies the risk. Risk impact and impact analyses are carried out and risk mitigation activities are identified, costed and temporarily planned.
- ***Risk Communication*** is between the team and management. Provide visibility and feedback data on current and emerging risk activities inside and outside the project

In addition, risk management has some benefits. The first of these allows the project or business issues to become clear and understandable from the beginning. Second, decisions ensure that they are supported by comprehensive analysis of available data. The third constantly and objectively monitors the structure and description of the work. Fourth, it allows for rapid, controlled and pre-assessed responses to risks that may occur with contingency planning. Fifth, it identifies specific risks, associates them with a project or business. The latter establishes a statistical historical risk profile to allow for better modeling for future projects and investments (Merna & Al-Thani, 2008).

Finally, the study describes some technical models that are based on risk management. First, Value-at-Risk; it is calculated from the probability distribution of gains over a period of time or the probability distribution of losses over a period of time (Hull, 2018). In other words, it measures the loss distribution in a summary way for the change in the firm's equity value over a fixed period of time, which is a day, a week or a year. Using the accounting identity that associates the firm's equity with the firm's assets and liabilities, the probability of loss is determined (Jarrow & Chatterjea, 2019). Second, the theory of exceed value; It plays an important methodological role in the risk management problems associated with insurance, reinsurance and finance. In order to review some of the basic ideas underlying this theory, the most important conclusions are obtained under the assumption that losses are distributed independently and in the same way. The results will always indicate losses as positive (Embrechts et al., 1999). Third, Modern portfolio theory; is a mathematical framework used to create a portfolio of assets at a given level of risk, so that the expected return for variance is maximized. What is important, according to this theory, is that both the risk and return of an asset are evaluated not only their own, but also how they contribute to the overall risk and return of a portfolio (Guégan & Hassani, 2019).

Fourth, Scenario analysis; is to determine the size, not the frequency of potential losses related to specific scenarios. For example, a 100-basis point shift in interest rates over a one-month period can consist of extreme changes in the value of a risk factor, such as credit margin, exchange rate, stock price, or commodity price. Therefore, it is calculated how much the portfolio can lose in a scenario and this is also known as the "stress test" (Crouhy et al., 2000). The last one, Tail value at risk (TVaR); the known at-risk tail value (TVaR) is a measure of risk associated with the more general at-risk value. Given that an event outside a certain level of probability has occurred, it quantifies the expected value of the loss. The first definition may not be a consistent measure of risk; however, the continuous distribution at the base is consistent, and the second definition is a consistent measure of risk. TVaR takes into account not only the probability of failure, but also the severity of failure, and TVaR is only a measure of the expectation in the tail of distribution (Guégan & Hassani, 2019).

Failure, Financial Failure, and Bankruptcy

Failure is defined as a deterioration in the activities of an enterprise and, accordingly, a decrease in the resources of the enterprise. The failure terms are replaced by terms such as business death, bankruptcy, collapse, downsizing and closure (Mellahi & Wilkinson, 2004). In addition to the fact that companies have to reconsider and change their financing decisions due to the inability to fulfill their obligations, it is also defined as failure to encounter undesirable situations such as failure to pay debts on time, decrease in creditworthiness, declaration of concordat, bankruptcy and request for postponement of bankruptcy (Çelik, 2018). Financial failure is also referred to as business failure, and this failure is expressed as the cessation or bankruptcy of business activities; lenders incurring losses after actions such as execution, foreclosure; the avoidance of paying debt and the reorganization of bankruptcy; and the voluntary settlement of the obligors and creditors (Altman & Hotchkiss, 2006). This failure causes all businesses to be subject to the risk of bankruptcy. This risk can have negative consequences, which have complex implications, both on all the activities of the enterprise and on other organizations with which it comes into contact. Failure to fulfill current activities and obligations that are due for the continuity of business activity is also called bankruptcy. Bankruptcy can also be defined as the inability of enterprises to face a financial banking transaction, respectively, to repay the amounts borrowed under agreements with third parties in a timely manner under a loan agreement (Bacovia, 2011).

At the same time, bankruptcy is a forced liquidation procedure of all the assets of the debtor, which is carried out by the bankruptcy bodies for the purpose of collecting the receivables of the creditors. The ability to pursue bankruptcy enterprises through bankruptcy is an opportunity granted to creditors (Pekcanitez et al., 2007, p. 227). In order to pursue bankruptcy against the debtor, the debtor must be subject to bankruptcy (TTK m.20).

Bad decisions that businesses often make in areas such as management, marketing and finance cause failure. Therefore, the specific reasons for bankruptcy, which is the result of the failure of enterprises, are explained as follows (Bradley & Cowdery, 2004).

- **Unrealistic unrealistic expectations;** It's because many businesses have the wrong idea about the amount of money to be created, assuming they will be successful from day one. It is not taking into account the percentage of reinvestment necessary for the continuation of the business. In addition, businesses need a year or more to become profitable.
- **Personal problems;** It is the most common personal problems of the business owner related to divorce and illness.
- **Missing Capital**; Business always has unforeseen problems or issues when starting a business. To achieve profitability, two to three times the estimated amount of capital is required. The lack of capital creates a deficiency in the achievement of profitability of the enterprise.
- **Natural disaster;** Disasters can be classified as anything that occurs naturally in the environment. While not common, natural disasters can play a significant role in business failures and bankruptcies.
- **Cash flow**; Lack of cash flow is the biggest indicator of failure. A lack of cash flow can cause a business to fall behind in wage payments, rent, insurance and loan payments. A lack of cash flow can also hinder the business's ability to reinvest for future profits, such as ordering products or materials and executing marketing. When a business borrows to pay off its past debts, this is often a sign of a future disaster and indicates that businesses that have not entered a state of profitability within eighteen months are at high risk of bankruptcy.
- **Bad Location**; It is common knowledge that for most businesses, the choice of location is a critical decision in determining success or failure. Marketing ideas such as the population, the number of competitors and the number of non-competing enterprises in the environment should be taken into account when choosing a business.
- **Poor Record Keeping**; Poor record-keeping by businesses makes it nearly impossible for owners to know the financial condition of the business.
- **Growing pains**; A sudden drop in demand during the period of expansion of businesses, possibly due to an economic downturn, can lead to stagnant excesses in inventory and expenses that create potential for unpaid bankruptcy.
- **Key Person Loss**; Many businesses rely heavily on one or a few select individuals. The loss of this key person can lead to bankruptcy.
- **Lack of Technology;** Whether technology has increased quality, efficiency or durability, it always plays an important role in the products and services offered to consumers. It is also important for businesses to remain competitive.
- **Poor planning**; Poor planning or a lack of complete planning can be the reason why businesses have a short life expectancy.
- **Trade credit**; The use of commercial credit is a common practice used to provide temporary financing in businesses. Because it is extremely important for the survival of the business, late payment or non-payment can lead to financial failure and possibly bankruptcy.
- **Tax and Regulatory Burdens;** The burdens imposed by tax laws and regulations have a significant impact on determining the success of businesses.

According to the Turkish Commercial Code, the indebtedness of the enterprise causes its bankruptcy (TTK m. 376/3; Kaya, 2021). On the other hand, according to Article 385 of the Enforcement and Bankruptcy Code of 2004, a debtor can request a concordat in order to be able to pay his debts or to get rid of a possible bankruptcy.

Bankruptcy in Turkey, Abolition of Bankruptcy Postponement and Concordat

Bankruptcy is a forced liquidation procedure of all the assets of the debtor, which is carried out by the bankruptcy bodies for the purpose of collecting the receivables of the creditors. The ability to pursue bankruptcy persons through bankruptcy is an opportunity granted to creditors (Pekcanitez et al., 2007, p. 227). According to Article 20 of the Turkish Commercial Code, in order to pursue bankruptcy against the debtor, the debtor must be subject to bankruptcy. As a rule, in our law, merchants are subject to bankruptcy and who will be considered a trader is specified in the Turkish commercial law.

Postponement of bankruptcy is an institution that allows the commercial court to temporarily give up the bankruptcy decision on a capital company or cooperative that is indebted under certain conditions, that is, to temporarily give up on it and serves to prevent bankruptcy (Atalay; 2007, p. 65). Bankruptcy postponement is one of the regulations contained in both the Enforcement Bankruptcy Code and the Turkish Commercial Code. When it is declared by the administration that the debts of capital companies and cooperatives are more than their assets, the court determines this situation and gives bankruptcy decision and the bankruptcy could be requested to be postponed by submitting a project to the court to improve the financial condition of the company/cooperatives. However, new regulations have been made in this regard in order to prevent the sudden increase in the number of bankruptcy postponement requests and the abuse of this situation. With the new regulation, bankruptcy postponement was abolished and the possibility of concordat was introduced in its place (Uzel, 2018).

Therefore, in accordance with Article 285 of the Execution and Bankruptcy Law, any debtor who is unable to pay his debts when they are due or is in danger of not being able to pay on time can request a concordat in order to be able to pay his debts by giving a maturity or to avoid a possible bankruptcy.

If the initiation of the concordat proceedings is requested by one of the creditors, a temporary respite decision is made if the debtor submits the documents and records specified in Article 286 of the Execution and Bankruptcy Law within a reasonable timeframe to be given by the court. In this case, the expense required for the preparation of documents and records is borne by the creditor. In the event that the documents and records are not submitted in a timely and complete manner, the temporary respite decision shall not be made, and the concordat request made by the creditor shall be rejected. If the documents and records are submitted in full, the court shall, with the temporary restraining order, appoint an interim concordat commissioner to closely examine whether the concordat is likely to succeed. Taking into account the number of creditors and the amount of receivables, three commissioners may be appointed when necessary. Such commissioner or commissioners shall be granted a temporary respite period of three months, and the court may, at the request of the debtor or the interim commissioner, extend the provisional period for a maximum of two months before the expiry of this three-month period, and the total duration of the temporary respite shall not exceed five months. A temporary respite has consequences for a definite respite. In Article 289 of the Enforcement and Bankruptcy Code, the definite respite is the stage after the temporary respite at which the court decides whether the proposed concordat is likely to be successful and whether the concordat should be ratified in this context. In this sense, while the temporary respite is a kind of preparatory stage for the concordat trial; the definite respite is the stage at which the concordat proceedings are held. If it is understood that the concordat is possible to succeed, the debtor is given a definite respite of one year. However, according to the Articles 291-292 of the Enforcement and Bankruptcy Code, in cases such as the improvement of the financial condition of the debtor or otherwise deteriorating beyond improvement, the debtor failing to comply with the instructions of the commissioner and the court, the definite respite may be lifted and if the debtor is subject to bankruptcy, the court may even decide on his bankruptcy ex officio.

Bankruptcy Prediction Methods

Before investing in a firm's share, an investor is concerned about the bankruptcy of the firm that causes the loss of all investments and uses bankruptcy estimation methods that are constructed for these firms with one piece of historical observations and evaluated by another piece of historical observations (Zhou, 2013). Therefore, since it is aimed to predict the companies without failing, some of the financial failure, in other words artificial intelligence and statistical bankruptcy estimation methods, are explained in this study by specifying them as follows.

1. **Fuzzy set theory:** Models uncertainty in data using fuzzy sets of data and correlates people's experimental knowledge to models. This method has low numerical requirements (Kumar & Ravi, 2007).
2. **Artificial neural networks:** This method is among the most popular artificial intellectual techniques and is inspired by other computationally classified models. At the same time, this method creates a similarity with the functioning human nerve. Many nonlinear relationships are analyzed using artificial neural networks and credit scores are accurately estimated with this method (Barboza et al., 2017). The most common artificial neural model is the multilayer back propagation algorithm, which is among the most popular techniques used in bankruptcy estimation and credit score evaluation (Tsai et al., 2014).
3. **Rough sets:** The theory of rough set sets is a proposed method for solving the bankruptcy estimation problem by considering the criteria of qualifications with sequential domains of influence. This method is based on assumptions, which is some information associated with any object of the universe, and objects characterized by similar information cannot be distinguished or noticed. This theory uses the upper and lower approach of a concept to model uncertainty in data, and approaches are two basic activities in this theory. In solving classification problems, rough sets are applied to extract decision rules from the data, and the stimulated decision rules are classified as precise and probable (Kumar & Ravi, 2007).
4. **Logistic regression:** This method is used to design broken models immediately after discriminant analysis and then offers two main advantages. The first is not to force any conditions so that the explanatory variables are optimal, and the second is to allow the use of qualitative variables. To design a distorted model, this method aims to compute a function that calculates the z-score for each firm. This score represents the possibility of disorder (Jardin, 2016).
5. **Decision trees**: Decision trees are used to design bankruptcy models for several years after the use of logistic regression (Jardin, 2016). This method forms part of "machine learning", an important area of artificial intelligence. The vast majority of decision tree algorithms are used to solve classified problems and regression problems. At the same time, all these algorithms form a binary tree on the training data given (Kumar & Ravi, 2007). The decision trees method, which creates

the rules new data based on historical data, is easy for people to understand. This method creates rules by combining the answers to the questions asked (Sönmez, 2015).

6. **Support vector machines:** This model reflects the initial input vector into the eigenspace of high dimension with linear and nonlinear core function and uses the separation hyperplane to distinguish between two or more materials of different classes. It also uses the hyperplane classifier to classify materials. This method appears to have excellent classification ability (Chen et al., 2014). Support vector machines apply the principle of structural risk minimization, which is known to have high generalization performance, and create a linear model to predict the decision function using its nonlinear boundaries based on support vectors. With this method, compared to classical methods, significantly better results are obtained in bankruptcy estimation (Shin et al., 2005). Because it serves as a promising alternative by combining the strengths of traditional statistical methods that are easy to analyze and are more theory drivers. In particular, this method is used for financial applications such as credit rating and time series estimation (Kumar & Ravi, 2007).
7. **Genetic algorithms:** This method is carried out for bankruptcy estimation and is applied in studies for one-year information before bankruptcy and three years before bankruptcy. The rules produced by genetic algorithms are used as an expert system and are easily understood (Kumar & Ravi, 2007).
8. **Data envelopment analysis**: It is a non-parametric performance valuation method defined to measure the relative effectiveness of organizational or decision-making units. This method applies linear programming to observe the outputs and inputs consumed by decision-making units and establishes an effective production boundary based on best practices. At the same time, in data envelopment analysis, is calculated by obtaining the rate of sum of the relative efficacy weighted outputs to total ratio of weighted inputs (Kumar & Ravi, 2007).
9. **Discriminant analysis**: It is one of the multivariate statistical methods proposed by Fisher in the 1930s. This method is one of the methods used to predict financial failure. In this method, mathematical techniques are used to distinguish groups from each other and reveal whether there is a significant difference between two or more groups depending on a group of variables (Çelik, 2010).
10. **From other models;** Some bankruptcy forecasting models are developed by researchers using various quantitative approaches based on accounting. For example; In the study of Beaver (1966), it is stated that the bankruptcy estimation is made 5 years before the failure of the firms with ratio analysis as a univariate model using the discriminant analysis method. Because univariate models try to predict financial failure by considering financial ratios one by one and produce contradictory results according to the examined ratios, Altman (1968) proposes the Z score model to be used in solving this problem. In this model, multiple discriminant analysis, which is one of the multivariate models that handle events in multiple dimensions, is used. With the model established as a result of the Altman (1968) study, estimation success is achieved by classifying the firms as financially unsuccessful and non-unsuccessful firms. The Z Score calculated for each firm states that firms with a score greater than 2.99 are in the "safe zone", that is, there is no risk of financial failure, and firms with a Z Score between 1.81 and 2.99 are in the "grey zone", that is, although the risk of financial failure is not very high, they should be cautious when investing. Businesses with a Z Score below 1.81 indicate that they are at high risk of financial failure. In his study Altman (1968), he achieves a successful classification performance of 95% for the estimation of financial failure one year ago and 72% for two years ago. The goal here is to calculate the discriminant scores for each observation in any firm after estimating the values of the discriminant coefficients and to divide the observations by groups according to this score (Altman. & Hotchkiss, 2006). Finally,

in this study of Ohlson (1980) is proposed the O score model to predict bankruptcy one year and two years before bankruptcy using logistic regression analysis method.

FUTURE RESEARCH DIRECTIONS

This study has some limitations and these limitations offer suggestions for future studies. In the study, risk, bankruptcy and bankruptcy predictions are evaluated theoretically, but in future studies, bankruptcy or failure predictions of companies in various sectors in different countries can be made. At the same time, determinants of bankruptcy or failure can be investigated in future studies. Finally, in future studies, the effect of bankruptcy or failure on firm performance or the effect of performance on firm bankruptcy or failure can be analyzed.

CONCLUSION AND RECOMMENDATIONS

The aim of this study is to explain bankruptcy by talking about risk, risk types and risk management and to talk about bankruptcy prediction models. The studies in the literature are examined and evaluated. Risk affects many aspects of human life and is lived with it every day. The probability of risk occurrence consists of parameters such as the severity of the impact, susceptibility to change and the degree of interdependence with other risk factors. Without any of these, the situation or event is not really considered a risk. Risk analysis is used to identify risk situations in modelling any investment. Therefore, risk management includes identifying risks, estimating how likely they are and how serious they may become, deciding what to do about them and implementing these decisions. The main reasons for the development of this risk management are their failure to meet the budgets, deadlines, quality and performance of projects or their inability to generate sufficient revenue to serve principal and interest payments. The lessons to be learned from each failed project or company are obtained better performance through risk management.

At the same time, in the literature, it is determined that the inability of firms to fulfil financial obligations is called bankruptcy. Many socio-economic problems arise with the financial failure of firms, and therefore bankruptcy estimation methods, which are constructed with one part of historical observations and evaluated with another part of historical observations, are used to predict firms without failing and these methods are evaluated in the literature.

Finally, this study presents some recommendations for firms and managers of companies. All levels of risks that firms will experience are effectively assessed, ensuring that all stakeholders are aware of the risks associated with the investment and predicting bankruptcy before the bankruptcy or failure of firms. Thus, the findings obtained from the literature offer important contributions to the company managers.

REFERENCES

Agarwal, V., & Taffler, R. (2008). Comparing the performance of market-based and accounting-based bankruptcy prediction models. *Journal of Banking & Finance*, *32*(8), 1541–1551. doi:10.1016/j.jbankfin.2007.07.014

Aksoy, A., & Tanrıöven, C. (2014). Sermaye piyasası yatırım araçları ve analizi (5th ed.). [Capital market investment instruments and analysis (5th ed.)]. Detay yayıncılık.

Altman, E. (1968). Financial ratios, discriminant analysis and the prediction of corporate bankruptcy. *The Journal of Finance*, *23*(4), 589–609. doi:10.1111/j.1540-6261.1968.tb00843.x

Altman, E. I., & Hotchkiss, E. (2006). Corporate financial distress and bankruptcy: Predict and avoid bankruptcy, analyze and invest in distressed debt (3rd ed.). Wiley finance series.

Atalay, O. (2007). *Borca Batıklık ve İflasın Ertelenmesi* [Indebtedness and Postponement of Bankruptcy]. Turhan Kitabevi.

Bacovia, G. (2011). Analysis models of the bankruptcy risk. *Economy Transdisciplinarity Cognition*, *14*(1), 248–259.

Barboza, F., Kimura, H., & Altman, E. (2017). Machine learning models and bankruptcy prediction. *Expert Systems with Applications*, *83*, 405–417. doi:10.1016/j.eswa.2017.04.006

Beaver, W. H. (1966). Financial Ratios as Predictors of Failure. *Journal of Accounting Research. Empirical Research in Accounting: Selected Studies*, *4*, 71–111. doi:10.2307/2490171

Bharath, S. T., & Shumway, T. (2004). *Forecasting default with the KMV-Merton model* [Working paper]. University of Michigan.

Black, F., & Scholes, M. (1973). The pricing of options and corporate liabilities. *Journal of Political Economy*, *6*(3), 637–654. doi:10.1086/260062

Bordeianu, G. D., Radu, F., Paraschivescu, M. D., & Păvăloaia, W. (2011). Analysis models of the bankruptcy risk. *Economy Transdisciplinarity Cognition*, *14*(1), 248–259.

Bradley, D. B., & Cowdery, C. (2004). Small business: Causes of bankruptcy. Technical Report, University of Central Arkansas.

Çelik, M. K. (2010). Bankaların finansal başarısızlıklarının geleneksel ve yeni yöntemlerle öngörüsü [Prediction of banks' financial failures by traditional and new methods]. *Yönetim ve Ekonomi*, *17*(2), 129–143.

Çelik, M. S. (2018). Altman Z-Skor modeli kullanılarak Bist-30 endeksinde yer alan imalat şirketlerinin finansal başarısızlık riskinin tahmin edilmesi [Estimating the risk of financial failure of manufacturing companies included in the Bist-30 index using the Altman Z-Score model]. *ICPESS, 5*.

Çelik, S., & Akarım, Y. D. (2012). Likidite riski yönetimi: Panel veri analizi ile İMKB bankacılık sektörü üzerine ampirik bir uygulama [Liquidity risk management: An empirical application on the ISE banking sector with panel data analysis]. *Eskişehir Osmangazi Üniversitesi Sosyal Bilimler Dergisi*, *13*(1), 1–17.

Chen, S., Goo, Y. J. J., & Shen, Z. D. (2014). A hybrid approach of stepwise regression, logistic regression, support vector machine, and decision tree for forecasting fraudulent financial statements. *The Scientific World Journal*, *9*(16), 1–9. doi:10.1155/2014/968712 PMID:25302338

Çıtak, S. (1999). *Geleneksel risk yönetiminden programlanmış menkul kıymet işlemlerine* [From traditional risk management to scheduled securities transactions]. Dünya yayıncılık.

Crouhy, M., Galai, D., & Mark, R. (2000). *Risk managemenet: Comprehensive chapters on market credit, and operational risks: Features an integrated VaR framework: Hedging strategies for reducing risk*. McGraw-Hill.

Eiser, J. R., Bostrom, A., Burton, I., Johnston, D. M., McClure, J., Paton, D., Pligt, J. V. D., & White, M. P. (2012). Risk interpretation and action: A conceptual framework for responses to natural hazards. *International Journal of Disaster Risk Reduction, 1*, 5–16. doi:10.1016/j.ijdrr.2012.05.002

Embrechts, P., Resnick, S. I., & Samorodnitsky, G. (1999). Extreme value theory as a risk management tool. *North American Actuarial Journal, 3*(2), 30–41. doi:10.1080/10920277.1999.10595797

Flanagan, R., & Norman, G. (1993). Risk management and construction. Blackwell Science.

Gratt, L. B. (1987). Risk Analysis or Risk Assessment: A proposal for consistent definitions. Uncertainty in Risk Management. In V. T. Covello, L. B. Lave, A. Moghissi, & V. R. R. Uppuluri (Eds.), *Risk Assessment, Risk Management and Decision Making* (pp. 241–249). Plenum Press.

Guégan, D., & Hassani, B. K. (2019). *Risk measurement: from quantitative measures to management decisions*. Springer. doi:10.1007/978-3-030-02680-6

Head, G. L. (1967). An alternative to defining risk as uncertainty. *The Journal of Risk and Insurance, 34*(2), 205–214. doi:10.2307/251319

Hillegeist, S. A., Keating, E. K., Cram, D. P., & Lundstedt, K. G. (2004). Assessing the Probability of Bankruptcy. *Review of Accounting Studies, 9*(1), 5–34. doi:10.1023/B:RAST.0000013627.90884.b7

Hull, J. C. (2018). Risk management and financial institutions (5th ed.). Wiley Finance Series.

İcra and İflas Kanunu (2018). *Enforcement and Bankruptcy Law No. 2004*. Official Gazette: Law no. 7101, 28/02/2018.

Jardin, P. D. (2016). A two-stage classification technique for bankruptcy prediction. *European Journal of Operational Research, 254*(1), 236–252. doi:10.1016/j.ejor.2016.03.008

Jarrow, R. A., & Chatterjea, A. (2019). *An introduction to derivative securities, financial markets, and risk Management* (2nd ed.). World Scientific Publishing. doi:10.1142/y0018

Kasser, J. E. (2020). *Systemic and Systematic Risk Management*. CRC Press. doi:10.1201/9780429025389

Kaya, A. (2021). *Borca batıklık sorunlarının çözümünde değerlemenin yeri* [The place of valuation in solving debt indebtedness problems]. https://www.dmflegal.com.tr/yayinlarimiz/borca-batiklik-sorunlarinin-cozumunde-degerlemenin-yeri

Kovacova, M., & Kliestikova, J. (2017). Modelling bankruptcy prediction models in Slovak companies. *SHS Web of Conferences, 39*. 10.1051hsconf/20173901013

Kumar, P. R., & Ravi, V. (2007). Bankruptcy prediction in banks and firms via statistical and intelligent techniques – A review. *European Journal of Operational Research, 180*(1), 1–28. doi:10.1016/j.ejor.2006.08.043

Marin, M. & Montréal, H. (2015). Can financial risk management help prevent bankruptcy? *Journal of Finance and Accountancy*. doi:10.1016/j.jfineco.2004.06.013

McNeil, A. J., Frey, R., & Embrechts, P. (2005). *Quantitative risk management: concepts, techniques and tools*. Princeton University Press.

Mellahi, K., & Wilkinson, A. (2004). Organizational failure: A critique of recent research and a proposed integrative framework. *International Journal of Management Reviews*, *5/6*(1), 21–41. doi:10.1111/j.1460-8545.2004.00095.x

Mellahi & Wilkinson. (2004). *Systemic and Systematic Risk Management*. CRC Press.

Merna, T., & Al-Thani, F. F. (2008). *Corporate risk management* (2nd ed.). John Wiley & Sons.

Merton, R. C. (1974). On the pricing of corporate debt: The risk structure of interest rates. *The Journal of Finance*, *29*(2), 449–470. doi:10.2307/2978814

Min, J. H., & Jeong, C. (2008). A binary classification method for bankruptcy prediction. *Expert Systems with Applications*, *36*(3), 5256–5263. doi:10.1016/j.eswa.2008.06.073

Ohlson, J. A. (1980). Financial Ratios and the Probabilistic Prediction of Bankruptcy. *Journal of Accounting Research*, *18*(1), 109–131. doi:10.2307/2490395

Olson, D. L., Delen, D., & Meng, Y. (2012). Comparative analysis of data minin methods for bankruptcy prediction. *Decision Support Systems*, *52*(2), 464–473. doi:10.1016/j.dss.2011.10.007

Özbilgin, İ. G. (2012). Risk ve risk çeşitleri. *Bilişim dergisi, 145*, 86-93. http://www.bilisimdergisi.org.tr/s145/pdf/86-93.pdf

Pekcanıtez, H., Atalay, O., & Özekes, M. (2007). *İcra ve İflas Hukuku Temel Bilgiler* [Enforcement and Bankruptcy Law Basics]. Yetkin Yayınları.

Rowe, W. D. (1977). *An Anatomy of Risk*. John Wiley.

Sayılgan, G. (1995). *Finansal risk yönetimi* [Financial risk management]. Ankara Üniversitesi SBF Dergisi.

Scholes, M. S. (2000). Crisis and Risk Management. *The American Economic Review*, *90*(2), 17–21. doi:10.1257/aer.90.2.17

Shin, K. S., Lee, T. S., & Kim, H. J. (2005). An application of support vector machines in bankruptcy prediction model. *Expert Systems with Applications*, *28*(1), 127–135. doi:10.1016/j.eswa.2004.08.009

Sönmez, F. (2015). Kredi skorunun belirlenmesinde yapay sinir ağları ve karar ağaçlarının kullanımı bir model önerisi [The use of artificial neural networks and decision trees to determine the credit score is a model proposal]. *Anadolu Bil Meslek Yüksekokulu Dergisi*, *37*, 1–22.

Tapiero, C. (2004). *Risk and financial management: Mathematical and computational methods*. John Wiley & Sons. doi:10.1002/0470020369

Thornhill, S., & Amit, R. (2003). Bankruptcy, firm age, and the resource-based view. *Organization Science*, *14*(5), 497–509. doi:10.1287/orsc.14.5.497.16761

Tsai, C. F., Hsu, Y. F., & Yen, D. C. (2014). A comparative study of classifier ensembles for bankruptcy prediction. *Applied Soft Computing*, *24*, 977–984. doi:10.1016/j.asoc.2014.08.047

Uzel, Ö. (2018). *İflas ertelemenin yürürlükten kaldırılması ve konkordato süreci*. http://www.uzeldanismanlik.com/iflas-ertelemenin-yururlukten-kaldirilmasi-ve-konkordato-sureci/

Wieczorek-Kosmala, M., Błach, J., & Trzesiok, J. (2018). Analysis of Bankruptcy Threat for Risk Management Purposes: A Model Approach. *International Journal of Financial Studies*, *6*(98), 1–17. doi:10.3390/ijfs6040098

Zhou, L. (2013). Performance of corporate bankruptcy prediction models on imbalanced dataset: The effect of sampling methods. *Knowledge-Based Systems*, *41*, 16–25. doi:10.1016/j.knosys.2012.12.007

KEY TERMS AND DEFINITIONS

Bankruptcy: It is a forced liquidation procedure of all the assets of the debtor, which is carried out by the bankruptcy bodies for the purpose of collecting the receivables of the creditors.

Bankruptcy Estimation Methods: These are fuzzy cluster theory, neural networks, decision trees, rough cluster theory, case-based reasoning, support vector machines, data envelopment analysis, soft computing, statistical techniques such as linear discriminant analysis (LDA), multivariate discriminant analysis (MDA), quadratic discriminant analysis (QDA), logit and factor analysis.

Failure: It is defined as a deterioration in the activities of an enterprise and, accordingly, a decrease in the resources of the enterprise. The failure terms are replaced by terms such as business death, bankruptcy, collapse, downsizing and closure.

Risk: It is used synonymously with the word uncertainty.

Risk Management: It is the discipline to live with the possibility of future events having adverse effects.

Risk Types: Risks are divided into many varieties. These are interest rate risk, market risk, political risk, financial risk, business risk, management risk, non-repayment risk, marketability risk, purchasing power risk, interest rate risk, exchange rate risk, structural delay risk, equity risk, corporate bond risk, liquidity risk, taxation risk, reinvestment risk, country risk, dynamic risk, structural risk, conditional risk, customer risk and interpretation risks.

Chapter 8
To Fail or Not to Fail?
Financial Examination of the Agriculture, Forestry, and Fishing Sector of Turkey

Gizay Daver
Zonguldak Bulent Ecevit University, Turkey

ABSTRACT

The ratio analyses are used to evaluate firms in the sector. Similarities and the differences between the DAP calculated ratios and the investment firm calculated ratios are shown. Companies are compared among each other and with the sector. Automated calculations and potential robo advisory directions are proposed. Auto calculations and comparisons are found to be reliable after 2018. Suggestions for the improvement of computer-assisted calculations are given. There are alternative ways to avoid bankruptcy and concordat. Also, there are choices between bankruptcy procedures, liquidation, and restructuring. The DAP is a useful tool to investigate a sector as a whole, but it is not enough to decide whether a firm failure is close or not. The given 35 equations on the financials of companies are powerful tools but not enough to decide. Policies play a key role in the agri-food industry worldwide. The effects of these policies cannot be observed by just looking at the financial statements.

INTRODUCTION

Turkey has great potential in agriculture, forestry, and fishery sectors in its geography with its arable lands, geopolitical location, and logistics network. It is debatable to what extent Turkey and Turks evaluate this potential. The formal name of the sector is known as "Agriculture, Forestry, and Fishing". Sub-sectors are "Crop and Animal Production Hunting and Related Service Activities", "Forestry and Logging", and "Fishing and Fisheries". This study covers the largest set by using the "Agriculture, Forestry and Fishing" sector definition.

In 2021, the number of companies, which was 3 in the real sector of agriculture, forestry, and fisheries, is decreasing. As of 2022, there are only 2 companies left representing the sector.

The company whose former title/name was "Taç Tarım Ürünleri Hayvancılık Gıda Sanayi ve Ticaret A.Ş." has decided to continue its life as "OTTO Holding A.Ş" by changing the title and sector. What are

DOI: 10.4018/978-1-6684-5181-6.ch008

the reasons underlying this decision? Are those firms performing better than their eliminated competitor or they are just lucky?

This study is organized to show the most recent developments in a selected Borsa İstanbul stock market, marketplace. The study is up to date and covers the most recent years 2021 and 2022. Also, it covers the name and ticker changes as well as the sector changes of the companies. One of the biggest contributions of the study is that the firms from the selected sector may draw lessons from the imperfection of the disqualified ones.

Fundamental financial ratios may reveal valuable information on these questions. Therefore, one path should be an investigation of the ratios. This path may be named "The ratio analysis direction". As another path, the price of a stock has valuable information. Finance theory suggests following "the signaling theory direction" as an alternative.

If the second path – the signaling theory direction- is chosen, there are several factors to be explained. First of all, considering the life of the OTTO, how the trading on the Equity Market in Borsa Istanbul is carried out should be explained. Each market has its own specialty. Markets, market definitions, and their symbols should be introduced. The difference between the BIST main market and Watch List should be given. The conditions for being quoted in the BIST main market should be specified as well as the Watch List. And after all these steps stock prices and public disclosure platform notifications should be monitored. Also, the news on the company should be monitored too. While conducting the study, the firms being listed on the Watch List are closer to bankruptcy than the ones in the BIST main market information should always be kept in the mind.

In this study first path -the ratio analysis direction- will be taken and the second path will be left as another study. Automation and computer-assisted calculated ratios will be presented. And the ways of using these calculations to predict firm failures will be addressed. Also, suggestions for the improvement of computer-assisted calculations will be given. By considering financial aspects and monitoring the firms in the sector, investment decision views may be altered.

1. BACKGROUND

Countries need to import foodstuffs to meet their increasing food needs. It is difficult for countries with limited funds to do this. In order to eliminate the bottleneck, they should attach importance to increasing agriculture and food production (Çelik, 2000).

The projections of the OECD-FAO (Food and Agriculture Organization of the United Nations) Agricultural outlook address agricultural issues. Sustainable development and productivity growth in agriculture and reduction of waste are the key points(OECD and Food and Agriculture Organization of the United Nations, 2017, 2021). These aims can be reached by implementing great planning in the sector.

The neighborhood is important as history showed to all humankind. The overall well-being of European citizens is seen as dependent on their ability to ensure that, next to economic growth and efficiency priorities, Europe in the long term offers a multitude of multifunctional territories with good social and environmental quality that is capable of meeting the different needs of its citizens(European Environment Agency, 2017). Countries must work together to ensure global food security and a healthy environment for the next generations. These aims can be reached by ensuring the accountability of firms in the sector.

Even when we limit the subject specifically to Turkey, there is a variety of documents regarding the infrastructure and superstructure of the agriculture sector such as strategic documents, investment incentives, and support given to agricultural activities.

Intending to position itself as a preferred regional base and supply center among global players, Turkey tries to encourage investments in the sector. Turkey offers incentives to potential agricultural and food investors. Meanwhile, current domestic investors in the agriculture sector face difficulties, such as some going into bankruptcy processes.

Incentives for agro-food investments are offered through the Ministry of Agriculture and Forestry. These incentives are communicated as lucrative incentives. Rural Development Support Program (2021 – 2025) and EU & TR granted funds are supported and communicated by different organizations. IPARD – II Program is mainly communicated through the Agriculture and Rural Development Support Institution.

Turkey can take advantage of its geopolitical and climatic location with the right policies both in the sector and throughout the economy of the country.

Ten reasons to invest in Turkey are listed as follows, robust economy, domestic and accessible markets, strategic location, favorable demographics, skilled and competitive labor force, continuous reform process, business friendliness, lucrative incentives, benign R&D ecosystem, and sectoral opportunities(Presidency of the Republic of Türkiye, 2022, p. 2).

The agro-food sector offers abundant opportunities with its $103 billion market value according to the Investment Office of the Presidency of the Republic of Türkiye. Export value of 19$ billion and around 200 countries export opportunities according to Turkstat, Ministry of Industry and Technology, Ministry of Agriculture and Forestry, OSD, ODD as of 2020, MAKFED, TESİD as of 2019, SASAD as of 2020, SHGM as of 2019(Presidency of the Republic of Türkiye, 2022, p. 20).

One of the key reasons to invest in the Turkish agro-food industry is given as follows, "Turkey has a strong and growing agricultural industry, offering opportunities in many areas"(Presidency of the Republic of Turkey, 2021, p. 1). Turkey is the largest country in Europe in terms of the agricultural economy due to 2019 data with its $49 billion production volume. In the same year, it is listed as the 10th largest country in the World in terms of the agricultural economy. In 2019, in the production quantities of leading commodities such as fruits, vegetables, coarse grains, dairy, and oils, Turkey has been listed as the 3rd largest agricultural producing country in the world(Presidency of the Republic of Turkey, 2021, p. 5).

It can clearly be seen from the represented data and information there is an adorable investment aura in Turkey. At this point, scientific questioning asks if it is so?

One must keep in mind that OECD outlooks are set on specific assumptions such as oil prices, GDP, population growth rate, etc. (OECD and Food and Agriculture Organization of the United Nations, 2021)

Among these aforementioned assumptions, finance theory has many strong tools for investment decisions. Two of the most known are ratio analyses and signals sent from firm managers to the public. These two aspects are covered briefly in this study and the pros and cons of the application of computer-assisted ratio analyses are discussed.

One of the companies out of three drew off the sector and left two may be forced to follow their past competitor. This conclusion may come true in the near future as the IZTAR ticker changed to IZINV and the company name changed to "İz Yatırım Holding A.Ş." from "Iz Hayvancılık Tarım Ve Gıda Sanayi Ticaret A.Ş."

The strength of companies in a country is important because of the agriculture negotiations. In determining the development level of the agricultural sector of the countries, the share of agriculture in employment and GDP values is important. As the level of development increases, the share of the agricultural sector in GDP and employment is expected to decrease(Özden & Gürgen, 2008). As an alternative, the number of agro-food companies listed on the stock market and their strength is an indicator of the power of that country.

1.1 Ratio Analyses

In the fundamentals of corporate finance, the financial statement analysis topic is considered an important topic. Financial ratios are broken down into leverage ratios, liquidity ratios, efficiency ratios, and profitability ratios. These are some main breakdowns to name, but not all of them. The Du Pont System is also considered very important along with the other financial ratios. The calculations of the ratios are relatively easy compared to the usage and the choosing of a benchmark to measure company performance.

Financial ratio calculation is a mechanical process that can be completed without any human interaction with the financial reports. Also, roboadvisory processes can be set up on these calculations. In the background, these calculations and how they are made must be shown to fully understand the company's look.

Sometimes reality is not as it's seen from the financial statements. Financial Accounting Standards Board's generally accepted accounting principles (GAAP) are being followed while preparing financial statements. Management's decisions on the reporting of the flexible conditions help them not to violate GAAP to reach different results(Keown, Martin, & Petty, 2020, p. 80). It must be noted that, although there is an international consensus, uniformity has not been fully achieved in all areas.

At the basics, the company's debt situation and how heavy it is shown by the leverage ratios. Firms' ability to lay their hands on cash, is measured using liquidity ratios. Efficiency or turnover ratios measure is a great sign of the company's productive usage of its assets. If there is an investment there is an expectation of profit and the return of investments are measured by using profitability ratios(Brealey, Myers, & Marcus, 2007).

In the appendix, the financial ratio formulas are given. They are presented in Turkish; because automated calculations of the ratios are done using financial statements prepared in Turkish. Along with the Turkish ratios, translations of the ratios are given. In order to clarify the topic to non-Turkish financial table users, the dangers of the ratios are going to be presented.

In the broadest sense, translated variations are used as if they are calculated in the same way. The liquidity ratio is somewhat similar to the quick ratio. But when we dig deeper, the calculation methodology of the liquidity ratio and the cash ratio differs from the generally represented ones. Such calculation divergences may be encountered so it is recommended to work on Turkish-prepared financial statements. Also, the importance of getting support from a local financial expert before making an international investment decision is obvious.

To make the point clearer, the international way of calculating the cash ratio is presented as using cash added to marketable securities on the numerator part of the equation. Although the name is the same, the calculation of the Turkish "cash ratio" has "Cash and Cash Equivalents, Cash Accounts Opened under Real Estate Projects, and Financial Investments" in the numerator. There is no guarantee that these two numerators will match each other.

In the literature, there is a vast amount of paper explaining and using the ratio analysis methodology. Just to name a few, Gümüş, Şakar, Akkın, & Şahin, (2017); TCMB, (2022); Yenisu, (2019) are the chosen ones to show how unique the ratios may be used and calculated. Also, ratios can be combined with other methods to evaluate the performance of companies. As an example, performance comparison study of Kanat, (2019) with the grey relational analysis method can be given. This study will not combine methods. It will strictly stick to the financial ratio calculation rules of the Central Securities Depository of the Turkish capital markets. In the appendix, the formulas for these calculations are given. In the following comparative financials, profitability, and multipliers tables, results gathered from the calculation methodologies of investment firms active in Turkey are given.

Even though the data of the study starts by the year 2016 when the XBRL type data gathering started, the limitations of comparative data for all firms limit the study from 2019/12 to the present.

Table 1. Financials 1

	Net Sales Quarterly (Mln TL)			Net Sales (Annualized) (Mln TL)			EBITDA (Quarterly) (Mln TL)			EBITDA (Annualized) (Mln TL)		
	IZINV	YAPRK	OTTO	IZINV	YAPRK	OTTO	IZINV	YAPRK	OTTO	IZINV	YAPRK	OTTO
2022/03	17.77	16.73	2.37	33.56	54.26	5.15	4.53	14	0.62	3.1	25.69	-0.16
2021/12	6.05	14.59	0	21.39	48.73	2.79	-0.22	8.67	-0.77	-0.65	14.99	-0.9
2021/09	5.54	12.1	0	21.86	44.21	3.75	-0.57	1.6	-0.1	0.7	8	0.45
2021/06	4.2	10.84	2.79	22.33	40.4	3.75	-0.65	1.43	-0.25	0.18	7.74	0.07
2021/03	5.6	11.2	0	22.11	38.26	1	0.78	3.29	-0.12	1.1	8.27	0.05
2020/12	6.52	10.06	0.96	19.68	35.47	1.02	1.13	1.68	0.59	0.98	9.87	0.06
2020/09	6.01	8.3	0		32.36	0.89	-1.08	1.34	-0.51		10.49	-0.48
2020/06	3.98	8.7	0.04	18.88	31.08	1.3	0.27	1.96	0.06	0.27	10.32	-0.25
2020/03	3.17	8.41	0.02		29.49	2.41	0.66	4.89	-0.1		9.49	0.29
2019/12	0	6.95	0.83	21.6	28.19	3.19	0	2.3	-1.51	2.27	6.08	-2.12

Source: Authors' own elaboration from scorecards (Halk Yatırım, 2022)

In Table 1 Net Sales Quarterly (Mln TL), Net Sales (Annualized) (Mln TL), EBITDA (Quarterly) (Mln TL), EBITDA (Annualized) (Mln TL) are presented for three firms in the sector. As is seen in the table some values are zero and some are missing. Zero values are reported as is. Empty cells have no data reported.

Table 2. Financials 2

	Net Financial Incomes / Expenses (Quarter) (Mln TL)			Net Financial Income / Expenses (Annualized) (Mln TL)			Net Profit Quarterly (Mln TL)			Net Profit (Annualized) (Mln TL)		
	IZINV	YAPRK	OTTO	IZINV	YAPRK	OTTO	IZINV	YAPRK	OTTO	IZINV	YAPRK	OTTO
2022/03	-0.91	0.36	-0.15	-3.1	2.3	-0.19	2.48	10.81	3.46	-2.34	19.88	4.49
2021/12	-0.74	1.79	0.09	-2.95	2.32	-0.32	-1.5	8.57	2.19	-5.2	11.14	0.85
2021/09	-0.73	-0.04	-0.11	-2.78	0.31	-0.63	-1.74	0.24	-1.1	-4.39	2.67	-3.37
2021/06	-0.72	0.19	-0.02	-2.4	0.79	-0.91	-1.58	0.25	-0.05	-4.2	3.3	-3.34
2021/03	-0.76	0.38	-0.29	-2.24	0.52	-0.89	-0.39	2.07	-0.18	-2.9	4.57	-3.41
2020/12	-0.56	-0.22	-0.22	-2	0.02	-0.61	-0.69	0.1	-2.03	-2.78	5.15	-1.94
2020/09	-0.36	0.44	-0.11	0	0.09	-0.57	-1.55	0.88	-0.86		5.66	-3.81
2020/06	-0.56	-0.08	0	-2.15	-0.3	0.4	-0.28	1.52	-0.12	-3.19	5.2	-0.34
2020/03	-0.51	-0.12	0	0	-0.1	-0.19	-0.26	2.64	1.29		3.93	-2.42
2019/12	0	-0.14	-0.19	-2.5	0.06	-0.19	0	0.62	-3.9	-3.38	1.81	-5.05

Source: Authors' own elaboration from scorecards (Halk Yatırım, 2022)

In Table 2 Net Financial Incomes / Expenses (Quarter) (Mln TL), Net Financial Income / Expenses (Annualized) (Mln TL), Net Profit Quarterly (Mln TL), Net Profit (Annualized) (Mln TL) are presented for three firms in the sector.

Table 3. Financials 3

	Total Debts (Mln TL)			Net Debt (Mln TL)			Net Working Capital (Mln TL)			Equity (Mln TL)			Total Assets (Mln TL)		
	IZINV	YAPRK	OTTO	IZINV	YAPRK	OTTO	IZINV	YAPRK	OTTO	IZINV	YAPRK	OTTO	IZINV	YAPRK	OTTO
2022/03	46.9	41.77	16.2	10.34	7.22	4.22	-0.88	7.01	-7.78	26.93	53.28	36.97	82.16	95.05	53.18
2021/12	43.42	33.7	19.76	15.58	10.64	4.81	-2.38	7.39	-8.49	24.79	42.47	33.5	76.14	76.17	53.26
2021/09	42.7	30.8	15.23	18.23	12.28	4.29	1.77	6.79	-5.62	26.55	33.89	9.81	77.18	64.69	25.04
2021/06	37.5	30.35	14.36	17.32	9.11	7.54	1.99	3.11	1.39	28.56	33.65	10.91	74.21	64	25.27
2021/03	33.38	29.61	14.76	13.9	9.31	8.4	0.21	4.02	-4.81	30.38	33.4	7.16	72.05	63.01	21.92
2020/12	31.85	28.41	16.99	18.8	9.14	8.69	5.96	4.11	-4.59	31.05	31.51	7.28	70.99	59.92	24.28
2020/09		28.9	15.41		9.02	6.5		3.74	-4.64		31.4	9.33		60.31	24.74
2020/06	27.85	27.99	14.99	18.73	6.45	6.48	8.02	0.56	-4.08	33.83	30.51	10.19	69.68	58.5	25.18
2020/03		26.93	14.78		6.56	6.2		1.57	-4.1		29.2	10.56		56.13	25.34
2019/12	27.85	19.07	19.46	15.48	6.58	6.2	5.55	2.07	-5.64	30.59	26.56	9.22	66.68	45.63	28.68

Source: Authors' own elaboration from scorecards (Halk Yatırım, 2022)

In Table 3 Total Debts (Mln TL), Net Debt (Mln TL), Net Working Capital (Mln TL), Equity (Mln TL), Total Assets (Mln TL) are presented for three firms in the sector.

Table 4. Profitability 1

	Gross Profit Margin (%) (Quarter)			Gross Profit Margin (%) (Annualized)			Operating Expense Margin (%) (Quarter)			Operating Expense Margin (%) (Annualized)		
	IZINV	YAPRK	OTTO	IZINV	YAPRK	OTTO	IZINV	YAPRK	OTTO	IZINV	YAPRK	OTTO
2022/03	26.19	89.97	45.12	10.53	53.8	9.43	2.85	8.04	21.82	5.71	8.23	12.47
2021/12	-2.06	68.55		-1.34	36.82	-20.87	7.17	7.66		8.6	8.32	21.25
2021/09	-8.76	17.98		5.5	22.79	-3.84	8.25	8.59		9.21	8.64	17.39
2021/06	-12.12	18.13	-14.93	2.89	23.9	-1.18	12.36	8.91	6.75	8.82	8.92	26.69
2021/03	14.88	33.95		7.01	26.16	23.32	7.66	8.34		8.94	8.82	117.19
2020/12	20.92	21.19	63.93	7.09	32.39	-1.01	9.34	8.72	25.24	10.01	8.82	76.66
2020/09	-17.32	21.17			37.49	-238.43	6.87	9.97			9.72	63.01
2020/06	9.9	26.62	-393.03	6.35	38.48	-111.18	13.2	8.45	39.73	11.7	9.66	4.9
2020/03	21.37	62.84	-1294.43		38.35	-55.79	13.36	8.18	402.84		10.33	5.63
2019/12		39.91	-178.78	16.32	28.07	-112.11		12.87	2.71	10.37	10.64	3.05

Source: Authors' own elaboration from scorecards (Halk Yatırım, 2022)

In Table 4 Gross Profit Margin (%) (Quarter), Gross Profit Margin (%) (Annualized),Operating Expense Margin (%) (Quarter), Operating Expense Margin (%) (Annualized) are presented for three firms in the sector.

Table 5. Profitability 2

	Equity Margin (%) (Quarter)			Equity Margin (%) (Annualized)			Net Profit Margin (%) (Quarterly)			Net Profit Margin (%) (Annualized)		
	IZINV	YAPRK	OTTO	IZINV	YAPRK	OTTO	IZINV	YAPRK	OTTO	IZINV	YAPRK	OTTO
2022/03	25.52	83.65	26.34	9.24	47.34	-3.03	13.93	64.61	146.34	-6.98	36.63	87.19
2021/12	-3.67	59.41		-3.06	30.75	-32.35	-24.89	58.76		-24.33	22.85	30.57
2021/09	-10.2	13.18		3.19	18.09	12.12	-31.36	2.02		-20.06	6.04	-89.78
2021/06	-15.39	13.2	-9.14	0.82	19.17	2	-37.51	2.29	-1.87	-18.81	8.17	-89.07
2021/03	13.93	29.4		4.98	21.62	4.64	-6.89	18.5		-13.13	11.96	-341.65
2020/12	17.3	16.66	60.83	4.98	27.83	6.34	-10.53	1.04	-210.93	-14.11	14.51	-190.84
2020/09	-17.93	16.18			32.43	-54.15	-25.83	10.55			17.5	-429.19
2020/06	6.8	22.52	171.2	1.44	33.19	-19.3	-7	17.49	-352.37	-16.92	16.72	-26.35
2020/03	20.81	58.2	-553.43		32.18	12.04	-8.16	31.44	6873.81		13.33	-100.61
2019/12		33.06	-181.49	10.5	21.58	-66.45		8.92	-467.87	-15.67	6.43	-158.25

Source: Authors' own elaboration from scorecards (Halk Yatırım, 2022)

In Table 5 Equity Margin (%) (Quarter), Equity Margin (%) (Annualized), Net Profit Margin (%) (Quarterly), Net Profit Margin (%) (Annualized) are presented for three firms in the sector.

Table 6. Profitability 3

	Return on Equity (%) (Annual)			Return on Assets (%)			Net Debt / EBITDA (x)			Net Finance Income (Expense) / EBITDA (x)			Net Debt / (Net Debt + Equity) (%)		
	IZINV	YAPRK	OTTO	IZINV	YAPRK	OTTO	IZINV	YAPRK	OTTO	IZINV	YAPRK	OTTO	IZINV	YAPRK	OTTO
2022/03	-8.18	45.86	20.36	3.21	13.68	9.22	3.34	0.28	-27.09	0.2	-0.03	0.25	27.75	11.93	10.25
2021/12	-18.64	30.11	4.18	-7.07	16.37	2.2	-23.81	0.71	-5.34	-3.32	-0.21	0.11	38.59	20.04	12.56
2021/09	-16.52	8.18	-35.19	-4.79	4.1	-5.36	26.18	1.54	9.43	-1.3	0.03	-1.11	40.72	26.59	30.42
2021/06	-13.47	10.29	-31.66	-2.73	3.79	-0.91	94.38	1.18	100.58	-1.12	-0.13	-0.06	37.75	21.31	40.87
2021/03	-9.56	14.62	-38.52	-0.54	3.48	-0.76	12.63	1.13	181.39	0.98	-0.12	-2.33	31.4	21.79	54
2020/12	-9.01	17.72	-23.53	-4.03	9.75	-7.33	19.17	0.93	134.62	0.5	0.13	0.38	37.71	22.48	54.4
2020/09		19.75	-40.85		9.73	0.36		0.86	-13.53	-0.33	-0.33	-0.22		22.32	41.08
2020/06	-9.92	18.55	-3.27	-0.78	8.11	4.21	68.81	0.63	-25.89	2.07	0.04	-0.01	35.64	17.45	38.86
2020/03		14.44	-22.94		5.42	5.1		0.69	21.39	0.78	0.02	-0.01		18.36	37
2019/12	-14.63	7.07	-43.05	-6.04	4.26	-16.55	6.82	1.08	-2.93		0.06	-0.13	33.6	19.85	40.22

Source: Authors' own elaboration from scorecards (Halk Yatırım, 2022)

In Table 6 Return on Equity (%) (Annual), Return on Assets (%), Net Debt / EBITDA (x), Net Finance Income (Expense) / EBITDA (x), Net Debt / (Net Debt + Equity) (%) are presented for three firms in the sector.

Table 7. Multipliers 1

	Price			Price Market Cap (Mln TL)			P/E			Market Value / Book Value		
	IZINV	YAPRK	OTTO	IZINV	YAPRK	OTTO	IZINV	YAPRK	OTTO	IZINV	YAPRK	OTTO
2022/03	20.32	32.37	33.78	315.89	460.08	239.16		23.15	53.24	11.73	8.64	6.47
2021/12	18.98	29.34	36.7	280.8	416.91	259.84		37.44	305.04	11.33	9.82	7.76
2021/09	23.3	29.66	24.58	344.71	421.46	174.03		157.88		12.98	12.43	17.75
2021/06	20	35.09	31.58	295.89	498.7	223.59		151.08		10.36	14.82	20.49
2021/03	18.45	53.84	25.5	272.96	765.38	180.54		167.3		8.99	22.91	25.22
2020/12	18	36.16	10.53	266.3	514.04	74.55		99.89		8.58	16.32	10.23
2020/09	8.69	29.29	17.23	128.56	416.42	121.99		73.55			13.26	13.08
2020/06	5.57	4.92	6.03	82.41	70.08	42.69		13.49		2.44	2.3	4.19
2020/03	1.85	3.39	1.8	27.37	48.35	12.74		12.3			1.66	1.21
2019/12	2.62	3.12	3.12	31.36	44.52	22.09		24.56		1.03	1.68	2.4

Source: Authors' own elaboration from scorecards (Halk Yatırım, 2022)

In Table 7 Price, Price Market Cap (Mln TL), P/E, Market Value / Book Value are presented for three firms in the sector.

Table 8. Multipliers 2

	Firm Value/EBITDA			Firm Value/Sales			Earnings Per Share			Earnings Per Share (Annualized)		
	IZINV	YAPRK	OTTO	IZINV	YAPRK	OTTO	IZINV	YAPRK	OTTO	IZINV	YAPRK	OTTO
2022/03	105.22	18.19	-1560.47	9.72	8.61	47.24	0.16	0.76	0.49	-0.15	1.4	0.63
2021/12	-452.94	28.53	-293.63	13.86	8.77	94.98	-0.1	0.6	0.31	-0.35	0.78	0.12
2021/09	521.13	54.24	392.31	16.6	9.81	47.55	-0.12	0.02	-0.16	-0.3	0.19	-0.48
2021/06	1706.93	65.58	3082.21	14.02	12.57	61.64	-0.11	0.02	-0.01	-0.28	0.23	-0.47
2021/03	260.62	93.66	4078.55	12.97	20.25	189.17	-0.03	0.29	-0.03	-0.2	0.64	-0.48
2020/12	290.77	53	1289.59	14.48	14.75	81.8	-0.05	0.01	-0.29	-0.19	0.72	-0.27
2020/09		40.54	-267.28		13.15	144.73	-0.1	0.12	-0.12	0	0.8	-0.54
2020/06	371.53	7.42	-196.52	5.36	2.46	37.93	-0.02	0.21	-0.02	-0.22	0.73	-0.05
2020/03		5.79	65.34		1.86	7.87	-0.02	0.37	0.18	0	0.55	-0.34
2019/12	20.65	8.4	-13.34	2.17	1.81	8.87	0	0.09	-0.55	-0.46	0.26	-0.71

Source: Authors' own elaboration from scorecards (Halk Yatırım, 2022)

In Table 8 Firm Value/EBITDA, Firm Value/Sales, Earnings Per Share, Earnings Per Share (Annualized) are presented for three firms in the sector.

Table 9. Multipliers 3

	Dividend Per Share			Dividend Efficiency			Receivables Collection Period (Days)			Debt Payment Period (Days)			Stock-Keeping Period (Days)		
	IZINV	YAPRK	OTTO	IZINV	YAPRK	OTTO	IZINV	YAPRK	OTTO	IZINV	YAPRK	OTTO	IZINV	YAPRK	OTTO
2022/03	0	0.03	0		0.07		96.22	29.77	135	2.68	4.5	1.58	113.06	44.09	77.52
2021/12	0	0.03	0		0.08		111.58	29.19	171.82	2.08	4.43	1.2	181.71	45.25	106.89
2021/09	0	0.03	0		0.08		103.47	28.38	177.8	1.47	4.23	1.77	166.02	49.39	61.64
2021/06	0	0.03	0		0.06		94.21	28.8	170.42	2.38	3.3	2.03	144.99	51.9	42.37
2021/03	0	0.03	0		0.04		84.02	29.47	620.69	1.94	3.78	0.36	138.18	51.16	109.59
2020/12	0	0.03	0		0.03		84.41	29.63	818.94	2.59	3.37	0.64	147.89	51.41	123.66
2020/09	0	0.03	0		0.04			31.21	1030.66		2.79	1.4		52.21	56.66
2020/06	0	0.03	0		0.22		56.79	31.18	719.96	2.57	2.44	1.57	149.9	52.38	63.08
2020/03	0	0.03	0		0.31			30.77	391.27		2.98	2.22		49.03	43.24
2019/12	0	0.04	0		0.41		53.28	30.66	309.21	2.4	3.09	7.12	139	48.67	23.2

Source: Authors' own elaboration from scorecards (Halk Yatırım, 2022)

In Table 9 Dividend Per Share, Dividend Efficiency, Receivables Collection Period (Days), Debt Payment Period (Days), Stock-Keeping Period (Days)are presented for three firms in the sector.

When all the tables are dug deep, the scale difference is obvious. But the performance difference is not as obvious as the scale. It can be seen that there are conflicting signals from the ratios.

1.2 Signaling Theory

In order to find funds for high-quality projects, knowledge transfer must take place. Moral hazard hinders the direct transfer of information. In any case, good project finance requires information exchange. By observing the entrepreneur's actions, information can be conveyed about whether the project is good or not. Insiders are willing to invest in a good project or a good company. This investment aspiration can serve as a signal to the credit market of the true quality of the project. Lenders value projects by evaluating signals. The entrepreneur's desire to invest in his/her own project indicates the quality of the project. As the share of the entrepreneur increases, the value of the firm increases. Contrary to Modigliani and Miller, it is argued that the value of the firm is related to the financial structure. Even in the absence of bankruptcy costs, a low level of firm debt indicates that the firm has riskier returns. Firms with riskier returns will have lower debt levels even when there are no bankruptcy costs. Signal theory is an approach that takes into account information asymmetry. The need to signal causes entrepreneurs to invest more in their firms than they are willing to make(Leland & Pyle, 1977).

In short, assuming that the capital markets are competitive, the financial structure of the firm is a signaling model of insider information. If the firm has potential, the entrepreneur prefers to invest in his/her own firm rather than holding the market portfolio.

2. FIRMS IN THE AGRICULTURE, FORESTRY, AND FISHING SECTOR OF TURKEY

In Turkey, as of 22.01.2022, there are three companies listed in Borsa Istanbul under the agriculture, forestry, and fishing sector. These companies are given in Table 10.

Table 10. Firms in the sector as of 22.01.2022

Rank / Number	Ticker Code	Company Title/Name
1	IZTAR	İZ HAYVANCILIK TARIM VE GIDA SANAYİ TİCARET A.Ş.
2	TACTR	OTTO HOLDİNG A.Ş.
3	YAPRK	YAPRAK SUT VE BESI ÇIFTLIKLERİ SANAYİ VE TİCARET A.Ş.

Source: Public Closure Platform (Kamuyu Aydınlatma Platformu (KAP), 2022)

The field of activities of the firms given in Table 10 are as follows:

The first one registered its activities as "Raising, care and feeding, milk production and sale of farm animals for milk production in the livestock sector, and apple and apple sapling cultivation and sale, storage in the agriculture sector".

The second one registered its activities as "Manufacturing milk, processed (pasteurized, sterilized, homogenized and/or high heat) (except solid or powder milk), manufacturing of other products made from milk (butter, yogurt, ayran, cream, etc.) (including whipped cream) (except solid or powder cream), manufacturing of bakery products (including bread, pita, simit, etc., excluding the manufacturing of fresh pastry products), manufacturing of pasta, vermicelli, couscous, and similar products (including filled or frozen), livestock breeding with milking (cow and buffalo breeding for its milk), Intermediations who wholesale live animals on fees or contractual basis".

The last one registered its activities as "The actual field of activity of the company is to operate the farm established for the purpose of producing milk, where the farm animals are raised, cared for and fed.".

All three firms are listed under the "Crop And Animal Production Hunting And Related Service Activities" subsector. The IZTAR & YAPRK are listed on the BIST main market and the TACTR is listed on the watch list. All firms are registered after 2004. None of the firms have two decades in the sector. The registration dates are 08.10.2010, 30.12.2011, and 17.12.2004 consequently.

In Turkey, the agricultural structure is dominated by small family businesses based on private ownership. Therefore this projection should not lead to misspecification problems(TOBB, 2013, p. 1).

2.1 Sources of the Data Used in the Study and Restrictions

The main role of the Central Registry Agency (CRA) is to act as the central securities depository of the Turkish capital market. In this study financial ratios calculated by "Data Analysis Platform" which is a subdivision of the Central Registry Agency is one of the sources. During the study, the DAP is used to represent "Data Analysis Platform".

DAP calculates periodical financial ratios, and also average ratios from 2016 to 2021 are covered.

The data is limited due to XBRL (eXtensible Business Reporting Language) type data collection. Public Disclosure System started collecting XBRL format data in 2016. The DAP of CRA follows a similar path to the Public Disclosure Platform(KAP) calculated series.

"In a nutshell, XBRL provides a language in which reporting terms can be authoritatively defined. Those terms can then be used to uniquely represent the contents of financial statements or other kinds of compliance, performance, and business reports. XBRL lets reporting information move between organizations rapidly, accurately, and digitally."(XBRL International, 2022). Giving further information on the XBRL exceeds the purpose of this study. For the ones intending to know more about the XBRL visiting the website is offered.

Financial ratios are calculated for four periods a year for periods of 3, 6, 9, and 12 months. They are published on the 10th working day following the last date of announcement of the consolidated financial reports of the relevant period, announced by CRA within the scope of the Capital Markets Board of Turkey (CMB) regulations, on the Public Disclosure Platform. In Turkey, for interim periods consolidated financials is not a necessity for all type of firms.

In the calculations of the financial ratios, the data in the "current period" column in the financial statements published on the Public Disclosure Platform for the relevant year and period are used, and the data in the "previous period" column and retrospective adjustments are not taken into account. Also, it must be noted that retrospective adjustments are not made in financial ratios.

"Periodic Financial Ratios" is the arithmetic average of the ratios of companies that have published their financial statements for the relevant year and period.

Mathematical restrictions are implied on the financial ratio data. Companies with zero numerators or denominators are not included in the calculations. Also, outliers are not included. For this reason, the number of companies may differ in the ratios calculated for the same period.

Interim periods are not annualized at the rates where "Statement of Financial Position" and "Profit or Loss Statement" are used together. Financial ratios for each period should be evaluated on their own or compared with the rates for the same period of the previous year.

Table 11. Equations and translations of the ratios gathered from DAP

Ratio in Turkish (Original Source)	Number of Eq.	Ratio in English
Cari oran	(Equation 1)	Current ratio
Likidite oranı	(Equation 2)	Liquidity ratio
Nakit oranı	(Equation 3)	Cash ratio
Stoklar/ Dönen Varlıklar (%)_1	(Equation 4)	Inventories/Current Assets_1 (%)
Stoklar/ Dönen Varlıklar (%)_2	(Equation 5)	Inventories/Current Assets_2 (%)
Dönen varlıklar / Varlıklar(%)	(Equation 6)	Current Assets/TotalAssets (%)
Maddi Duran Varlıklar/ Varlıklar(%)	(Equation 7)	(Tangible) Fixed Assets/TotalAssets (%)
Maddi olmayan Duran Varlıklar/ Varlıklar(%)	(Equation 8)	Intangible Assets/TotalAssets (%)
Toplam Yükümlülükler/ Varlıklar(%)	(Equation 9)	"Financial Leverage Ratio\" " or Liabilities/TotalAssets (%)
Kısa Vadeli Yükümlülükler/ Varlıklar(%)	(Equation 10)	"Short-Term Liabilities"/TotalAssets (%)
Uzun Vadeli Yükümlülükler/ Varlıklar(%)	(Equation 11)	"Long-Term Liabilities"/TotalAssets (%)
Özkaynaklar / Varlıklar(%)	(Equation 12)	Equities/TotalAssets (%)
Özkaynaklar / Toplam Yükümlülükler(%)	(Equation 13)	Equities/Liabilities(%)
Stok Devir Hızı_1	(Equation 14)	Inventory Turnover Ratio_1
Stok Devir Hızı_2	(Equation 15)	Inventory Turnover Ratio_2
Ticari Alacaklar Devir Hızı	(Equation 16)	"Trade Receivable Turnover Ratio"
Özkaynak Devir Hızı	(Equation 18)	"Equity Turnover Ratio"
Aktif Devir Hızı	(Equation 17)	"Assets Turnover Ratio"
Dönem Karı (Zararı)/ Varlıklar (Aktif Karlılığı) [%)	(Equation 19)	Return on Assets(%)
Dönem Karı (Zararı)/ Özkaynaklar (Özkaynak Karlılığı) (%)	(Equation 20)	Return on Equity(%)
Net Kar Marjı(%)	(Equation 21)	Net Profit Margin (%)
Satışların Maliyeti/ Toplam Hasılat(%)	(Equation 22)	Cost of Sales/Revenues (%)
Brüt KarMarjı(%)	(Equation 23)	Gross Profit Margin (%)
Esas Faaliyet Kar Marjı(%)	(Equation 24)	Operating Profit Margin (%)
Gen.Yön.Gid. / Toplam Hasılat(%)	(Equation 25)	General and Administrative expenses/Revenues (%)
Pazarlama Gid. / Toplam Hasılat(%)	(Equation 26)	Marketing expenses/Revenues (%)
Gen.Yön+ Pazarlama+ ARGE Gid. / Toplam Hasılat(%)	(Equation 29)	(G&A+ Marketing+R&D expenses)/Revenues (%)
Gen.Yön+ Pazarlama+ ARGE Gid. / Dönem Karı (Zararı) (%)	(Equation 30)	(G&A+ Marketing+R&D expenses)/[Term profit(loss)] (%)
Finansman Gid. / Toplam Hasılat(%)	(Equation 28)	Financing expenses/Revenues (%)
Toplam Varlıklar Değişim oranı(%)	(Equation 31)	Total Assets Change Rate(%)
Toplam Yükümlülükler Değişim oranı(%)	(Equation 32)	Total Liability Change Rate(%)
Özkaynak Değişim oranı(%)	(Equation 33)	Equity Change Rate(%)
Toplam Hasılat Değişim oranı(%)	(Equation 34)	Revenue Change Rate(%)
Dönem Karı Değişim oranı(%)	(Equation 35)	Term profit Change Rate(%)

In Table 11 the Turkish English translation of sector ratios and their calculation methodology are given.

Due to the calculation methodology of DAP, only sector averages can be reached. These averages are compared to the firm-specific ratios. It must be mentioned that investment firm-based calculations may differ from the automated calculations of DAP. These differences arise from the calculation methodology. One using the ratios should consider this possible difference in mind while analyzing the sector and firms in the sector.

2.2 Sector Averages

In this section data gathered from DAP are presented.

Table 12. 2022 and 2021 ratios

	2022/1 (3 Monthly)		2021/4(Annual)		2021/3 (9 Monthly)		2021/2 (6 Monthly)		2021/1 (3 Monthly)	
	Comp.	Average	Comp.	Average	Comp.	Average	Comp.	Average	Comp.	Average
Current ratio	1	1.09	2	0.79	3	0.62	3	0.62	3	0.52
Liquidity ratio	1	0.65	2	0.35	3	0.28	3	0.27	3	0.24
Cash ratio	1	0.46	2	0.15	3	0.07	3	0.07	3	0.09
Inventories/Current Assets_1 (%)	1	15.75	2	33.99	3	37.17	3	36.70	2	33.65
Inventories/Current Assets_2 (%)	1	30.33	2	46.62	3	44.64	3	45.16	2	44.34
Current Assets/TotalAssets (%)	1	35.12	2	30.79	3	26.48	3	24.40	3	18.57
(Tangible) Fixed Assets/TotalAssets (%)	1	17.94	2	33.79	3	50.14	3	51.40	3	56.74
Intangible Assets/TotalAssets (%)	1	0.01	2	0.81	2	0.80	2	0.83	2	0.86
"Financial Leverage Ratio\" " or Liabilities/TotalAssets (%)	1	43.95	2	50.64	3	54.59	3	51.59	3	53.56
"Short-Term Liabilities"/TotalAssets (%)	1	32.14	2	41.90	3	44.39	3	41.04	3	41.56
"Long-Term Liabilities"/TotalAssets (%)	1	11.81	2	8.74	3	10.20	3	10.55	3	12.00
Equities/TotalAssets (%)	1	56.05	2	49.36	3	45.41	3	48.41	3	46.44
Equities/Liabilities(%)	1	127.54	2	100.68	3	85.06	3	94.92	3	92.38
Inventory Turnover Ratio_1	1	2.45	2	4.84	3	4.00	3	3.11	2	1.26
Inventory Turnover Ratio_2	1	1.34	2	3.27	3	3.34	3	2.65	2	0.86
"Trade Receivable Turnover Ratio"	1	3.11	2	7.76	3	4.56	3	3.31	2	2.10
"Equity Turnover Ratio"	1	0.35	2	0.96	3	0.60	3	0.41	2	0.24
"Assets Turnover Ratio"	1	0.20	2	0.50	3	0.29	3	0.20	2	0.13
Return on Assets(%)	1	12.63	2	4.80	3	-2.04	3	0.15	3	0.82
Return on Equity(%)	1	22.59	2	8.13	3	-5.83	3	0.03	3	1.23
Net Profit Margin (%)	1	64.61	2	-0.21	3	-21.23	3	-5.07	2	8.43
Cost of Sales/Revenues (%)	1	79.12	2	90.16	3	103.56	3	98.82	2	83.68
Gross Profit Margin (%)	1	89.97	2	17.74	3	-1.69	3	4.85	2	24.41
Operating Profit Margin (%)	1	85.77	2	9.37	3	-11.88	3	6.04	2	18.59
General and Administrative expenses/Revenues (%)	1	8.04	2	8.40	3	10.78	3	9.77	2	7.94
Marketing expenses/Revenues (%)			1	0.12	1	0.10	1	0.12	1	0.11
(G&A+ Marketing+R&D expenses)/Revenues (%)	1	8.04	2	8.40	3	10.81	3	9.81	2	8.00

Continued on following page

Table 12. Continued

	2022/1 (3 Monthly)		2021/4(Annual)		2021/3 (9 Monthly)		2021/2 (6 Monthly)		2021/1 (3 Monthly)	
	Comp.	Average	Comp.	Average	Comp.	Average	Comp.	Average	Comp.	Average
(G&A+ Marketing+R&D expenses)/[Term profit(loss)] (%)	1	12.45	2	-0.25	3	14.89	3	-36.04	3	-162.59
Financing expenses/Revenues (%)	1	1.43	2	7.85	3	10.41	3	9.22	2	7.62
Total Assets Change Rate(%)	1	50.85	2	17.18	2	4.24	3	5.42	2	-0.62
Total Liability Change Rate(%)	1	41.09	2	27.48	2	2.69	3	12.96	2	4.92
Equity Change Rate(%)	1	59.50	2	9.18	2	6.53	3	1.71	2	-8.92
Revenue Change Rate(%)	1	49.36	2	23.03	2	2541.72	3	1704.98	2	-33.38
Term profit Change Rate(%)	1	421.66	2	106.80	2	-814.11	3	9.12	2	-67.71

Source: Authors' own elaboration from the Data Analysis Platform(DAP)

In Table 12 latest sector ratios of 2022 are presented with the 2021 ratios.

Table 13. 2020 ratios

	2020/4(Annual)		2020/3 (9 Monthly)		2020/2 (6 Monthly)		2020/1 (3 Monthly)	
	Comp.	Average	Comp.	Average	Comp.	Average	Comp.	Average
Current ratio	3	0.59	2	0.62	3	0.65	2	0.62
Liquidity ratio	3	0.27	2	0.32	3	0.31	2	0.39
Cash ratio	3	0.08	2	0.14	3	0.14	2	0.21
Inventories/Current Assets_1 (%)	2	40.28	2	21.25	3	30.04	2	15.09
Inventories/Current Assets_2 (%)	2	49.62	2	29.46	3	37.47	2	21.59
Current Assets/TotalAssets (%)	3	21.37	2	21.90	3	20.97	2	21.68
(Tangible) Fixed Assets/TotalAssets (%)	3	54.40	2	55.57	3	54.72	2	54.50
Intangible Assets/TotalAssets (%)	2	0.86		0.00	2	0.88		0.00
"Financial Leverage Ratio\" " or Liabilities/ TotalAssets (%)	3	54.09	2	55.11	3	49.12	2	53.14
"Short-Term Liabilities"/TotalAssets (%)	3	39.96	2	37.81	3	37.17	2	40.94
"Long-Term Liabilities"/TotalAssets (%)	3	14.13	2	17.30	3	11.95	2	12.21
Equities/TotalAssets (%)	3	45.91	2	44.89	3	50.88	2	46.86
Equities/Liabilities(%)	3	92.23	2	84.59	3	109.06	2	89.96
Inventory Turnover Ratio_1	3	4.27	2	2.98	3	1.77	2	1.27
Inventory Turnover Ratio_2	3	3.54	2	2.19	3	1.30	2	0.88
"Trade Receivable Turnover Ratio"	3	5.83	2	4.87	3	2.90	2	1.53
"Equity Turnover Ratio"	3	0.62	2	0.44	3	0.26	2	0.15
"Assets Turnover Ratio"	3	0.33	2	0.24	3	0.15	2	0.08
Return on Assets(%)	3	-0.42	2	4.93	3	3.56	2	4.99
Return on Equity(%)	3	-4.09	2	9.18	3	7.65	2	11.27
Net Profit Margin (%)	3	-63.05	2	93.29	3	589.95	2	3452.62
Cost of Sales/Revenues (%)	3	94.97	2	670.51	3	327.06	2	737.06

Continued on following page

Table 13. Continued

	2020/4(Annual)		2020/3 (9 Monthly)		2020/2 (6 Monthly)		2020/1 (3 Monthly)	
	Comp.	Average	Comp.	Average	Comp.	Average	Comp.	Average
Gross Profit Margin (%)	3	12.82	2	-560.28	3	-214.35	2	-615.80
Operating Profit Margin (%)	3	-49.36	2	412.32	3	701.30	2	3408.39
General and Administrative expenses/Revenues (%)	3	31.59	2	500.50	3	46.24	2	205.51
Marketing expenses/Revenues (%)	1	0.73						
(G&A+ Marketing+R&D expenses)/Revenues (%)	3	31.83	2	500.50	3	46.24	2	205.51
(G&A+ Marketing+R&D expenses)/[Term profit(loss)] (%)	3	-19.16	2	319.84	3	-41.03	2	15.95
Financing expenses/Revenues (%)	3	24.16	2	356.71	3	174.44	2	3.52
Total Assets Change Rate(%)	3	7.48		39.27	3	5.95		35.70
Total Liability Change Rate(%)	3	16.89		66.36	3	7.19		67.21
Equity Change Rate(%)	3	-0.51		21.12	3	7.49		15.61
Revenue Change Rate(%)	3	-17.06		19.59	3	-34.83		18.24
Term profit Change Rate(%)	3	37.47		322.75	3	122.82		404.66

Source: Authors' own elaboration from the Data Analysis Platform(DAP)

In Table 13 the average of the sector ratios for 2020 are presented.

Table 14. 2019 ratios

	2019/4 (Annual)		2019/3 (9 Monthly)		2019/2 (6 Monthly)		2019/1 (3 Monthly)	
	Comp.	Average	Comp.	Average	Comp.	Average	Comp.	Average
Current ratio	3	0.61	1	0.94	3	0.73	1	1.02
Liquidity ratio	3	0.21	1	0.21	3	0.33	1	0.46
Cash ratio	3	0.01	1	0.03	3	0.11	1	0.22
Inventories/Current Assets_1 (%)	3	35.44	1	33.33	3	22.63	1	17.63
Inventories/Current Assets_2 (%)	3	42.70	1	52.43	3	32.45	1	40.22
Current Assets/TotalAssets (%)	3	20.33	1	27.10	3	23.71	1	27.30
(Tangible) Fixed Assets/TotalAssets (%)	3	53.58	1	25.40	3	52.34	1	25.21
Intangible Assets/TotalAssets (%)	3	0.61	1	0.00	3	0.61	1	0.00
"Financial Leverage Ratio\" " or Liabilities/TotalAssets (%)	3	50.47	1	40.12	3	49.95	1	38.93
"Short-Term Liabilities"/TotalAssets (%)	3	38.09	1	28.77	3	32.96	1	26.82
"Long-Term Liabilities"/TotalAssets (%)	3	12.39	1	11.35	3	16.99	1	12.11
Equities/TotalAssets (%)	3	49.53	1	59.88	3	50.05	1	61.07
Equities/Liabilities(%)	3	108.68	1	149.23	3	108.08	1	156.85
Inventory Turnover Ratio_1	3	6.62	1	4.89	3	4.43	1	2.28
Inventory Turnover Ratio_2	3	5.24	1	2.85	3	3.27	1	1.12
"Trade Receivable Turnover Ratio"	3	6.50	1	9.58	3	3.38	1	3.03
"Equity Turnover Ratio"	3	0.70	1	0.84	3	0.35	1	0.28
"Assets Turnover Ratio"	3	0.38	1	0.51	3	0.19	1	0.18

Continued on following page

Table 14. Continued

	2019/4 (Annual)		2019/3 (9 Monthly)		2019/2 (6 Monthly)		2019/1 (3 Monthly)	
	Comp.	Average	Comp.	Average	Comp.	Average	Comp.	Average
Return on Assets(%)	3	-5.76	1	2.88	3	-3.35	1	1.30
Return on Equity(%)	3	-15.13	1	4.71	3	-8.82	1	2.10
Net Profit Margin (%)	3	-54.93	1	5.61	3	-59.93	1	7.37
Cost of Sales/Revenues (%)	3	128.34	1	81.14	3	129.16	1	82.46
Gross Profit Margin (%)	3	-22.57	1	24.19	3	-23.28	1	26.54
Operating Profit Margin (%)	3	-55.48	1	19.52	3	-34.78	1	24.31
General and Administrative expenses/Revenues (%)	3	7.65	1	9.91	3	8.55	1	9.02
Marketing expenses/Revenues (%)	1	1.12			2	0.31		
(G&A+ Marketing+R&D expenses)/Revenues (%)	3	8.02	1	9.91	3	8.75	1	9.02
(G&A+ Marketing+R&D expenses)/[Term profit(loss)] (%)	3	27.91	1	176.64	3	-32.60	1	122.41
Financing expenses/Revenues (%)	3	6.66	1	0.97	3	15.74	1	0.84
Total Assets Change Rate(%)	3	16.98	1	5.32	3	15.77	1	8.37
Total Liability Change Rate(%)	3	16.52	1	4.66	3	16.12	1	16.25
Equity Change Rate(%)	3	19.61	1	5.77	3	17.54	1	3.88
Revenue Change Rate(%)	3	2.22	1	24.73	3	-8.61	1	29.90
Term profit Change Rate(%)	3	-81.01	1	-48.78	3	-444.70	1	-71.77

Source: Authors' own elaboration from the Data Analysis Platform(DAP)

In Table 14 the average of the sector ratios for 2019 are presented.

Table 15. 2018 ratios

	2018/4 (Annual)		2018/3 (9 Monthly)		2018/2 (6 Monthly)		2018/1 (3 Monthly)	
	Comp.	Average	Comp.	Average	Comp.	Average	Comp.	Average
Current ratio	3	0.68	1	1.07	3	0.81	1	1.21
Liquidity ratio	3	0.22	1	0.41	3	0.34	1	0.46
Cash ratio	3	0.03	1	0.26	3	0.14	1	0.23
Inventories/Current Assets_1 (%)	3	29.35	1	23.60	3	34.86	1	17.32
Inventories/Current Assets_2 (%)	3	42.52	1	46.13	3	44.77	1	42.03
Current Assets/TotalAssets (%)	3	22.86	1	29.10	3	25.18	1	26.04
(Tangible) Fixed Assets/TotalAssets (%)	3	47.15	1	26.10	3	46.32	1	26.79
Intangible Assets/TotalAssets (%)	3	0.90	1	0.01	3	0.92	1	0.02
"Financial Leverage Ratio\" " or Liabilities/TotalAssets (%)	3	49.20	1	40.38	3	48.00	1	36.29
"Short-Term Liabilities"/TotalAssets (%)	3	37.13	1	27.21	3	32.81	1	21.54
"Long-Term Liabilities"/TotalAssets (%)	3	12.07	1	13.17	3	15.19	1	14.75
Equities/TotalAssets (%)	3	50.80	1	59.62	3	52.00	1	63.71
Equities/Liabilities(%)	3	110.12	1	147.65	3	111.98	1	175.52
Inventory Turnover Ratio_1	3	4.05	1	5.13	3	1.93	1	1.96
Inventory Turnover Ratio_2	3	2.77	1	2.73	3	1.28	1	0.96
"Trade Receivable Turnover Ratio"	3	8.23	1	10.29	3	4.59	1	3.12

Continued on following page

Table 15. Continued

	2018/4 (Annual)		2018/3 (9 Monthly)		2018/2 (6 Monthly)		2018/1 (3 Monthly)	
	Comp.	Average	Comp.	Average	Comp.	Average	Comp.	Average
"Equity Turnover Ratio"	3	0.73	1	0.73	3	0.40	1	0.23
"Assets Turnover Ratio"	3	0.39	1	0.44	3	0.22	1	0.15
Return on Assets(%)	3	0.87	1	6.01	3	3.71	1	4.98
Return on Equity(%)	3	0.72	1	9.91	3	6.63	1	7.94
Net Profit Margin (%)	3	-9.26	1	13.67	3	15.26	1	33.90
Cost of Sales/Revenues (%)	3	85.73	1	83.28	3	67.16	1	79.41
Gross Profit Margin (%)	3	21.51	1	35.23	3	42.11	1	70.69
Operating Profit Margin (%)	3	2.98	1	31.57	3	28.57	1	65.73
General and Administrative expenses/Revenues (%)	3	9.08	1	10.18	3	8.31	1	9.42
Marketing expenses/Revenues (%)	2	1.53	1		2	1.26		
(G&A+ Marketing+R&D expenses)/Revenues (%)	3	10.10	1	10.18	3	9.15	1	9.42
(G&A+ Marketing+R&D expenses)/[Term profit(loss)] (%)	3	93.72	1	74.50	3	67.72	1	27.78
Financing expenses/Revenues (%)	3	12.61	1	1.31	3	11.08	1	1.28
Total Assets Change Rate(%)	3	6.16	1	12.53	3	12.86	1	10.87
Total Liability Change Rate(%)	3	11.63	1	17.23	3	15.18	1	11.90
Equity Change Rate(%)	3	0.34	1	9.56	3	14.96	1	10.29
Revenue Change Rate(%)	3	28.20	1	27.27	3	40.36	1	25.24
Term profit Change Rate(%)	3	-810.00	1	45.35	3	-141.50	1	45.34

Source: Authors' own elaboration from the Data Analysis Platform(DAP)

In Table 15 the average of the sector ratios for 2018 are presented.

Table 16. 2017 ratios

	2017/4 (Annual)		2017/3 (9 Monthly)		2017/2 (6 Monthly)		2017/1 (3 Monthly)	
	Comp.	Average	Comp.	Average	Comp.	Average	Comp.	Average
Current ratio	3	0.75	1	1.11	3	0.76	1	1.38
Liquidity ratio	3	0.26	1	0.29	3	0.30	1	0.41
Cash ratio	3	0.09	1	0.13	3	0.09	1	0.17
Inventories/Current Assets_1 (%)	3	42.56	1	23.26	3	29.84	1	17.42
Inventories/Current Assets_2 (%)	3	53.68	1	47.51	3	44.94	1	45.37
Current Assets/TotalAssets (%)	3	23.25	1	27.85	3	22.14	1	27.05
(Tangible) Fixed Assets/TotalAssets (%)	3	50.80	1	28.30	3	50.65	1	29.48
Intangible Assets/TotalAssets (%)	3	1.03	1	0.03	3	1.07	1	0.04
"Financial Leverage Ratio\" " or Liabilities/TotalAssets (%)	3	46.40	1	38.76	3	48.29	1	35.96
"Short-Term Liabilities"/TotalAssets (%)	3	32.23	1	25.05	3	33.38	1	19.59
"Long-Term Liabilities"/TotalAssets (%)	3	14.17	1	13.71	3	14.91	1	16.37
Equities/TotalAssets (%)	3	53.60	1	61.24	3	51.71	1	64.04
Equities/Liabilities(%)	3	119.25	1	157.98	3	115.77	1	178.09
Inventory Turnover Ratio_1	3	3.95	1	5.16	3	2.76	1	1.83

Continued on following page

Table 16. Continued

	2017/4 (Annual)		2017/3 (9 Monthly)		2017/2 (6 Monthly)		2017/1 (3 Monthly)	
	Comp.	Average	Comp.	Average	Comp.	Average	Comp.	Average
Inventory Turnover Ratio_2	3	2.80	1	2.64	3	1.79	1	0.84
"Trade Receivable Turnover Ratio"	3	8.23	1	9.55	3	5.42	1	3.20
"Equity Turnover Ratio"	3	0.61	1	0.62	3	0.32	1	0.20
"Assets Turnover Ratio"	3	0.34	1	0.38	3	0.18	1	0.13
Return on Assets(%)	3	1.67	1	4.59	3	0.40	1	3.77
Return on Equity(%)	3	2.72	1	7.43	3	0.15	1	5.96
Net Profit Margin (%)	3	3.43	1	11.97	3	-3. 51	1	29.21
Cost of Sales/Revenues (%)	3	84.27	1	88.36	3	88.20	1	80.27
Gross Profit Margin (%)	3	24.65	1	39.96	3	18.56	1	61.24
Operating Profit Margin (%)	3	24.79	1	34.14	3	8.98	1	55.78
General and Administrative expenses/Revenues (%)	3	11.30	1	11.36	3	10.84	1	11.60
Marketing expenses/Revenues (%)	1	1.30			1	1.18		
(G&A+ Marketing+R&D expenses)/Revenues (%)	3	11.73	1	11.36	3	11.23	1	11.60
(G&A+ Marketing+R&D expenses)/[Term profit(loss)] (%)	3	2680.70	1	94.94	3	-66.32	1	39.71
Financing expenses/Revenues (%)	3	13.90	1	1.87	3	9.49	1	2.52
Total Assets Change Rate(%)	3	5.58	1	15.53	3	2.72		
Total Liability Change Rate(%)	3	4.44	1	24.50	3	11.45		
Equity Change Rate(%)	3	10.45	1	10.49	3	-4.01		
Revenue Change Rate(%)	3	1.22	1	45.44	3	4.47		
Term profit Change Rate(%)	3	-53.49	1	142.92	3	-103.70		

Source: Authors' own elaboration from the Data Analysis Platform(DAP)

In Table 16 the average of the sector ratios for 2017 are presented.

Table 17. 2016 ratios

	2016/4 (Annual)		2016/3 (9 Monthly)		2016/2 (6 Monthly)	
	Comp.	Average	Comp.	Average	Comp.	Average
Current ratio	3	0.72	1	1.31	3	0.92
Liquidity ratio	3	0.27	1	0.33	3	0.31
Cash ratio	3	0.08	1	0.18	3	0.13
Inventories/Current Assets_1 (%)	3	24.00	1	27.84	3	19.46
Inventories/Current Assets_2 (%)	3	32.89	1	47.46	3	33.11
Current Assets/TotalAssets (%)	3	20.46	1	26.78	3	22.11
(Tangible) Fixed Assets/TotalAssets (%)	3	53.47	1	32.29	3	51.22
Intangible Assets/TotalAssets (%)	3	1.14	1	0.06	3	1.12
"Financial Leverage Ratio\" " or Liabilities/TotalAssets (%)	3	48.08	1	35.97	3	44.72
"Short-Term Liabilities"/TotalAssets (%)	3	32.09	1	20.50	3	27.10
"Long-Term Liabilities"/TotalAssets (%)	3	15.99	1	15.47	3	17.62
Equities/TotalAssets (%)	3	51.92	1	64.03	3	55.28
Equities/Liabilities(%)	3	115.79	1	178.02	3	134.39

Continued on following page

Table 17. Continued

	2016/4 (Annual)		2016/3 (9 Monthly)		2016/2 (6 Monthly)	
	Comp.	**Average**	**Comp.**	**Average**	**Comp.**	**Average**
Inventory Turnover Ratio_1	3	8.45	1	3.66	3	8.34
Inventory Turnover Ratio_2	3	7.00	1	2.08	3	3.37
"Trade Receivable Turnover Ratio"	3	12.08	1	9.75	3	4.87
"Equity Turnover Ratio"	3	0.86	1	0.46	3	0.41
"Assets Turnover Ratio"	3	0.47	1	0.31	3	0.23
Return on Assets(%)	3	-3.64	1	2.19	3	0.35
Return on Equity(%)	3	-8.58	1	3.31	3	-0.25
Net Profit Margin (%)	3	-18.94	1	7.17	3	-6.70
Cost of Sales/Revenues (%)	3	96.95	1	84.61	3	88.33
Gross Profit Margin (%)	3	12.11	1	36.07	3	19.76
Operating Profit Margin (%)	3	-3.95	1	27.46	3	4.33
General and Administrative expenses/Revenues (%)	3	13.40	1	14.72	3	12.75
Marketing expenses/Revenues (%)						
(G&A+ Marketing+R&D expenses)/Revenues (%)	3	13.40	1	14.72	3	12.75
(G&A+ Marketing+R&D expenses)/[Term profit(loss)] (%)	3	-12.78	1	205.42	3	149.88
Financing expenses/Revenues (%)	3	12.51	1	1.66	3	9.54
Total Assets Change Rate(%)						
Total Liability Change Rate(%)						
Equity Change Rate(%)						
Revenue Change Rate(%)						
Term profit Change Rate(%)						

Source: Authors' own elaboration from the Data Analysis Platform(DAP)

In Table 17 the average of the sector ratios for 2016 are presented.

It is known that international financial reporting standards are followed throughout the preparation of DAP-based ratios. This is the strength of the system. The weakness of the system are the lack of multilingual presentation and metadata formation. According to the author, the most important points to be developed are these weaknesses.

3. DISCUSSION

Automated calculations of the interpreted ratios are given in tables 12 to 17. These calculations represent sector averages. And the number of companies given for the related period explains how many firms were used to calculate the sector average for the related ratio.

DAP gives an insight into the situation of the sector. By using the traditional comparison methodology, one may decide whether the company is performing well or bad. At this stage, the DAP platform does not assist users at this comparison point. Even it does not provide initial calculations for the firms. One may only list the historical changes in the selected ratio.

As averages are calculated by using companies listed under a sector list, some companies will perform better, and some will perform worse. The DAP listings would be extended to show how companies are performing relative to the sector. This automated comparison may assist investors in their decisions.

The companies listed under a sector sometimes do not fall into the same market indices. This is an important point to be considered. To clarify the point, the difference between the BIST main market and Watch List is given as follows: Based on the Listing Directive of Borsa İstanbul, equities of the corporations will be traded in Watchlist in the presence of certain conditions that will result in exclusion from BIST Stars, Main or SubMarket. The conditions for being quoted in the BIST main market are specified as well as the Watch List. Companies with a market capitalization of shares in an actual free float from 75 to 300 million TL are listed on BIST Main market. The companies on the Watch List are riskier than the main market. The firms on the Watch List are closer to bankruptcy than the ones in the BIST main market. But one must not conclude that if a firm is listed on the watch list that will go through the concordat process of declaring bankruptcy.

There are alternative ways to avoid bankruptcy and concordat. Also, there are choices between bankruptcy procedures, liquidation, and restructuring. These are risk exposures of running a business.

Sources of failed business may be listed as, risk management failures, misleading financial statements, not accepting professional management procedures into business activities, cash management issues, writing losses, and not operating profitably. Also not following ethical codes, in business activities can be listed as the main reason for failed business activities.

Altman's Z-score is a historical prediction model for bankruptcy and these automated calculations may be altered to show these calculations.

Automated calculations and early deviation signals from sector averages may be an appropriate way to foresee coming bankruptcy processes. The DAP is a useful tool to investigate a sector as a whole but it is not enough to decide whether a firm failure is close or not. Given thirty-five equations on the financials of companies are powerful tools but not enough to decide.

Investment firms follow different ratios while conducting score cards. The DAP may be developed and extended in a way that will cover the multipliers, financials, and other measures that are followed by investment firms.

The DAP average calculations differ between periods. Although there are more firms in the sector the ratios are calculated using fewer of them. The reason for these limited calculations is sometimes timing problems. Financial statements should be structured to reflect user needs and they must be reliable. Quarterly financials of all firms may lack independent audit processes. Computers may miss this important point.

One of the main contributions of this study is presenting the calculation methodology of DAP ratios to international investors. Equation 27 cannot be observed among the ratios presented in the study. The main reason for this is the lack of research and development facilities in the agriculture, forestry, and fishing sector of Turkey. We should remember why to invest in Turkey notes. With an appropriate R&D strategy, there is great potential.

The power of the Turkish agro-food industry may be misleading to potential investors due to its presentation according to the NACE codes. This part includes the exploitation of vegetable and animal resources, which consists of the activities of growing crops, raising and feeding animals, felling and logging timber, and extracting plants, animals or products of animal origin from a farm or their natural habitat. Companies listed on Turkish stock markets may either be listed under manufacturing firms.

Macroeconomic and policy assumptions must be kept in mind during the investment decision-making processes in the sector. Policies play a key role in the agri-food industry worldwide. The effects of these policies cannot be observed by just looking at the financial statements.

REFERENCES

Brealey, R. A., Myers, S. C., & Marcus, A. J. (2007). *Fundamentals of corporate finance* (5th ed.). McGraw-Hill Irwin.

Çelik, N. (2000). *Tarımda Girdi Kullanımı ve Verimliliğe Etkileri* [Input Use in Agriculture and Its Effects on Productivity]. Devlet Planlama Teşkilatı (DPT). Retrieved from https://www.sbb.gov.tr/wp-content/uploads/2018/11/NebiCelik.pdf

European Environment Agency. (2017). *EEA Report No 10/2017 - Landscapes in transition - An account of 25 years of land cover change in Europe*. Retrieved from https://www.eea.europa.eu/publications/landscapes-in-transition

Gümüş, U. T., Şakar, Z., Akkın, G., & Şahin, M. (2017). Finansal Analizde Kullanılan Oranlar ve Firma Değer İlişkisi: BİST'de İşlem Gören Çimento Firmaları Üzerine Bir Analiz [Ratios Used in Financial Analysis and Firm Value Relationship: An Analysis on Cement Companies Traded in BIST]. *Karadeniz Sosyal Bilimler Dergisi, 9*(16), 1–23. Retrieved from https://dergipark.org.tr/en/pub/ksbd/issue/31387/344614

Halk Yatırım. (2022). *Skor Kart* [Shoes Map]; Retrieved May 27, 2022, from https://analizim.halkyatirim.com.tr/Financial/ScoreCardDetail

Kamuyu Aydınlatma Platformu (KAP). (2022). *KAP Sectors*. Retrieved May 28, 2022, from https://www.kap.org.tr/en/Sektorler

Kanat, E. (2019). Gri İlişkisel Analiz Yöntemiyle Kamu ve Özel Bankaların Performanslarının Karşılaştırılması [Comparison of Performance of Public and Private Banks with Gray Relational Analysis Method]. *Akademik Sosyal Araştırmalar Dergisi, 7*(96), 135–146.

Keown, A., Martin, J., & Petty, W. (2020). *Foundations of Finance - The logic and Practice of Financial Management* (10th ed.). Pearson Education, Inc.

Leland, H. E., & Pyle, D. H. (1977). Informational Asymmetries, Financial Structure, and Financial Intermediation. *The Journal of Finance*, *32*(2), 371. doi:10.2307/2326770

Merkezi Kayıt Istanbul. (2022). *Finansal Oran Hesaplama Kuralları* [Financial Ratio Calculation Rules]. Retrieved from https://www.vap.org.tr/sites/default/files/2022-01/finansal_oran_hesaplama_kurallari_ocak_2022.pdf

OECD and Food and Agriculture Organization of the United Nations. (2017). *OECD-FAO Agricultural Outlook 2017-2026* (OECD-FAO Agricultural Outlook). OECD. doi:10.1787/AGR_OUTLOOK-2017-EN

OECD and Food and Agriculture Organization of the United Nations. (2021). *OECD-FAO Agricultural Outlook 2021-2030* (OECD-FAO Agricultural Outlook). OECD. doi:10.1787/19428846-EN

Özden, C., & Gürgen, Y. (2008). Türkiye Ve Avrupa Birliğinde Süt Hayvancılığının Mevcut Durumu İle Avrupa Birliği Üyelik Sürecinin Polonya Hayvancılığına Olan Etkilerinin İncelenmesi [Examination of the Current Status of Dairy Livestock in Turkey and the European Union and the Effects of the European Union Membership Process on Polish Livestock]. *Çukurova Üniversitesi Fen Bilimleri Enstitüsü - Fen Ve Mühendislik Bilimleri Dergisi, 17*(8), 68–78. Retrieved from https://fbe.cu.edu.tr/storage/fbeyedek/makaleler/2008-17-8-8.pdf

Presidency of the Republic of Turkey. (2021). *Why Invest in Turkish Agro-food Industry?* Retrieved from https://www.invest.gov.tr/tr/library/publications/lists/investpublications/tarim-gida-sektoru-raporu.pdf

Presidency of the Republic of Türkiye. (2022). *Why Invest in Türkiye*. Retrieved from https://www.invest.gov.tr/tr/library/publications/lists/investpublications/neden-turkiyeye-yatirim-yapmali.pdf

TCMB. (2022). *Oran Formülleri*. Retrieved June 9, 2022, from https://www3.tcmb.gov.tr/sektor/dosyalar/menu/ratios_tr.pdf

TOBB. (2013). *Türkiye Tarım Sektörü Raporu* [Turkey Agricultural Sector Report]. TOBB.

XBRL International. (2022). *An Introduction to XBRL*. Retrieved May 29, 2022, from https://www.xbrl.org/the-standard/what/an-introduction-to-xbrl/

Yenisu, E. (2019). Finansal Tabloların Oran Analizi İle İncelenmesi: ADESE Örneği [Finansal Tabloların Oran Analizi İle İncelenmesi: ADESE Örneği]. *Aksaray Üniversitesi Sosyal Bilimler Enstitüsü Dergisi, 3*(1), 19–45. doi:10.38122/ased.537634

KEY TERMS AND DEFINITIONS

Data Analysis Platform (DAP): The platform which was established under the Central Registry Agency of İstanbul. A wide range of data and statistics on Turkey's markets are presented. Just to name a few, storage data, investor statistics, corporate governance data, indices, financial ratios, and academic studies are listed.

MAKFED: Basically, it refers to the Turkish Machinery Federation, which works to achieve the three objectives listed. 1-To contribute to the progress and development of the Turkish Machinery Manufacturing Sector together with other sub-sectors, 2-Strengthening the sector in global competition by developing together with its sub-industry, 3-The formation of all sectoral policies and practices related to the Machinery Industry.

ODD: It refers to the Automotive Distributors Association, which works to ensure the continuity and development of the sector by increasing the ownership of land vehicles in Turkey.

OSD: An institution operating with the mission of creating policies, informing and directing relevant institutions in this direction, and taking part in policy implementation in order to increase national and international competitiveness in line with the common interests of the automotive industry in Turkey.

SASAD: Defense Industry Manufacturers Association was established in Ankara in 1990 with the suggestion and support of the Ministry of National Defense. At the beginning of 2012, manufacturers in the field of civil aviation and space were also included in the working area of the association and the name of the association was changed to Defense and Aviation Industry Manufacturers Association.

SHGM: It refers to the General Directorate of Civil Aviation, which organizes and supervises the civil aviation sector, continues its activities with the mission of "Ensuring the Reliability and Sustainable Development of Turkish Civil Aviation" and the vision of "Having a Strong, Autonomous and Participatory Institutional Structure in the Field of Civil Aviation, an Effective and Reputable Position at the Global Level".

TESID: TESID is the abbreviation of the Turkish Electronics Industrialists Association that brings together business people from the Public, Electronics Industry, Information Technologies, and related service sectors in Turkey. It is the meeting point of the Electronic Industry.

APPENDIX

The ratios are translated from Turkish calculations. Original source is Merkezi Kayıt Istanbul, (2022).

$$Current\ Ratio = \frac{Current\ Assets}{"Short\text{-}Term\ Liabilities"} \tag{1}$$

$$Liquidity\ Ratio = \frac{\left(\begin{array}{l} Cash\ and\ Cash\ Equivalents + Cash\ Accounts\ Opened\ within\ the\ Scope\ of \\ Real\ Estate\ Projects + Financial\ Investments + Financial\ Assets\ Given \\ as\ Collateral + Trade\ Receivables + Receivables\ from\ Financial\ Sector \\ Activities + "Freely\ Available\ Collaterals\ Non\text{-}Cash" + CBRT\ Account \\ +Derivative\ Instruments + Financial\ Assets\ Related\ to\ Concession \\ Agreements + Natural\ Assets + Other\ Receivables\ from\ Customer \\ Agreements"\ Short\text{-}Term\ Liabilities" \end{array}\right)}{Short\text{-}Term\ Liabilities} \tag{2}$$

$$Cash\ Ratio = \frac{\begin{array}{l}(Cash\ and\ Cash\ Equivalents + Cash\ Accounts\ Opened\ within\ the \\ Scope\ of\ Real\ Estate\ Projects + Financial\ Investments\end{array}}{Short\text{-}Term\ Liabilities} \tag{3}$$

$$Inventories\ /\ Current\ Assets\_1(\%) = 100 * \frac{"Short\text{-}Term\ Inventories"}{Current\ Assets} \tag{4}$$

$$Inventories\ /\ Current\ Assets\_2(\%) = 100 * \frac{\begin{array}{l}"Short\text{-}Term\ Inventories" \\ +"Short\text{-}Term\ Live\ Assets" \\ +"Short\text{-}Term\ Project\ Holdings"\end{array}}{Current\ Assets} \tag{5}$$

$$Current\ Assets\ /\ Total\ Assets(\%) = 100 * \frac{Current\ Assets}{Total\ Assets} \tag{6}$$

$$\left(Tangible\right) Fixed\ Assets\ /\ Total\ Assets\left(\%\right) = 100 * \frac{\left(Tangible\right) Fixed\ Assets}{Total\ Assets} \tag{7}$$

$$Intangible\ Assets\ /\ Total\ Assets\left(\%\right) = 100 * \frac{Intangible\ Assets}{Total\ Assets} \tag{8}$$

$$"Financial\ Leverage\ Ratio"\ or\ Liabilities\ /\ Total\ Assets\left(\%\right) = 100 * \frac{Liabilities}{Total\ Assets} \tag{9}$$

$$"Short\text{-}Term\ Liabilities"/\ Total\ Assets\left(\%\right) = 100 * \frac{"Short\text{-}Term\ Liabilities"}{Total\ Assets} \tag{10}$$

$$"Long\text{-}Term\ Liabilities"/\ Total\ Assets\left(\%\right) = 100 * \frac{"Long\text{-}Term\ Liabilities"}{Total\ Assets} \tag{11}$$

$$Equities\ /\ Total\ Assets\left(\%\right) = 100 * \frac{Equities}{Total\ Assets} \tag{12}$$

$$Equities\ /\ Liabilities\left(\%\right) = 100 * \frac{Equities}{Total\ Liabilities} \tag{13}$$

$$Inventory\ Turnover\ Ratio\_1 = \frac{Cost\ of\ Goods\ Sold}{\left[\left(Inventories\right)_{Beginning\ of\ Term} + \left(Inventories\right)_{End\ of\ Term}\right] / 2} \tag{14}$$

$$Inventory\ Turnover\ Ratio\_2 = \frac{Cost\ of\ Goods\ Sold}{\left[\begin{array}{l}\left(\begin{array}{l}"Inventories" + "Live\ Assets"\\ + "Project\ Holdings"\end{array}\right)_{Beginning\ of\ Term}\\ + \left(\begin{array}{l}"Inventories" + "Live\ Assets"\\ + "Project\ Holdings"\end{array}\right)_{End\ of\ Term}\end{array}\right] / 2} \quad (15)$$

$$"Trade\ Receivable\ Turnover\ Ratio" = \frac{Revenues}{\left[\begin{array}{l}\left("Short\text{-}Term\ Trade\ Receivables"\right)_{Beginning\ of\ Term}\\ + \left("Short\text{-}Term\ Trade\ Receivables"\right)_{End\ of\ Term}\end{array}\right] / 2} \quad (16)$$

$$"Assets\ Turnover\ Ratio" = \frac{\left(Revenues + Financial\ Sector\ Activity\ Revenues\right)}{\begin{array}{c}[\left("Total\ Assets"\right)_{Beginning\ of\ Term}\\ + \left("Total\ Assets"\right)_{End\ of\ Term}] / 2\end{array}} \quad (17)$$

$$"Equity\ Turnover\ Ratio" = \frac{\left(Revenues + Revenues\ from\ Financial\ Sector\ Activities\right)}{\left[\begin{array}{l}\left("Total\ Equity"\right)_{Beginning\ of\ Term}\\ + \left("Total\ Equity"\right)_{End\ of\ Term}\end{array}\right] / 2} \quad (18)$$

$$Return\ on\ Assets\left(\%\right) = \frac{Term\ profit\left(loss\right)}{\left[\left("Total\ Assets"\right)_{Beginning\ of\ Term} + \left("Total\ Assets"\right)_{End\ of\ Term}\right] / 2} \quad (19)$$

$$Return\ on\ Equity\left(\%\right) = \frac{Term\ profit\left(loss\right)}{\left[\left(Equity\right)_{Beginning\ of\ Term} + \left(Equity\right)_{End\ of\ Term}\right] / 2} \quad (20)$$

$$Net\ Profit\ Margin\left(\%\right) = 100 * \frac{Term\ profit\left(loss\right)}{\left[Revenue + Finance\ Sector\ Activity\ Revenue\right]} \tag{21}$$

$$Cost\ of\ Sales\ /\ Revenues\left(\%\right) = 100 * \frac{\left[Cost\ of\ Sales + Cost\ of\ Financial\ Sector\ Activities\right]}{\left[Revenue + Finance\ Sector\ Activity\ Revenue\right]} \tag{22}$$

$$Gross\ Profit\ Margin\left(\%\right) = 100 * \frac{Gross\ profit\left(loss\right)}{\left[Revenue + Finance\ Sector\ Activity\ Revenue\right]} \tag{23}$$

$$Operating\ Profit\ Margin\left(\%\right) = 100 * \frac{Operating\ profit\left(loss\right)}{\left[Revenue + Finance\ Sector\ Activity\ Revenue\right]} \tag{24}$$

$$General\ and\ Administrative\ expenses\ /\ Revenues\left(\%\right) = 100 * \frac{General\ and\ Administrative\ expenses}{\left[Revenue + Finance\ Sector\ Activity\ Revenue\right]} \tag{25}$$

$$Marketing\ expenses\ /\ Revenues\left(\%\right) = 100 * \frac{Marketing\ expenses}{\left[Revenue + Finance\ Sector\ Activity\ Revenue\right]} \tag{26}$$

$$"R\&D"\ expenses\ /\ Revenues\left(\%\right) = 100 * \frac{"R\&D"\ expenses}{\left[Revenue + Finance\ Sector\ Activity\ Revenue\right]} \tag{27}$$

$$Financing\ expenses\ /\ Revenues\left(\%\right) = 100 * \frac{Financing\ expenses}{\left[Revenue + Finance\ Sector\ Activity\ Revenue\right]} \tag{28}$$

$$\left(G\&A + Marketing + R\&D\,expenses\right) / \,Revenues\left(\%\right) = 100 * \frac{\begin{pmatrix} G\&A + Marketing \\ +R\&D\,expenses \end{pmatrix}}{\begin{bmatrix} Revenue + Finance\,Sector \\ Activity\,Revenue \end{bmatrix}} \tag{29}$$

$$\left(G\&A + Marketing + R\&D\,expenses\right) / \left[Term\,profit\left(loss\right)\right]\left(\%\right) = 100 * \frac{\begin{pmatrix} G\&A + Marketing \\ +R\&D\,expenses \end{pmatrix}}{Term\,profit\left(loss\right)} \tag{30}$$

$$Total\,Assets\,Change\,Rate\left(\%\right) = 100 * \frac{\begin{bmatrix} \left(Total\,Assets\right)_{Current\,Period} \\ -\left(Total\,Assets\right)_{Same\,Period\,Previous\,Year} \end{bmatrix}}{\left(Total\,Assets\right)_{Same\,Period\,Previous\,Year}} \tag{31}$$

$$Total\,Liability\,Change\,Rate\left(\%\right) = 100 * \frac{\begin{bmatrix} \left(Total\,Liability\right)_{Current\,Period} \\ -\left(Total\,Liability\right)_{Same\,Period\,Previous\,Year} \end{bmatrix}}{\left(Total\,Liability\right)_{Same\,Period\,Previous\,Year}} \tag{32}$$

$$Equity\,Change\,Rate\left(\%\right) = 100 * \frac{\left[\left(Equity\right)_{Current\,Period} - \left(Equity\right)_{Same\,Period\,Previous\,Year}\right]}{\left(Equity\right)_{Same\,Period\,Previous\,Year}} \tag{33}$$

$$Revenue\ Change\ Rate(\%) = 100 * \frac{\left[\begin{pmatrix} Revenue \\ +Finance\ Sector\ Activity\ Revenue \end{pmatrix}_{Current\ Period} - \begin{pmatrix} Revenue \\ +Finance\ Sector\ Activity\ Revenue \end{pmatrix}_{Same\ Period\ Previous\ Year}\right]}{\begin{pmatrix} Revenue \\ +Finance\ Sector\ Activity\ Revenue \end{pmatrix}_{Same\ Period\ Previous\ Year}} \quad (34)$$

$$Term\ profit\ Change\ Rate(\%) = 100 * \frac{\left[(Term\ profit)_{Current\ Period} - (Term\ profit)_{Same\ Period\ Previous\ Year}\right]}{(Term\ profit)_{Same\ Period\ Previous\ Year}} \quad (35)$$

Chapter 9
The Effect of External Factors on Financially Distressed Companies:
An Analysis on Borsa Instanbul

Aslihan Yetim
https://orcid.org/0000-0003-0996-0035
Atatürk Üniversitesi, Turkey

Bekir Elmas
Atatürk Üniversitesi, Turkey

ABSTRACT

The aim of this study is to examine the causality relationship between external factors and financial risk situations of companies experiencing financial distress among companies traded on Borsa Istanbul. In the study covering the periods of 2016-2021, financial ratios measuring liquidity risk and capital structure risk were used from the financial statements for 20 periods. In addition, 20-period data in quarterly periods were utilized for inflation, interest rates, and exchange rates as external factors. In the study where Toda Yamamoto causality test was used as a method, the relationship between the financial risks of the companies subject to the application and the situations affected by external factors was analyzed. As a result of the study, it has been determined that the most encountered causal relationship is from foreign exchange to liquidity and CPI to leverage, while the least encountered causal relationship is from CPI to liquidity and interest to leverage.

INTRODUCTION

To date, many studies have been carried out to predict the state of financial distress or to determine the micro factors causing financial distress based on the micro information of companies. However, macroeconomic conditions and the financial situation of the country can cause companies to experience

DOI: 10.4018/978-1-6684-5181-6.ch009

financial distress. In order to develop restructuring strategies in bankrupt companies, managers need to have a good understanding of micro factors and financial performance, as well as macroeconomic conditions within the company, and develop strategies accordingly. In addition, the relationship between the internal factors and external factors of the companies should be evaluated well. Therefore, it is important for financial analysts to make their evaluations by considering macro conditions. In a period when the economy is in its normal course, micro factors, financial performance, or profitability of companies may appear to be in good condition. However, economic stagnation and fluctuations in macroeconomic factors can expose companies to undesirable consequences. The exchange rate fluctuations in the Turkish economy in recent years, the increases in inflation, and the rise in interest rates have negatively affected the general economy as well as companies, which are an important part of the economy.

When long-term planning is not carried out effectively in companies, the probability of financial distress or financial failure increases (Ross et al., 2002, p. 95). The concepts of financial failure or financial distress are more flexible concepts than bankruptcy, and enable the scope of the research to be broadened. Bankruptcy is the process that begins with financial distress and ends with applying to the court. There is no certainty that every company that is experiencing financial distress will go into bankruptcy. In various studies, the concepts of financial distress, financial failure, or bankruptcy are defined as the inability of the company to pay its debts to the creditors, the writing of a blank check, the appointment of a trustee to the company, and the loss of the company for three consecutive years (Aktaş, 1997, pp. 5-6). The fact that financial difficulties have begun in a company foreshadows that bankruptcy may occur for the company (Ross et al., 2002, p.371).

In the studies included in the literature, situations such as the company's negative net working capital, inability to pay its debt to creditors, and default of its bonds are described as financial distress or financial distress indicators (Karels and Arun, 1987, p. 575). The fact that the liabilities of a company exceed its total assets, that is, its equity has reached a negative value, means that the company has become bankrupt (İçerli and Akkaya, 2006, p. 414).

The causes that lead companies to financial distress can occur at every stage of company activities. It is possible to divide these causes into two, as causes originating from within the company or causes originating from outside the company. Internal causes are usually those caused by managers. The reason for the emergence of financial difficulties within the company is the insufficient capital of the company and the excessive short-term borrowing of the company. On the other hand, external causes are: the negative effects on the long-term borrowings of companies as a result of the continuous increase in interest rates and inflation, and the decrease in demand as a result of the increase in prices, the fluctuations in exchange rates causing foreign raw materials or goods to become expensive, changes in import and export policies, natural disasters, wars, and changes in the world market (Uzun, 2005, pp. 160-163).

The increase in interest rates has a negative effect on the decrease in disposable income and causes companies to borrow at higher borrowing costs. In the opposite case, disposable income is positively affected and the growth potential of companies increases (Gögül and Yaman, 2020, p. 263). In a country where the exchange rate risk is high due to fluctuations in exchange rates and the currency is destabilized, the possibility of profit or loss for companies in all sectors is revealed. The losses incurred because of the exchange rate risk cause the costs of companies to increase and its profits to decrease (Eyüboğlu and Eyüboğlu, 2018, p. 9). One of the most important effects of inflation on companies is that it becomes more expensive for companies to access goods and services due to the decrease in the purchasing power of money. In an environment where inflation is high, companies may prefer to borrow more because they need capital. In this case, the financial expenses and costs of the companies increase (Tunçsiper and Köroğlu, 2006, pp. 48-49).

In the economic crisis experienced in 2001, both the high interest rates and the fluctuations in exchange rates led to the bankruptcy of companies (Poyraz and Uçma, 2006, p. 4). When a company's fixed costs increase, its liquid assets decrease, and in periods of economic recession, the possibility of experiencing financial distress increases and its revenues become more sensitive to these situations (Khaliq et al., 2014, p.141). A high leverage ratio of a company operating in the intensive industrial sector may expose this company to higher financial distress costs (Purnanandam, 2008, p. 708).

The aim of this study is to examine the relationship between firm-specific micro factors (financial risk situations) and macroeconomic factors (namely interest rates, inflation rates, and exchange rates), which are the main indicators of the economy, in the context of companies experiencing financial distress. Since it is theoretically known that companies are affected by macroeconomic conditions, the aim of this study is to expand the academic literature. In addition, there has been no study observed in the literature examining such a relationship using the Toda Yamamoto method. In the introduction, the concepts of financial distress and bankruptcy are explained, the causes of financial distress and financial risks are explained. In the following parts of the study, literature review and the purpose, scope and importance of the study are given, then information about the methodology, data set and method of the study is presented and the findings are expressed. The study is completed with conclusions and recommendations.

1. LITERATURE REVIEW

When the literature is examined, considering that financial distress is a situation that occurs before bankruptcy, this study focuses on companies that are in financial distress and have a negative equity value, that is, they have gone bankrupt according to book value. Studies in the literature have generally focused on detecting financial distress situations of companies before bankruptcy with early warning indicators or financial ratios that determine financial distress. In addition, macroeconomic variables have been taken into account in some foreign or domestic studies. The relationship between bankruptcy and interest has been touched upon, or macroeconomic variables other than interest have been noted in foreign studies.

Table 1. Literature review

Authors/Year	Period	Country/Company	Method	Result
Poyraz and Uçma (2006)	1992-2003	Turkey/BIST	Altman Z-score	As a result of the study, it was determined that the agricultural products and food sectors were not adversely affected by the crisis periods, there was an inefficiency in the tourism sector in general, and the textile and transportation sector was affected quite negatively during the financial crisis.
McNamara, Duncan, and Kelly (2011)	1985-2000	Australian Securities Exchange	Principal Component Analysis	This study aimed to evaluate macroeconomic variables and firm-specific variables together to explain corporate failure. According to the results of the study, macro variables were found to be 10% more effective in explaining financial success.
Hwang, Chung, and Ku (2013)	May 1987 – April 2010	Taiwan	Logit Model with autocorrelation structure	This study aimed to predict the recurrent financial distresses of Taiwan industrial firms using the data set. As a result of the study, it was found that the method accurately gives the possibilities of financial distress and is a useful method to prevent credit losses.
Tinoco and Wilson (2013)	1980 – 2011	England London Stock Exchange	Panel Logit	In the study, accounting, market, and macroeconomic variables were taken into account when estimating financial distress or bankruptcy. As a result of the study, it was determined that although market variables cannot be included in the financial statements, they act as a complement in default prediction.
Khaliq, Altarturi, Thaker, Harun, and Nahar (2014)	2008 – 2012	Malaysia Stock Exchange	Z-Score	In the study, the financial distress of companies traded in the Malaysia Stock Exchange was measured. As a result of the study, it was determined that there is a significant relationship between the current ratios of firms and the Z-scores of debt ratios that determine financial distress.
Geng, Bose, and Chen (2015)	2001 – 2008	China Shanghai Stock Exchange	Neural network Model	In the study, the financial distress situations of 107 Chinese companies were examined with 31 financial indicators. As a result of the study, it was determined that financial indicators such as net profit margin, return on total assets, earnings per share, and cash flow per share play an important role in predicting the deterioration in profitability.
Altman, Iwanicz-Drozdowska, Laitinien, and Suvas (2017)	2007 – 2010	European and non-European	Z Score (Multiple Discriminant Analysis)	In their study, the application performance for 31 companies in Europe and 3 companies outside Europe was examined on an international scale. As a result of the study, it was determined that the Z-score model showed a successful performance for all countries in the study.
Ege, Topaloğlu, and Erkol (2017)	2011 – 2015	Turkey BIST	Fulmer H Score	In the study, the relationship between the financial failure status and financial performance of the manufacturing industry companies in the BIST 100 Index was examined. As a result of the study, it was determined that there is a positive and significant relationship between these two representation values.

Continued on following page

Table 1. Continued

Authors/Year	Period	Country/Company	Method	Result
Kaya and Açdoyuran (2017)	August 2002 – September 2015	Turkey	ARDL	In the study, the relationship between financial distress and oil prices was examined. The financial distress index and the Brent Oil price were used as variables in the study. According to the results of the study, it was found that there is a negative relationship between financial distress and oil prices.
Mariano, İzadi, and Pratt (2020)	2010 – 2018	England	Binomial Logistic Regression	In the study, the probability of financial distress of listed companies in the UK was investigated. According to the results obtained in the study, it was determined that companies with low ownership concentration and low degree of independence are more likely to be in financial distress.
Barışık and Budak (2021)	January 2010 – February 2020	Turkey	Bootstrap Toda Yamamoto	In the study, the relationship between company bankruptcies and interest rates was examined. The number of opened/closed companies obtained from the Union of Chambers and Commodity Exchanges of Turkey and the interest rates obtained from the Central Bank of the Republic of Turkey (CBRT) were used as data. As a result of the study, a unidirectional causality relationship was determined from the interest rate to the number of closed companies.
Dinh, Powell, and Vo (2021)	1997 – 2016	ASEAN Countries	Market-Based Approach	In the study, corporate financial distress was estimated. While choosing the companies, companies that faced distress in terms of interest coverage ratio and non-performing loans were selected. As a result of the study, it was determined that the interest coverage ratio is an early warning indicator for the next period, but this situation differs between countries.
Jan (2021)	2000 – 2019	Taiwan	Deep Learning Algorithm	This study aimed to predict financial distress effectively. The data of 86 companies with financial distress and 258 companies without financial distress registered in the Taiwan Economic Journal (TEJ) database were analyzed. As a result of the study, it was determined that the model reached the highest level of financial distress estimation at a rate of 94.23%.
Rahman, Sa, and Masud (2021)	2009 – 2017	USA – Public Firms	Logistic Regression and F score	The study aimed to determine the companies with high risk of paying debt. As a result of the study, it was determined that there is a significant relationship between the F-score and the probability of companies going into financial distress. In addition, in the study, it was found that the companies with a risk of financial distress had negative cash flow and the profitability of the assets decreased in the year prior to default.
Tekin (2021)	2010 – 2019	Turkey BIST	Altman Z score Cointegration Analysis Panel Causality Analysis	In the study, the relationship between the financial failure status of technology companies traded in Borsa Istanbul and their stock prices was examined. According to the results of the study, it was determined that there is a positive relationship between Z-scores and stock prices.

In this study, unlike the studies in the literature, whether macroeconomic factors affect micro factors in companies were examined and the causal relationship between them was investigated. Since it is theoretically known that companies are affected by macroeconomic conditions, the aim of this study is to expand the academic literature. In addition, there has been no study observed in the literature examining such a relationship using the Toda Yamamoto method. Among the companies traded in Borsa Istanbul, the companies experiencing financial distress were selected among the Public Disclosure Platform (PDP) notifications, and attention was paid to comply with some criteria. These criteria are: negative equity, three consecutive years of loss, and the company being placed in the Watchlist Market. At least two of these criteria were taken into account when selecting the companies. Thus, whether the financial risks of the companies operating in Borsa Istanbul and experiencing financial distress are affected by macroeconomic conditions is attempted to be identified by the causality relationship.

2. METHODOLOGY

In this section, information about the purpose, scope, importance, data set, and method of the study is given.

Purpose, Scope, Importance

The aim of the study is to examine the causality relationship between external factors and financial risk situations of companies traded in Borsa Istanbul, which are found to have financial distress regardless of sector and index. In the study, quarterly financial statement data for the years 2016-2021, quarterly exchange rates, inflation figures, and interest rates were used. In the study, an examination was conducted for 10 companies that were found to be experiencing financial distress. Before the causality test, the ADF (Augmented Dickey-Fuller) unit root test was applied to determine the degree of stationarity of the series. In the study, a unidirectional causality relationship is investigated from macroeconomic variables to the ratios related to the financial structure of the company. Since 2017, there have been fluctuations in exchange rates and inflation, interest rates, and exchange rates have gradually increased. Therefore, it is inevitable for companies not to be affected by such an economic environment. In this unfavorable economic environment, especially for financially distressed companies, liquidity problems may increase and companies may face difficulty in paying their debts. For this reason, the relationships of interest, inflation, foreign exchange, liquidity, and leverage variables were examined in the study starting from 2016, one year before 2017.

The theoretical and empirical examination conducted in the field shows that besides the internal factors that cause companies to get into financial distress, there are external factors as well. In general, studies related to determining the financial failure or financial distress levels of companies and financial ratios indicating financial distress have been carried out in the literature. In similar studies in the literature on the subject, the relationship between bankruptcy and interest (Barışık and Budak, 2021), the relationship between macroeconomic variables (inflation and interest rates) and firm-specific variables (share price index) (McNamara et al., 2011), and the utility of combining macroeconomic variables, market variables, and accounting-based variables (Tinoco & Wilson, 2013) were examined.

Unlike other studies in the literature, in this study, the causality relationship between the financial risks of the companies regarding their liquidity and capital structures (debt payment risk) and macroeconomic variables was examined. In previous studies, no study was found in which the causality relationship of external factors and internal factors was examined using the Toda Yamamoto method. Therefore, since it is known that external factors are a factor affecting the financial risk level of a company in the theoretical framework, it is intended that this study will contribute to the literature. Based on this information, the fact that the study aims to expand the academic literature reveals the importance of the study.

Data Set

The financial table data for the determination of the financial ratios displaying the financial risks of the companies in the study were obtained from the PDP. Data on inflation, interest rates, and exchange rates were obtained from the CBRT. The CPI (General Level - quarterly period) as the inflation rate, interest rates applied to commercial loans as an interest rate (TL, Current Data, % - quarterly period) and the CPI-based real effective exchange rate (2003=100 - quarterly period) for the exchange rate were taken into account. Among the companies operating in Borsa Istanbul, 8 companies were determined to be in financial distress, without distinction of sector and index, and were included in the study.

The studies considered in the literature for financial distress indicators are given in Table 2.

Table 2. A literature review on the indicators of financial distress

Authors/Year	Brief Content of the Study	Indicators of Financial Distress Considered
(2005) **Dilek ALTAŞ,** **Selay GİRAY**	Financial failure was detected by using multivariate statistical methods for companies operating in the textile sector.	Having closed the relevant period as a loss was used as an indicator of financial distress.
(2006) **M. Yılmaz İÇERLİ,** **G. Cenk AKKAYA**	Companies that succeeded and failed financially were identified using financial ratios.	In the study, having made losses for 3 consecutive years and being bankrupt was assessed as a financial failure. In addition, by means of the Z test, whether there was a significant difference between financially successful and unsuccessful companies was determined.
(2008) **Ender COŞKUN,** **Güven SAYILGAN**	In the study, they made an application on the indirect financial distress costs of the companies in the Istanbul Stock Exchange (ISE).	In the study where a two-stage financial distress detection was made, the financial distress indicators discussed in the second stage are as follows: Incurring a loss for 3 consecutive years, Negative equity, Bankruptcy, Permanent suspension of trading Being listed in the Watchlist Market (close monitoring market).
(2012) **Metin BAŞ,** **Zeki ÇAKMAK**	In the study, they determined the financial failures of companies operating in the textile and leather sector with the help of Grey Relational Analysis and logistic regression.	In the study, 21 financial ratios consisting of financial structure, liquidity, activity and profitability ratios were evaluated as financial failure criteria.
(2015) **Geng vd.**	They sought to identify the financial distress indicators of companies traded on the China Stock Exchange.	In this study, three situations were considered when identifying the companies experiencing financial distress. These are the fact that a listed company has incurred a loss for 2 consecutive years, the equity of the company is lower than the registered capital, the operations of a company are stopped and it becomes impossible to resume its activities within 3 months due to reasons such as natural disasters, accidents and lawsuits.

Continued on following page

Table 2. Continued

Authors/Year	Brief Content of the Study	Indicators of Financial Distress Considered
(2015) Seval SELİMOĞLU, Abdullah ORHAN	They determined the financial failures of companies operating in the weaving, clothing, and leather sectors in BIST with the help of ratio analysis and discriminant analysis.	The Altman Z-score was used as an indicator of financial failure in the study. Companies with a value of less than 1.81 and which incurred a loss in the relevant year were classified as companies that experienced financial failure.
(2016) Ender COŞKUN, Abdulvahap ÖZCAN	They determined the efficiency levels of companies experiencing financial distress.	Companies engaged in financial restructuring, Companies stating that they have made debt restructuring in the material event disclosure, Companies that incurred a loss for 3 consecutive years, Bankrupt companies, Companies with negative equity, Companies that suspended permanently, Companies that are placed in the Watchlist Market (close monitoring market), Companies that announce enforcement, foreclosure, debt, restructuring.
(2017) Kadri Cemil AKYÜZ, İbrahim YILDIRIM, İlker AKYÜZ, Turan TUGAY	They determined the financial failure levels of the companies in the paper and paper products industry sector in BIST with the help of ratio analysis and discriminant analysis.	In the study, by applying Altman's Z-score, companies that were below the value of 1.81 and companies that declared losses in the relevant year were evaluated as financially distressed.
(2018) Arhan S. ERTAN, Ömer ERSAN	They identified the factors that determine financial failure of companies in the Turkish manufacturing sector.	In the study, companies that were listed in the Watchlist market by the BIST Board of Directors were taken into account. The criteria for entry into the Watchlist market are as follows: • Absence or negative auditor opinion in the last 2 reports. • Filing an application for bankruptcy postponement. • Suspension of activities for more than 3 months. • Enforcement proceedings or insolvency.
(2019) Muhammed Fatih YÜRÜK, İbrahim Halil Ekşi	They identified the financial failures of companies in the BIST Manufacturing sector by using artificial intelligence methods.	Bankruptcy. Being in the BIST Watchlist Market. Suspension of activities. Loss for 2 consecutive years. Loss of 10% of total assets.

While selecting the companies, selection criteria were established based on the studies in the literature. Accordingly, financial distress indicators that are commonly considered in the studies examined are listed as follows.

- Having incurred a loss for three consecutive years,
- Having negative equity,
- Taking part in the BIST Watchlist market.

Companies that had the characteristics of at least two of the above-mentioned financial distress indicators and that suffered financial distress for 3 consecutive years were selected. In addition, a notification search covering the years 2021-2022 was carried out in PDP for these selected companies. As a result of this notification search, some material event notifications, which can be considered as an indicator of financial distress and support the criteria listed earlier, were also taken into account. These material event notifications are as follows:

- Partial or complete cessation of activities or their impossibility,
- Non-current financial asset sale
- Non-current asset sale
- Capital increase-decrease (Rights Issue)
- Unusual price and volume movements

In the study, financial ratios indicating liquidity and capital structure risk were again based on the literature and net working capital/total assets and market value of equity/total liabilities ratios used in Altman's Z-score method were employed (Elmas, 2017, p. 289). The net working capital/total assets ratio shows the liquidity status of the company, while the market value of equity/total liabilities ratio shows the power of leverage and financial structure of the company (Karadeniz and Öcek, 2019, p. 197).

In this study, the financial distress indicators taken into account when determining the companies and the companies included in the study are listed in Table 3.

Table 3. Companies included in the study and financial distress indicators considered

Company Code	Company Name	Profit/Loss Status	Traded Market	Material Event Notification
CRFSA	CARREFOURSA CARREFOUR SABANCI TİCARET MERKEZİ A.Ş.	Last 6 years	Main Market	Non-current Financial Asset Sale Non-current Asset Sale Rights Issue Negative equity between Q1 2019 – Q4 2021
CASA	CASA EMTİA PETROL KİMYEVİ VE TÜREVLERİ SANAYİ TİCARET A.Ş.	2016, 2017, 2018	Watchlist Market	Rights Issue Unusual Price and Volume Movements
UTYPA	UTOPYA TURİZM İNŞAAT İŞLETMECİLİK TİCARET A.Ş.	2016, 2017, 2018, 2019, 2020	Watchlist Market	Non-current Asset Sale
BRMEN	BİRLİK MENSUCAT TİCARET VE SANAYİ İŞLETMESİ A.Ş.	Last 6 years	Watchlist Market	Unusual Price and Volume Movements Negative equity between Q1 2020 – Q4 2021
KERVN	KERVANSARAY YATIRIM HOLDİNG A.Ş.	Last 6 years	Watchlist Market	Unusual Price and Volume Movements On 22.02.2022, a debt assignment and structuring agreement was signed. Negative equity between Q1 2020 – Q4 2021
UFUK	UFUK YATIRIM YÖNETİM VE GAYRİMENKUL A.Ş.	2017, 2018, 2019	Watchlist Market	Unusual Price and Volume Movements
ETILR	ETİLER GIDA VE TİCARİ YATIRIMLAR SANAYİ VE TİCARET A.Ş.	2017, 2018, 2019	Watchlist Market	Unusual Price and Volume Movements
EMNIS	EMİNİŞ AMBALAJ SANAYİ VE TİCARET A.Ş.	2016, 2017, 2018, 2019	Watchlist Market	Unusual Price and Volume Movements On 22.06.2020, concordat was declared and a restructuring was carried out. Negative equity between Q2 2018 – Q3 2020

Method

In the study, Toda Yamamoto test was used as a method to examine the causality relationship between liquidity and capital risks of companies and macroeconomic variables.

In order to be able to make statistical inferences in economic time series, unit root tests or cointegration tests are performed beforehand. Since there are some pre-test biases in the observations made accordingly, it may negatively affect the results of the hypotheses. However, in some studies, these tests are necessary in order to reach a statistical result. With the method they developed, Toda and Yamamoto presented a simple method for eliminating the problems that occur in the hypotheses when unit roots are involved in the VAR process. Thus, in time series, data are estimated using the var model with level values, and it is possible to make an application without regarding integration and cointegration by determining the criteria with the WALD coefficient (Toda and Yamamoto, 1995, pp. 226-227). Toda Yamamoto is a highly applicable method because it does not require pre-testing compared to other methods. With this method, causality analysis can be performed regardless of the cointegration relationship of series of the same or different degrees (Çalışkan, Karabacak, & Meçik, 2017, p. 50).

In order to reach the maximum order of integration (Dmax) in the Toda Yamamoto causality test, unit root tests should be performed for the series before the application of the method. After determining the optimal lag length (k) in the model, a new estimation model is created as (k + Dmax). As the last step in the Toda Yamamoto causality test based on the VAR model, the MWALD coefficient test is performed and the resulting chi-square values are analyzed in Excel again in accordance with the degree of freedom (k). Thus, the resulting table values are interpreted according to the test statistics. According to the H0 hypothesis, there is no causality between the variables. According to the H1 (alternative hypothesis) hypothesis, there is causality between the variables. If the value of the test statistic is greater than the table value, the H0 hypothesis is rejected. The formula structure of the model is as follows (Yenilmez and Erdem, 2018, p. 13):

$$Y_t = \varpi + \sum_{i=1}^{k} \alpha_{1i} X_{t-i} + \sum_{i=1}^{k} \beta_{1i} Y_{t-i} + \sum_{j=m+1}^{d\max} \delta_{1i} X_{t-i} + \sum_{j=m+1}^{d\max} \theta_{1i} Y_{t-i} + \varepsilon_{1t} \quad (1)$$

$$X_t = \partial + \sum_{i=1}^{k} \alpha_{2i} X_{t-i} + \sum_{i=1}^{k} \beta_{2i} Y_{t-i} + \sum_{j=m+1}^{d\max} \delta_{2i} X_{t-i} + \sum_{j=m+1}^{d\max} \theta_{2i} Y_{t-i} + \varepsilon_{2t} \quad (2)$$

FINDINGS

In the study, the causality relationship of negative economic developments after 2016 on the liquidity and leverage structure of companies experiencing financial distress was examined. The ADF unit root test was applied for the series before the Toda Yamamoto causality test was performed. Since the macroeconomic data are valid for each company, ADF unit root tests were performed only for the first company and the D_{max} value was determined as 2. Therefore, ADF was not applied for other periods. The ADF unit root test applied for the CRFSA company is given in the following table. Other businesses are attached.

Table 4. CRFSA company ADF unit root test results

Test Statistics	Constant			Constant With Trend			D_{max}
Variables	**Level**	**1st Difference**	**2nd Difference**	**Level**	**1st Difference**	**2nd Difference**	
Interest	-3.2981**	-2.717*	-4.8732***	-3.1974	-2.887	-4.7556***	2
CPI	2.2835	-2.1046	-4.8594***	-1.1498	-2.620	-4.7725***	2
Foreign Exchange	-0.1997	-5.7874***	-5.9432***	-3.321*	-5.635***	-5.8452***	2
Liquidity	-3.7583***	-4.5459***	-5.5783***	-3.5482*	-4.503***	-2.9983	1
Leverage	-1.9231	-4.9963***	-4.8577***	-2.9645	-5.171***	-4.7037***	2

Note: (***), (**) and (*) values indicate significance levels of 1%, 5% and 10%, respectively.

As a result of unit root tests, D_{max} value was found to be 2. The lag length determined by the causality test was found to be k=1. Thus, it was determined as k+ D_{max} =3 and the estimation was made according to the number 3 in practice. Then, the chi-square values according to the degree of freedom 1 in Excel were calculated as probability values using the CHIDIST formula. The tables presenting the results of the causality analysis are as follows.

Table 5. The causality relationship from ınterest to leverage

From Interest ® To Leverage			
Companies	**Chi-sq**	**Probability Value (Excel)**	**Decision (%5)**
CRFSA	14.77718	0.000120991	Causality
CASA	16.53254	4.78223E-05	No Causality
UTPYA	21.86806	2.92055E-06	No Causality
BRMEN	79.66375	4.4387E-19	No Causality
KERVN	9.373054	0.002201983	Causality
UFUK	23.72118	1.1135E-06	No Causality
ETILR	33.20391	8.29835E-09	No Causality
EMNIS	7.436246	0.006392309	Causality

When the causality relationship from interest to leverage was examined, it was seen that there is a causal relationship in KERVN and EMNIS companies. In this case, there is no causal relationship from interest to leverage in the majority of companies experiencing financial distress. It was determined that the leverage structure of the companies other than these 3 companies is not affected by the interest rates.

Table 6. The causality relationship from foreign exchange to leverage

From Foreign Exchange ® To Leverage				
Companies	**Chi-sq**	**Probability Value (Excel)**	**Decision (%5)**	
CRFSA	2.421622	0.119670963	No Causality	
CASA	18.63463	1.58318E-05	No Causality	
UTPYA	4.352276	0.036959522	Causality	
BRMEN	81.06883	2.17991E-19	No Causality	
KERVN	8.170278	0.004258238	Causality	
UFUK	3.638388	0.056461577	No Causality	
ETILR	13.68984	0.000215618	Causality	
EMNIS	4.243129	0.039409471	Causality	

When the causality relationship from foreign exchange to leverage was examined, it was observed that there is a causal relationship in UTPYA, KERVN, ETILR and EMNIS companies. It was determined that the leverage structure of the companies other than these 4 companies is not affected by the exchange rates.

Table 7. The causality relationship from CPI to leverage

From CPI ® To Leverage			
Companies	**Chi-sq**	**Probability Value (Excel)**	**Decision (%5)**
CRFSA	8.555765	0.003444297	Causality
CASA	3.955186	0.046727154	Causality
UTPYA	3.273991	0.070386196	No Causality
BRMEN	73.39387	1.06195E-17	No Causality
KERVN	3.602157	0.057704654	No Causality
UFUK	32.16309	1.41758E-08	No Causality
ETILR	13.27233	0.000269352	Causality
EMNIS	7.376608	0.006607768	Causality

When the causality relationship from CPI to leverage was examined, it was realized that there is a causal relationship in CRFSA, CASA, ETILR and EMNIS companies. In this case, while there is a causal relationship from CPI to leverage in half of the companies experiencing financial distress, there is no such relationship in the other half. It was determined that the leverage structure of the other 4 companies, excluding these 4 companies, is not affected by the CPI. It was realized that the leverage structure of the companies is affected more by the CPI than by exchange rates and interest rates.

Table 8. The causality relationship from interest to liquidity

From Interest ® To Liquidity			
Companies	**Chi-sq**	**Probability Value (Excel)**	**Decision (%5)**
CRFSA	5.953245	0.01469022	Causality
CASA	96.79168	7.70191E-23	No Causality
UTPYA	34.52009	4.21875E-09	No Causality
BRMEN	13.48702	0.000240219	Causality
KERVN	65.55685	5.64615E-16	No Causality
UFUK	29.47075	5.6767E-08	No Causality
ETILR	22.54892	2.0486E-06	No Causality
EMNIS	42.71671	6.32695E-11	No Causality

When the relationship of causality from interest to liquidity was examined, it was found that there is a causal relationship in CRFSA and BRMEN companies. In this case, there is no causal relationship between interest and liquidity in the majority of companies experiencing financial distress. It was determined that the liquidity structure of the companies other than these 2 companies is not affected by interest rates.

Table 9. The causality relationship from foreign exchange to liquidity

From Foreign Exchange® To Liquidity			
Companies	**Chi-sq**	**Probability Value (Excel)**	**Decision (%5)**
CRFSA	2.329418	0.126949333	No Causality
CASA	43.29669	4.70379E-11	No Causality
UTPYA	39.02244	4.18962E-10	No Causality
BRMEN	8.278966	0.004010696	Causality
KERVN	15.05643	0.000104344	Causality
UFUK	32.83238	1.00458E-08	No Causality
ETILR	8.443233	0.003664043	Causality
EMNIS	1.077129	0.299340707	No Causality

When the causality relationship between foreign exchange and liquidity was examined, it was found that there is a causal relationship in BRMEN, KERVN and ETILR companies. It was determined that the liquidity structure of the other 5 companies, excluding these 3 companies, is not affected by the foreign exchange rates.

Table 10. The causality relationship from CPI to liquidity

From CPI® To Liquidity			
Companies	**Chi-sq**	**Probability Value (Excel)**	**Decision (%5)**
CRFSA	3.48569	0.06190155	No Causality
CASA	14.7585	0.000122195	Causality
UTPYA	54.99744	1.20687E-13	No Causality
BRMEN	23.49585	1.25183E-06	No Causality
KERVN	35.41737	2.66103E-09	No Causality
UFUK	15.81286	6.99256E-05	No Causality
ETILR	6.818628	0.009021185	Causality
EMNIS	44.033	3.22886E-11	No Causality

When the causality relationship from CPI to liquidity was examined, it was determined that there is a causal relationship in CASA and ETILR companies. In this case, there is no causal relationship from CPI to liquidity in the majority of companies experiencing financial distress. It was determined that the liquidity structure of the companies other than these 2 companies is not affected by the CPI.

DIRECTIONS FOR FUTURE RESEARCH

In this study, the relationship between the financial status of the companies and the macroeconomic variables was discussed. In the study in which the Toda Yamamoto causality test was applied, it was determined that the majority of companies experiencing financial distress were related to macroeconomic variables. Therefore, this study made it possible to investigate the sources of financial distress of companies in more detail by moving to a further point. Future studies can contribute to the development of the academic literature on this subject by examining the companies by separating them by sector, investigating the effect of exchange rates on exporting companies, and diversifying the methods to be used.

CONCLUSION

In this study, the causality relationship between the liquidity and leverage structure (which shows the internal conditions of the companies) and the external factors was examined. These external factors consist of inflation rates (CPI), exchange rates (CPI-based real effective rate) and interest rates (interest rates applied to Commercial Loans). According to the findings of the study, the liquidity and leverage ratios of companies are generally affected by external factors.

When the causality relationships between the leverage ratio and macroeconomic variables are examined, causality is discovered running from interest to leverage in CRFSA, KERVN and EMNIS companies, from foreign exchange to leverage in UTPYA, KERVN, ETILR and EMNIS companies, and from CPI to leverage in CRFSA, CASA, ETILR and EMNIS companies. The leverage structure in the EMNIS Company is affected by all three external factors.

When the causality relationship between the liquidity structure and macroeconomic variables is examined, causality is found running from interest to liquidity in CRFSA and BRMEN companies. A causal relationship running from foreign exchange to liquidity was determined in BRMEN, KERVN and ETILR companies. A causal relationship from CPI to liquidity was determined in CASA and ETILR companies.

When the causality relations of companies are examined in general, it has been determined that while ETIR company are the company most affected by macroeconomic variables, UFUK company has no causal relationship with any macroeconomic variable. When the variables are looked at in general, the most encountered causal relationship is from foreign exchange to leverage and from CPI to leverage. The least encountered causal relationship is from CPI to liquidity and from interest to liquidity. Therefore, the liquidity structure of the companies is mostly affected by the exchange rates. Leverage structure, on the other hand, is most affected by CPI and foreign exchange.

According to these results, while the variable that managers should pay the most attention to for the liquidity situation of companies experiencing financial difficulties is exchange rates, the variable that they should pay the most attention to for the leverage structure is the CPI and foreign exchange. The decrease in the value of TL causes the raw materials or goods supplied from outside to become expensive and more cash to come out of the company. This confirms the fact that there is a causal relationship from foreign currency to liquidity in most of the companies. When TL assets decrease, companies may have difficulty in paying their short-term debts. If the borrowing rate from different currencies is high, the TL assets of the company may be insufficient. In addition, due to the depreciation of TL, companies may have problems in clearing their debts due to rising foreign exchange prices. It will be beneficial for companies to increase their foreign exchange assets or reduce their foreign currency borrowings.

When interest rates are high, borrowing costs increase. This situation causes both liquidity and leverage to be negatively affected. A causal relationship running from interest to leverage was identified only in 3 companies. According to this result, the leverage structure of most companies is affected by rising inflation rather than interest rates.

In most of the companies subject to the study, there was no causal relationship running from CPI to liquidity. Reduced purchasing power causes access to goods and services to be more expensive. However, such a causal relationship was not found in 6 companies. In addition, in periods of high inflation, companies need capital intensively. Therefore, companies can resort to borrowing more in such an environment, leading to greater utilization of leverage. Correspondingly, according to this study, there is a causal relationship from CPI to leverage in most of the companies.

Sudden price increases due to foreign exchange or inflation cause a negative impact on cash flow and an increase in costs due to the inability of companies to reflect these changes to their customers. Therefore, it causes companies to experience difficulties in fulfilling their financial obligations. Companies need to be prepared for these changes in a negative economic environment. In order for companies not to fall into financial distress in such an economic environment, some of the measures to be taken are: to keep cash reserves high, to find cheap markets for imported raw materials or goods, to reduce borrowing in currencies other than TL, to avoid financing long-term debts with short-term assets, and thus to avoid the need for frequent refinancing. These and similar measures will reduce the risk of financial distress for companies.

Increasing the short-term financial investments of the companies to a certain extent, investing in rising financial instruments, and increasing the use of derivative financial instruments will contribute positively to the financial structure of a company. Tangible non-current assets in a company provide more advantages in terms of borrowing than intangible non-current assets. It provides an advantage at the point of paying off debts in companies with a high value of tangible non-current assets and financial distress.

REFERENCES

Aktaş, R. (1997). *Mali başarsızlık (İşletme riski) tahmin modelleri* [Financial failure (Business risk) forecast models]. Türkiye İş Bankası Kültür Yayınları.

Akyüz, K. C., Yıldırım, İ., Akyüz, İ., & Tugay, T. (2017). 'Borsa İstanbul'da İşlem Gören Kâğıt Ve Kâğıt Ürünleri Sanayi İşletmelerinin Finansal Başarısızlık Düzeylerinin Oran Analizi Ve Diskriminant Analizi Yöntemleri Kullanılarak Ölçülmesi [Measurement of Financial Failure Levels of Paper and Paper Products Industrial Enterprises Traded on Borsa İstanbul by Using Ratio Analysis and Discriminant Analysis Methods]. *Düzce Üniversitesi Orman Fakültesi Ormancılık Dergisi*, *13*(1), 60–74.

Altaş, D., & Giray, S. (2005). Mali Başarısızlığın Çok Değişkenli İstatistiksel Yöntemlerle Belirlenmesi: Tekstil Sektörü Örneği [Determination of Financial Failure by Multivariate Statistical Methods: The Case of the Textile Sector]. *Marmara Üniversitesi Sosyal Bilimler Dergisi*, *2*, 13–28.

Altman, E. I., Iwanicz-Drozdowska, M., Laitinen, E. K., & Suvas, A. (2017). 'Financial Distress Prediction in An International Context: A Review and Empirical Analysis of Altman's Z-Score Model. *Journal of International Financial Management & Accounting*, *28*(2), 131–171. doi:10.1111/jifm.12053

Barışık, S., & Budak, S. (2021). Türkiye'de İşletme İflasları ve Faiz İlişkisi [Business Bankruptcies and Interest Relationship in Turkey]. *Third Sector Social Economic Review*, *56*(4), 2198–2212.

Baş, M., & Çakmak, Z. (2012). Gri İlişkisel Analiz Ve Lojistik Regresyon Analizi İle İşletmelerde Finansal Başarısızlığın Belirlenmesi ve Bir Uygulama [Determination of Financial Failure in Enterprises with Gray Relational Analysis and Logistic Regression Analysis and an Application]. *Anadolu Üniversitesi Sosyal Bilimler Dergisi*, *12*(3), 63–81.

Çalışkan, Ş., Karabacak, M., & Meçik, O. (2017). Türkiye Ekonomisinde Eğitim Harcamaları ve Ekonomik Büyüme İlişkisi: Bootstrap Toda-Yamamoto Nedensellik Testi Yaklaşımı [The Relationship Between Education Expenditures and Economic Growth in the Turkish Economy: Bootstrap Toda-Yamamoto Causality Test Approach]. *Kocaeli Üniversitesi Sosyal Bilimler Enstitüsü Dergisi, KOSBED*, *33*(1), 45–56.

Coşkun, E., & Özcan, A. (2016). *Finansal Sıkıntı Sürecinde Şirketlerin Etkinlik Düzeylerinin Belirlenmesi (No. 16001)* [Determination of the Effectiveness Levels of Companies in the Process of Financial Hardship (No. 16001)]. WERI-World Economic Research Institute. doi:10.22440/EconWorld.WP.2016.001

Coşkun, E., & Sayılgan, G. (2008). Finansal Sıkıntının Dolaylı Maliyetleri: İMKB'de İşlem Gören Şirketlerde Bir Uygulama [Indirect Costs of Financial Distress: An Application in Companies Traded on the ISE]. *Gazi Üniversitesi İktisadi ve İdari Bilimler Fakültesi Dergisi*, *10*(3), 45–66.

Dinh, D. V., Powell, R. J., & Vo, D. H. (2021). Forecasting Corporate Financial Distress in The Southeast Asian Countries: A Market-Based Approach. *Journal of Asian Economics*, *74*, 101293. doi:10.1016/j.asieco.2021.101293

Ege, İ., Topaloğlu, E. E., & Erkol, A. Y. (2017). Fulmer Modeline Dayalı Finansal Başarısızlık İle Finansal Performans İlişkisi: İmalat Sanayi Üzerine Bir Uygulama [The Relationship Between Financial Failure and Financial Performance Based on the Fulmer Model: An Application on the Manufacturing Industry]. *Muhasebe ve Finansman Dergisi*, (74), 119–132. doi:10.25095/mufad.396862

Elmas, B. (2017). Finansal Tablolar Analizi, 3 [Financial Statement Analysis, 3]. Nobel Akademik Yayıncılık Eğitim Danışmanlık.

Ertan, A. S., & Ersan, Ö. (2018). Finansal Başarısızlığı Belirleyen Etkenler: Türkiye İmalat Sektörü Örneği [Factors Determining Financial Failure: The Case of the Turkish Manufacturing Sector]. *Marmara Üniversitesi İktisadi ve İdari Bilimler Dergisi*, *40*(2), 181–207.

Eyüboğlu, S., & Eyüboğlu, K. (2018). Borsa İstanbul Sektör Endeksleri İle Döviz Kurları Arasındaki İlişkilerin İncelenmesi: ARDL Modeli [Investigation of the Relations Between Borsa İstanbul Sector Indices and Exchange Rates: The ARDL Model]. *Ömer Halisdemir Üniversitesi İktisadi ve İdari Bilimler Fakültesi Dergisi, 11*(1), 8-28.

Geng, R., Bose, I., & Chen, X. (2015). Prediction of financial distress: An empirical study of listed Chinese companies using data mining. *European Journal of Operational Research*, *241*(1), 236–247. doi:10.1016/j.ejor.2014.08.016

Gögül, P. K., & Yaman, D. (n.d.). Hisse Senedi Fiyatına Etki Eden Makroekonomik Faktörlerin İncelenmesi: Simetrik Ve Asimetrik Nedensellik Sınaması (2006-2020 Dönemi) [Investigation of Macroeconomic Factors Affecting Stock Price: Symmetric and Asymmetric Causality Test (2006-2020 Period)]. *Sakarya İktisat Dergisi*, *9*(4), 258–276.

Hwang, R. C., Chung, H., & Ku, J. Y. (2013). Predicting Recurrent Financial Distresses With Autocorrelation Structure: An Empirical Analysis From An Emerging Market. *Journal of Financial Services Research*, *43*(3), 321–341. doi:10.100710693-012-0136-0

İçerli, M. Y., & Akkaya, G. C. (2006). Finansal Açıdan Başarılı Olan İşletmelerle Başarısız Olan İşletmeler Arasında Finansal Oranlar Yardımıyla Farklılıkların Tespiti [Detecting Differences Between Financially Successful Businesses and Failing Businesses with the Help of Financial Ratios]. *Atatürk Üniversitesi İktisadi ve İdari Bilimler Dergisi*, *20*(1), 413–421.

Jan, C. L. (2021). Financial Information Asymmetry: Using Deep Learning Algorithms to Predict Financial Distress. Symmetry. *Symmetry*, *13*(3), 443. doi:10.3390ym13030443

Karadeniz, E., & Öcek, C. (2019). Finansal Başarısızlık Riski Taşıyan İle Taşımayan İşletmelerin Finansal Oranlarının Karşılaştırmalı Analizi: Borsa İstanbul Turizm İşletmelerinde Bir Araştırma [Comparative Analysis of the Financial Ratios of Enterprises with and Not at Risk of Financial Failure: A Study in Borsa İstanbul Tourism Enterprises]. *Seyahat Ve Otel İşletmeciliği Dergisi*, *16*(2), 191–206. doi:10.24010oid.600207

Karels, G. V., & Prakash, A. J. (1987). Multivariate Normality and Forecasting of Business Bankruptcy. *Journal of Business Finance & Accounting*, *14*(4), 573–593. doi:10.1111/j.1468-5957.1987.tb00113.x

Kaya, E., & Açdoyuran, B. (2017). Petrol Fiyatları Ve Finansal Sıkıntı Arasındaki İlişki: Türkiye İçin Bir ARDL Yaklaşımı [The Relationship Between Oil Prices and Financial Distress: An ARDL Approach for Turkey]. *Sosyal Ekonomik Araştırmalar Dergisi*, *17*(33), 134–155. doi:10.30976usead.327648

Khaliq, A., Altarturi, B. H. M., Thaker, H. M. T., Harun, M. Y., & Nahar, N. (2014). Identifying Financial distress firms: A case study of Malaysia's government linked companies (GLC). *International Journal of Economics, Finance and Management*, *3*(3).

Mariano, S. S. G., Izadi, J., & Pratt, M. (2021). Can we predict the likelihood of financial distress in companies from their corporate governance and borrowing? *International Journal of Accounting & Information Management.*

McNamara, R., Duncan, K., & Kelly, S. (2011, November). Micro and Macro Determinants of Financial Distress. In *15th International Business Research Conference*, Sydney, Australia.

Poyraz, E., & Uçma, T. (2006). Türkiye'de Faaliyet Gösteren İhracatçı Sektörlerin Mali Kriz Ortamlarında Finansal Başarısızlıklarının Altman (Z-Score) Modeli Yardımıyla Ölçülmesi [Measurement of Financial Failures of Exporter Sectors Operating in Turkey in Financial Crisis Environments with the Help of Altman (Z-Score) Model]. *Muhasebe ve Finansman Dergisi*, (32).

Purnanandam, A. (2008). Financial Distress and Corporate Risk Management: Theory and Evidence. *Journal of Financial Economics*, *87*(3), 706–739. doi:10.1016/j.jfineco.2007.04.003

Rahman, M., Sa, C. L., & Kaium Masud, M. (2021). Predicting Firms' Financial Distress: An Empirical Analysis Using The F-Score Model. *Journal of Risk and Financial Management*, *14*(5), 199. doi:10.3390/jrfm14050199

Ross, S. A., Westerfield, R. W., & Jaffe, J. (2002). *Corporate Finance*. McGraw Hill Irwin.

Selimoğlu, S., & Orhan, A. (2015). Finansal Başarısızlığın Oran Analizi Ve Diskriminant Analizi Kullanılarak Ölçümlenmesi: BİST'de İşlem Gören Dokuma, Giyim Eşyası Ve Deri İşletmeleri Üzerine Bir Araştırma [Measuring Financial Failure Using Ratio Analysis and Discriminant Analysis: A Study on Weaving, Apparel and Leather Enterprises Traded at BIST]. *Muhasebe ve Finansman Dergisi*, (66), 21–40. doi:10.25095/mufad.396529

Tekin, B. (2021). Finansal Başarısızlık Ve Hisse Senedi Fiyatı İlişkisi: Xutek Endeksinde Panel Eşbütünleşme Ve Nedensellik Analizleri [The Relationship Between Financial Failure and Stock Price: Panel Cointegration and Causality Analysis in Xutek Index]. *Finans Ekonomi ve Sosyal Araştırmalar Dergisi*, *6*(4), 780–790.

Tinoco, M. H., & Wilson, N. (2013). Financial Distress and Bankruptcy Prediction among Listed Companies Using Accounting, Market and Macroeconomic Variables. *International Review of Financial Analysis*, *30*, 394–419. doi:10.1016/j.irfa.2013.02.013

Toda, H. Y., & Yamamoto, T. (1995). Statistical Inference in Vector Autoregressions with Possibly Integrated Processes. *Journal of Econometrics*, *66*(1-2), 225–250. doi:10.1016/0304-4076(94)01616-8

Tunçsiper, B., & Köroğlu, Ö. (2006). Enflasyonun Otomotiv Sektöründeki İşletmeler Üzerindeki Etkisi: Balıkesir İli Örneği [The Impact of Inflation on Enterprises in the Automotive Sector: The Case of Balıkesir Province]. *Balıkesir Üniversitesi Sosyal Bilimler Enstitüsü Dergisi*, *9*(15), 43–65.

Uzun, E. (2005). İşletmelerde Finansal Başarısızlığın Teorik Olarak İrdelenmesi [Theoretical Investigation of Financial Failure in Business]. *Muhasebe ve Finansman Dergisi*, (27), 158–168.

Yenilmez, F., & Erdem, M. S. (2018). Türkiye ve Avrupa Birliği'nde Ekonomik Büyüme İle Enerji Tüketimi Arasındaki İlişki: Toda-Yamamoto Nedensellik Testi [The Relationship Between Economic Growth and Energy Consumption in Turkey and the European Union: Toda-Yamamoto Causality Test]. *Eskişehir Osmangazi Üniversitesi Sosyal Bilimler Dergisi*, *19*(1), 71–95. doi:10.17494/ogusbd.457078

Yürük, M. F., & Ekşi, İ. H. (2019). Yapay Zekâ Yöntemleri ile İşletmelerin Finansal Başarısızlığının Tahmin Edilmesi: BIST İmalat Sektörü Uygulaması [Estimating the Financial Failure of Enterprises with Artificial Intelligence Methods: BIST Manufacturing Sector Application]. *Mukaddime*, *10*(1), 393–422.

APPENDIX

Table 11. CASA company ADF unit root test results

Test Statistics	Constant			Constant With Trend			D_{max}
Variables	Level	1st Difference	2nd Difference	Level	1st Difference	2nd Difference	
Interest	-3.29814	-2.71699	-4.87315	-3.19742	-2.88741	-4.75557	2
CPI	2.28349	-2.10458	-4.85938	-1.14984	-2.61984	-4.77247	2
Foreign Exchange	-0.19973	-5.78736	-5.94316	-3.32101	-5.63478	-5.84519	2
Liquidity	-1.92218	-5.37262	-5.9457	-1.90545	-5.24115	-3.99448	2
Leverage	-4.12635	-3.42856	-3.02647	-3.93515	-3.53857	-2.86879	0

Table 12. UTPYA company ADF unit root test results

Test Statistics	Constant			Constant With Trend			D_{max}
Variables	Level	1st Difference	2nd Difference	Level	1st Difference	2nd Difference	
Interest	-3.29814	-2.71699	-4.87315	-3.19742	-2.88741	-4.75557	2
CPI	2.28349	-2.10458	-4.85938	-1.14984	-2.61984	-4.77247	2
Foreign Exchange	-0.19973	-5.78736	-5.94316	-3.32101	-5.63478	-5.84519	2
Liquidity	-4.06163	-1.50578	-1.51888	-4.07421	-1.43667	-1.55489	0
Leverage	-1.68532	-4.59795	-3.49422	-1.40076	-4.79609	-3.72221	2

Table 13. BRMEN company ADF unit root test results

Test Statistics	Constant			Constant With Trend			D_{max}
Variables	Level	1st Difference	2nd Difference	Level	1st Difference	2nd Difference	
Interest	-3.29814	-2.71699	-4.87315	-3.19742	-2.88741	-4.75557	2
CPI	2.28349	-2.10458	-4.85938	-1.14984	-2.61984	-4.77247	2
Foreign Exchange	-0.19973	-5.78736	-5.94316	-3.32101	-5.63478	-5.84519	2
Liquidity	-0.31613	-4.74226	-3.88069	-2.38867	-5.19024	-3.84154	2
Leverage	-0.3513	-5.61781	-8.29628	-2.13184	-4.49887	-8.04779	2

Table 14. KERVN company ADF unit root test results

Test Statistics	Constant			Constant with Trend			D_{max}
Variables	**Level**	**1st Difference**	**2nd Difference**	**Level**	**1st Difference**	**2nd Difference**	
Interest	-3.29814	-2.71699	-4.87315	-3.19742	-2.88741	-4.75557	2
CPI	2.28349	-2.10458	-4.85938	-1.14984	-2.61984	-4.77247	2
Foreign Exchange	-0.19973	-5.78736	-5.94316	-3.32101	-5.63478	-5.84519	2
Liquidity	-1.21644	-3.98178	-1.13854	-1.69705	-3.87812	-1.0778	1
Leverage	-1.12183	-3.81277	-3.95693	-2.52648	-3.66043	-3.83306	2

Table 15. UFUK company ADF unit root test results

Test Statistics	Constant			Constant With Trend			D_{max}
Variables	**Level**	**1st Difference**	**2nd Difference**	**Level**	**1st Difference**	**2nd Difference**	
Interest	-3.29814	-2.71699	-4.87315	-3.19742	-2.88741	-4.75557	2
CPI	2.28349	-2.10458	-4.85938	-1.14984	-2.61984	-4.77247	2
Foreign Exchange	-0.19973	-5.78736	-5.94316	-3.32101	-5.63478	-5.84519	2
Liquidity	-2.41341	-8.31478	-6.15686	-5.40089	-7.74468	-6.01806	2
Leverage	-2.46818	-3.0643	-4.5599	-3.37105	-2.99284	-4.51401	2

Table 16. ETILR company ADF unit root test results

Test Statistics	Constant			Constant With Trend			D_{max}
Variables	**Level**	**1st Difference**	**2nd Difference**	**Level**	**1st Difference**	**2nd Difference**	
Interest	-3.29814	-2.71699	-4.87315	-3.19742	-2.88741	-4.75557	2
CPI	2.28349	-2.10458	-4.85938	-1.14984	-2.61984	-4.77247	2
Foreign Exchange	-0.19973	-5.78736	-5.94316	-3.32101	-5.63478	-5.84519	2
Liquidity	-1.18667	-3.81301	-6.58244	-1.55936	-3.99154	-6.43801	2
Leverage	-3.49436	-4.29989	-7.61464	-4.66975	-4.26023	-7.51309	2

Table 17. EMNIS company ADF unit root test results

Test Statistics	Constant			Constant With Trend			D_{max}
Variables	**Level**	**1st Difference**	**2nd Difference**	**Level**	**1st Difference**	**2nd Difference**	
Interest	-3.29814	-2.71699	-4.87315	-3.19742	-2.88741	-4.75557	2
CPI	2.28349	-2.10458	-4.85938	-1.14984	-2.61984	-4.77247	2
Foreign Exchange	-0.19973	-5.78736	-5.94316	-3.32101	-5.63478	-5.84519	2
Liquidity	-1.4333	-4.84243	-5.12386	-2.76155	-4.76775	-4.96193	2
Leverage	-1.15481	-3.9242	-7.5301	-0.9813	-3.96871	-3.35225	1

Chapter 10
Economic Impact of COVID-19: Challenges and Opportunities

Zainab Hamid
University of Kashmir, India

Shawkat Ahmad Shah
University of Kashmir, India

ABSTRACT

The novel coronavirus (COVID-19) poses unprecedented challenges to global economy and international development and has become a humanitarian crisis affecting millions of lives and livelihoods throughout the world. It affects almost every economic activity and operation and at the same time poses a threat to every sector of the economy, people, places, and businesses. COVID-19 brought not only crisis, disruptions, and challenges but also bred fertile ground for opportunities, innovations, and digitalization of economic sectors. In this context, this chapter focuses keenly on the economic impacts of the COVID-19 crisis, including the economic challenges and opportunities it creates, and accordingly, recommendations have been presented.

INTRODUCTION

The world Health Organization declared COVID -19 a pandemic in January 2020, due to the severity of illness and that it spreads quickly across countries and/or continents. Covid-19 is a global crisis, as this infectious virus quickly spreads because of the hyper globalization and in return it shakes every corner of the world, society, healthy organizations, educational system, economies, government and what not. As per World Trade Organization (WTO, 2020) due to this pandemic merchandise trade fall between 13% and 33% and the figure is worse as far as commercial services are considered. While as per International Monetary Fund (IMF, 2020) there is a 3% contraction of global economy- (cited in Lamy & Pedrosa, 2020). Global economy in 2020 has reduced by 5.3% but grows by 8.0% in 2021 as per another report (Congressional Research Service, 2021). Further this report (Congressional Research Service, 2021) also revealed that economic growth has fallen rapidly in second quarter of 2020 but regains

DOI: 10.4018/978-1-6684-5181-6.ch010

quickly in the third quarter and is mostly recovering since. While in 2021, world economy experienced strong rebound, but due to the fresh threats from COVID 19 variants economic growth is forecasted to decline from 5.5% last year 2021 to 4.1% in 2022 and will further fall to 3.2% in 2023 (United Nations [UN], 2022). Moreover, UN (2022) also highlighted that global economy is continuously facing COVID-19 and its new variants (Delta & Omicron) which further leads to escalation in inflation, debt, policy uncertainty, poverty, unemployment and income equality and will continuously disrupt economic activities. According to International Labour Organizations (ILO, 2022) global unemployment will reach to 207 million in 2022(cited in "Global Unemployment", 2022. *India today*), which means the rate is almost 21 million higher than the rate in year 2019. Henceforth, this figure warns of slow and uncertain recovery of labour market worldwide. India today newspaper in another report ("Explained: Impact of Omicron Variant", 2021) highlighted that Omicron variant has become a new concern for Organization for Economic Cooperation and Development (OECD) as it could cause severe economy slowdown and could impact economic recovery worldwide. This report also mentioned that if Omicron becomes more severe and dominant COVID variant it could trigger further challenges and risks to already struggling supply chains, result in inflation over a extended period of time and compels government organizations to implement strict restrictions on mobility and lockdowns and subsequently further disruptions in demand for goods and services could affect economic activities badly. As per this report, travel and tourism sector, aviation, restaurant and other ancillary sectors are also witnessing significant fall and these sectors are already experiencing a heat of previous waves of COVID-19 ("Explained: Impact of Omicron Variant" 2021. *India Today).*

"What we are seeing is an economy that functions right through these waves of COVID",-US Federal Reserve Chairman Jerome Powell (cited in John & Schneider, 2022).

International Monetary Fund (IMF, 2022) in World Economic Outlook Update under the title "*Rising Caseloads-A Disrupted Recovery and Higher Inflation*" revealed that due to high spread of new variant of COVID19 pandemic i.e. Omicron, nations have re-imposed lockdowns and restrictions and world economy has reached in weaker position than expected earlier. The IMF (2022) further suggested that global growth expected to moderate from 5.9% in 2021 to 4.4% in 2022 and probably to go slow down by 3.8% in 2023, highlighting a significant fall in the two largest economies of the world. In addition to this, rise in energy prices and disruptions in supply could also cause more unremitting inflation than forecasted before in countries like USA, in emerging markets and also in various developing countries. While China is also experiencing limited growth prospects because of ongoing downturn in real estate sector and also because of slow recovery in private consumptions (International Monetary Fund, 2022). Similarly, Curran and Kennedy (2021) also revealed that the omicron variant of COVID19 pandemic deteriorates plans of policymakers to shift their focus on inflation rather than on weak demand. These researchers mentioned that imposition of restrictions on mobility and on travel blows costumer and corporate world and lessening activities in holiday seasons to curb the virus spread shakes many economies of world. Expectations for interest –rate raises over the coming years and markets shifted quickly to price in economic blow and before emerging of omicron variant economists expected a transition in demand from durable goods towards services like travel, leisure and tourism but that assumption may now be delayed and undermines global recovery (Curran, et al. 2021). European Investment bank (2022) also highlighted that as the pandemic and its variants continue, uncertainty about future poses broad challenge to economic activity like investment. European Investment bank (2022) further showed that 5%

companies planned to reduce investment in coming year and 43% companies have firm belief that the pandemic would negatively affect their investment plans, while 20% firms estimate to decline employment due to the pandemic crisis.

According to Ozkazanc-Pan and Pullen (2020) due to COVID-19 pandemic not only hundreds and thousands of people lost their precious lives around the world, but health, educational, political system and economic organizations are disrupted, with alarming rate of unemployment, poverty and deepening of pre-existing inequalities. Further these researchers advocated that fear and uncertainty in business, absence of good governance and care for individual all leads to racial, social, economic, political and health adversities. Other researchers however indicated that Covid-19 outbreak not only disrupts and threatens health system, business and economy on large scale but also poses unparallel challenges for individual's current work and their careers (Restubog, Ocampo & Wang, 2020). The authors further mentioned that Novel Coronavirus that continues to create chaos worldwide, results in harsh workplace conditions in many companies, firms and industries in the form of lack of social and work support, rise in work demands, irregular work shifts, insufficient work benefits and inadequate and poor access to healthcare services. In addition, economic abatement will continue compels people to endure layoffs, downsizing, involuntary unemployment, job insecurity across various sectors such as in travel and tourism, food services, manufacturing and retailing etc (Restubog, et al. 2020). As this pandemic has arises need for social distancing and imposing remote policies to ensure work at home, which further creates incongruence in work family roles and disturbs work family balance (Restubog, Ocampo & Wang, 2020).

The news about the Omicron variant may actually be a reminder of how shortsighted that failure has been. We are spending to support our economies, while we are failing to vaccinate the whole world. As a result, the world really is not looking better - Laurence Boon, chief economist of OCED (cited in "Explained: Impact of Omicron Variant" 2021. India Today).

As per International Labour Standards (ILO, 2020) the most vulnerable in the labour market are 1.6 billion informal workers who are significantly affected by lockdown and other COVID- related restrictions and measures. Among informal economy workers, women workforce as compared to their man counterparts is significantly impacted by this pandemic. And in the present economic crises, small entrepreneurs and self-employed workers of retail trade, hospitality and food service sector are more susceptible to high risk disruptions across the globe (ILO, 2020). In this context ILO (2020) has forwarded policy framework which is based on four pillars to fight and curb against COVID-19 threats-

First Pillar is stimulating the economy and employment, which involves -

- Activating fiscal policy.
- Accommodating monetary policy.
- Lending and encouraging financial support to specific sectors particularly health organization.

Second Pillar is supporting enterprises, jobs and incomes, which comprises-

- Extension in social protection for all.
- Execution of employment retention procedures.
- Give financial and other relief for entrepreneurs.

Third Pillar is protecting workers in the workplace, includes-

- Ensure protection of all workforces at the workplaces.
- Strengthening of Occupational Safety and Health (OSH) measures.
- Adaption of work arrangements in the form of teleworking etc.
- Prevention of work discrimination and exclusion.
- Equality in healthcare access.
- Expand in access to paid leave.

Fourth Pillar deals with relying on social dialogue for solutions with focus on following aspects-

- Improve the capacity and resilience of employers and worker's organizations.
- Improve and strengthen the capacity and power of governments.
- Reinforce social dialogue, strengthen collective bargaining and improve labour relations institutions and processes.

COVID-19 outbreak which has impacted hundreds of millions of people around the world directly or indirectly and its affect will continuously to be prolonged, and its impact on work, people's career and career development is a complex phenomenon that calls from reflective solution (Rudolph & Zacher, 2020). While these researchers (Zacher & Rudolph, 2021) in their other study have suggested that this outbreak not only pose medical and economic crises but also challenges various components of wellbeing such as life satisfaction, positive affect as well as negative affect which in turn can also influence individuals' resources, their competences and effectiveness in long run. As per other researcher like Mair (2020) coronavirus is partly a problem of our economic structure and at the same time is a socially driven phenomenon. Further mentioned researcher narrated that its clear COVID virus is the actual cause of current chaos but regulating and managing its effect need us to understand complex human behaviour as well as its broad economic background. Mair (2020) also mentioned that it is possible to handle and tackle COVID19 effectively if all individuals lessen economic activities, as the logic is simple when people mix in households, and in workplace, or on journeys they spread infections. But on the other hand, imposition of lockdown to curb moment of people has its destructive consequences on the global economy as the main objective of businesses is to make profit but due to lockdown they can't produce and sell anything, in this way they won't make any profit and revenue and are less able to employee individuals (Mair, et al. 2020). Accordingly, people lost their jobs or due to the fear of losing jobs they will consume less and the whole vicious circle start again and ultimately whole economy spiral into depression phase- (Mair, 2020).

COVID pandemic is triggering unprecedented challenges and threats to all shapes and sizes of business particularly those who are in their initial stages of operations (i.e. startups) (Waldron, 2020). High level changes in customers behaviour and buying power, combined with supply chain disruptions and restrictions on offices across the globe compelled business into "do or die" situation, where success and survival depends on adoption of new digital technologies, future-proof management businesses and other effective communication tools (Waldron, 2020). Apart from affecting public health and livelihood throughout the world, COVID-19 has major disruptive consequences for poor and vulnerable population (Ramalingam & Prabhu, 2020). This crisis has direct impact on health and mortality rate and has indirect impact on social, economic and political sector. In addition, COVID-19 also creates opportunities for new solutions and approaches and for investments related to health sectors (Ramalingam and Prabhu, 2020). These researchers have also highlighted the role of innovation as an effective response to the Coronavirus pandemic.

Tourism sector is a significant contributor of many economies around the globe and a labor-intensive industry (as its main source of employment particularly for less skilled and educated employees), shares approximately 6.9% of employment rate in the Organization for Economic Co-operation and development (OECD, 2020). Moreover, this sector contains employment opportunities to many seasonal, part time workers, students, migrants, women's, geriatric population etc in urban, rural and remote areas where other employment opportunities are less and scare (OECD, 2020). However, COVID-19 pandemic substantially impacts and hits tourism economy, with 60-80 per cent reduction in this sector worldwide and in this context many recovery measures were introduced accordingly for instances, lifting of travel restrictions and lockdowns, bring back travellers confidence and reassess and revaluate tourism industry (OECD, 2020).

Coronavirus which has reached almost every corner of the country around the world left economies and businesses of nations counting the cost and the economic impact of pandemic are presented under the following headings (Jones, Palumbo & Brown, 2021)-

The Impact of Coronavirus on Stock Markets

Huge shifts in stock markets impacts the value of pensions and persons savings accounts. Lockdowns, other movement restrictions and delay in vaccination programmes made market volatile and unstable and as the COVID19 cases grew FTSE, DOW Jones and Nikkei etc saw big drop and/or fall (Jones, Palumbo & Brown, 2021).

World Economies Struggling With Rising Unemployment (A Difficult Year for Job Seekers)

Because of this pandemic outbreak most of the people have lost their jobs and have experienced cut down in their incomes. In major economies unemployment rate has increased at alarming rate and the percentage of generation of new job opportunities remains very low (Jones, Palumbo & Brown, 2021).

New Vaccination Is Still Very Low in Many Countries

Majority Of Countries Are in a Recession Phase

International Monterey Fund (IMF) has declared decline in world economy as the worst since the Great Depression (1930). The only major country whose economy registered a growth in 2020 was China by 2.3% (Jones, Palumbo & Brown, 2021).

The Impact on Travel Industry

Due to the pandemic travel industry suffers badly and faces huge damage with commercial flights remain very low as customers were seen cancelling business and holiday trips. New variants of coronavirus also compile many nations to follow strict travel restrictions. So it can be said that travel industry is still away from recovery mode (Jones, Palumbo & Brown, 2021).

Hospitality Sector Has Shut Down Globally

The hospitality is one of those sectors which have been hit hard by this pandemic outbreak and millions of related jobs and various companies get bankrupt. Apart from this, over 35 million hotels and rental houses globally have marked a decline in reservations (Jones, Palumbo & Brown, 2021). And lockdowns and other restrictions results in drastic fall in economic activities and one of them is investment.

The World Tourism Industry Is Collapsing

In 2020, billions of dollars have been lost worldwide in the tourism sector and many analysts forecast that international travel and tourism industry won't return to the normal level until around 2025 (Jones, Palumbo & Brown, 2021).

The Impact on Shoppers and Shopping Behaviour

Huge drop in shoppers have been witnessed as shoppers stayed at homes, and with emergence of new variants and increase in COVID-19 cases have made problem even very worse (Jones, Palumbo & Brown, 2021). Reports have revealed that about 67% customers show resistance to travel more than 5 kilometres for shopping purpose (Jones, et al. 2021). So to avoid threats from infectious virus people are forced to change their shopping styles and behaviours which in turn has significantly boosted and enhanced online e-commerce sector with global revenue of approximately $3.9 trillion in 2020 (Jones, Palumbo & Brown, 2021).

The Rise of Pharmaceutical Industries

Governments throughout the world have invested billions of dollars for COVID vaccination and other related treatment options. Vaccines like Moderna, Novavax and AstraZeneca have registered significant rises (Jones, Palumbo & Brown, 2021).

The COVID pandemic runs in phases and waves, with each phase brought different kind of needs, demands and requirements that has significantly impacted workers, entrepreneurs, consumers and partners (Saueressig, 2021). The first wave was characterised by the challenges in the form of reacting to the crisis, human impact and the urgent needs (Saueressig, et al. 2021). The most affected businesses by the first wave of COVID pandemic were those whose supply chains were based on constituents and/or components manufactured in pandemic hotspots, as well as those who have abrupt swings in demands and/or supply such as manufactures of personal protective equipment (PPE) kits, facial masks and of office equipments, and certain consumer product producers (Saueressig, 2021). While second wave was marked by coping and responding to the effect on businesses and finding solutions, with extension in attention towards helping consumers to manage the COVID pandemic's impact on their businesses and other firms seek to keep lean activities and operation so to preserve and protect their revenue and cash flow (Saueressig, 2021). Third wave comprises looking forward, come out of the COVID crisis strongly, be more resilient and transformed-businesses have been changed abruptly with the emerging of new ways of working, and e-commerce and collaborative has been in growing trend (Saueressig, 2021).

The COVID-19 pandemic hit hard European economy and trigger slower growth and recovery as compared to the global economy, with real Gross Domestic Product (GDP) growth in the euro area range from 3.6% to 4.2% in 2021, and this figure represents European Unions are significantly lagging behind the recovery of China with Gross Domestic Product (GDP) of 7.9% in year 2021 (De Vet, et al. 2021). Notable differences were found in performance among and within various work sectors. For instances, overall digital industry as well as healthcare sector performed well and companies manufacturing electric vehicles were less affected by COVID crisis as compared to overall sectors (De Vet, et al. 2021). Other industries associated with chemicals, construction, food and drinks showed v-shaped recovery from the COVID crisis and automotive and textile sector also showed recovery despite the shocks (De Vet, et al. 2021). Whereas other sectors due to the restriction on mobility, and lockdowns experienced abrupt shock by crisis such as tourism, cultural and creative industries and aerospace industries and these are more likely to face futher disruptions from the unprecedented crisis as these industries involve human contact and interactions (De Vet, et al. 2021).

Madgavkar, et al (2020) reflected in their research study that women workforce as compared to man are more vulnerable to coronavirus related economics impacts because of already prevailing gender inequalities. They have further estimated that the rates of Job loss in female workers are about 1.8 times higher than male counterparts globally. This figure implies that women's job are falling faster than average irrespective of the fact that both women and man work in different domains (Madgavkar, et al. 2020).

Ramvilas et al. (2021) focus on holistic solutions like optimising research funding, and collaborations and supporting, encouraging and strengthening big data analytics etc as a post Pandemic response. Whereas per other author Lalani (2021) the year 2020 is remarked as the year of pandemic and this outbreak is followed by opportunities, innovativeness and inventions witnessed in healthcare sector and manufacturing industry .The author further stated that pandemic which tremble all economies of world, also leads to high rate of unemployment, decline in economic growth and shook all the pillars of world economy in the form of exports, consumption, manufacturing and so on and other economic crisis related to capital, availability of manpower and other factors of production all adds fuel to fire. Even though the Government and policy makers worldwide are taking innovative roads maps and launched various programmes successfully such as upgradation of e-commerce etc but still thoroughly and comprehensive analysis of the various ongoing and upcoming challenges needed to get started, with focus on encouraging private and public partnership. All these start-ups will surely lay the foundation for recovery of world economy- (Lalani, 2021).

COVID19 and its variants affected both lives and livelihood and consequently have made realized the need for digital transformation at workplaces, new skills for workforce and even new strategies to tackle and manage crises (Branicki, 2020). In turn digitalization has been modifying the ways employees interact at the workplace, the expectation from their employees and the career paths and how, when and where work is conducted (Antonacopoulou & Georgiadou, 2021). Moreover, as per these researchers COVID-19 pandemic has disturbed our living and working patterns as well as the ways to relate and interact with each other. In connection with this, corporation has become more than a workplace and leadership has become inclusive (leading from home) rather than relational process. Thus, there is a paradigm shift in work, its meaning and significance, in corporation, leadership and even in social structures (Antonacopoulou and Georgiadou, 2021). The COVID-19 which poses a threat to various aspect of human lives throughout the world, and to curb its effects many hard hit countries and other nations took various safety measures such as lockdowns, shutdowns of business sector, closing of educational organizations(schools, colleges, & universities), social distancing and regulations of hygiene to control quick spread of COVID virus. All these measures were seen to have significant impacts on peoples working lives, work arrangements, regular employment relationships, subcontracted labor and other new types of working like gig economy (Spurk & Straub, 2020).

"The workplace is a social environment and business in any form is a social phenomenon"- Robin Dunbar Emeritus Professor of Experimental Psychology, University of Oxford (cited in "Coronavirus" 2020. BBC WORKLIFE).

The COVID-19 outbreak has prompted businesses throughout the world to develop and experiment with new, sophisticated and modern technologies to reduce risks and threats associated with this ongoing menace. For example in many countries robots were designed to deliver medicines, food and other basic services, while other countries develop drones and spray machines to spray disinfectants and spray employees safely at workplaces (Lalani, 2021). With the help of artificial intelligence and other advanced technologies countries all around the world were able to develop and test potential and effective vaccines, whereas shortage in personal protective equipments (PPE) has encouraged small enterprisers to startup its manufacturing and enables them to earn a lot of profit-(Lalani, et al. 2021).

ECONOMIC CHALLENGES OF COVID-19

According to researchers Rudolph and Zacher (2020) Global pandemic (COVID-19) activates '*uncertain times*' and its influence can be understood as career "*shock*" to whole humanity. And accordingly it brought with itself many alarming challenges which are mentioned below-

- Due to rise in COVID-19 cases, initially restrictions were put on international trade that was related to travel restrictions not export ban (Lamy & Pedrosa, 2020). However as national lockdowns has been lifted, so international trade should restart again as soon as possible. And this challenge needed to address by international community.
- Immunity passport must be given serious thought for at least those workers who are working at international transportations like sea crews, pilots etc (Lamy & Pedrosa, 2020).
- Medical and scientific initiatives need to be taken by both public and private organizations in order to facilitate international tour and travel (Lamy & Pedrosa, 2020).
- As such trillions of dollars as stimulus packages are disbursed across Globe so to provide financial support to businesses and general masses, however lack of clear rules and regulations regarding policies could result in trade friction and other allied problems that further becomes a big challenge for WHO and other international organizations that needs to get resolve as soon as possible (Lamy & Pedrosa, 2020).
- Government also needs to come forward to discuss reforms associated with the World Trade Organization (WTO) agreement on subsidies and other countervailing procedures (Lamy & Pedrosa, 2020).
- Managing world supply chain practices associated with speed, and efficiency and effectiveness also requires attention. Accordingly governments, costumers and workforce has to give consider-

ation to risk involvements in supply chain crises in terms of fragility that may range from accepting of much more inventories to diversification and so on (Lamy & Pedrosa, 2020).

- Unclear WTO policies on export restrictions also possess big challenge that needs to tackle as it favours no one (Lamy & Pedrosa, 2020).
- Coronavirus undoubtly gets highly spreads because of higher globalization but it's not World Health Organization (WHO) and World Trade Organization (WTO) that supplies hospital beds, health professionals (doctors, technicians and nurses), and provides medicines, oxygen cylinders, ventilators as well as PPE(Personal Protective Equipment) (Lamy & Pedrosa, 2020). Rather all the responsibilities and duties are met by domestic government who determine and decide their policies, programmes and interventions. International bodies in the form of WHO and WTO and others allied organizations could only give timely warnings, technical assistance and dispute settlements (Lamy, et al. 2020).
- According to International Labour Organization (ILO, 2022) Global unemployment has reached to 207 million, a number approximately 21 million higher rate than in 2019 (cited in "Global Unemployment", 2022. *India today*). This report also depicts slow and uncertain recovery due to continuity in COVID-19 pandemic and it is subsequently going to have significant impact on international labour markets.
- Emerging new variants of COVID-19 results in prolong and long-lasting pandemic crisis and could escalate worldwide novel economic disturbances and disruptions (International Monetary Fund, 2022). Moreover, disturbance in supply chain, instability in energy prices, localized wage pressure causes more uncertainty about inflation, and other global risks and crises may shoot up as geopolitical conflicts and/or tension remains elevated and ongoing global climate catastrophe predicts alarming upcoming natural disasters (International Monetary Fund, 2022).
- There is a disproportionate impact of the new COVID-19 variants (Delta and Omicron) across group of workers, world of work and countries due to the involvement of higher uncertainty. These difference are escalating inequalities within and among countries and challenging the economic, financial and social segment of every corner of world, irrespective of development status (cited in "Global Unemployment", 2022. *India today*).
- The huge significant difference of COVID-19 crises can be felt on women's employment. Moreover shutting down of education and training institutions due to pandemic have long term consequences for youth more especially the younger population without access to internet facility (cited in "Global Unemployment", 2022. *India today*).
- When this COVID crisis is over people are less likely to return to normalcy, so all individuals need to learn with this contagious virus and its effect on people, business, society, health and educational organizations (Saueressig, 2021).
- Government and all other related stakeholders need to provide support and help to companies and industries to bring back workers to their workplaces, to facilitate required travel recommendations and to diagnose potential risks for workers (Saueressig, 2021).
- Humanity is going to face novel challenges resulted by geopolitical events, wars, climate changes, health issues and other crises, so accordingly companies and other businesses requires to manage and adjust to continuous changes, adaptability to new circumstance and challenges, and to show resilient while facing any kind of distress (Saueressig, 2021).
- One main challenge for policy makers in battling the blow economy will be the fact that they have only few options left after 2020's stimulus effort (Curran & Kennedy, 2021). Only few central

banks have tightened monetary policy since the end of 2020's recession and world's benchmarks remain around zero which implies they have limited space to rescue again, with governments around globe are already struggling rising debut burdens (Curran & Kennedy, 2021).

- COVID-pandemic prompts more digitalisation of work, online jobs and e-commerce, but at the same time transition in jobs will require new kinds of skills, training and ultimately leads to elimination of many workforces who are unable to meet growing demands of new jobs (European Investment bank, 2022).
- One of the major challenge for economist is how the important interconnected components and factors of the tourism supply chain will function and to operate together and also to provide flawless experience to tourists (OECD, 2020).

In addition to above mention challenges, COVID-19 pandemic cause's unexceptional challenges for businesses and governments around the world in the form of digital disruption, diversity and inclusion, workforce and skills etc and in this context PricewaterhouseCoopers (PWC, 2022) has focused on five areas of post COVID-19 pandemic-

Business resilience-*Redefining crisis reaction that exist stronger from crisis* (PWC, 2022).

COVID-19 outbreak results in unexceptional impact for which already prevailing crisis plans and teams were non-prepared. But if getting right insight from the pandemic and develop resilience and preparation for next crisis, businesses have an opportunity to turn the COVID pandemic disruption into advantage (PWC, 2022). And for long term resilience three key lessons need to implement by businesses:

- Planning and preparation for inevitable crisis by designing a crisis response team, and crisis response plan associated with strategy, goals, objective as well as developing an integrated resilience programme (PWC, 2022).
- For effective crisis management, there should be integration between resilience competencies and teams and coordinates the tools, tactics and technologies (PWC, 2022).
- Establishment of high level of governance, readdressing and reanalysing of crisis management structure as well reinforcing and cultivating resilience culture (PWC, 2022).

Future of work-*Rethinking how employees are going to work in the post pandemic world* (PricewaterhouseCoopers[PWC], 2022).

The COVID pandemic has changed the global workforce forever. And managements and leaders of businesses are expected to reskill employees particularly in digital sector, emphasis should also be given on inclusivity and job security (PWC, 2022).

Future supply chain capabilities– *Extension of focus from logistic to customer insight* (PricewaterhouseCoopers[PWC], 2022).

The impact of COVID19 pandemic has been felt throughout world supply chains. An extension of future supply chain competitiveness ahead of the physical supply chain has been seen, that comprises comprehension of consumers experiences and to utilize them in order to shape strategy (PWC, 2022). This domain emphasis on three key aspects mentioned below:

- Establish a reflective understanding of customer's needs and aspirations and to investigate on how to deliver outstanding services to them without any compromise on cost and responsiveness.

- Mapping of consumers journey through the value chain and creation of an ecosystem so to sustain customer interactions and involvement.
- Develop a human centric and /or human friendly approach to digital world, utilize proper digital qualities at the right times to prioritise important promises and demands of customers.

Finance and liquidity-*Formulating what the post COVID-19 pandemic implies for cash flow* (PricewaterhouseCoopers[PWC], 2022).

As business operations are recovering at unpredictable speed from the COVID crisis, companies will require to re-examine ways and strategies for their revenues and cash flow. Companies and businesses who are endure to plan and manage their cash and liquidity positions in a sustained, controlled and in responsive way will be better able to optimize the opportunities as recovery get stronger (PWC, 2022).

Economic Opportunities

Apart from earlier mentioned challenges brought by Covid-19, this pandemic also creates many economic and other allied opportunities which are discussed below-

- COVID-19 gives more opportunities to business and companies to invest in digital technology and transform the world economy to flourish in new and more digitalization.
- COVID-19 crises that have become a shared experience for all humanity can be counterattacked by multilateral actions. As there is a probability of re-emergence of risk that the virus can reinfect the whole population again, there is a need of establishing new international organization that could perform risk assessment, monitoring and notification (Lamy & Pedrosa, 2020).
- The global pandemic provides opportunity to learn from this COVID crisis and in anticipation we should prepare ourselves to handle these catastrophes effectively by developing efficient and helpful strategies to save the future generations (Lamy & Pedrosa, 2020).
- As per Director of International Labour Organization (ILO), (2022) "sustainable recovery is possible if it's based on the principles of decent work at health and safety sector, equity, social protection and social dialogue" (cited in "Global Unemployment", 2022. *India today*).
- Policy and interventions should be in line with the criteria of inclusive, sustainable, resilience and human centred recovery from the COVID-19 crisis both at national and international levels (cited in "Global Unemployment", 2022. *India today*).
- COVID-pandemic has created various career opportunities and flexible type of work environment, online platform in the form of gig work which results in more boundaryless work environment, individualized and whole life careers (Spurk & Straub, 2020).
- Investigating employees experience regarding the effects of novel coronavirus crises can prove fruitful to aware and inform various stakeholders as how to improve work conditions and flexible employment relations for longer term (Spurk & Straub, 2020).
- Employees experience during Corona pandemic and afterwards will make conscious contracting firms and online platforms about the demands of workers (Spurk & Straub, 2020). Moreover, those information and insight can be utilized to align infrastructure and services with sustainability and could decline lessening of workforce by providing support, suitable work conditions and effective work environment for promoting their work performance and thereby enhancing quality and satisfaction of workers (Spurk & Straub, 2020).

- Vocational trainers and researchers in behavioural sciences can also contribute to provide insight and information to all involved stakeholders in order to support long term and sustainable career development of workforce (Spurk & Straub, 2020).
- Workforces' experiences during and after COVID pandemic will reveal the risks, challenges and opportunities of flexible employment and the significant role of potential factors and stakeholders like unions, federal officers and union leaders etc in order to develop efficient, sustainable and effective new policies, rules and regulations which will be worker friendly, supportive and conducive for employees (Spurk & Straub, 2020).
- Workforces experience during COVID pandemic will also help employees to understand the effects of work environment and conditions on their health status, opportunities for career development, enhancement of quality and empowerment of workers like appeal for workers rights and awareness of self-care (Spurk & Straub, 2020).
- One of the sectors where pandemic crisis is posing unprecedented opportunity for potential growth and development is digitalisation and it also triggers opportunity to rethink of tourism industry for the future, supports low carbon transition, and endorsing digital transformation of the sector in order to establish a stronger, more sustainable and resilient tourism sector (OECD, 2020).
- Government at national levels has introduced unprecedented initiatives and emergency response to provide income to tourism workforce, and supports tourism businesses to restart their operations and activities, and to assist tourist workers (OECD, 2020).
- Government and policy makers throughout the world are taking abrupt measures and extraordinary initiatives to focus on health issues and to curb economic impact of COVID 19 disruptions on businesses and employees. And these governments' responses come in the form of economy wide stimulus packages such as providing liquidity and fiscal reliefs in the form of loans, tax postponements, other guarantee schemes etc to small businesses and health organizations OECD, 2020). Tourism sector and its workforces is one of the sectors which are widely benefiting from these economic stimulus packages and tourism specific measures which are meant to facilitate its recovery (OECD, 2020).
- Online business has been escalating significantly, collaborative working is in demand more than ever and leaders are recognizing the fact that companies, industries and firms are more resilient to bounce back and that when operating in networks, business activities and operations become more sustainable (Saueressig, 2021).
- Digitalization of customers, supply chain interactions and internal operations has been escalated by companies and firms, and customers are given more opportunity to reassess their process and to reallocate resources as per need (Saueressig, 2021).
- The post COVID-pandemic opportunity for enterprises is to realize that those who have the ability to adapt to changing environment and to adjust with the growing demand and to shape the next normal, will be the utmost successful (Saueressig, 2021).
- COVID-19 crisis while triggering new challenges but at the same time creates new opportunities for businesses particularly who are in their initial stage of operations, to tackle new constraints and difficulties prevails in the market and accordingly respond to changing needs, aspirations and preferences of consumers (Waldron, 2020).
- During current COVID disruptions, ecommerce and food delivery services has increased at high pace and a trends of ordering goods and products through online is expected to remain long lasting even after demise of COVID-19 pandemic. As COVID-19 causes persistent and consistent

modification in the markets, in costumer's need, and habit, accordingly creates precious and helpful opportunities for businesses and startups that are able to adapt and adjust with these changes (Waldron, 2020).

- Researchers also suggested that COVID-19 pandemic posing various opportunities for companies and businesses characterised by agility and willing to adapt and also result in emergence of various successful innovative start-ups (Waldron, 2020).
- Due to continuity in COVID-pandemic and its new variants, more attention has been given to effective global health strategy and in this connection, equal access to vaccination, tests and treatments has become an essential tools and/or instruments to decline the risks and threats associated with COVID and its variants (International Monetary Fund, 2022). So accordingly this calls for amplified production of supplies of mentioned requirement, effective delivery system of nations and fair international distribution.
- Additionally, many countries need to revise their monetary policies so to have tight grip on inflation and, fiscal policy will require to focus more on health and social spending and to provide assistance and support to the worst affected (International Monetary Fund, 2022). Accordingly international organization will need to preserve liquidity and accelerate systematic debt restructurings, revise and readdress climate related policies in order to curb the risks of disastrous climate changes and save the world from further global crisis (International Monetary Fund, 2022).
- Transition in jobs could benefit some areas more than the others, although policy makers must readdress regional disparity as well as to encourage social cohesion (European Investment bank, 2022).
- Greening of organizations (awareness regarding environmental issues) and digitalisation will generate more new job opportunities and, overall effect on employment rate could be positive one (European Investment bank, 2022).
- COVID-19 crisis has substantial impact on global economy and accordingly stimulates remarkable, extraordinary and unprecedented policy response around the globe (De Vet, et al. 2021).
- The recovery package from COVID crisis creates unique opportunities to facilitate the competitiveness of industries by focusing on making them more green, digital as well as resilient (De Vet, et al. 2021). And the effectiveness and efficiency of recovery and resilience plans and policies can be judged from the perspective if these policies take into consideration basic economic and sector specific aspects (De Vet, et al. 2021).
- COVID-19 pandemic generated opportunities especially for certain sectors of economy, because of the fact that customers and businesses have drastically and radically modified their behaviours out of this outbreak (De Vet, et al. 2021).

CONCLUSION

As the coronavirus (COVID-19) pandemic and its variants (Delta & Omicron) continues and still keeps global economy in its grip, and it's too early to estimate and assess full impacts of this COVID crisis- either positive or negative (De Vet, Nigohosyan, Ferrer, Gross, Kuehl & Flickenschild, 2021). In this context it's recommended that government both at national and international level should conduct an objective, empirical, extensive as well comprehensive analysis and investigation on economic impact, challenges and opportunities of COVID 19 so to pave the wave for development of intervention models and effective policies accordingly to curb the negative impact of COVID pandemic as well as to promote economic growth, progress and flourishing of business activities.

REFERENCES

Antonacopoulou, E. P., & Georgiadou, A. (2021). Leading through social distancing: The future of work, corporations and leadership from home. *Gender, Work and Organization*, *28*(2), 749–767. doi:10.1111/gwao.12533

Branicki, L. J. (2020). COVID-19, ethics of care and feminist crisis management. *Gender, Work and Organization*, *27*(5), 872–883. doi:10.1111/gwao.12491 PMID:32837015

Congressional Research Service. (2021, November). *Global Economic Effects of COVID-19*. https://sgp.fas.org/crs/row/R46270.pdf

Coronavirus: How the world of work may change forever. (2020, October 23). *BBC WORKLIFE*. https://www.bbc.com/worklife/article/20201023-coronavirus-how-will-the-pandemic-change-the-way-we-work

Curran, E., & Kennedy, S. (2021, November 29). Worst case scenario: Economists analyse how omicron will impact recovery. *Business Standard*. https://www.business-standard.com/article/international/how-covid-variant-omicron-will-impact-global-recovery-economists-evaluate-121112900293_1.html

De Vet, J. M., Nigohosyan, D., Ferrer, J. N., Gross, A. K., Kuehl, S., & Flickenschild, M. (2021). Impacts of the COVID-19 Pandemic on EU Industries.European Parliament.

European Investment Bank. (2021, January). *EIB Investment Report 2020/2021: Building a smart and green Europe in the COVID-19 era*. https://www.eib.org/en/publications/investment-report-2020

Explained: Impact of Omicron variant on global economy. (2021, December 2). *India Today*. https://www.indiatoday.in/business/story/omicron-coronavirus-variant-global-economy-impact-explained-1883353-2021-12-02

Global unemployment to reach 207 million in 2022, says ILO report. (2022, January 21). *India Today*. https://www.indiatoday.in/business/story/global-unemployment-to-reach-207-million-in-2022-says-ilo-report-1902576-2022-01-21

International Labour Organization. (2020, April). *ILO Monitor: COVID-19 and the world of work. Third edition Updated estimates and analysis*. https://www.ilo.org/wcmsp5/groups/public/---dgreports/---dcomm/documents/briefingnote/wcms_743146.pdf

International Monetary Fund (World Economic Outlook Update). (2022, January). *Rising Caseloads, A Disrupted Recovery, and Higher Inflation*. https://www.imf.org/en/Publications/WEO/Issues/2022/01/25/world-economic-outlook-update-january-2022

John, M., & Schneider, H. (2022, January 18). Analysis: With Omicron, global economy spots chance to push past COVID. *Reuters*. https://www.reuters.com/markets/europe/with-omicron-global-economy-spots-chance-push-past-covid-2022-01-18/

Jones, L., Palumbo, D., & Brown, D. (2021, January 24). Coronavirus: How the pandemic has changed the world economy. *BBC News*. https://www.bbc.com/news/business-51706225#:~:text=The%20IMF%20estimates%20that%20the,grow%20in%202020%20was%20China.&text=The%20IMF%20is%2C%20however%2C%20predicting,growth%20of%205.2%25%20in%202021

Lalani, M. (2021). Post COVID 19-Economic Opportunities & Challenges in India: Crisis that led to innovations and the road ahead. *PalArch's Journal of Archaeology of Egypt/Egyptology, 18*(7), 2081-2085.

Lamy, P., & Pedrosa, E. (2020). *Economics: Trade and Connectivity in the Post-COVID-19 World*. Challenges and Opportunities in the Post-COVID-19 World (World Economic Forum). https://www3.weforum.org/docs/WEF_Challenges_and_Opportunities_Post_COVID_19.pdf

Madgavkar, A., White, O., Krishnan, M., Mahajan, D., & Azcue, X. (2020). *COVID-19 and gender equality: Countering the regressive effects*. McKinsey Global Institute.

Mair, S. (2020, March 30). What will the world be like after coronavirus? Four possible futures. *The Conversation*. https://theconversation.com/what-will-the-world-be-like-after-coronavirus-four-possible-futures-134085

OECD. (2020). *Tourism policy responses to the coronavirus (COVID-19)*. https://read.oecd-ilibrary.org/view/?ref=124_124984-7uf8nm95se&title=Covid-19_Tourism_Policy_Responses

Özkazanç-Pan, B., & Pullen, A. (2020). Gendered labour and work, even in pandemic times. *Gender, Work and Organization, 27*(5), 675–676. doi:10.1111/gwao.12516 PMID:32904841

PricewaterhouseCoopers (PWC). (2021, December). *Learning from the impacts of COVID-19 and leading the recovery*. https://www.pwc.com/gx/en/issues/crisis-solutions/covid-19.html

Ramalingam, B., & Prabhu, J. (2020). Innovation, development and COVID-19: Challenges, opportunities and ways forward. *OECD Tackling Coronavirus (COVID-19): Contributing to a Global Effort*, 1-14.

Ramvilas, G., Dhyani, S., Kumar, B., Sinha, N., Raghavan, R., Selvaraj, G., Divakar, N., Anoop, V. K., Shalu, K., Sinha, A., Kulkarni, A., Das, S., & Molur, S. (2021). Insights on COVID-19 impacts, challenges and opportunities for India's biodiversity research: From complexity to building adaptations. *Biological Conservation, 255*, 109003. doi:10.1016/j.biocon.2021.109003 PMID:35125501

Restubog, S. L. D., Ocampo, A. C. G., & Wang, L. (2020). Taking control amidst the chaos: Emotion regulation during the COVID-19 pandemic. *Journal of Vocational Behavior, 119*, 103440. doi:10.1016/j.jvb.2020.103440 PMID:32390659

Rudolph, C. W., & Zacher, H. (2020). COVID-19 and careers: On the futility of generational explanations. *Journal of Vocational Behavior, 119*, 103433. doi:10.1016/j.jvb.2020.103433 PMID:32390654

Saueressig, T. (2021, March 29). The Co-Existence of Challenge and Opportunity for Businesses. *SAP News*. https://news.sap.com/2021/03/co-existence-businesses-challenges-and-opportunities/

Spurk, D., & Straub, C. (2020). Flexible employment relationships and careers in times of the COVID-19 pandemic. *Journal of Vocational Behavior*, *119*, 103435. doi:10.1016/j.jvb.2020.103435 PMID:32382161

The World Bank. (2020, June). *The Global Economic Outlook During the COVID-19 Pandemic: A Changed World*. https://www.worldbank.org/en/news/feature/2020/06/08/the-global-economic-outlook-during-the-covid-19-pandemic-a-changed-world

United Nations. (2022, January). *COVID-19 variants, rising debt, threaten global economic growth: World Bank*. https://news.un.org/en/story/2022/01/1109702

Waldron, J. (2020, November 4). Challenges and Opportunities for Startups in the Time of COVID-19. *metasfresh*. https://metasfresh.com/en/2020/11/04/challenges-and-opportunities-for-startups-in-the-time-of-covid-19/

Zacher, H., & Rudolph, C. W. (2021). Individual differences and changes in subjective wellbeing during the early stages of the COVID-19 pandemic. *The American Psychologist*, *76*(1), 50–62. doi:10.1037/amp0000702 PMID:32700938

KEY TERMS AND DEFINITIONS

COVID-19: An illness (infectious disease) triggered by coronavirus SARS-CoV-2 that causes respiratory tract infection.

Digitalisation: It's a process of inclusion of digital technologies into business, and social sector with the objective of improving them and their revenue streams.

Economic: The branch of social science deals with production, distribution, and consumption of resources such as wealth.

Gross Domestic Product: It is defined as monetary measure of the market value of the total goods produced and services provided in an economy over a specific period of time.

International Labour Organization: International Labour Organization is a part of the United Nations which is concerned with the world of work by framing international labour standards, promotes social protection and rights at work settings and encourages equal employment opportunities.

Liquidity: It means availability and accessibility of assets, capital or cash to a company or market.

Organization for Economic Co-Operation and Development (OECD): It's an intergovernmental economic organization which promotes economic progress and world trade by creating opportunity to compare policy experiences, solve common problems, connects, and coordinates national and international policies of its member countries.

Pandemic: It's an infectious disease outbreak that spreads quickly across countries and/or continents. Its more severe than epidemic as it affects more people, larger area, and causes high mortality rate.

Supply Chain: It's a network or a system that exists between company and its suppliers involved in production and distribution of specific products and services.

Chapter 11
Evaluation of the Concordation Process in Turkey in Terms of Tax Applications

Cihan Kayacık
Zonguldak Bülent Ecevit Üniversitesi, Turkey

ABSTRACT

Any debtor who cannot pay his debts even though they are due or is in danger of not being able to pay on time can request a concordat. In the concordat process, tax-related practices and results concern more than one area. Therefore, it would be useful to consider the tax consequences of the concordat application as a whole. In addition, the concordat process will be discussed in terms of debtor and creditor. The consequences of the concordat by the creditor are in some cases "doubtful debt" and generally "worthless credit" being accepted and written off as an expense. In terms of the debtor, the resulting amount of "withdrawal receivable" must be followed in a provision account for three years and amortized with the losses incurred in these years. In addition, according to Article 308/g of the Execution and Bankruptcy Law, it also provides privileges in terms of fees, stamp duty, and BITT. However, the concordat decision accepted by the court is not obligatory for public receivables within the scope of Law No. 6183.

INTRODUCTION

Concordat regulates the rights and obligations of the creditor and debtor and partially protects them in line with the assurances it provides to the creditors in order to prevent honest debtors from going bankrupt. Therefore, it has consequences for the debtor and creditor. In the study, the consequences of the concordat for the debtor and the creditor will be discussed, and in addition to these, the results of the concordat in the tax field will be explained.

Before the bankruptcy or concordat decision, companies are expected to calculate their bankruptcy risks, determine which category they are in, and make decisions accordingly. According to the results of the analysis, it can decide to continue its activities without declaring bankruptcy or concordat. However, they may decide to declare a concordat if it is possible to get out of the insolvent situation according to

DOI: 10.4018/978-1-6684-5181-6.ch011

the risk results. In case it is not possible to save the company from bankruptcy situations, bankruptcy decision can also be taken. While capital companies and cooperatives can apply for bankruptcy, real persons can apply to the concordat together with legal entities. When declaring a concordat, companies have to choose one of the concordat types in return for their debts. By choosing one of the maturity concordat, deductible concordat or mixed concordat types, the debts are paid, and the activities are continued. Extending the maturities of debts is considered as a maturity concordat; The renunciation of some of the creditors' receivables is considered as a reduction concordat. Extending the maturity of the debts and giving up some of the creditors' receivables are also considered as mixed concordat. Evaluated concordat types provide ease of payment for the debtor, and also provide for the creditor to receive some of their receivables rather than losing all of them.

In the event that legal entities or natural persons declare a concordat, they must undertake to pay their debts honestly. In the concordat, it is necessary to request a concordat on the condition that it does not cause the other party to be in a difficult situation. In the improvement project submitted to the court, 2/3 of the creditors must approve the payment offer. In case the court approves the concordat, it is ensured that legal or real persons pay all debts according to the proposal submitted (Demir, 2019, p.62). It is important for companies to calculate their bankruptcy risks before going bankrupt or declaring concordat in order to continue their activities, to decide to go bankrupt or to declare bankruptcy.

Definition and Types of Concordat

Concordat is a compulsory enforcement institution, which is approved by the commercial court with the acceptance of the majority of the creditors, covering all the ordinary debts of an honest debtor (Gercek, 2017, p.299). In such a situation, unprivileged creditors give up some of their receivables. The debtor avoids paying the rest by paying his debts at the rate determined by the concordat (Karakış & Taş, 2001). In this case, honest debtors avoid falling into bankruptcy. It also protects the debtor, who is in economic distress, by preventing them from being followed through foreclosure. In the concordat process, the creditor has the opportunity to collect more receivables compared to bankruptcy (Konca, 2018, p.7).

In order for the concordat project to be accepted, a certain majority of the creditors must approve the proposal in the concordat and this proposal must be accepted by the court (Uyar, 2018, p.1). Concordat is an institution accepted to protect the debtors in the event that things go wrong and regular cash flow cannot be provided due to reasons beyond the debtor's own will (Kuru, 2013, p. 680).

It is possible to divide the concordat into two as in-court and out-of-court concordat. However, there are also types of concordat according to different situations. When evaluated according to the time it was made, it is divided into two and these are; are considered as bankruptcy and non-bankruptcy (ordinary) concordat. When evaluated according to its content, it is divided into three. It is possible to list these as discount (discount) concordat, maturity (respite) concordat and mixed concordat. When evaluated according to the way of arrangement, it is divided into two and it is possible to list them as ordinary concordat and concordat by abandonment of assets. Arrangements regarding in-court concordat, deductible concordat and ordinary concordat form the scope of this study.

Thanks to the concordat, the debtor firm continues its activities and provides a significant benefit in terms of collecting the receivables of the creditors even if it is possible to pay their receivables in a longer period of time, not on the due date. The activities of the debtor are carried out under the supervision of the concordat commissioners and in this process, the debtor will not be able to reduce his assets. Thus, the trust of creditors will be won.

The assets of the debtor company are protected during the temporary-definitive period. Since the debtor carries out his activities with the knowledge of the concordat commissioners during the concordat process, he will not be able to make any pledge regarding his assets without the permission of the authorized and authorized court . In addition, in this process, the debtor cannot transfer or donate to third parties his real estate and assets necessary for the continuation of his activities and cannot be a guarantor (Uyar, 2018).

With the amendment made in the Enforcement and Bankruptcy Law in 2018, the "postponement of bankruptcy" was abolished, thus making the concordat more applicable (Kuşoğlu 2018, p. 51). While the creditors did not have much say in the postponement of the bankruptcy, the process was carried out between the debtor and the court. Accordingly, abuse and judicial problems caused the suspension of bankruptcy to be lifted. With the abolition of the postponement of bankruptcy, some arrangements were made regarding the agreements between the creditors and the debtor, and the "concordat" based on the acceptance of this agreement by the court (Yavuz, 2018, p. 93). When the debtor cannot pay his debts in due time or there is a danger of not being able to pay, it is ensured that the debtor can pay his debts by giving additional time or discounting his debts. Thus, it can request a concordat in order to avoid bankruptcy (EBL art. 285). In addition, the creditors have the right to demand the initiation of the concordat process with a petition along with their reasons. The commercial court of first instance is authorized as the competent court in this regard (EBL art. 285).

CLASSIFICATION OF CONCORDAT

The classification of the concordat may differ according to the application form. When the classification of the concordat is made according to the time of its announcement, it is possible to examine it under three headings as ordinary (without bankruptcy) concordat, bankruptcy concordat and concordat by abandonment of assets. When the concordat is classified according to the place it is made, it is possible to divide it into two as out-of-court concordat and in-court concordat. The classification made according to how the debts will be paid represents the most general classification form. In this classification, it is possible to talk about the maturity concordat in case the debts are paid by dividing into maturities, the discount concordat in case the debts are paid at a discount, and the mixed concordat in the payment of the debts both in terms and by discount (Uyar, 2018).

Types of Concordat by the Time of Announcement

Whether or not the company goes bankrupt during the application to the concordat is important in classifying it according to the time it was announced. In case the firm does not go bankrupt, the bankruptcy concordat will not be mentioned. Since the main purpose of the concordat institution is to get rid of bankruptcy, non-bankruptcy ordinary concordat is more common in practice (Uyar, 2018).

Ordinary (Non-Bankruptcy) Concordat

The type of concordat offered by debtors who are not subject to bankruptcy and debtors who are subject to bankruptcy but have not yet been bankrupt is called ordinary concordat. Ordinary or non-bankruptcy concordat can be considered as the most common concordat type in practice. It is a type of concordat made before the bankruptcy process starts, in order to save the company from going bankrupt. The main purpose of the concordat is to get rid of bankruptcy for the company and to earn more income for the creditors than in the case of bankruptcy. Therefore, Ordinary (Non-Bankruptcy) concordat can also be expressed as the type of concordat that best serves the purpose of the concordat institution. (Kale, 2017, p. 4).

Bankruptcy Concordat

In-bankruptcy concordat is the name given to the type of concordat declared by the natural or legal person subject to bankruptcy while the bankruptcy process continues. The purpose of the bankruptcy concordat is to get rid of the debtor's bankruptcy. However, for this to happen, certain conditions must be met. It is possible to list them as follows:

In the concordat project of the bankrupt, explaining the reasons that led to his bankruptcy, creditors may be more advantageous when a concordat is announced. Demonstrating evidence of the possibility of collecting a larger portion of the receivables it has to convince the creditors of this situation (Kale, 2017, p.96).

In order to apply for concordat after bankruptcy, the bankruptcy must be finalized. (Uyar, 2018, p.221) After the bankruptcy, a concordat commissioner is not appointed in the concordat and his duties are fulfilled by the bankruptcy administration or the bankruptcy office. Definitive and temporary respite periods will not be given as the debtor has lost his power of saving on his assets. In addition, there is no need to establish a board of creditors, as a meeting of creditors is held during the bankruptcy process.

Concordat With Abandonment of Assets

In the concordat by abandoning the assets, the debtor loses some or all of his power of disposition on the assets and this power passes to the creditors. In line with this authority, the creditors have the opportunity to collect their receivables by liquidating the debtor's assets together with the liquidation officers. The authority to choose the liquidators belongs to the creditors. In order for creditors and liquidators to exercise their power of disposition over the debtor's assets, there must be a court decision in this direction. In this concordat process, with the finalization of the decision of the commercial court of first instance, the power of disposition on the assets of the debtor will be partially or completely eliminated. At the end of the concordat process, the power of disposition on the debtor's assets passes to the creditors, and the creditors fulfill their power of disposition on the debtor's assets through the concordat liquidators (Kuru, 2013, p. 1542).

Types of Concordat by Place of Placement

It is evaluated whether there is an official institution's intervention during the concordat request according to the place of concordat. These types of concordat constitute whether the concordat is made by applying to the court or an agreement is made between the creditors and the debtor within the framework of private law without applying to any official institution (Uyar, 2018, p. 20).

In-court (Judicial) Concordat

The agreement to be made between the debtor and the creditors, who have problems in paying their debts during the in-court concordat process, must be made under the supervision of the court in accordance with the provisions of the Enforcement and Bankruptcy Law. In this type of concordat, the court decision is binding. Namely, if the court decision is approved, even if the creditors do not accept the concordat project, the result binds all the creditors as the court approves the concordat. However, when the court gives a temporary respite decision, this will be valid for all of the creditors. All the proceedings that have been opened will be stopped regardless of the approval of the creditors and no new follow-ups can be started regarding the previous debts (Uyar, 2018, p.20).

Out-of-Court (Non-judicial-Private) Concordat

In an out-of-court concordat, an agreement is made between the person who has difficulties in paying their debts and their creditors without the intervention of any official institution. In line with the freedom of contract, the debtor can make an agreement with all of the creditors, as well as with only certain creditors. The concordat will have consequences for the creditors who accept the contract. For the creditors who do not accept the concordat, there is no such thing as the suspension of the proceedings and the inability to open new proceedings (Uyar, 2018, p.20).

Types of Concordat by Content

Concordat types are divided into three according to their content. It is possible to list these as maturity concordat, discount (discount) concordat and mixed concordat.

Maturity Concordat

In the maturity concordat, it is a type of concordat that arises as a result of the agreement of the debtor and the creditor to pay the debt in a certain maturity and in installments. It is subject to the condition that the debt will be paid in a certain installment and maturity. Since those who request a concordat do not have the power to pay their debts in one go, it is preferred to pay in a certain maturity and in installments, and this provides convenience for the business (Eroğlu, 2018, p. 23). If all the debts can be paid with the maturity concordat, a deduction concordat cannot be requested. However, it is still left to the competent and authorized court for approval (Uyar, 2018, p. 20).

Deduction (Discount) Concordat

The division of debts into maturities may not be a solution for the debtor, who is in a difficult situation economically, to get rid of the situation he is in. Therefore, the contribution of creditors is required in order to pay at least a part of the debt. In such cases, the discount (reduction) concordat is one of the tools to be applied to pay at least some of the debts and to get rid of the debtor's economic hardship. The deduction concordat is based on the principle that the creditor gives up a certain part of the amount to be received. Creditors give up their receivables other than the discount rate agreed with the debtor (Tanriver, 1993, p.12).

The amount of debt must be more than the financial capacity of the company requesting a reduction concordat. In the concordat project, the debtor's current economic conditions should be evaluated and it should be explained how much of his debts he can pay and when these conditions are met, he will be saved from bankruptcy. If the creditors accept the project, they accept that only a certain part of their receivables will be collected from the debtor. With the payment of the rate accepted in the concordat, the debtor is considered to have paid all of his debts (Berkin, 1972, p.571).

Mixed Concordat

The type of concordat that occurs when the maturity concordat and the discount concordat are realized together is called mixed concordat. In the payment of debts, both types of concordat are used according to their content. In the concordat project, if the creditors are offered to pay the debts with both discount and maturity, a mixed concordat will be realized (Uyar, 2018, pp.21-22). Mixed concordat is the most preferred concordat type in practice (Pekcanıtez and Erdönmez, 2018, p.6).

EVALUATION OF THE CONCORDAT PROCESS IN TERMS OF TAX PRACTICES

Some transactions carried out during the concordat process reveal the tax receivable. These will be evaluated separately in terms of income and corporate tax, value added tax, stamp tax and fees law. In addition, during the concordat process, tax offices cannot initiate proceedings for tax debts and liens are stopped.

In Terms of Income and Corporate Tax

The transactions to be made by companies and individuals who are creditors during the concordat process cause changes in the Income and Corporate Tax base. The creditor waived in the concordat is recorded as an expense for the creditor. The creditor company records this waived receivable as expense in Account 689 Other Extraordinary Expenses and Losses. When this waived amount of receivables is evaluated in terms of tax base account, it is considered as legally unacceptable expenses.

When evaluated in terms of the debtor, the receivable given up in the concordat is in the nature of income. According to Article 324 of the Tax Procedure Law, the debtor transfers the receivables, which are canceled by agreement or at the end of the concordat process, to a special reserve account. If this account is not amortized with a loss starting from the end of the year in which the receivable is forfeited, it is transferred to the profit account at the end of the 3rd year. As a result of this situation, the amount of receivables waived is added to the tax base. However, in case of loss, the amount of receivables waived is deducted from the financial loss.

In Terms of Value Added Tax (VAT)

When the concordat process is evaluated in terms of VAT applications, it is seen that there is no direct effect. The VAT amounts calculated for the debtor company, discount or receivables waived by the creditor need to be adjusted.

In Terms of Stamp Duty

When evaluated in terms of stamp duty, transactions made within the scope of the approved concordat project are exempted from stamp duty. Istisna is specific to the transactions in the concordat process and the debtors and creditors in the concordat project. Stamp taxes paid by the debtor company are expensed in "770 General Administrative Expenses Account".

In Terms of Fees Law

Those who request a concordat must deposit the fees determined by the court at the time of application to the court in advance. In case the request is rejected by the court, the remaining amount after deducting the costs from the fee paid is returned to the claimant. In case of temporary respite, final respite or interim injunction, it is not possible to refund the fees.

Over the money agreed to be paid to the concordat creditors (2.27 per thousand); At the end of the restructuring, the debtor company is required to make a fee payment on the money agreed to be paid to the pledged creditors (1,13 per thousand).

In Terms of Banking and Insurance Transactions Tax

When evaluated in terms of Banking and Insurance transactions tax, the transactions made during the concordat process are exempted from this tax.

In terms of Resource Utilization Support Fund

The loans to be extended to the debtor within the scope of the approved concordat project are deemed exempt from the Resource Utilization Support Fund. However, Resource Utilization Support Fund, restructuring of loans etc. will not be calculated in such cases.

TAX CONSEQUENCES OF THE CONCORDAT

In the process of the concordat, tax-related consequences emerge. In order for the concordat to become binding, the concordat project must be approved. Concordat is not applied for public receivables (Kuşoğlu, 2018, p.53). According to Article 101 of AATUHK, " *Concordat approved by the public administration is not obligatory for public receivables, even if a bankruptcy request is made* ". The tax consequences of the concordat will be evaluated separately for the creditor and the debtor.

Consequences for the Creditor

In the Turkish tax legislation, the accrual principle is valid in the acquisition of income in commercial and agricultural earnings. According to the accrual basis, if the income is finalized in terms of its nature and amount and has reached the payment stage, it is considered as income even if it is not collected (Şenyüz, Yüce & Gerçek, 2019b, p.8). Although the earnings are considered as income as of the period in which they are earned, it is possible that in some cases their collection may become doubtful or impossible. These receivables, which are doubtful or impossible to collect, should be taxed as income if corrections are not allowed in the records. The "worthless receivables", arranged to avoid this situation, made it possible to write off the uncollectible receivables under certain conditions and to set a provision for "doubtful receivables" under certain conditions (Kuşoğlu 2018, p.54).

Allocating Provision for Doubtful Receivables

In practice, there are various opinions regarding the existence of a doubtful situation in the concordat process. The following explanations are included in the Circular No. VUK-112/2019-2 published by the Revenue Administration on 14 February 2019 on the differences. The explanation includes different arrangements for temporary and definite respite.

For the receivables that are transferred to the litigation and execution phase before the temporary respite decision, there is no need to make corrections if provision for doubtful receivables has been reserved. In addition, provision for doubtful receivables can be set aside as of the accounting period in which the temporary respite decision is announced, for receivables that have not been transferred to the litigation or enforcement phase before the respite decision. The reason for this situation was stated as "the inability to follow up with the temporary respite decision. If the concordat is rejected by the court in the temporary respite, correction is required (VUK Circular 112/2019-2). After the definitive deadline has been given, there is no need to make any adjustments to the provisions previously made. In the VUK application, for the receivable that has become doubtful, in the relevant period Since it is not possible to take into account the unreserved provision in the following accounting periods, if no provision for doubtful receivables has been set aside as of the accounting period in which the temporary respite decision is announced, no provision for doubtful receivables can be set aside in the next accounting period, in case the final respite decision is announced (VUK Circular 112/2019-2).

In case the final respite decision is revoked in case the debtor's financial situation improves, there is no need to correct the provisions set aside for the receivables that were transferred to the litigation and execution phase before the temporary respite decision, whereas the provision accounts set aside for the temporary respite decision should be adjusted as of the accounting period in which the decision to reject the concordat was announced. If the concordat request is rejected upon the ex officio decision of the debtor's bankruptcy, there is no need to make any adjustments to the previously reserved provisions, since the doubtful state of receivables will continue in the receivables recorded at the bankruptcy desk. For secured receivables, provision for doubtful receivables will only be applied for the portion exceeding the collateral. (VUK Circular 112/2019-2).

Transaction as a Bad Receivable

Receivables that are not collected are considered as worthless receivables if it is revealed by a judicial decision or a document that gives an opinion. With the realization of this situation, it loses its savings values and is destroyed by being recorded as a loss over its registered values. It is seen that the concordat agreement, which shows that the receivable is waived within the framework of the judicial decisions and rulings regarding the "conclusive document" accepted outside the court decision, is accepted as a convincing document (Kuşoğlu 2018: 55).

Before the approval of the concordat project, it is necessary to specify how much of the creditors' receivables have been waived and the calendar within which the debtor will pay his debts. The portion of the receivables that is waived in favor of the debtor will be a worthless receivable, and the worthless receivable and the provision for this receivable will be destroyed in accordance with the "worthless receivable" provision as of the accounting period in which the concordat is approved (VUK Circular 112/2019-2).

With the concordat project approved by the court, a new debt relationship is established between the creditor and the debtor. In this context, the old debt will be renewed in terms of maturity / amount and these receivables will not be considered as doubtful receivables. The provisions set aside for the said receivables should be corrected as of the accounting period in which the approval decision of the concordat is announced (VUK Circular 112/2019-2).

In the accounting of the records, the profit and loss account for the period is made by using the provision for doubtful trade receivables and other extraordinary expenses and losses. Since both situations have a reducing effect on the tax base, it is important to perform the transactions at the right time in order to avoid tax loss.

Consequences for the Borrower

As a result of the concordat, the creditor gives up a part of the receivable and writes a loss for the receivable that has become worthless. The debtor of this receivable must also write off the debt that he has been freed from paying as profit (Apalı, 2018, p.216). The accounts need to be adjusted, as some of the amounts that were previously considered expenses are no longer required to be paid . As a result, the tax base will increase for the debtor and an additional tax liability will arise.

Status in Terms of Recognition and Effect on Tax

Concordat is clearly referred to in the TPL regarding the issue of "abandoned receivables". Accordingly, a special provision account is used in the debtor's books for the receivables whose collection is canceled due to a settlement or a concordat. This account must be amortized with a loss within three years. If not, it is transferred to the profit account.

Although the debtor does not have a complete problem in paying the debt, some businesses may give up some or all of the debt in order to make their job easier. The debtor's renunciation of receivables caused a decrease in liabilities and this situation led to an increase in equity. Therefore, foreclosed receivables have the appearance of profit for the debtor. The legislator accepted that the resulting profit should be added to the profit in the following years, not in the year the transaction occurred. The case of the creditor's renunciation causes the taxation process to be postponed for a certain period of time in terms of the tax administration (Durusoy, 2005). This situation can be considered as a tax deferral.

Although it is accepted in practice that the receivable forgone can be deducted from the losses of the next year (years), it is not possible to deduct the receivables from the foreclosed regardless of the source of the previous year's losses.

Follow-up of the Borrower and Late Charge

In Turkey, procedures regarding the follow-up and collection of public receivables are carried out within the framework of the provisions of the Law No. 6183 on the Procedure for the Collection of Public Receivables (AATUHK). In some cases, AATUHK cannot be followed under this law. Giving a temporary or final respite to the debtor during the concordat process is one of these situations (Yavuz, 2018, p.93). Accordingly, no proceedings can be made against the debtor within the time limit given by the court, and the proceedings that have already started are stopped. Those within the scope of AATUHK are also included in these ongoing follow-ups. However, the statute of limitations and forfeiture periods do not operate (EİK Art. 294). For this reason, the statute of limitations for collection of public receivables will also cease within temporary and definite deadlines (Yavuz, 2018, p.96).

Unless otherwise stated in the approved concordat project, interest processing ceases for the pledged receivables as of the final deadline (EİK, art. 294). The late fee is taken within the scope of AATUHK and should not be considered as interest. In Article 52 of the AATUHK, the provision of "the application period is the period until the day when the deferment of the public receivable is postponed, the bankruptcy is filed in case of bankruptcy, and this situation is fixed in case of insolvency" . Accordingly, it has been determined in which cases the late fee will not apply. In the bankruptcy postponement arrangement, although there was no clear provision in the law, it was accepted that the delay increment would not work (See. Biyan, 2009). This practice has been abolished and no new provision has been added in the concordat stating that it will not work. For this reason, the late fee will continue to apply for public receivables.

With the amendment of Law No. 7101, it has been regulated that "precautionary injunction" decisions cannot be applied within the concordat period. Thus, the differences of opinion regarding the "Injunctive Injunction" decisions came to an end. However, it is important that this situation, which may negatively affect the success of the concordat, is eliminated (Akil, 2019, p.243).

CONCLUSION

The fact that real persons as well as legal persons can apply can be shown as the biggest feature that distinguishes concordat from bankruptcy. While capital companies and cooperatives filed for bankruptcy, real persons along with capital companies and cooperatives were subject to concordat. Legal entities earn income as a result of the activities of their companies and the values of their companies are calculated on this income. The earnings and values obtained cannot be evaluated independently of each other in this context. This connection reaches a certain level of benefit together with the legal entities themselves, their partners, employees and final consumers. Legal entities face certain risks for various reasons while performing their activities. Real persons, on the other hand, may request a concordat in order to pay their debts and benefit from concordat types such as legal entities in cases where they are guarantors because they are not merchants, they give bail or they cannot afford to pay due to high debts. With the abolition of the Bankruptcy Postponement Institution, the institution of concordat was made functional instead of this institution.

Concordat is an agreement in which honest and prudent debtors participate in order to protect their commercial reputation from the moment they fall into financial difficulties when their financial situation deteriorates. In cases where the debtor cannot make the payments in due time and has difficulty in paying, he can apply for a concordat, provided that he can pay his debts in certain terms with a maturity concordat and can make a payment from a certain amount with a discount concordat. In addition, it is possible to extend the maturities with a mixed concordat and can make applications to pay their debts at a certain rate. Creditor parties can also request a concordat on behalf of the debtor, and they can do this by applying to the Commercial Courts of First Instance. With the functionalization of the concordat institution, an institution has emerged that includes the agreement of the two parties and protects and observes the interests of the debtor and creditor.

REFERENCES

Akil, C. (2019). *Konkordato Süresinin Alacaklılar Açısından Sonuçları (7101 Sayılı Kanun İle Yapılan Değişikliklere Göre)* [The Consequences of the Concordat Term in Terms of Creditors (According to the Amendments Made with the Law No. 7101 dated 28.02.2018)]. TBB Journal.

Apali, İ. (2018). Vergi usul kanunu açisindan konkordato ilani kapsaminda vazgeçilen alacaklarin değerlendirilmesi ve muhasebeleştirilmesi [Evaluation and accounting of abandoned receivables within the scope of concordat announcement in terms of tax procedure law]. *Mali Çözüm Dergisi*, *28*, 211–219.

Berkin, N. M. (1972). *İflas Hukuku (4. Baskı b.)* [Bankruptcy Law (4th Edition b.)]. Faculties Printing House.

Biyan, O. (2009). *İflasın Ertelenmesi ve Vergi Hukukuna Etkisi* [Postponement of Bankruptcy and Its Effect on Tax Law]. http://www.ozgurbiyan.com/2009/10/iflasin-ertelenen-ve-vergi-hukuna-etkisi/

Demir, G. (2019). *İflasın Ertelenmesi ve Konkordato* [Postponement of Bankruptcy and Concordat] [Unpublished Master Thesis]. Işık University Institute of Social Sciences, Istanbul, Turkey.

Durusoy, R. Y. (2005). *Vazgeçilen Talepler ve Uygulama Örneği* [An Example of Abandoned Claims and Implementation]. https://www.verginet.net/dtt/1/RefikYasarDurusoyYMMAdoptedCreditsAndApplicationIliskinB_9150.aspx

Eroğlu, O. (2018). *Uygulamada Konkordato, Seçkin Yayınları, 1* [Concordat in Practice, Distinguished Publications, 1]. Basım.

Gercek, A. (2017). *Kamu Alacaklarının Tahsil Hukuku, 5. Baskı* [Collection Law of Public Claims, 5th Edition]. Ekin Publishing and Distribution.

Kale, S. (2017). Sorularla konkordato (iflas dışı ve iflas içi adi konkordato) [Concordat with questions (non-bankruptcy and in-bankruptcy ordinary concordat)]. In *Vergi Hukuku Açısından Konkordato Müessesesi ve Sonuçları* [Concordat Institution and Its Consequences in terms of Tax Law]. Vergi Dünyası Dergisi.

Konca, N. K. (2018). *Konkordato uygulamalarına ilişkin beklentiler ve riskler* [Expectations and Risks Regarding Concordat Practices]. SETA Vakfı Yayınları.

Kuru, B. (2013). *İcra ve iflâs hukuku: el kitabı* [Enforcement and bankruptcy law: handbook]. Adalet Yayınevi.

Kuşoğlu, M. V. (2018). Konkordato Kapsamındaki Alacak ve Borçların Değerlemesi [Valuation of Receivables and Payables within the Scope of Concordat]. *Vergi Sorunları Dergisi*, (362), 51–58.

Özdemir, M. (2018). Konkordatonun muhasebe işlemlerine etkisi [The Effect of Concordat on Accounting Transactions]. *Giresun Üniversitesi İktisadi ve İdari Bilimler Dergisi*, *4*(2), 1–12.

Pekcanıtez, H., & Erdönmez, G. (2018). *7101 Sayılı Kanun Çerçevesinde Konkordato* [Concordat within the framework of Law No. 7101]. Vedat Kitapçılık.

Şenyüz, D., Yüce, M., & Gercek, A. (2019a). *Tax Law (General Provisions)* (10th ed.). Ekin Publishing Distribution.

Şenyüz, D., Yüce, M., & Gercek, A. (2019b). *Turkish Tax System* (16th ed.). Ekin Publishing Distribution.

Tanriver, S. (1993). *Trustee in composition*. Yetkin Publishing House.

Uyar, T. (2019). *Yeni Konkordato Hukukumuzun Temel İlkeleri* [Basic Principles of Our New Concordat Law]. Türkiye Barolar Birliği Yayınları.

Yavuz, M. (2018). Konkordato Talebi Üzerine Mahkemece Verilen Mühlet Kararlarının Amme Alacaklarına Etkisi [The Effect of the Decision of the Court on the Concordat Request on Public Claims]. *Vergi Sorunları Dergisi*, (362), 92–98.

KEY TERMS AND DEFINITIONS

Concordat: It is a compulsory enforcement institution approved by the commercial court and accepted on the condition of providing the qualified majority of its receivables, covering all ordinary debts of an honest debtor.

In-Bankruptcy Concordat: In case the real or legal person is subject to bankruptcy, it is the type of concordat declared while the bankruptcy process continues.

Non-Bankruptcy Concordat: The type of concordat applied to get rid of bankruptcy before the bankruptcy procedure starts for the company.

Tax: These are compulsory, unrequited, final, monetary payments received from individuals and institutions with the ability to pay, in proportion to their ability to pay, in order to finance the public expenditures of institutions and/or to solve the socio-economic problems they are in.

Chapter 12
The Effect of Bankruptcy Risk and Financial Stress on Firm Value:
The Role and Importance of Audit in Preventing Bankruptcy

Nazan Güngör Karyağdı
Vocational School of Social Sciences, Turkey

Ahmet Şit
Faculty of Social Sciences and Humanities, Turkey

ABSTRACT

The aim of this study is to investigate the effects of firm bankruptcy risk and auditing factors on the market value of firms and to investigate the effect of auditing on firm bankruptcy risk. The period of the research is 2011-2021. In the study on BIST Sustainability-25 Index, in the first model, the dependent variable is the market value/book value; the independent variables are Springate S Score, Fulmer H Score, Altman Z Score, Çolakoğlu MFA Score; the ratio of the number of independent auditor members to the total number of members; the number of members in the supervisory board; and the number of early risk detection committee members.

INTRODUCTION

Another important purpose of businesses whose main purpose is to make a profit and maximize profit is the continuity of the business. The fact that one of the basic concepts of accounting is the continuity principle reinforces this aim. However, from time to time, businesses may suffer losses due to their distance from corporate governance principles or systematic risks outside themselves. Businesses that make losses for a long time will face the risk of financial failure and bankruptcy. For this reason, measuring

DOI: 10.4018/978-1-6684-5181-6.ch012

the bankruptcy risk of enterprises will contribute to both the early detection of risk and the recovery of businesses from bankruptcy.

The bankruptcy risk of companies is affected by internal factors such as insufficient working capital, deterioration in the financial balance due to excessive borrowing, the inadequacy of internal control, lack of knowledge and experience of management, insufficient sales, etc.; Exchange rate fluctuations, decisions made by policymakers, diplomatic problems between countries, external factors such as import and export regimes, etc. also affect them (Uzun, 2005, p. 159).

For this reason, it is vital for companies to identify and measure risk beforehand. The following methods have been used to identify and measure risk in businesses:

- Altman Z Score
- Zeta model
- Lev (1969) Measuring Balance Sheet Distortion model
- Contingent demands approach (CCA) modern finance theory
- Cash management theory
- Chaos Theory
- Faulty Company Model
- Beaver model
- Springate model
- Ohlson Score model
- Weiber model
- Fulmer model
- CA-Score
- Tamari model
- Meyer and Pifer model
- Wilcox model
- Deakin model
- Edmister model
- Blum model
- Sinkey model
- Taffler and Tisshaw model

When these models are examined, it is seen that each model emerges to develop and differentiate another model from a different perspective. In this study, Altman Z Score, Springate model, and Fulmer model were used, while the Çolak Mfa score, which is not very common in the literature, was also used to determine the risk of bankruptcy.

The Altman Z Score was coined by Altman in 1968. Thanks to this method, which is based on Multiple Discriminant analysis, it eliminates some negative situations such as the fact that companies have the power to analyze all their features simultaneously and the ratios are misclassified and the reliability level is low (Altman, 1968, pp. 591-594).

The Springate model, on the other hand, was applied to industrial enterprises in Canada based on multiple discriminant analyses. In this analysis, 4 different financial ratios were used to distinguish successful/unsuccessful businesses (Rajasekar, Ashraf, & Deo, 2014, p. 103; Haseley, 2012, p. 18). In some studies, it is seen that the results of the model show similar results with Altman.

The Fulmer model was introduced in 1994 by John G. Fulmer. This ratio was applied to 30 successful and 30 unsuccessful companies in the USA w average total assets of $450 million using 40 different financial ratios (Yazdanfar and Nilsson, 2008, p. 3).

The Çolak Mfa score, on the other hand, was determined as a score belonging to different real sector companies whose shares are traded in BIST by using multiple different analyses. This method refers to the linear equation that separates the financial ratios of companies that have financial problems one or two years ago from the financial ratios of the same period in companies that do not have problems (Çolak, 2020).

The aim of this study is to investigate the effect of bankruptcy risks of companies in the BIST Sustainability Index on firm value and to investigate the importance of auditing in preventing bankruptcy risk. The study, it is also aimed to investigate whether the active work of committees such as independent auditing and early detection of risk have an effect on the bankruptcy risks of businesses. BIST Sustainability Index was created with a mission that produces policies for the sustainability and corporate governance risks of companies. It is an index calculated from November 4, 2014. Companies to be included in this index must have a General Sustainability Rating of 50 and above, a score of 40 or higher for each main heading, and a score of 26 or higher for at least 8 categories related to the categories. However, the conditions for being included in the BIST Sustainable 25 Index are slightly more severe (BIST, 2022). The period of the study is the period of 2011-2021 and the data are used annually. As a method, GMM was used because the size of the firm is larger than the time dimension.

LITERATURE REVIEW

The risk of bankruptcy of businesses has strategic importance for companies as it negatively affects the purpose of continuity. For this reason, it is seen that there are many studies on bankruptcy in both national and international literature. Some of these studies can be briefly summarized as follows:

Carter et al. (2006) examined the data of companies for the years 1992-2003, based on companies operating in the air transport sector in the USA, in their study where they wanted to examine the effects of hedging on firm value. The results show that hedging is positively associated with firm value.

Sun (2007) aimed to include the evaluation of the auditor's opinions on bankruptcy in his article. As a result of the evaluation of the opinions handled with statistical models, it has been seen that the evaluation of variables such as financial distress, industry failure rate, abnormal stock returns, market value by the auditors is very important in terms of making predictions about bankruptcy.

Hotchkiss et al. (2008) aimed to conduct research on the organization of firms in default and financial distress. In their studies, they emphasized the necessity of reviewing financial problems, debts and credit restructuring and eliminating the corporate governance problems to be experienced with them.

Abid and Mseddi (2010) wanted to examine the effects of financial leverage degrees and financial risks on firm value. Non-financial in the USA in the 1995 -1999 periods examined companies. In their studies where firm leverage and internal business risk explain changes in firm value when firm sales are negatively related to the market portfolio when firm sales are positively correlated with the market portfolio, the degree of operating leverage is embedded in internal business risk and most of the increase in firm value is found. It has also been determined that it can be explained by the internal business risk and the degree of financial leverage.

Uğur (2011) determined the aim of his study as revealing the effect of financial risks on firm value. In the study, financial statements of companies traded in the ISE for the period 2007-2008 were used. Multiple regression analysis was used to test the research hypotheses; Analyzes were made using the SPSS18 program. The results show that company management does not take into account the contribution of stock market investors to the management of financial risks, both to the competitiveness of the companies and to their income. Therefore, it has been revealed that financial risk management does not contribute to the value of the firm.

Gonzalez and Yun (2013) stated that the purpose of their study is to examine whether there is a relationship between risk management and firm value of firms. In the study, the data of the companies operating in the field of electricity and natural gas distribution for the years 1960-2007 were examined. As a result of the analysis made in the study, it was concluded that there is a positive relationship between risk management and firm value.

In their article, Casero et al. (2014) wanted to measure the importance and reliability of auditing in predicting the bankruptcy of financial institutions. With the analysis made, it emphasizes the importance of auditing to business stakeholders against foreseen bankruptcies and gives various signals in this context. The data of 42 financial companies traded in the USA for the period 1998-2011 were examined. According to the results, it has emerged that auditors' knowledge, expertise and use of data mining methods can be effective in preventing bankruptcy, but auditors need to consider more information to support audit opinions, especially in some clients.

Li et al. (2014) wanted to examine the relationship between corporate risk management and firm value, which firms use against their financial risks such as bankruptcy risk. Within the scope of the study, they used the 2010 return on equity of 135 insurance companies operating in China to represent the firm value. According to the results, it was seen that risk management, which is thought to be effective in reducing financial risks, and firm value were positive and significant in the Pearson correlation matrix, but the correlation level was statistically below the significance level in the regression analysis.

Azim, Hassan, and Zakia (2015) examined the relationship between public disclosure of risks, risk management and firm value; They tried to analyze the situation of the companies whose stocks are traded on the Egyptian Stock Exchange. As a result of the analysis, it was determined that there is a significant and positive relationship between risk management and firm value determined based on Tobin Q.

Şenol and Karaca (2017) aimed to examine the effects of financial risks experienced in companies on company values. In this context, they analyzed the 2008-2015 periods of 35 companies whose stocks are traded in Borsa Istanbul. As a result of their analysis, there is a significant and negative relationship between exchange rate and liquidity risks and Tobin Q; It has been determined that there is no significant relationship between leverage and credit risks. While a significant and positive relationship was found between Market Value/Book Value (PD/DD) and leverage and credit risks; It was determined that there is a significant and negative relationship between liquidity risk and PD/BV.

Elitas et al. (2017) aimed to examine the relationship between financial distress and ownership structure in their study. In addition, the researchers, who aim to evaluate the possibility of encountering financial difficulties in the enterprises subject to audit in the study, are included in the BIST Industrial Index. They analyzed the data of 112 companies whose stocks are traded. Researchers examining the data for the years 2009-2015 used the Z Altman score to measure the risk of financial distress. According to the empirical findings obtained as a result of the study, a negative relationship was found between capital concentration and free float ratio and financial distress, and a positive relationship between institutional investor ownership and financial distress. In addition, no statistically significant relationship was found between foreign investor ownership and financial distress. Another important result obtained from the study is that the probability of financial distress of companies under supervision is quite low. Surveillance and supervision seem to play an important role in reducing financial difficulties.

In his article Topaloğlu (2018), taking into account the relationship between the financial risks experienced by the companies and the firm value, examined the companies that were included in the Borsa Istanbul 100 index and whose stocks were traded continuously between the years 2012-2017. Three different models were created in the analysis; firm value was tried to be measured using Tobin Q, Market Value/Book Value and Price/Earnings ratios. In the analysis, there is a significant and negative relationship between capital and liquidity risks and Tobin Q; It has been determined that there is no relationship with exchange rate, credit and interest risk. There is a negative and significant relationship between credit risk and Market Value/Book Value ratio; It is concluded that there is no significant relationship with interest, capital, exchange rate and liquidity risks. Another result obtained as a result of the analyzes is that there is a significant and negative relationship between exchange rate and credit risks and Price/Earnings ratio; It is determined that there is no significant relationship with interest, capital and liquidity risks.

Oluwaseyi et al. (2020) aimed to examine the effect of firms' financial risks on the firm value of banks. They analyzed the data of 63 commercial banks operating in ASEAN-5 countries using the panel data regression model. GMM dynamic estimation was used in the study, in which a total of 567 observations were examined. Empirical evidence suggests that the agency ratio and liquidity risk have a significant positive effect on firm value; liquid asset ratio has a negative effect on firm value. Another important result of the study is that operational and interest rate risks have negative effects on firm value.

Alimbekova et al. (2020) wanted to reveal the importance of auditing in preventing bankruptcy risks in their article. Within the scope of the study, possible ways were investigated in order to increase the value of auditing in preventing the bankruptcy of companies in the tourism industry. In the study, a questionnaire was applied to 108 Kazakh tourism companies. According to the survey results, the risk of bankruptcy among travel companies is very high, which can be reduced by a comprehensive audit.

Sari et al. (2022) wanted to examine the effects of financial distress on bankruptcy risk in their article. In this respect, it has been revealed that the Hero Supermarket company, which is discussed in the study in which the X-Score Zmijewski model, Z-Score Altman model and S-Score models are used, is experiencing financial difficulties. They argued that in order to improve the situation, the management should engage in operational improvement efforts in financial decisions.

In the literature summary above, it is seen that different studies have been carried out on bankruptcy risk and firm value. However, the fact that the number of studies in which the Çolak MFA Score is used for variables, especially in bankruptcy risk, is not high, highlights the originality of the study. In addition, the lack of studies that relate it to the role of auditing in the prevention of bankruptcy indicates the originality of the study. It is expected to contribute to the literature in these aspects.

DATA AND METHODOLOGY

The aim of this study is to investigate the effect of the bankruptcy risk of the companies in the BIST-100 Index on the firm value and to determine the role and importance of auditing in minimizing the risk. The period of the research is the period of 2011-2021 and the data are used annually. The variables used in the study are shown in Table 1.

Table 1. Variables used in the study

	Short Name	Variable	Source
Dependent Variables	PDDD	Market Value / Book Value	Finnet, TR Investing
Independent Variables	RS	Springate S Score	
	HS	Fulmer H Score	
	ZS	Altman Z Score	
	MFAS	Colak Mfa Score	
	BDUTUS	Ratio of Number of Independent Auditors to Total Number of Members	KAP, Annual Reports of Companies
	DKUS	Number of Audit Committee Members	
	ERSK	Number of Early Risk Detection Committee Members	

Since some of the variables are quarterly and some annual data will not give healthy results in terms of comparison in the analysis, annual data of the companies have been used. BIST Sustainability 25 Index was used as a sample in the study.

BIST Sustainability Index is a platform that guides companies by developing policy recommendations against the risks that may arise in the environmental, social and corporate governance headings of the stock market, and provides information on companies' sustainability policies. Borsa İstanbul and Refinitiv Information Ltd. Sti. As a result of the agreement signed between Refinitiv company, the sustainability evaluation criteria of Refinitiv are taken into consideration in determining the companies to be included in this index.

BIST Sustainability Index started to be calculated as of 04.11.2014 and BIST Sustainability-25 Index started to be calculated as of 21.11.2022. With this new limited index, the aim is to create an index consisting of companies with high sustainability performance, certain asset sizes and liquid assets. In order for a company to be included in the BIST Sustainability-25 Index, its general sustainability score must be 70 and above, the score for each main heading of the companies must be 60 and above, and the score for at least 8 categories must be 50 and above (BIST, 2022).

There are 25 companies in the BIST Sustainability-25 Index. However, Akbank, İşbank and Türkiye Sınai ve Kalkınma Bankası, which are included in this index, were not included in the study since banks differ in terms of presentation and content of their financial statements compared to companies operating in the real sector. The period of the study is 2011-2021. The data of the Energy and Mavi clothing companies were not included in the analysis since they do not have data for the period of 2011-2016. The companies included in the study are shown in Table 2.

Table 2. Companies included in the study as a sample

Arçelik A.Ş.	Kordsa Teknik
Aselsan	Logo Yaz. San. Ve Tic. A.Ş.
Çimsa Çim. San. ve Tic. A.Ş.	Migros
Doğan Şirketler Grubu	Otokar
Doğuş Oto. Ser. Ve Tic. A.Ş.	Şişecam
ENKA	TAV Havalimanları
Erdemir	Tekfen Holding
Ford Otomotiv San. A.Ş.	THY
Hacı Ömer Sabancı Holding	Türk Traktör
Koç Holding	Vestel Elektronik San.

Panel data analysis was used, in which the study was conducted on a firm basis and more than one firm was compared. However, since the size of the firm (n) is larger than the time dimension (t), the GMM (Generalized Moments Method), one of the dynamic panel data analysis techniques, was used.

The GMM method was introduced by Arellano-Bond in 1991, and the System GMM estimator method was developed by Arellano-Bover in 1995. As seen in the literature study, there is a dynamic relationship between the bankruptcy risks of firms and firm value/financial performance. In other words, the current situation will be the cause of the past and the reason for the situations to be experienced in the future. Therefore, while investigating the relationship between the variables, the lagged values of the variables should also be given. The disadvantages of the relationship between the lagged value of the dependent variable and the error term will be eliminated if lagged variables are used as intervening variables in dynamic panel data analysis (Değirmen and Karaçoban, 2019). These methods can be used in the following situations (Roodman, 2009:86):

- Less time cross section,
- The company/country section (n) is larger than the time section (t).
- In the case of a linear functional relationship
- If the current value of the dependent variable is based on its past data,
- In case the series are heterogeneous,
- In case of autocorrelation and varying variance in the series,
- In case of cross-section dependence in the series,
- It can be used where the independent variables are not strictly exogenous.

The equation of the model that forms the basis of the study is as follows (Han ve Phillips, 2010: 3):

$$PDDD_{i,t=} \alpha \, PDDD \, i,t_{-1+\beta 1} \, RS \, i,t +_{\beta 2} HS \, i,t +_{\beta 3} ZS \, i,t$$

$$_{+}\beta 4 \, MFAS \, i,t_{+\beta}5 \, BDUTUS \, i,t_{+\beta}6 \, DKUS \, i,t_{+\beta}7 \, ERSK \, i,t_{+\varepsilon} \, i,t \quad (1)$$

In the formula, PDDD represents Market Value / Book Value, RS represents Springate S Score, HS represents Fulmer H Score, ZS represents Altman Z Score, MFAS represents Çolak Mfa Score, BDUTUS represents Ratio of Number of Independent Auditors to Total Number of Members, DKUS represents Number of Audit Committee Members, ERSK represents Number of Early Risk Detection Committee Members and ε represents Error margins.

In the other model, the effect of auditing on bankruptcy risk is investigated. And the formula for this model is as follows:

$$ZS\ i_{,t} = \alpha\ ZS\ i_{,t-1} + \beta 1\ BDUTUS\ i,t + \beta 2\ DKUS\ i,t + \beta 3\ ERSK\ i,t + \varepsilon\ i,t$$

Results

The frequency values of the variables are given in Table 3.

Table 3. Frequency values of variables

Variables	Obs	Mean	Std. Dev.	Min	Max
PDDD	220	3.916133	16.19388	0.375	207.8233
RS	220	1.004893	0.3574846	0.1225	2.22
HS	220	9.138986	1.451975	0	14.14
ZS	220	1.128367	0.5541836	-0.07	2.505
MFAS	220	-2.60533	17.97641	-237.17	0.86666
BDUTUS	220	0.2762273	0.1145922	0	0.64
DKUS	220	1.859091	0.6573498	0	4
ERSK	220	2	1.256944	0	5

While positive things are said on behalf of the index for the market value / book value ratio of the firms, it is seen that the variables that show the bankruptcy risk of the firms are generally at low levels.

Correlation test results expressing the relationship between variables are as shown in Table 4.

Table 4. Correlation test results

	PDDD	RS	HS	ZS	MFAS	BDUTUS	DKUS	ERSK
PDDD	1.0000							
RS	0.0655	1.0000						
HS	-0.0477	0.0991	1.0000					
ZS	0.0150	0.7469	0.2236	1.0000				
MFAS	-0.9857	0.0220	0.0136	0.0678	1.0000			
BDUTUS	0.0298	0.0872	0.2728	0.0149	-0.0437	1.0000		
DKUS	-0.0180	-0.0714	0.1644	0.0935	-0.0030	0.5051	1.0000	
ERSK	0.1402	-0.0303	0.1122	-0.0788	-0.1572	0.3421	0.5195	1.0000

As seen in Table 4, it is seen that there is a moderate relationship between the variables, except for the relationship only between MFAS and PDDD. The relationship between MFAS and PDDD is opposite and strong. This shows that there is an inverse relationship between the PDDD variable and MFAS.

The results of the GMM test, which is one of the dynamic panel methods to determine the coefficient of the relationship between the variables, are given in Table 5.

Table 5. GMM test results (dependent variable: market value/book value)

Dep. Var.: PDDD		Difference GMM		System GMM	
		Coef	Prob	Coef	Prob
Independent Variables	PDDD (t-1)	-0,2283162	0.000	-0.1903114	0.000
	RS	0.2245121	0.532	3.134427	0.000 ***
	HS	-0.0286396	0.466	-0.59043	0.001 ***
	ZS	1.838016	0.000 ***	-0.1725898	0.862
	MFAS	-1.001262	0.000 ***	-0.9772711	0.000 ***
	BDUTUS	-2.660985	0.000 ***	-4.489099	0.018 **
	DKUS	0.06093	0.724	-0.1433546	0.662
	ERSK	0. 2006154	0.001 ***	0.2626716	0. 000 ***
		Wald: 101.07 *** Sargan: 11.73346 AR1: 0.6965 AR2: 0.1127		Wald: 173.07 *** Sargan: 8.139899 AR1: 0.4518 AR2: 0.1215	

***,** and * express respectively 1%, 5% and 10% significance levels.

According to the Difference GMM estimator results; Altman Z Score, Çolakoğlu Mfa Score, the ratio of Independent Auditors to the total number of members, early risk detection committee variables have a strong effect at a 1% significance level on the market value/book value of the firms. A 1-unit increase in the Altman Z score increases the firms' market value/book value by 1.83 units; a 1-unit increase in the early risk detection committee increases the companies' market value/book value by 0.2 units. 1-unit increase in Çolakoğlu MFA score increases the market value/book value of the companies by 1 unit; A 1-unit increase in the ratio of the Number of Independent Auditors to the total number of members reduces the market value/book value of the firm by 2.66 units.

According to the System GMM estimator results; The strong effect of Springate R Score, Fulmer H score, Çolakoğlu Mfa Score, early risk detection committee's market value/book value at a 1% significance level; The number of audit committee members has a 5% significant effect on the market value/book value of the firms. A 1-unit increase in Springate's R Score increases market cap/book value to 3.13; a 1-unit increase in the early risk detection committee increases the companies' market value/book value by 0.26. A 1-unit increase in the Fulmer H score will increase the market value/book value of the firms by 0.59 units; A 1-unit increase in the Çolakoğlu MFA score increases the market value/book value of the firms by 0.97 units; A 1-unit increase in the ratio of the Number of Independent Auditors to the total number of members reduces the market value/book value of the firms by 4.48 units.

Table 6. GMM test results (dependent variable: Altman Z Score)

Dep. Var.: ZS		Difference GMM		System GMM	
		Coef	Prob	Coef	Prob
Independent Variables	ZS (t-1)	0.6614966	0.000	0.8093182	0.000
	BDUTUS	0.0471908	0.792	0.3194203	0.256
	DKUS	-0.024919	0.168	-0.0088629	0.656
	ERSK	0.0242682	0.001 ***	-0.008343	0.319
		Wald: 620.99 *** Sargan: 16.51556 AR1: 0.0083 AR2: 0.2888		Wald: 2050.14*** Sargan: 16.82582 AR1: 0.0091 AR2: 0.3195	

*** express 1% significance levels.

In the model where the bankruptcy risk is the dependent variable, only the Number of Early Risk Detection Committees has a strong effect at the 1% significance level on the Altman Z-Score, which represents the bankruptcy risk. A 1-unit increase in the number of early risk detection committees increased the Altman Z score by 0.02.

CONCLUSION

Bankruptcy is the biggest obstacle to the continuity objective, which is one of the main objectives of the companies. For this reason, companies are expected to follow policies that will minimize the risk of bankruptcy.

In this study, the effect of bankruptcy risk and auditing on firm value and the importance of auditing in preventing bankruptcy risk are investigated. The period of the study is 2011-2021. The BIST Sustainability-25 Index, which has the strictest rules in line with the continuity purpose of the companies, was used as the sample index. However, since the banks differ in terms of the presentation of the financial statements, and the data of Enerjisa and Mavi Giyim companies were disclosed to the public after 2016, the analysis was not included. Market Value/ Book Value representing the firm value as the dependent variable in the study; Springate S Score, Fulmer H Score, Altman Z Score, Colak Mfa Score, Ratio of Number of Independent Auditors to Total Number of Members, Number of Audit Committee Members, Number of Early Risk Detection Committee Members were used as independent variables representing bankruptcy risk. As a method, GMM, one of the dynamic panel data analysis methods, was used.

According to the Difference GMM estimator results; A 1-unit increase in the Altman Z score increases the market value/book value of the firms by 1.83 units; 1 unit increase in the early risk detection committee increases the market value/book value of the companies by 0.2 units. 1 unit increase in Çolakoğlu MFA score increases the market value/book value of the companies by 1 unit; A 1-unit increase in the ratio of the Number of Independent Auditors to the total number of members decreases the market value/book value of the firm by 2.66 units.

According to the System GMM estimator results; A 1-unit increase in Springate's R Score increases market cap/book value to 3.13; 1 unit increase in the early risk detection committee increases the market value/book value of the companies by 0.26. A 1-unit increase in the Fulmer H score will increase the market value/book value of the firms by 0.59 units; A 1-unit increase in the Çolakoğlu MFA score increases the market value/book value of the firms by 0.97 units; A 1-unit increase in the ratio of the Number of Independent Auditors to the total number of members reduces the market value/book value of the firms by 4.48 units.

In line with these results, companies that want to increase the market value/book value ratio, which is one of the main financial performance indicators of publicly traded companies, should increase their Altman Z Score. Looking at the components that the Altman Z Score consists of, the highest weight is the ratio of Net sales to total assets. Therefore, it is vital for companies to increase their sales. In this direction, it is very important to produce better quality products and to realize accurate pricing and an effective marketing strategy. The number of early risk detection committees also positively affects the market value/market value. As the number of members in this committee increases, the firm's risk will be minimized and the firm's value will increase. Decreasing the Çolakoğlu MFA Score will increase the market value/book value ratio of the companies. Financial liability in the share of the components of the ration will adversely affect the value of the firm due to the risks and costs it brings as the foreign resource decreases. The decrease in the number of Independent Auditors to the total number of members will also increase the value of the firm. In other words, the decrease in the number of independent members in the company, the fact that the number of members of the board of directors is within the company instead of being independent of outside the company will increase the market value/book value ratio of the company. Increasing the Springate R Score will also positively affect the dependent variable. The fact that working capital is predominant in the components of this ratio shows that working capital will increase the short-term added value of companies if it is used efficiently. In addition, the share of sales, equity and profitability ratios, as in the Altman Z Score, will positively affect the value of the company.

In the other model, a 1-unit increase in the number of Early Risk Detection Committees increased the Altman Z score by 0.02. In other words, as the number of early risk detection committees of the companies increases, it will cause an increase on the company's Z score. The increase in the Z-score indicates that the firms move away from the risk of bankruptcy. For this reason, companies will minimize their risk by increasing the number of early risk detection committees.

In line with these results, it is seen that the risk of bankruptcy has a negative effect on the value of the firm in general. It is a vital necessity for companies to stay away from bankruptcy risk level by keeping their ratios, which constitute the variables showing bankruptcy risk, high.

In addition, it is of great importance for companies to have an Early Risk Committee in order to detect a possible risk beforehand and prevent the company before it becomes more impressive. It is an important issue for all companies to use these committees more actively, to reduce their risks and increase company values by including more independent and qualified people in this committee. The fact that the study was applied only on the BIST Sustainability Index and there are many variables that show the risk of bankruptcy, while using only 4 variables can be expressed as the limitations of the study. The study can be improved by increasing the bankruptcy risk variable and applying different indices as a sample.

REFERENCES

Abid, F., & Mseddi, S. (2010). The Impact of Operating and Financial Leverages and Intrinsic Business Risk on Firm Value. *International Research Journal of Finance and Economics*, *44*(44), 129–142.

Alimbekova, G., Kanterbayeva, S., Abdildin, S., Yerzhanova, A., & Kydyrbayeva, S. (2021). Audit as a Tool for Preventing Bankruptcy Risks and Evaluating Development Prospects for Tourism Industry Companies. *Journal of Environmental Management and Tourism, 12*(6), 1617–1626. doi:10.14505// jemt.12.6(54).17

Altman, E. I. (1968). Financial ratios, Discriminant Analysis and The Prediction Of Corporate Bankruptcy. *The Journal of Finance, 23*(4), 589–609. doi:10.1111/j.1540-6261.1968.tb00843.x

Azim, A., Hassan, M., & Zakia, A. (2015). Risk Management And Disclosure And Their Impact on Firm Value: The Case of Egypt, International Journal of Business, Accounting, &. *Finance, 9*(1), 30–43.

Borsa İstanbul. (2022). *Sürdürülebilirlik Endeksleri*. https:// www.borsaistanbul.com/tr/sayfa/165/bist-surdurulebil irlik-endeksleri

Büyükoğlu, B., Buyuran, B., & Ekşi, İ. H. (2022). Ekonomik Özgürlük ve Borçlanma Faiz Oranları Arasındaki İlişkinin Analizi. *Alanya Akademik Bakış, 6*(3), 2667-2682.

Carter, D. A., Rogers, D. A., & Simkins, B. J. (2006). Does Hedging Affect Firm Value? Evidence from The US Airline Industry. *Financial Management, 35*(1), 53–86. doi:10.1111/j.1755-053X.2006.tb00131.x

Casero, C., Panaro, D., & Trucco, S. (2014). A Statistical Analysis of Reliability of Audit Opinions as Bankruptcy Predictors. *Journal of Modern Accounting and Auditing, 10*(9), 917–931.

Çolak, M. S. (2017). *Bilançolara Yeni Bir Bakış: Firmalar İçin Finansal Risk Değerlemesi*. https://tcmbblog.org/wps/wcm/connect/blog/tr/main+menu/anali zler/bilancolara_yeni_bir_bakis

Elitaş, B. L., Doğan, M., & Kevser, M. (2017). Finansal Sıkıntı ve Sahiplik Yapısı Arasındaki İlişki: Borsa İstanbul Üzerine Bir Araştırma. *İşletme Araştırmaları Dergisi, 9*(4), 787-804.

Gonzalez, F. P., & Yun, H. (2013). Risk Management and Firm Value: Evidence from Weather Derivatives. *The Journal of Finance, 68*(5), 2143–2176. doi:10.1111/jofi.12061

Han, C., & Phillips, P. C. (2010). Gmm Estimation For Dynamic Panels With Fixed Effects and Strong Instruments At Unity. *Econometric Theory, 26*(1), 119–151. doi:10.1017/S026646660909063X

Hotchkiss, E. S., Kose, J., Mooradian, R., & Thorburn, K. (2009). *Bankruptcy and the Resolution of Financial Distress. In Handbook of Empirical Corporate Finance*. North Holland.

Li, Q., Wu, Y., Ojiako, U., Marshall, A., & Chipulu, M. (2014). Enterprise Risk Management and Firm value within Chine's Insurance Industry. *Acta Commercii, 14*(1), 1–10. doi:10.4102/ac.v14i1.198

Öcek, C. (2018). *Konaklama İşletmelerinde Finansal Başarısızlık Riskinin Ölçümü: Türkiye ve Avrupa'daki Halka Açık Konaklama İşletmelerinin Karşılaştırmalı Analizi*. Mersin Üniversitesi Sosyal Bilimler Enstitüsü Turizm İşletmeciliği Anabilim Dalı Yüksek Lisans Tezi.

Oluwaseyi, O., Islam, A., Zukime, M., Junoh, M., Yusoff, W., & Iqbal, M. M. (2020). Revisiting the Impact of Intrinsic Financial Risks on the Firm Value of Banks in ASEAN-5 Countries: A Panel Data Approach. *Banks and Bank Systems, 15*(2), 200–213. doi:10.21511/bbs.15(2).2020.18

Roodman, D. (2009). How to do xtabond2: An introduction to difference and system GMM in Stata. *The Stata Journal*, *9*(1), 86–136. doi:10.1177/1536867X0900900106

Sari, K. R., Martini, R., Almira, N., Hartati, S., & Husin, F. (2022). Prediction of Bankruptcy Risk Using Financial Distress Analysis. *Golden Ratio of Finance Management*, *2*(2), 77–86. doi:10.52970/grfm.v2i2.127

Şenol, Z., & Karaca, S. S. (2017). Finansal Risklerin Firma Değeri Üzerine Etkisi: BİST Örneği. *Gazi İktisat ve İşletme Dergisi*, *3*(1), 1–18.

Sun, L. (2007). A Re-Evaluation of Auditors' Opinions Versus Statistical Models in Bankruptcy Prediction. *Review of Quantitative Finance and Accounting*, (28), 55–78.

Topaloğlu, E. E. (2018). Finansal Riskler ile Firma Değeri Arasındaki İlişkinin Belirlenmesi: Borsa İstanbul Firmaları Üzerine Bir Uygulama. *Mehmet Akif Ersoy Üniversitesi İktisadi ve İdari Bilimler Fakültesi Dergisi*, *5*(2), 288–301.

Uğur, S. (2011). *Finansal Risk Yönetiminin Firma Değeri Üzerine Etkileri (Yayımlanmış Doktora Tezi).* İstanbul Üniversitesi Sosyal Bilimler Enstitüsü.

Ural, K. (2020). *İflas Tahmin Yöntemlerinin Karşılaştırılması: Borsa İstanbul Üretim Şirketlerinde Uygulama.* Yaşar Üniversitesi Sosyal Bilimler Enstitüsü İşletme Anabilim Dalı Doktora Tezi.

Uzun, E. (2005). İşletmelerde finansal başarısızlığın teorik olarak irdelenmesi. *Muhasebe ve Finansman Dergisi*, (27), 158–168.

KEY TERMS AND DEFINITIONS

Audit: Auditing is very important for the efficiency and continuity of companies. The purpose of the audit here is to investigate the ownership of the independent audit mechanism.

Bankruptcy Risk: Indexes are created with different weights with the ratios obtained from the financial statements of the companies. These indices are expected to be above certain reference values.

BIST Sustainability-25 Index: It is a platform that guides companies by developing policy recommendations against risks that may arise from different aspects of the stock market and provides information about companies' sustainability policies.

GMM (Generalized Method of Moments): It is a predictive method used in panel data analysis. It is a dynamic panel method. It is especially used when the company cross section is larger than the time cross section.

Chapter 13
Measuring Financial Stress in the Turkish Banking Sector and Its Evaluation in the Context of the Economic Crisis

Emrah Öget
https://orcid.org/0000-0002-7659-4357
Zonguldak Bülent Ecevit University, Turkey

ABSTRACT

This study develops the Turkey banking sector stress index for the period of 2012-2021. For this, sector beta, volatility, return on assets, capital adequacy ratio, and asset quality variables were used. The variables were combined with the variance equal-weight method, and a single index was constructed. The reliability of the index was evaluated in terms of whether it detects the years shown as the economic crisis years by the experts. As a result, it has been determined that the index detects the exchange rate crisis that broke out in Turkey in 2018 and the global economic crisis caused by COVID-19, the effects of which began to appear in 2020. In addition, it is predicted that there may be an increase in the number of concordats and bankruptcies in years when the stress index is high. It has been determined that the Turkish banking sector is resistant to crises.

INTRODUCTION

Some of the important crises for Türkiye in the last 10 years are the exchange rate crisis that broke out in 2018 and the global economic crisis caused by Covid-19 that reflections have seen in 2020. Crises cause financial disruption. Banks are the most important factor in financial markets (Akın, 2017: 28). The number of companies working with banks is high and if they don't fulfill their obligations, crises occur in the banking sector. In the ongoing process, the crisis in the banking sector causes real economic losses and economic crises (Akın, 2017: 34). Therefore, it is thought that the financial disruption of the banks may be an early harbinger of the crises. For this reason, in this study, a stress index has been

DOI: 10.4018/978-1-6684-5181-6.ch013

tried to be developed to detect a financial disruption in the Türkiye banking sector. Stress is caused by exogenous forces acting on a system. This exogenous force can cause changes in the functioning of the system, as well as cause changes that may harm the system itself. Such a change is considered a crisis (Geetha et al., 2021: 2252).

Motivations in trying to develop a reliable stress index for the Türkiye banking sector: The index can predict crises, reveal the fragility of the banking sector, and help policymakers in taking precautionary decisions. For these purposes, in the second part of the study, similar studies in the literature related to the stress index were examined. In the third part of the study, the data and the variables used to develop the stress index are explained. In the fourth section, after computing the stress index, the reliability of the index was evaluated. In the last part, the results of the study were mentioned and suggestions were made for future studies.

LITERATURE REVIEW

Hanschel and Monnin (2005) used the stock price index of banks, yield spreads for bank-issued bonds, total interbank deposits, return on assets, bank capital, provision rate, total assets and the number of bank branches variables to measure the stress of the Swiss banking sector for the period 1987-2002. Then, by combining all the variables with the variance equal-weight method, they created a single index showing the stress of the Swiss banking sector. As a result, it was stated that the index caught the stress of the years that were shown as crisis years by experts. The researchers also built a regression model to predict the index and found that the variables of Swiss and European GDP, loan and investment rates, stock price index, and house price explain a large part of the stress level in the banking sector.

Geršl and Heřmánek (2007) aimed to construct a financial stability index for the Czech Republic banking sector for the period 1997-2007. For this, they used capital adequacy, asset quality, profitability, liquidity, interest rate risk, and foreign exchange risk variables. All variables were given different weights and the variables were combined with the variance weighting method. As a result, they revealed that the Czech Republic's banking sector has good resilience to potential shocks.

Dridi, El Ghourabi and Limam (2010) used total deposits, variation in bank capital, loans to the private sector, foreign liabilities of banks, and total assets variables to measure the financial stress in the Tunisian banking sector for the period 1975-2006. They preferred the variance equal-weight method to combine the variables. They proposed a stress index model based on the theory of extreme value to predict the stress of the banking sector. As a result, it has been stated that this model can be used to accurately describe stress periods.

Puddu (2013) studied various alternative approaches to constructing the US banking sector stress index. Monthly data for the period 1984-2007 were used in the study. The variables used in the study are banks' return on assets, net interest margin, the ratio of net loan losses to average total loans, the ratio of non-performing loans to total loans, the ratio of loan loss reserve to total loans, and a number of the failed commercial banks. He developed two models based on signaling and a zero-inflated Poisson approach to construct the index and compared the results with the variance equal-weight and factor analysis approaches. As a result, it has been revealed that the index constructed based on zero-inflated Poisson outperforms other approaches in capturing stress in the industry.

Morni and Masih (2017) used the stock price index, lending spread, total interbank deposits, banks' total capital and reserves, and amount of non-performing loans over total loans variables to measure the stress in the Malaysian banking sector for the period 2000-2015. Combining all variables with the variance equal-weight method, the researchers used cointegrating vector autoregressive (VAR) and autoregressive distributed lag (ARDL) estimators to measure the macroeconomic determinants of stress in banks. As a result, it has been determined that private sector demands, GDP, gross fixed capital formation, housing price index, and stock market variables are the determinants of the bank stress index.

Nadri, Ebrahimi and Fadaie (2018) used monthly banking sector data to construct the financial stress index in Iran for the period 2007-2017. In the study, the variables of return on assets, return on equity, total non-performing loans to total loans, the ratio of liquid liabilities to liquid assets, the ratio of total liabilities to total assets, and the ratio of interbank funds to liquid assets were used. An index was constructed by bringing together all variables with the variance equal-weight method, and the long and short-term relationships between macroeconomic variables and the index were tried to be determined by VECM and ARIMA models. As a result, a long-term relationship was determined between inflation, GDP growth rate, unemployment rates and the stress index. It has been revealed that there is a bidirectional causality relationship between the stress index and the unemployment rate.

Babar et al. (2019) aimed to develop a financial stress index for the Pakistan banking sector by using monthly, quarterly and annual financial data for the period 2001-2011. For this, they used the variables of the return on assets, return on equity, quality of assets, unrequited liabilities, interest margin, liquid assets versus liquid liabilities and liquid assets versus interbank funds. Then, they combined all variables with variance equal-weight, linear probability and logistic regression methods and constructed indices with three different methods and compared these indices. As a result, they revealed that profitability, liquid assets versus liquid liabilities, asset quality, unrequited liabilities, interest margin, and interbank funds versus liquid assets variables contributed significantly to the determination of financial stress of commercial banks by all indices.

Geetha et al. (2021) used default probabilities, volatility, sector beta, capital adequacy ratio and return on assets variables as internal and external factors to measure financial stress in US banking sector for the period 2007-2016. Then, a single index was constructed by combining all variables with the variance equal-weight model, and it was revealed that this index could be used to predict the crises in the coming years.

DATA AND METHODOLOGY

In order to construct the Türkiye banking sector stress index, the variables frequently used by researchers in the literature were preferred. These variables are the beta of the banking sector, volatility, return on assets, capital adequacy ratio, and asset quality. After arranging the 10-year data for the 2012-2021 period, the variance equal-weight method was used to construct the index. Return on assets, capital adequacy ratio and asset quality data are retrieved from the monthly bulletin of the Banking Regulation and Supervision Agency (BDDK) (https://www.bddk.org.tr/BultenAylik). XBANK and BIST100 daily closing prices were used for calculations beta of Türkiye banking sector and volatility, and related data were obtained from Borsa Istanbul DataStore (https://datastore.borsaistanbul.com/).

Volatility

It is assumed that large fluctuations in stock prices indicate financial instability and create tension between banks (Geetha et al., 2021: 2253). For this reason, annual volatility was calculated with the help of formula (1) by using the daily closing prices of the Türkiye banking sector index (XBANK).

$$\sqrt{\frac{1}{N-1}\sum_{i=1}^{N}\left(x_i-\overline{x}\right)^2} \tag{1}$$

In this formula $x_i = x_1, x_2, \ldots, x_n$ represents the daily closing prices and $\overline{x}$ the average of closing prices.

Beta

Beta is a risk measure that shows the sensitivity of stock returns to market returns. Market risk can affect all companies, but some sectors may be less sensitive to market shocks. If the sector is highly sensitive to market risk, it is estimated that the relevant sector will be highly affected by macroeconomic events. For this reason, banking sector beta has been included in the study to determine the tension in the sector in case of possible crises. Sector beta was calculated with the help of formula (2);

$$\beta = \frac{\text{cov}\left(b,m\right)}{\text{var}\left(m\right)} \tag{2}$$

where, β represents the banking sector beta, b represents the XBANK index return for the banking sector return, and m represents the BIST100 return for the market return.

Return on Assets (ROA)

Return on assets shows the effectiveness of company assets in generating profit. The unprofitability of the banking sector indicates a problem and is associated with high stress (Hanschel and Monnin, 2005: 433; Babar et al., 2019: 4). Therefore, the return on assets of the banking sector was included in the study. Return on assets is calculated with the help of formula (3);

$$ROA = \frac{Net\,income}{Total\,assets} \tag{3}$$

Capital Adequacy Ratio (CAR)

Capital adequacy ratio is a measure of bank capital. According to Geršl and Heřmánek (2007: 71), capital adequacy indicators show the resilience of the banking sector to shocks. In addition, it is stated that the decrease in this rate increases the stress of the bank (Geetha et al., 2021: 2253). Therefore, the capital adequacy ratio is included in the index. The capital adequacy ratio is calculated with the help of formula (4);

$$CAR = \frac{Total\ Equity}{Risk\ weighted\ assets} \tag{4}$$

where risk-weighted assets consist of the amount subject to credit risk, operational risk and market risk.

Asset Quality

Asset quality shows the status of assets and various ratios are used to show the status of assets. In this study, as in other similar studies, the ratio of non-performing loans to total cash loans (NPL) was used as an indicator of asset quality (Puddu, 2013: Morni ve Masih, 2017). According to Puddu (2013: 8) the higher this ratio, the higher the distress in the banking sector. According to Morni and Masih (2017: 10), one of the most important indicators of a crisis is the increase in this rate. For these reasons, this rate was included in the study. NPL ratio, which is an indicator of asset quality, is calculated with the help of formula (5);

$$NPL = \frac{Outstanding\ Loans}{Total\ Cash\ Loans} \tag{5}$$

ESTABLISHMENT AND EVALUATION OF THE STRESS INDEX

After the relevant data were arranged, the literature was followed and the data were combined with the variance equal weight method, and a single indicator was obtained. In the data aggregation process with the variance equal-weighting method, the formula (6) was followed and the variables that had a stress-reducing effect were excluded from the variables that had a stress-increasing effect; where, a represents the variables that have a stress-increasing effect, and b represents the variables that have a stress-reducing effect. x_{it} is the value of the variable i at time t, $\overline{x}_i$ is the mean value of the variable i and σ is the standard deviation. The stress index values obtained after combining the data with the variance equal-weight method are shown in Figure 1.

$$I_t = \sum_{i=1}^{a} \frac{x_{it} - \overline{x}_i}{\sigma} - \sum_{i=1}^{b} \frac{x_{it} - \overline{x}_i}{\sigma} \tag{6}$$

Figure 1. Stress Index in Türkiye Banking Sector

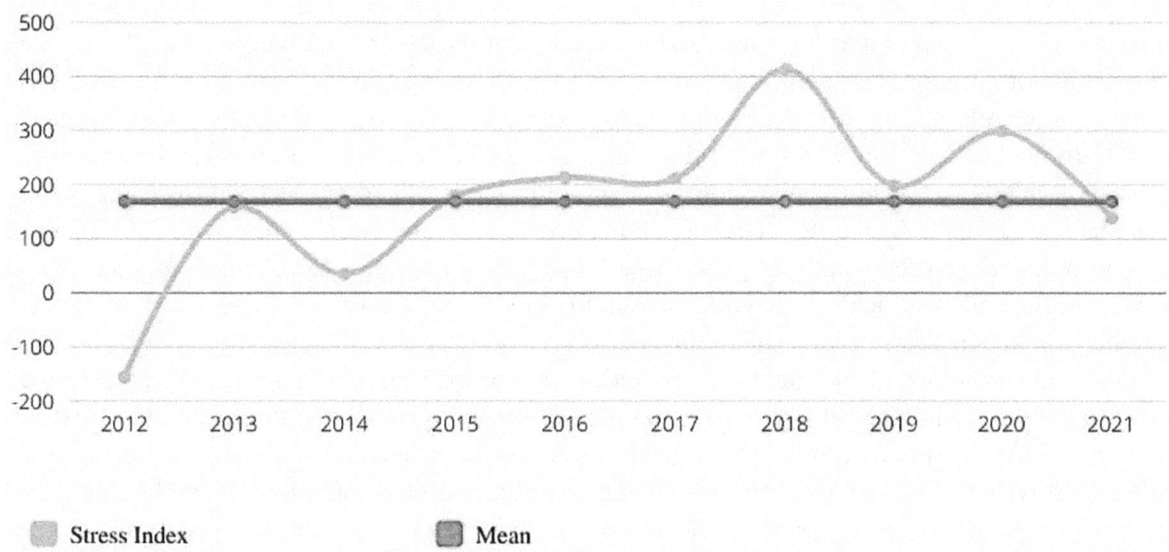

Figure 1 shows the stress index of the Türkiye banking sector for each year between the years 2012-2021 and the average stress index values of the last 10 years. It is seen that the stress index exceeded the average for the first time in 2015 and reached the highest level in 2018. The other year in which the stress index is at a high level is 2020. The year 2018, when the stress index was high, was shown by experts and researchers as the year in which the currency crisis was experienced in Türkiye (Gürgen, 2018; Akçay, 2018; Yokuş and Ay, 2020; Şen and Taşdelen, 2019; Şanlı, 2021). The year 2020, another year with a high-stress index, was evaluated as a global economic crisis by researchers (Örki, Tol, and Arıkan, 2021; Küçükoğlu, 2021; Küçükbay, Uysal and Çırak, 2021). The reason for this is shown as Covid-19, which started in China in 2019 and turned into a global epidemic in March 2020. In the IMF World Economic Outlook October 2020 report, it is estimated that global economic growth will be -4.4 percent for 2020 and 5.2 percent for 2021 (IMF, 2020, p. XV). The fact that the IMF has a negative growth expectation for 2020 also explains the high-stress index in 2020.

It can be said that the policy rate hikes that started in the USA at the end of 2015 caused deterioration in the financial structures of developing countries (Gürgen, 2018, p. 449). Therefore, the fact that the stress index rose above the average for the first time in 2015 can be explained by the policy interest rate increases in the USA. When the findings are evaluated in terms of the currency crisis in 2018; It is stated that the exchange rate crisis causes money and debt crises and deterioration in the basic macroeconomic indicators in Türkiye (Şanlı, 2021, p. 141). In parallel with the deterioration in macroeconomic indicators, Gürgen (2018: 450) stated that the high-interest rate environment increased the number of bankruptcies and concordats. Although the data on the number of companies declaring concordat for all years could not be reached, the years when the concordat announcements were high were reflected in the media. According to the information obtained from the news reflected in the media, while 1094 companies declared concordat in 2018, this number was 899 in 2019 (Cumhuriyet, 2020; Sözcü, 2020; Haberglobal, 2020).

RESULTS AND DISCUSSIONS

In this study, it has tried to develop a reliable stress index for the Türkiye banking sector. Due to banks' relationship with economic growth, it is thought that the stress level in the banking sector may reflect the crises in the relevant country. As a result, in this study, it was seen that the stress index constructed for the Türkiye banking sector identified the years described as a crisis by experts and researchers. It has been revealed that the stress index constructed for the Türkiye banking sector reflects the currency crisis that started in 2018 and the global economic crisis caused by the pandemic in 2020. Therefore, it has been understood that combining the variables of volatility, sector beta, return on assets, capital adequacy ratio, and asset quality used to construct the index with the variance equal-weight method is a reliable practice in terms of identifying the crises.

In the evaluation carried out after the stress index was constructed, it was predicted that there would be an increase in the number of concordats and bankruptcies in years when the stress index was high. However, the absence of any concordat and bankruptcy processes in banks in the relevant period shows that the Türkiye banking sector is quite strong and resistant to crises. Therefore, it can be said that the high level of stress in the banking sector reflects the economic crises in the relevant country and increases the risks of bankruptcy of other companies outside the sector. For this reason, it is recommended to introduce government policies to prevent the bankruptcy of companies in years when the stress index is high.

It is recommended to reveal the relationships between macroeconomic variables and the stress index in future studies on the subject. The factors that have the most impact on the increase in the stress level can be determined by revealing the determinants of the stress index and policies towards the factors that increase the stress level can be studied to reduce the effect of the crises experienced.

REFERENCES

Akçay, Ü. (2018). *Beş Soruda 2018-2019 Ekonomik Krizi* [The 2018-2019 Economic Crisis in Five Questions]. Retrieved from https://www.gazeteduvar.com.tr/yazarlar/2018/12/13/bes-soruda-2018-2019-ekonomik-krizi

Akın, F. (2017). Türk bankacılık sektörünün yapısı ve sorunları [The structure and problems of the Turkish banking sector]. *İş ve Hayat*, *4*(8), 54-73. Retrieved from https://dergipark.org.tr/tr/pub/isvehayat/issue/48947/678738

Babar, S., Latief, R., Ashraf, S., & Nawaz, S. (2019). Financial stability index for the financial sector of Pakistan. *Economies*, *7*(81), 1–24. doi:10.3390/economies7030081

BDDK. (n.d.). *Aylık Bankacılık Sektörü Verileri* [Monthly Banking Industry Data]. Retrieved from https://www.bddk.org.tr/BultenAylik

Borsa İstanbul DataStore. (n.d.). *Pay Piyasası Verileri* [Equity Market Data]. Retrieved from https://datastore.borsaistanbul.com/

Cumhuriyet. (2020). *2019'da 899 şirket konkordato ilan etti* [In 2019, 899 companies declared concordats]. Retrieved from https://www.cumhuriyet.com.tr/haber/2019da-899-sirket-konkordato-ilan-etti-1715448

Dridi, A., El Ghourabi, M., & Limam, M. (2010). On monitoring financial stress index with extreme value theory. *Quantitative Finance*, *12*(3), 329–339. doi:10.1080/14697681003792229

Geetha, K., Maria Suganthi, L., Vasanthi, K., & Kavitha, B. (2021). Financial stress testing in US banking sector. *Materials Today: Proceedings*, *37*, 2252–2255. doi:10.1016/j.matpr.2020.07.700

Geršl, A., & Heřmánek, J. (2007). Financial stability indicators: Advantages and disadvantages of their use in the assessment of financial system stability. In CNB Financial Stability Report 2006 (pp. 69-79). Czech National Bank.

Gürgen, A. R. (2018). Türkiye'nin 2018 krizi: Nereden nereye? [Turkey's 2018 crisis: From where to where?]. *Mülkiye Dergisi*, *42*(3), 449-452. Retrieved from https://dergipark.org.tr/tr/pub/mulkiye/issue/44591/676021

Haberglobal. (2020). *Türkiye'de şimdiye kadar kaç firma konkordato ilan etti?* [How many companies have declared concordats in Turkey so far?]. Retrieved from https://haberglobal.com.tr/ekonomi/turkiye-kac-firma-konkordato-ilan-etti-konkordato-nedir-24979

Hanschel, E., & Monnin, P. (2005). Measuring and forecasting stress in the banking sector: evidence from Switzerland. *BIS Work.*, *22*, 431–449. Retrieved from https://www.researchgate.net/publication/4735258_Measuring_and_forecasting_stress_in_the_banking_sector_Evidence_from_Switzerland/citations

IMF. (2020). *World economic outlook. A long and difficult ascent*. Retrieved from https://www.imf.org/en/Publications/WEO/Issues/2020/09/30/world-economic-outlook-october-2020

Küçükbay, F., Uysal, D., & Çırak, A. N. (2021). Covid-19 salgının Dünya ekonomisi üzerindeki etkisinin değerlendirilmesi [Assessment of the impact of the Covid-19 pandemic on the world economy]. *Journal of Aksaray University Faculty of Economics and Administrative Sciences*, *13*(4), 15–20. doi:10.52791/aksarayiibd.985481

Küçükoğlu, S. (2021). Covid-19 pandemi sürecinin küresel ekonomik göstergeleri ve Türkiye'de bankacılık ve finans sektörüne etkileri [Global economic indicators of the Covid-19 pandemic process and its effects on the banking and financial sector in Turkey]. *İstanbul Ticaret Üniversitesi Sosyal Bilimler Dergisi*, *20*(42), 1269-1291. Doi: doi:10.46928/iticusbe.870711

Morni, F., & Masih, M. (2017). *Predicting stress in the banking sector: Malaysian evidence.* MPRA Paper 108445. Retrieved from https://mpra.ub.uni-muenchen.de/id/eprint/108445

Nadri, K., Ebrahimi, S., & Fadaie, A. (2018). Assessment of financial stability in the banking sector in Iran. *Journal of Monetary Economics*, *13*(4), 501–523. https://www.researchgate.net/publication/345733270_Assessment_of_Financial_Stability_in_the_Banking_Sector_in_Iran

Örki, A., Tol, M. A., & Arıkan, N. (2021). 2020 Küresel ekonomik krizi ve kendi kendine yeterli olma konusunda farklı yaklaşımlar: 2020 Ocak – 2020 Mayıs [Different approaches to the 2020 global economic crisis and self-sufficiency: January 2020 – May 2020]. *International Journal of Society Researches, 17*, 3676-3698. Doi: doi:10.26466/opus.776585

Puddu, S. (2013). *Optimal weights and stress banking indexes.* IRENE Working Papers 13-02. IRENE Institute of Economic Research. Retrieved from https://ideas.repec.org/p/irn/wpaper/13-02.html

Şanlı, O. (2021). Türkiye'de 1994, 2001 ve 2018-2021 kur krizlerinin yeni nesil kriz teorileri çerçevesinde incelenmesi [Investigation of the 1994, 2001 and 2018-2021 currency crises in Turkey within the framework of new generation crisis theories]. Aydın Faculty of Economics Journal, 6(2), 117-158. Doi: doi:10.53839/aifd.988000

Şen, A. F., & Taşdelen, H. (2019). Haberde söylem üretimi: 2018 döviz kuru krizinin haber medyasındaki yansımaları [Discourse production in the news: The reflections of the 2018 exchange rate crisis in the news media]. *Akdeniz Üniversitesi İletişim Fakültesi Dergisi,* (31), 254-275. Doi: doi:10.31123/akil.532292

Sözcü. (2020). *2019 yılında 900'e yakın şirket konkordato ilan etti!* [In 2019, nearly 900 companies declared concordats!]. Retrieved from https://www.sozcu.com.tr/2020/ekonomi/2019-yilinda-900e-yakin-sirket-konkordato-ilan-etti-5578534/

Yokuş, T., & Ay, A. (2020). Kur krizleri ve Türkiye: 2006-2018 dönemi [Exchange Crises and Turkey: 2006-2018 period]. *Journal of Management and Economies Research, 18*(1), 295–316. doi:10.11611/yead.608003

KEY TERMS AND DEFINITIONS

CAR: It is a measure of bank capital.

Economic Crisis: Abnormal fluctuations in the prices of goods, services, production, and foreign exchange.

Sector Beta: It is a measure of the yield volatility of the relevant sector relative to the whole market.

Stress Index: It is to reveal the current instability in financial markets and to show it with a single variable.

Volatility: It is the variability in the price of the security. High volatility is an indicator of uncertainty.

Chapter 14
Formulation of Altman's Index (AIN) and Financial Performance Index (FPI):
An Empirical Study on Wal-Mart (1987-2016)

Debasish Roy
https://orcid.org/0000-0002-0706-9743
Sikkim University, India

ABSTRACT

This chapter's objectives are two-fold: first, to technically modify Altman's model and formulate Altman's index (AIN) in such a manner that only two out of five stipulated financial ratios would suffice the major purpose of projection of soundness of any business organization's financial health; and second, to formulate a financial performance index (FPI) consisting of five financial ratios treated as independent variables that would help to provide a holistic overview of a firm's performance regardless of its functional domain. Since the much-discussed and strongly valid issue of non-normality is closely associated with the financial ratios in the macroeconomic perspective (group of industries), in order to avoid the underlying controversy, the microeconomic approach is followed considering a single firm, Wal-Mart, primarily for two reasons: first, for its financial soundness and, second, it can be used for a comparative study with a financially bankrupt firm by using the financial ratios as common variables to derive the "specific" condition for bankruptcy.

DOI: 10.4018/978-1-6684-5181-6.ch014

INTRODUCTION

Altman (1968) used Multiple Discriminant Analysis (MDA) for bankruptcy prediction of business firms with a specific objective in mind and that was to broadly classify 66 firms in two equal sections of 33 firms each, i.e., one section of 33 firms were classified under Chapter X of the National Bankruptcy Act during the period 1946 - 1965, and the other section consisted of equal number of firms under non-bankruptcy with asset sizes ranging from $1 million to $25 million. This particular technique helped to successfully compare the major underlying difference (in terms of financial ratios) between the bankrupt and non-bankrupt firms. The final discriminant function was expressed as the linear equation below:

$$Z = 0.012X_1 + 0.014X_2 + 0.033X_3 + 0.006X_4 + 0.999X_5$$

where

X_1 = Working Capital (WC) to Total Assets (TA) ratio,
X_2 = Retained Earnings (RE) to Total Assets (TA) ratio,
X_3 = Earnings before Income Taxes (EBITA) to Total Assets (TA) ratio,
X_4 = Market Value of Equity (MVE) to Book Value of Debt (BVD) ratio, and
X_5 = Net Sales (NS) to Total Assets (TA) ratio.

Clearly, Altman's Z – Score model was formulated on a *macro* perspective comprised of five independent variables. Although quite competent in its own merit, Altman's model requires estimations of five different financial ratios which at times, may be time – consuming and difficult to 'handle' in terms of calculations. In this research paper, an attempt has been made to simplify the existing Altman's model by keeping its basic foundation intact while dealing with the same 5 independent variables simultaneously. Although this study has been done on a single business firm (*micro* perspective), i.e., Wal-Mart; the regression relationships could be replicated in macro perspective also (for a group of firms).

In order to streamline the existing Altman's model, the first step was to pick the most common *element* out of the five ratios regardless of the choice between numerators and denominators. The obvious choice was Total Assets (TA).

Now since TA is the common choice for denominators for 4 out of 5 financial ratios, hence statistically, there remains a probability of some degree of correlation between TA and those 4 numerators, namely., Working Capital (WC), Retained Earnings (RE), Earnings before Income Taxes (EBITA), and Net Sales (NS) respectively (Lev and Sunder, 1979). Keeping in mind the same hypothesis, a probe for correlation between Market Value of Equity (MVE) and Book Value of Debt (BVD) could be conducted for the fourth independent variable. Thus for 4 out of 5 independent variables, i.e., X_1, X_2, X_3, and X_5, the common denominator TA is treated as the *dependent* variable and the remaining 4 numerators WC, RE, EBITA, and NS are treated as *independent* variables. For the remaining variable X_4, the numerator MVE is treated as the *dependent* variable and BVD is treated as the *independent* variable. The reasons for choosing TA and MVE as dependent variables are quite straightforward as follows:

1. An increase / decrease in Working Capital (WC) [defined as the difference between Current Assets (CA) and Current Liabilities (CL)] would certainly affect changes in the volume of Total Assets (TA) of a firm as both CA and CL are parts of the same balance sheet and CA is an integral part for estimation of TA. In a similar fashion, RE is an integral part of Total Liabilities and Equities (TLE) and finally, as per one of the rules of standard accounting, TA and TLE must balance. Hence WC and RE should maintain a statistically significant correlation to TA. On the other hand, EBITA and NS are integral parts of financial statements of income and both contribute directly to appreciate TA;
2. The formula for calculating Book Value of Debt (BVD) may be expressed as:
    a. Book Value of Debt (BVD) = Long-term Debt (LD) + Accrued Liabilities (ACRLB) + Accrued Income Taxes (ACRIT) + Current Portion of Long-term Debt (CPLD)

On the other hand, Market Value of Equity (MVE) may be expressed as:

Market Value of Equity (MVE) = Market price of stock × Number of shares outstanding.

Both BVD and MVE go hand in hand to increase / decrease the total amount of TLE. Moreover, any change in the value of BVD would directly affect MVE as equities are also treated as a part of the total liabilities for a business organization.

Formally,

$$TA = f(WC, RE, EBITA, NS) \tag{1}$$

and

$$MVE = g(BVD) \tag{2}$$

Thus, if statistically significant linear regression equations could be formed between the dependent and independent variables of equations (1) and (2) respectively, then all the independent variables could be expressed in terms of two dependent variables TA and MVE respectively and the initial objective of formation of Altman's Index (AIN) (named in honor of Edward Altman) can be fulfilled. In contrary to the notion of bankruptcy prediction, AIN should be treated as an indicator of the firm's financial strength where higher value contemplates greater individual strength both internally and externally (in case of market segment). The other objective of this research work is aimed at formulation of a Financial Performance Index (FPI) based on five major financial ratios, namely., Return on Assets (ROA), Return on Equity (ROE), Cash Flow Adequacy Ratio (CFAR), Debt Ratio (DR), and Net Profit Ratio (NPR) respectively. A conscious choice has been made in the selection of financial ratios in order to formulate FPI. According to Fraser and Ormiston (2015), financial ratios may be broadly classified into *five* categories. Their definitions are quoted as below (Fraser and Ormiston, 2015):

- **Liquidity ratios:** "which measure a firm's ability to meet cash needs as they arise",
- **Activity ratios:** "which measure the liquidity of specific assets and the efficiency of managing assets",

- **Leverage ratios:** "which measure the extent of a firm's financing with debt relative to equity and its ability to cover interest and other fixed charges",
- **Profitability ratios:** "which measure the overall performance of a firm and its efficiency in managing assets, liabilities, and equity", and
- **Market ratios:** "which measure returns to stockholders, and the value the marketplace puts on a company's stock".

Since leverage and profitability ratios encompass the broad gamut of firm's financing of debts and interest payments along with measuring of firm's performance in managing assets, liabilities, and equity; hence in order to formulate FPI, the leverage and profitability ratios are taken into consideration. The remaining three kinds of ratios simply provide supporting roles to leverage and profitability ratios when the vital issues of firm's financial performance, long – term solvency and bankruptcy come into play. Thus, formally, the FPI function may be expressed as:

$$FPI = \phi(ROA, ROE, CFAR, DR, NPR) \tag{3}$$

In order to test the validity of hypotheses as stated above, regression analyses were individually performed at 5 percent level of significance or better for the independent variables. The FPI has been formulated with *no* preconceived notion in mind, rather it has been based on a *heuristic* approach and involved iteration of regression analysis under Ordinary Least Squares (OLS) method in order to achieve statistically significant results for the coefficients of the independent variables and check the non-spuriousness of the regression analysis as well.

LITERATURE REVIEW

Lev and Sunder's (1979) seminal work emphasized on the fact that the use of financial ratios was "necessarily based on a hypothesis (either explicitly specified or implicitly assumed) about the relationship between the numerator variable (e.g., income) and the denominator size variable (e.g., equity)". According to Barnes (1987), if the ratio takes the form $y = a + bx \quad (a \neq 0)$, the ratio does not satisfactorily control for size. Whittington (1980) and Barnes (1982) suggested in his earlier work that in order to get rid of the misinformation arising from the linear relationship between the variables, regression analysis should be used.

Bird and McHugh's (1977) empirical study established the fact that the distribution of ratios within an industry may be approximated by a normal distribution in majority of the cases barring the exceptions of Quick Ratios which were substantially non – normal.

Walker *et al.* (1979) proposed that Decomposition Measures (DM) were significantly correlated to overall structural changes in the financial data of the financial statements and the decomposition analysis could be used as a supplementary or replacement tool for monitoring financial statements. Houghton and Woodliff's (1987) work emphasized on the findings that "the financial ratios of failed firms were significantly different to those of non – failed firms in the years preceding failure. In relation to the tests of relative 'success', the cross – validated discriminant function outperformed a random model at a significance level of 0.05. Hence it was concluded that, for the information set used, the financial ratios of firms which experienced different levels of Earnings per Share were significantly different in the preceding years". Chen and Shimerda's (1981) important study revealed the fact that inclusion of more than one ratio from a common factor "leads to multicollinearity among ratios and distorts the relationship between the dependent and independent variables".

They have suggested that a minimum number of ratios and one ratio in most cases should be selected to represent each factor for statistical analysis. However, according to their opinion, the question of selecting the 'appropriate' ratio for representing a factor does not have a definite guideline and yet to be resolved. Apart from Altman's MDA model, Boritz *et al.*'s (1995) model consists of a 14 – factor neural network which threw new light on the prediction of bankruptcy of firms.

Bellovary *et al.* (2007) stressed on the fact that the future research should be concentrated on refinement of existing bankruptcy models and *not* on development of new models.

According to their bankruptcy study spanning the time period 1930 - 2000, the neural network models (Messier and Hansen, 1988; Guan, 1993; Tsukuda and Baba, 1994) displayed maximum accuracy in bankruptcy prediction ranging from 71 percent to 100 percent. They concluded that a large number of factors do not necessarily increase a model's predictability. Contrary to Jo *et al.*'s (1997) model which consisted of 57 factors which yielded 86 percent accuracy rate, Beaver's (1966) model with just one ratio produced an accuracy rate of 92 percent. Even as per Jones' (1987) words: "using too many ratios can actually make a model less useful".

Platt *et al.* (1994) researched on the effect of temporal distortion on the accuracy of a bankruptcy prediction model for 124 business firms in US Oil & Gas sector out of which 35 were bankrupt and remaining 89 were non-bankrupt during the time period 1982 – 1988.

They used a multivariate logit model as below:

$$P(B) = 1 / [1 + e^{-(a + bFR + cRR)}] \tag{4}$$

where

P = Probability of bankruptcy,
B = Bankruptcy [Dummy variable (d) = 1 for bankrupt companies, 0 otherwise],
FR = A set of financial ratios,
RR = A set of reserve disclosure ratios,
a, b, c = Estimated parameters.

The results of their study demonstrated the fact that a superior model may be developed by creating real (deflated) ratios of accounting reserve disclosure data and also by introducing external economic factors. The empirical results showed that the model containing real financial and reserve ratios coupled with economic indicators provided the best classification accuracy across bankrupt and non-bankrupt firms.

Watts (1977) in his paper had an interesting observation that individual practitioners in U.S. and Australia did agree privately with the idea that the contents of the financial statements are the individual outcome of gratification of own self-interests. Although he doubted that practicing professionals would not accept this matter publicly, but students who were looking for alternate accounting procedures might not continue with the traditional methods.

Apart from Altman's Z – score, the other extremely valuable research which opened new vistas in the study of bankruptcy prediction was of Ohlson's (1980). As per his research, there are *four* factors derived from financial statements which are statistically significant for assessing the probability of bankruptcy, and they are: (i) Size of the firm, (ii) Total Liabilities (TL) to Total Assets (TA) ratio (TLTR) / Debt Ratio, (iii) Net Income (NI) to Total Assets (TA) ratio (NITA) and / or Funds provided by Operations (FU) to Total Liabilities (TL) ratio (FUTL), and (iv) Working Capital (WC) to Total Assets (TA) (WCTA) or WCTA and Current Liabilities (CL) to Current Assets (CA) (CLCA) jointly.

Lau *et al.* (1995) in their study showed that empirical ratio distributions have different shapes and should be modeled by different dfs' (degrees of freedom) and β_2s' (kurtosis).

Johnson's (1979) research revealed the fact that based on multivariate analysis, financial ratio factor patterns were common to both retail and manufacturing firms and they were: (i) Return on Investment, (ii) Financial leverage, (iii) Capital intensiveness, (iv) Inventory intensiveness, (v) Cash position, (vi) Receivables intensiveness, (vii) Short-term liquidity, and (viii) Decomposition measures.

Mossman et al. (1998) in their research based on a sample of bankruptcies for the time period 1980 – 1991 compared four types of bankruptcy models based on financial ratios, cash flows, stock returns, and return standard deviations came to a conclusion that none of the existing model of bankruptcy adequately predicts the outcome within a very short span of time.

Laitinen's (2018) interesting research highlighted on the roles of financial ratios when their numerators and denominators change over time. Laitinen had worked on two broad categories of ratios, i.e., (a) Pure Ratio ($R = x / y$ form), and (b) Pure Component Ratio [$R = (x - z) / y$ form] for a sample of 9160 active and 81 bankrupt firms for a time period of 10 years. The study showed that the growth of Net Sales played a central role in changes of financial ratios. Five ratios belonging to profitability and cash – flow measures displayed sensitivity to changes in sales growth rates. In case of bankrupt firms, the rate of sales growth was often approximately zero or negative.

Campbell *et al.* (2011) in their research paper tried to investigate the pricing of financially distressed stocks in two steps: First, they tried to present a model of financial stress, and second, they tried to venture into the history of investing in distressed stock portfolios. They formulated an equation of financial distress by using logit model following Shumway (2001), Chava and Jarrow (2004), and Campbell *et al.* (2001). The probability of failing a firm in the forthcoming month has been expressed as:

$$P_{t-1}(Y_{it} = 1) = 1 / [1 + e^{(-\alpha - \beta x_{i,t-1})}] \quad (5)$$

where Y_{it} is equal to 1 if the firm fails and equals 0 if it is active, and $\beta_{i,t-1}$ is the linear combination of exploratory variables. Their findings suggested that "distressed firms are those that have recently made losses, have high leverage, low and volatile recent returns, and have levels of market-to-book and low share prices". The additional findings corroborated that fact that the distressed stocks underperformed the S&P500 and were characterized by high levels of volatility and high market betas.

Ko *et al.* (2001) used Composite Rule Induction System (CRIS; Liang, 1992) to derive rules for predicting corporate financial distress in Taiwan. Apart from that, they compared the prediction performances of CRIS, neural computing, and the logit model. The empirical results of their study indicated that both CRIS and neural computing outperformed the logit model in predicting financial distress.

Beaver *et al.* (2005) in their attempt to study the secular change in the predictive ability of financial ratios for bankruptcy resulted in two major findings: (a) Barring minor changes, the robustness of predictive models was strong over time, and (b) The slight decline in the predictive ability of the financial ratios was offset by improvement of the predictive ability of the market-related variables.

Lyandres and Zhdanov's (2013) research shed light on the impact of investment opportunities on firm related to bankruptcy prediction. They concluded that "Firm's investment opportunities affect their shareholders' willingness to default on debt obligations. The more valuable the investment opportunities, the longer the shareholders are able / willing to wait before bankruptcy".

Finally, du Jardin *et al.* (2019) in their research paper used Accuracy Ratio to forecast corporate bankruptcy. The Accuracy Ratio may be defined as:

Accuracy = (CF + CNF) / (NF + NNF)

where CF = Correct classification rate of failed firms, CNF = Correct classification rate of non-failed firms, NF = Number of failed firms, and NNF = Number of non-failed firms.

By using this ratio, the researchers concluded that the reliability of bankruptcy model could be improved to a great extent and the improvement could be observed up to three years prior bankruptcy.

Recent research by Cindik and Armutlulu (2021) to study financial distress of companies by the help of *four* different models, i.e.; Altman Z – Score, Revised Altman Z – Score by applying *Linear Discriminant Analysis* (Altman *et al.*, 2017) which yielded the following equation as:

$$Z'' = 6.56X_1 + 3.26X_2 + 6.72X_3 + 1.05X_4$$

where X_1 = Working Capital / Total Assets, X_2 = Retained Earnings / Total Assets, X_3 = Earnings Before Interest and Taxes / Total Assets, X_4 = Book Value of Equity / Total Assets, and Z'' = Modified Z – Score, Quadratic Discriminant Analysis, and Random Forest Machine Learning Model respectively on 80 Turkish firms for the time period of 6 years (2013 – 2018) showed that the Random Forest Model surpassed the other 3 models in terms of accuracy level (95%) by using the Altman variables.

Hence from the discussion above, it may be clearly inferred that the accounting domain related to financial ratios and bankruptcy still remains a 'virgin' territory to investigate and explore as well. Thus, this research work acts as a bridge to connect two contradictory factors, i.e., prediction of financial distress and financial soundness of a business firm through defining the limits of a *multiplier* which has not been explored previously.

METHODOLOGY

Before the constructions of Altman's Index (AIN), Modified Altman's Index (MAI), and Financial Performance Index (FPI) for Wal-Mart, it should be necessary to distinguish between the former group of indices and other major indices which deal in the financial ratios, namely, Piotroski's F-Score (2000), Mohanram's G-Score (2005), and Sloan ratio (1996) respectively. The F-Score is an aggregation of the individual binary signals which ranges from 0 to 9 indicating the relative degree of responsiveness to higher mean return on Book-to-Market (BM) stocks. On the other hand, G-Score is the sum of 8 fundamental signals tailored for high – growth BM firms to projects their returns based on long-short strategies.

Finally, the Sloan ratio helps us to analyze the fact whether stock prices could accurately reflect their future earnings contained in the accrual and cash flow components of current earnings. The Sloan Ratio (SR) may be defined as:

$$SR = \left(NI - CFO - CFI\right) / TA$$

where

NI = Net Income of the firm,
CFO = Cash from Operations for the firm,
CFI = Cash from Investing for the firm, and
TA = Total Assets of the firm.

He advocated that the businesses with a high accrual ratio significantly underperform as compared to businesses with a low accrual ratio.

The three indices mentioned above provide us an idea that their primary domain of functioning is related to the (expected) return on stocks and their associated 'natures'. However, in stark contrast to these indices; AIN, MAI, and FPI primarily *focus* on the nature of financial health / soundness of a firm regardless of its domain of operation(s). Even the lean phases of a firm's business cycle (within a given time period) may be interpreted by the help of AIN and MAI also. Moreover, it might be repetitive to mention that F-Score, G-Score, and SR were formulated in a *macroeconomic* perspective whereas AIN, MAI, and FPI are formulated by strictly keeping *microeconomic* perspective in mind.

Apart from that, I have introduced the concept of *Net Sales elasticity of Working Capital* $\left(\frac{NS}{WC} \times \frac{dWC}{dNS}\right)$ to predict the propensity to bankruptcy of a firm based on a comparative study which is a novel approach in the study of financial accounting as a whole.

The necessary steps for the entire procedure are stated below:

- In the first step, the four variables, i.e., Working Capital (WC), Retained Earnings (RE), Earnings before Income Taxes (EBITA), Net Sales (NS), and Total Assets (TA) are documented:

Table 1. Documentation of Current Assets (CA), Current Liabilities (CL), Working Capital (WC), Retained Earnings (RE), Earnings before Income Taxes (EBITA), Net Sales (NS), and Total Assets (TA) respectively for Wal-Mart (1987 – 2016)

Year	CA	CL	WC	RE	EBITA	NS	TA
1987	2353	1340	1013	1470	846	11909	4049
1988	2905	1744	1161	2030	1069	15959	5132
1989	3631	2066	1565	2777	1325	20649	6360
1990	4713	2845	1868	3728	1707	25811	8198
1991	6415	3990	2425	4836	2043	32602	11389
1992	8575	5004	3571	6249	2553	43887	15443
1993	10198	6754	3444	8002	3166	55484	20565
1994	12114	7406	4708	9987	3691	67344	26441
1995	15338	9973	5365	12213	4262	82494	32819
1996	17331	11454	5877	14394	4346	93627	37541
1997	17993	10957	7036	16768	4877	104859	39604
1998	19352	14460	4892	18167	5719	117958	45384
1999	21132	16762	4370	20741	7323	137634	49996
2000	24356	25803	-1447	25129	9083	165013	70349
2001	26555	28949	-2394	30169	10116	191329	78130
2002	27878	27282	596	34441	10751	217799	83527
2003	30483	32617	-2134	37924	12368	244524	94685
2004	34421	37840	-3419	40206	14193	256329	105405
2005	38491	42888	-4397	43854	16105	285222	120223
2006	43825	48825	-5000	49105	17535	308945	138187
2007	46588	51754	-5166	55818	18968	344992	151193
2008	48020	58478	-10458	57319	20198	374307	163514
2009	48959	55390	-6431	63660	20867	401244	163429
2010	48032	55543	-7511	66357	22118	405132	170407
2011	52012	58603	-6591	63967	23538	418952	180782
2012	54975	62300	-7325	68691	24332	443416	193406
2013	59940	71818	-11878	72978	25662	465604	203105
2014	61185	69345	-8160	76566	24656	473076	204751
2015	63278	65253	-1975	85777	24799	482229	203490
2016	60239	64619	-4380	90021	21638	478614	199581

- Since according to my hypothesis, TA is dependent on WC, RE, EBITA, and NS; hence, X_1, X_2, X_3, and X_5 could be expressed as pure component ratios (Laitinen, 2018) in terms of linear regression equations respectively as:

$$TA = a_1 \pm b_1 WC \tag{6}$$

$$TA = a_2 \pm b_2 RE \tag{7}$$

$$TA = a_3 \pm b_3 EBITA \tag{8}$$

and

$$TA = a_5 \pm b_5 NS \tag{9}$$

where a_1, a_2, a_3, a_5 are intercepts of respective regression lines, and b_1, b_2, b_3, b_5 are slopes of those regression lines;

- In the third step, X_4 is also expressed a pure component ratio in terms of linear regression equation in a similar fashion:

$$MVE = a_4 \pm b_4 BVD \tag{10}$$

where a_4, b_4 have their usual interpretations;

- In the next step, regression analyses were performed for equations: (6) – (10) and as per the regression results; WC, RE, EBITA, and NS were expressed in terms of TA and MVE was expressed in terms of BVD (by simple method of substitution). In the process, variables X_1, X_2, X_3, and X_5 were simplified and expressed in terms of TA only and X_4 was separately expressed as a linear equation of BVD.

Table 2. Documentation of Salaries (SAL), Taxes (TAX), Others (OTH), Accrued Liabilities (ACRLB), Accrued Income Taxes (ACRIT), Current Portion of Long-term Debt (CPLD), Long-term Debt (LD), Book Value of Debt (BVD), and Market Value of Equity (MVE) respectively for Wal-Mart (1987 – 2016)

Year	SAL	TAX	OTH	ACRLB	ACRIT	CPLD	LD	BVD	MVE
1987	63	46	160	269	133	1	179	582	28
1988	89	81	230	400	121	2	186	709	56
1989	127	107	281	515	121	2	184	822	56
1990	157	134	340	631	179	2	185	997	57
1991	189	0	539	728	184	6	740	1658	114
1992	216	0	613	829	227	5	1722	2783	115
1993	0	0	0	1042	191	14	3073	4320	230
1994	0	0	0	1473	183	20	6156	7832	230
1995	0	0	0	1819	365	23	7871	10078	230
1996	0	0	0	2091	123	271	8508	10993	229
1997	0	0	0	2413	298	523	7709	10943	228
1998	0	0	0	3628	565	1039	7191	12423	224
1999	0	0	0	4998	501	900	6908	13307	445
2000	0	0	0	6161	1129	1964	13672	22926	446
2001	0	0	0	6355	841	4234	12501	23931	447
2002	0	0	0	7174	1343	2257	15687	26461	445
2003	0	0	0	8945	739	4538	16607	30829	440
2004	0	0	0	10342	1377	2904	17102	31725	431
2005	0	0	0	12155	1281	3759	20087	37282	423
2006	0	0	0	13465	1340	4595	26429	45829	417
2007	0	0	0	14675	706	5428	27222	48031	413
2008	0	0	0	15799	1016	5913	29799	52527	397
2009	0	0	0	18112	677	5848	31349	55986	393
2010	0	0	0	18734	1365	4050	33231	57380	378
2011	0	0	0	18701	157	4655	40692	64205	352
2012	0	0	0	18154	1164	1975	44070	65363	342
2013	0	0	0	18808	2211	5587	38394	65000	332
2014	0	0	0	18793	966	4103	41771	65633	323
2015	0	0	0	19152	1021	4810	41086	66069	323
2016	0	0	0	19607	521	2745	38214	61087	317

Now the Altman's Index (AIN) is formulated on year-to-year basis for Wal-Mart by the help of *Weighted Arithmetic Mean* with equal weight of 0.2 or 20 percent for each of the 5 variables (Das, 2008). The individual values for these 5 variables are estimated by simply plugging the values of TA and BVD in the linear equations.

Table 3. Estimation of variables X_1, X_2, X_3, X_4, X_5, and Altman's Index (AIN) respectively for Wal-Mart (1987 – 2016)

Year	TA	BVD	X1	X2	X3	X4	X5	AIN
1987	4049	582	1.51918	0.39	0.25352	0.32946	4.55091	1.40861
1988	5132	709	1.181	0.39	0.2257	0.27098	4.07566	1.22867
1989	6360	822	0.93688	0.39	0.20561	0.23414	3.73259	1.09984
1990	8198	997	0.70815	0.39	0.18679	0.19357	3.41114	0.97793
1991	11389	1658	0.48639	0.39	0.16854	0.1176	3.0995	0.8524
1992	15443	2783	0.33683	0.39	0.15623	0.07127	2.88932	0.76873
1993	20565	4320	0.23218	0.39	0.14762	0.04698	2.74225	0.71181
1994	26441	7832	0.16207	0.39	0.14185	0.02726	2.64372	0.67298
1995	32819	10078	0.11437	0.39	0.13792	0.02185	2.57669	0.64817
1996	37541	10993	0.08951	0.39	0.13588	0.02028	2.54175	0.63548
1997	39604	10943	0.0805	0.39	0.13514	0.02036	2.52909	0.63102
1998	45384	12423	0.05964	0.39	0.13342	0.01829	2.49977	0.62022
1999	49996	13307	0.04645	0.39	0.13233	0.01728	2.48124	0.61346
2000	70349	22926	0.0089	0.39	0.12924	0.01129	2.42847	0.59358
2001	78130	23931	-0.0003	0.39	0.12849	0.01094	2.41556	0.58894
2002	83527	26461	-0.0057	0.39	0.12805	0.01018	2.40802	0.58612
2003	94685	30829	-0.0148	0.39	0.12729	0.00916	2.39515	0.58136
2004	105405	31725	-0.0218	0.39	0.12672	0.00899	2.38536	0.57786
2005	120223	37282	-0.0294	0.39	0.1261	0.0081	2.3747	0.57391
2006	138187	45829	-0.0364	0.39	0.12552	0.00715	2.36484	0.57022
2007	151193	48031	-0.0404	0.39	0.12519	0.00696	2.35916	0.56818
2008	163514	52527	-0.0437	0.39	0.12492	0.00662	2.35462	0.5665
2009	163429	55986	-0.0436	0.39	0.12492	0.00639	2.35465	0.56647
2010	170407	57380	-0.0453	0.39	0.12479	0.00631	2.35236	0.56564
2011	180782	64205	-0.0474	0.39	0.12461	0.00596	2.34929	0.56448
2012	193406	65363	-0.0498	0.39	0.12442	0.00591	2.346	0.56331
2013	203105	65000	-0.0514	0.39	0.12428	0.00592	2.34375	0.56251
2014	204751	65633	-0.0516	0.39	0.12426	0.00589	2.34339	0.56238
2015	203490	66069	-0.0514	0.39	0.12428	0.00588	2.34366	0.56247
2016	199581	61087	-0.0508	0.39	0.12433	0.00611	2.34454	0.56283

The regression equation of TA on WC (Refer to Table 4), regression equation of TA on RE (Refer to Table 5), regression equation of TA on EBITA (Refer to Table 6), regression equation of MVE on BVD (Refer to Table 7), and regression equation of TA on NS (Refer to Table 8) are documented in support of establishing the regressionary relationships between the dependent and independent variables;

Table 4. Regression results of Total Assets (TA) on Working Capital (WC) for Wal-Mart [Independent variable (X Variable 1): Working Capital (WC)

SUMMARY OUTPUT

Regression Statistics	
Multiple R	0.8600627
R Square	0.7397079
Adjusted R Square	0.7304117
Standard Error	38001.205
Observations	30

ANOVA

	df	*SS*	*MS*	*F*	*Significance F*
Regression	1	1.14908E+11	1.1E+11	79.5714	1.12576E-09
Residual	28	40434564494	1.4E+09		
Total	29	1.55343E+11			

	Coefficients	*Standard Error*	*t Stat*	*P-value*	*Lower 95%*	*Upper 95%*	*Lower 95.0%*	*Upper 95.0%*
Intercept	77863.206	7176.723284	10.8494	1.5E-11	63162.35466	92564.057	63162.35466	92564.0567
X Variable 1	-12.04632	1.350441912	-8.9203	1.1E-09	-14.81257804	-9.280068	-14.812578	-9.2800684

Table 5. Regression results of Total Assets (TA) on Retained Earnings (RE) for Wal-Mart [Independent variable (X Variable 1): Retained Earnings (RE)]

SUMMARY OUTPUT

Regression Statistics	
Multiple R	0.9912131
R Square	0.9825034
Adjusted R Square	0.9818785
Standard Error	9852.4418
Observations	30

ANOVA

	df	*SS*	*MS*	*F*	*Significance F*
Regression	1	1.52625E+11	1.5E+11	1572.31	3.79679E-26
Residual	28	2717977055	9.7E+07		
Total	29	1.55343E+11			

	Coefficients	*Standard Error*	*t Stat*	*P-value*	*Lower 95%*	*Upper 95%*	*Lower 95.0%*	*Upper 95.0%*
Intercept	1140.5971	2957.672076	0.38564	0.70268	-4917.91945	7199.1136	-4917.91945	7199.1136
X Variable 1	2.5780058	0.065015196	39.6524	3.8E-26	2.444828183	2.7111834	2.44482818	2.711183365

Table 6. Regression results of Total Assets (TA) on Earnings before Income Taxes (EBITA) for Wal-Mart [Independent variable (X Variable 1): Earnings before Income Taxes (EBITA)]

SUMMARY OUTPUT

Regression Statistics	
Multiple R	0.9963955
R Square	0.9928039
Adjusted R Square	0.9925469
Standard Error	6318.5151
Observations	30

ANOVA

	df	*SS*	*MS*	*F*	*Significance F*
Regression	1	1.54225E+11	1.5E+11	3863	1.49726E-31
Residual	28	1117861724	4E+07		
Total	29	1.55343E+11			

	Coefficients	*Standard Error*	*t Stat*	*P-value*	*Lower 95%*	*Upper 95%*	*Lower 95.0%*	*Upper 95.0%*
Intercept	-4389.1865	1961.827258	-2.2373	0.03341	-8407.80744	-370.5656	-8407.80744	-370.56561
X Variable 1	8.222114	0.132288144	62.1531	1.5E-31	7.951133982	8.4930939	7.951133982	8.49309393

Table 7. Regression results of Market Value of Equity (MVE) on Book Value of Debt (BVD) for Wal-Mart [Independent variable (X Variable 1): Book Value of Debt (BVD)]

SUMMARY OUTPUT

Regression Statistics	
Multiple R	0.6314986
R Square	0.3987905
Adjusted R Square	0.3773188
Standard Error	108.20478
Observations	30

ANOVA

	df	*SS*	*MS*	*F*	*Significance F*
Regression	1	217455.2722	217455	18.5728	0.000182288
Residual	28	327831.6944	11708.3		
Total	29	545286.9667			

	Coefficients	*Standard Error*	*t Stat*	*P-value*	*Lower 95%*	*Upper 95%*	*Lower 95.0%*	*Upper 95.0%*
Intercept	190.38178	31.36423772	6.07003	1.5E-06	126.1350552	254.6285	126.1350552	254.628511
X Variable 1	0.0035084	0.000814091	4.30962	0.00018	0.001840829	0.005176	0.001840829	0.00517601

Table 8. Regression results of Total assets (TA) on Net Sales (NS) for Wal-Mart [Independent variable (X Variable 1): Net Sales (NS)]

SUMMARY OUTPUT								
Regression Statistics								
Multiple R	0.9986102							
R Square	0.9972223							
Adjusted R Square	0.9971231							
Standard Error	3925.6151							
Observations	30							
ANOVA								
	df	*SS*	*MS*	*F*	*Significance F*			
Regression	1	1.54912E+11	1.5E+11	10052.4	2.43552E-37			
Residual	28	431492706.3	1.5E+07					
Total	29	1.55343E+11						
	Coefficients	*Standard Error*	*t Stat*	*P-value*	*Lower 95%*	*Upper 95%*	*Lower 95.0%*	*Upper 95.0%*
Intercept	-3966.5794	1213.686947	-3.2682	0.00286	-6452.70435	-1480.454	-6452.70435	-1480.4544
X Variable 1	0.4353638	0.004342283	100.261	2.4E-37	0.426469025	0.4442586	0.426469025	0.44425855

In this context, the Altman's Z – Equation (AZE) is expressed as a linear regression equation of TA on BVD (Refer to Table 9). The AZE helps to explore the query whether BVD of a firm can affect its TA.

Table 9. Regression results of Total assets (TA) on Book Value of Debt (BVD) for Wal-Mart [Independent variable (X Variable 1): Book Value of Debt (BVD)]

SUMMARY OUTPUT								
Regression Statistics								
Multiple R	0.99760151							
R Square	0.99520876							
Adjusted R Square	0.99503765							
Standard Error	5155.73534							
Observations	30							
ANOVA								
	df	*SS*	*MS*	*F*	*Significance F*			
Regression	1	1.54599E+11	1.5E+11	5816	5.0318E-34			
Residual	28	744284993.9	2.7E+07					
Total	29	1.55343E+11						
	Coefficients	*Standard Error*	*t Stat*	*P-value*	*Lower 95%*	*Upper 95%*	*Lower 95.0%*	*Upper 95.0%*
Intercept	5715.4842	1494.441431	3.8245	0.00067	2654.259739	8776.7087	2654.259739	8776.708656
X Variable 1	2.95821314	0.038789763	76.2627	5E-34	2.878755911	3.0376704	2.878755911	3.037670364

In continuation to AZE, the Modified Altman's Index (MAI) is formulated by applying *Chain Index* method with **Base Year = 1986** and using *Link Indices (LI)* for estimation with BVD as the independent and TA as the dependent variable (Das, 2008).

Table 10. Estimation of year wise Link Index (LI) and Modified Altman's Index (MAI) for Wal-Mart (1987 – 2016)

Year	BVD	TA	LI	ACIN
1986	469	3104	100	100
1987	582	4049	124.094	124.094
1988	709	5132	121.821	151.173
1989	822	6360	115.938	175.267
1990	997	8198	121.29	212.58
1991	1658	11389	166.299	353.518
1992	2783	15443	167.853	593.39
1993	4320	20565	155.228	921.109
1994	7832	26441	181.296	1669.94
1995	10078	32819	128.677	2148.83
1996	10993	37541	109.079	2343.92
1997	10943	39604	99.5452	2333.26
1998	12423	45384	113.525	2648.83
1999	13307	49996	107.116	2837.31
2000	22926	70349	172.285	4888.27
2001	23931	78130	104.384	5102.56
2002	26461	83527	110.572	5642
2003	30829	94685	116.507	6573.35
2004	31725	105405	102.906	6764.39
2005	37282	120223	117.516	7949.25
2006	45829	138187	122.925	9771.64
2007	48031	151193	104.805	10241.2
2008	52527	163514	109.361	11199.8
2009	55986	163429	106.585	11937.3
2010	57380	170407	102.49	12234.5
2011	64205	180782	111.894	13689.8
2012	65363	193406	101.804	13936.7
2013	65000	203105	99.4446	13859.3
2014	65633	204751	100.974	13994.2
2015	66069	203490	100.664	14087.2
2016	61087	199581	92.4594	13024.9

The major reasons for inclusion of MAI in the form of chain index are as follows:

- The chain index is more *realistic* in nature than the fixed base index, since the effects of all intermediate years are taken into consideration,
- The chain base method enables comparison between two adjacent time periods through the link indices. This is far more useful in business and commerce than the indirect comparison through a remote fixed base (Das, 2008).

Finally, the Financial Performance Index (FPI) for Wal-Mart is formulated by estimating the *Geometric Mean (GM)* of five ratios (Insert Table 16), i.e., Return on Assets (ROA), Return on Equity (ROE), Cash Flow Adequacy Ratio (CFAR), Debt Ratio (DR), and Net Profit Ratio (NPR) respectively (Refer to Tables 11, 12, 13, 14, and 15).

Table 11. Documentation of Net Income (NI), Net Sales (NS), and Return on Assets (ROA) for Wal-Mart (1987 – 2016)

Year	NI	NS	ROA
1987	450	11909	0.11114
1988	628	15959	0.12237
1989	837	20649	0.1316
1990	1076	25811	0.13125
1991	1291	32602	0.11335
1992	1608	43887	0.10412
1993	1995	55484	0.09701
1994	2333	67344	0.08823
1995	2681	82494	0.08169
1996	2740	93627	0.07299
1997	3056	104859	0.07716
1998	3526	117958	0.07769
1999	4430	137634	0.08861
2000	5377	165013	0.07643
2001	6295	191329	0.08057
2002	6671	217799	0.07987
2003	8039	244524	0.0849
2004	9054	256329	0.0859
2005	10267	285222	0.0854
2006	11231	308945	0.08127
2007	11284	344992	0.07463
2008	12731	374307	0.07786
2009	13400	401244	0.08199
2010	14370	405132	0.08433
2011	16389	418952	0.09066
2012	15699	443416	0.08117
2013	16999	465604	0.0837
2014	16022	473076	0.07825
2015	16363	482229	0.08041
2016	14694	478614	0.07362

Table 12. Documentation of Net Income (NI), Total Stockholders' Equity (TE), and Return on Equity (ROE) for Wal-Mart (1987 – 2016)

Year	NI	TE	ROE
1987	450	1690	0.26627
1988	628	2257	0.27825
1989	837	3008	0.27826
1990	1076	3966	0.27131
1991	1291	5365	0.24063
1992	1608	6990	0.23004
1993	1995	8759	0.22777
1994	2333	10753	0.21696
1995	2681	12726	0.21067
1996	2740	14756	0.18569
1997	3056	17143	0.17827
1998	3526	18503	0.19056
1999	4430	21112	0.20983
2000	5377	25834	0.20814
2001	6295	31343	0.20084
2002	6671	35102	0.19005
2003	8039	39337	0.20436
2004	9054	43623	0.20755
2005	10267	49396	0.20785
2006	11231	53171	0.21122
2007	11284	61573	0.18326
2008	12731	64608	0.19705
2009	13400	65285	0.20525
2010	14370	72648	0.1978
2011	16389	71247	0.23003
2012	15699	75761	0.20722
2013	16999	81738	0.20797
2014	16022	81339	0.19698
2015	16363	85937	0.19041
2016	14694	83611	0.17574

Table 13. Documentation of Cash Flow from Operating Activities (CFOA), Capital Expenditure (CE), Debt Repayments (DRP), Dividends Paid (DIV), and Cash Flow Adequacy Ratio (CFAR) for Wal-Mart (1987 – 2016)

Year	CFOA	CE	DRP	DIV	CFAR
1987	265	376	17	48	0.60091
1988	459	531	42	68	0.71607
1989	734	502	107	90	1.05007
1990	867	756	25	124	0.95801
1991	1296	1489	134	159	0.72727
1992	1357	1894	75	195	0.62708
1993	1278	3499	68	241	0.33561
1994	2195	3960	470	299	0.46416
1995	2906	3154	107	391	0.79573
1996	2383	2729	207	458	0.70212
1997	5930	1301	3073	481	1.22142
1998	7123	4421	648	611	1.25405
1999	7580	2832	1176	693	1.61242
2000	8194	17129	996	890	0.43092
2001	9604	5582	3714	1070	0.92649
2002	10260	4074	5219	1249	0.97325
2003	13005	8553	1487	1328	1.144
2004	15996	6782	3846	1569	1.31147
2005	15044	10748	2335	2214	0.98346
2006	17635	12630	3673	2511	0.93733
2007	20235	10243	7291	2802	0.99503
2008	20642	10889	9066	3586	0.87685
2009	23147	-1014	9484	3746	1.89481
2010	26249	12184	7412	4217	1.1023
2011	23643	12699	4443	4437	1.09565
2012	24255	13510	5181	5048	1.02174
2013	25591	12898	1976	5361	1.26469
2014	23257	13115	5654	6139	0.93372
2015	28564	12174	13482	6185	0.89708
2016	27389	11477	5664	6294	1.16872

Table 14. Documentation of Total Liabilities (TL), Total Assets (TA) and Debt Ratio (DR) for Wal-Mart (1987 – 2016)

Year	TL	TA	DR
1987	2359	4049	0.58261
1988	2875	5132	0.56021
1989	3352	6360	0.52704
1990	4232	8198	0.51622
1991	6024	11389	0.52893
1992	8453	15443	0.54737
1993	11806	20565	0.57408
1994	15688	26441	0.59332
1995	20093	32819	0.61224
1996	22785	37541	0.60694
1997	22461	39604	0.56714
1998	26881	45384	0.5923
1999	28884	49996	0.57773
2000	44515	70349	0.63277
2001	46787	78130	0.59884
2002	48425	83527	0.57975
2003	55348	94685	0.58455
2004	61782	105405	0.58614
2005	70827	120223	0.58913
2006	85016	138187	0.61522
2007	89620	151193	0.59275
2008	98906	163514	0.60488
2009	98144	163429	0.60053
2010	97759	170407	0.57368
2011	109535	180782	0.6059
2012	117645	193406	0.60828
2013	121367	203105	0.59756
2014	123412	204751	0.60274
2015	117553	203490	0.57768
2016	115970	199581	0.58107

Table 15. Documentation of Net Income (NI), Net Sales (NS) and Net Profit Ratio (NPR) for Wal-Mart (1987 – 2016)

Year	NI	NS	NPR
1987	450	11909	0.03779
1988	628	15959	0.03935
1989	837	20649	0.04053
1990	1076	25811	0.04169
1991	1291	32602	0.0396
1992	1608	43887	0.03664
1993	1995	55484	0.03596
1994	2333	67344	0.03464
1995	2681	82494	0.0325
1996	2740	93627	0.02927
1997	3056	104859	0.02914
1998	3526	117958	0.02989
1999	4430	137634	0.03219
2000	5377	165013	0.03259
2001	6295	191329	0.0329
2002	6671	217799	0.03063
2003	8039	244524	0.03288
2004	9054	256329	0.03532
2005	10267	285222	0.036
2006	11231	308945	0.03635
2007	11284	344992	0.03271
2008	12731	374307	0.03401
2009	13400	401244	0.0334
2010	14370	405132	0.03547
2011	16389	418952	0.03912
2012	15699	443416	0.0354
2013	16999	465604	0.03651
2014	16022	473076	0.03387
2015	16363	482229	0.03393
2016	14694	478614	0.0307

RESULTS AND FINDINGS

The major results and findings of this study are described as follows:

- In reference to equations: (6) – (9), the necessary regression equations are given below:

$$TA = 77863 - 12WC \tag{11}$$

$$TA = 2.58RE \tag{12}$$

$$TA = -4389 + 8.22EBITA \tag{13}$$

$$TA = 3966.58 + 0.435NS \tag{14}$$

By using equations: (11) – (14), the following linear relations could be established:

$$WC = (77863 - TA)\,/\,12$$

$$RE = TA\,/\,2.58$$

$$EBITA = (4389 + TA)\,/\,8.22$$

$$NS = (-3966.58 + TA)\,/\,0.435$$

Thus, by substituting the values of WC, RE, EBITA, and NS for the four variables X_1, X_2, X_3, and X_5 respectively, the following results could be obtained:

$$X_1 = WC\,/\,TA = (77863 - TA)\,/\,12TA \tag{15}$$

$$X_2 = RE\,/\,TA = TA\,/\,2.58TA = 0.39 \tag{16}$$

$$X_3 = EBITA\,/\,TA = (4389 + TA)\,/\,8.22TA \tag{17}$$

and

$$X_5 = NS / TA = (-3966.58 + TA) / 0.435TA \tag{18}$$

Now in relation to equation: (10), the linear relationship between MVE and BVD could be expressed as:

$$MVE = 190 + 0.003BVD \tag{19}$$

Thus, in a similar fashion, by substituting the value of MVE in case of fourth variable X_4, it may be written as below:

$$X_4 = MVE / BVD = (190 + 0.003BVD) / BVD \tag{20}$$

- Now the Altman's Index (AIN) is formulated by applying the formula of *Weighted Arithmetic Mean* with equal weight of 20 percent for each of the 5 variables (Das, 2008).

Formally,

$$AIN = 0.2(X_1 + X_2 + X_3 + X_4 + X_5) \tag{21}$$

The summarized statistical results led to some interesting findings, such as; the recorded *maximum* value of the observed sample set was 1.4086 (Year: 1987) and the *minimum* value was 0.56238 (Year: 2014) setting a trend of continual decline in the value of AIN. The *range* of the observations was 0.84622 with *Mean* 0.68620, *Standard Deviation (S.D.)* 0.21571, and *Coefficient of Variation (C.V.)* 0.31435. The very high values of S.D. and C.V. contemplated the fact that for the time period of 30 years, there had been a huge fluctuation for the values of AIN (Refer to Table 3).

The regression of AIN on X_1 is as follows:

$$AIN = 0.59 + 0.54X_1$$

Table 16. Regression results of Altman's Index (AIN) on X_1 for Wal-Mart [Independent variable (X Variable 1): X_1]

SUMMARY OUTPUT								
Regression Statistics								
Multiple R	0.999958							
R Square	0.999916							
Adjusted R Square	0.999913							
Standard Error	0.0020124							
Observations	30							
ANOVA								
	df	*SS*	*MS*	*F*	*Significance F*			
Regression	1	1.349269525	1.34927	333187	1.30791E-58			
Residual	28	0.000113389	4E-06					
Total	29	1.349382913						
	Coefficients	*Standard Error*	*t Stat*	*P-value*	*Lower 95%*	*Upper 95%*	*Lower 95.0%*	*Upper 95.0%*
Intercept	0.5891815	0.000404028	1458.27	7E-70	0.588353922	0.59000915	0.58835392	0.59000915
X Variable 1	0.5411816	0.00093756	577.223	1.3E-58	0.539261113	0.54310212	0.53926111	0.54310212

The downward trend for the values of AIN indicated towards the withered financial strength of the company;

- The Altman's Z – Equation (AZE) may be expressed as:

$$TA = 5715 + 3BVD \tag{22}$$

Equation: (22) contemplates the fact that for Wal-Mart, Total assets (TA) is highly sensitive to changes in the value of Book Value of Debt (BVD), in fact, it is 300%.

The BVD elasticity of TA (e) may be expressed as:

$$e = (BVD \,/\, TA) \times \left(\frac{dTA}{dBVD}\right) = 3 \times (BVD \,/\, TA) > 0$$

as

$$\frac{dTA}{dBVD} = 3; TA, BVD > 0$$

- The Modified Altman's Index (MAI) is formulated in the following manner:

- In the first step, the two required variables BVD and TA are plotted annually. The Link Index (LI) is calculated for the entire time series by using *Laspeyres' Index Number* formula with preceding year as the base. The LI and MAI are held as 100 for the Base Year 1986,
- For the next year (1987), the LI is denoted by I_{01} and MAI is denoted by I'_{01} (by using Chain Index formula) and they are estimated as:

Link Index (LI) for year 1: $I_{01} = [(BVD_1 \times TA_0) / (BVD_0 \times TA_0)] \times 100$,

Link Index (LI) for year 2: $I_{12} = [(BVD_2 \times TA_1) / (BVD_1 \times TA_1)] \times 100$, and so on.

The Modified Altman's Index (MAI) for base year 0 (1986): $I'_{01} = I_{01}$,

The MAI for year 1 (with reference to year 0): $I'_{02} = I_{01} \times I_{12}$, and so on (Das, 2008).

Proceeding likewise, the LI and MAI for 1987 were both 124.094. For the year 1988, the LI was 121.821 and MAI was 151.173 respectively and, in this manner, the MAIs' for the time- period of 30 years were estimated. A perusal of the LIs' and MAIs' corroborate the same findings as the AINs', i.e., the growth trends for both the LIs' and MAIs' are *inconsistent* and for the time span of 4 years (2013 – 2016) the growth rates have absolutely flattened. Two out of those four years (2013 and 2016) had seen negative growth rates with LIs' of 99.4446 and 92.4594 respectively contemplating declining financial strength for Wal-Mart;

- The regressions of AIN on the variables X_1, X_3, X_4, and X_5 respectively yield the following results (Refer to Table 17):

$$AIN = 0.59 + 0.541X_1 \quad (23)$$

Table 17. Regression results of Altman's Index (AIN) on X_3 for Wal-Mart [Independent variable (X Variable 1): X_3]

SUMMARY OUTPUT								
Regression Statistics								
Multiple R	0.99995798							
R Square	0.99991597							
Adjusted R Square	0.99991297							
Standard Error	0.00201236							
Observations	30							
ANOVA								
	df	*SS*	*MS*	*F*	*Significance F*			
Regression	1	1.349269525	1.34927	333187	1.30791E-58			
Residual	28	0.000113389	4E-06					
Total	29	1.349382913						
	Coefficients	*Standard Error*	*t Stat*	*P-value*	*Lower 95%*	*Upper 95%*	*Lower 95.0%*	*Upper 95.0%*
Intercept	-0.2559857	0.001673117	-153	1.8E-42	-0.25941297	-0.252559	-0.25941297	-0.25255852
X Variable 1	6.57656566	0.011393453	577.223	1.3E-58	6.553227234	6.5999041	6.55322723	6.599904094

$$AIN = -0.26 + 6.58X_3 \tag{24}$$

Table 18. Regression results of Altman's Index (AIN) on X_4 for Wal-Mart [Independent variable (X Variable 1): X_4]

SUMMARY OUTPUT								
Regression Statistics								
Multiple R	0.9945987							
R Square	0.9892267							
Adjusted R Square	0.9888419							
Standard Error	0.0227858							
Observations	30							
ANOVA								
	df	*SS*	*MS*	*F*	*Significance F*			
Regression	1	1.334845569	1.33485	2571.01	4.26164E-29			
Residual	28	0.014537344	0.00052					
Total	29	1.349382913						
	Coefficients	*Standard Error*	*t Stat*	*P-value*	*Lower 95%*	*Upper 95%*	*Lower 95.0%*	*Upper 95.0%*
Intercept	0.5623025	0.004824657	116.548	3.6E-39	0.552419686	0.5721854	0.55241969	0.572185407
X Variable 1	2.4501007	0.048320557	50.7051	4.3E-29	2.351120484	2.5490808	2.35112048	2.549080832

$$AIN = 0.562 + 2.45X_4 \tag{25}$$

and

Table 19. Regression results of Altman's Index (AIN) on X_5 for Wal-Mart [Independent variable (X Variable 1): X_5]

SUMMARY OUTPUT								
Regression Statistics								
Multiple R	0.99995798							
R Square	0.99991597							
Adjusted R Square	0.99991297							
Standard Error	0.00201236							
Observations	30							
ANOVA								
	df	*SS*	*MS*	*F*	*Significance F*			
Regression	1	1.349269525	1.34927	333187	1.30791E-58			
Residual	28	0.000113389	4E-06					
Total	29	1.349382913						
	Coefficients	*Standard Error*	*t Stat*	*P-value*	*Lower 95%*	*Upper 95%*	*Lower 95.0%*	*Upper 95.0%*
Intercept	-0.3411889	0.001817411	-187.73	5.9E-45	-0.344911686	-0.3374661	-0.34491169	-0.33746609
X Variable 1	0.3850933	0.000667148	577.223	1.3E-58	0.38372671	0.3864599	0.38372671	0.386459891

$$AIN = -0.342 + 0.385X_5 \quad (26)$$

Since the values of X_2 is exactly *collinear*, hence there is no question of regression analysis for the said variable.

Table 20. Documentation of Current Ratio (CR) and Debt Ratio (DR) for Wal-Mart (1987 – 2016)

Year	CR	DR
1987	1.75597	0.58261
1988	1.66571	0.56021
1989	1.7575	0.52704
1990	1.65659	0.51622
1991	1.60777	0.52893
1992	1.71363	0.54737
1993	1.50992	0.57408
1994	1.6357	0.59332
1995	1.53795	0.61224
1996	1.5131	0.60694
1997	1.64215	0.56714
1998	1.33831	0.5923
1999	1.26071	0.57773
2000	0.94392	0.63277
2001	0.9173	0.59884
2002	1.02185	0.57975
2003	0.93457	0.58455
2004	0.90965	0.58614
2005	0.89748	0.58913
2006	0.89759	0.61522
2007	0.90018	0.59275
2008	0.82116	0.60488
2009	0.8839	0.60053
2010	0.86477	0.57368
2011	0.88753	0.6059
2012	0.88242	0.60828
2013	0.83461	0.59756
2014	0.88233	0.60274
2015	0.96973	0.57768
2016	0.93222	0.58107

- By taking total differential of equations: (23), (24), and (26), we have:

$$dAIN = 0.541dX_1 = 0.541[(TAdWC - WCdTA) / TA^2]$$
$$= (0.541 / TA^2) \times [TAdWC\{1 - (WCdTA / TAdWC)\}]$$
$$\rightarrow dAIN / dWC = (0.541 / TA)[1 - \varepsilon]$$

$dAIN / dEBITA = (6.58 / TA)[1 - \lambda]$, and $dAIN / dNS = (0.385 / TA)[1 - \rho]$

where

$$\varepsilon = (WC / TA) \times \frac{dTA}{dWC} = \text{Working Capital Elasticity of Total Assets,}$$

$$\lambda = (EBITA / TA) \times \frac{dTA}{dEBITA} = \text{EBITA Elasticity of Total Assets, and}$$

$$\rho = (NS / TA) \times \frac{dTA}{dNS} = \text{Net Sales Elasticity of Total Assets.}$$

Thus, it follows as:

$$\frac{dEBITA}{dWC} = (0.541 / 6.58) \times [(1 - \varepsilon) / (1 - \lambda)] = 0.08[(1 - \varepsilon) / (1 - \lambda)]$$
$$\rightarrow \frac{dWC}{dEBITA} = 12.5[(1 - \lambda) / (1 - \varepsilon)]$$

Similarly,

$$\frac{dNS}{dEBITA} = (6.58 / 0.385) \times [(1 - \lambda) / (1 - \rho)] = 17[(1 - \lambda) / (1 - \rho)]$$
$$\rightarrow \frac{dEBITA}{dNS} = 0.06[(1 - \rho) / (1 - \lambda)]$$

Finally,

$$\frac{dWC}{dEBITA} \times \frac{dEBITA}{dNS} = \frac{dWC}{dNS} = 0.75[(1 - \rho) / (1 - \varepsilon)] \qquad (27)$$

Equation: (27) establishes an important relationship between Net Sales (NS) and Working Capital (WC) for Wal-Mart. The positivity condition for growth rate of WC with respect to NS requires either

$0 \le \rho, \varepsilon \le 1$ or $\rho, \varepsilon > 1$. This multiplier could be used as a *predictor* for the financial health of any firm regardless of its functional domain.

Hence, the *primary* condition for both non-bankruptcy and financial robustness, the multiplier ($\frac{dWC}{dNS}$) must be *greater than 1*. In case the multiplier is a *positive fraction*, i.e.,

$0 < \frac{dWC}{dNS} < 1$, it ensures non-bankruptcy of the firm accompanied by retarded growth. However, if it is *negative*, it should be treated as a herald for the company's bankruptcy;

- Now let for a population N (μ, σ²): $E(x_i) = \mu$, $Var(x_i) = E(x_i - \mu)^2 = \sigma^2$ Hence $S^2 = \sum (x_i - \overline{x})^2 / n$

Now it may be written that (Das, 2008):

$$s^2 = \frac{n}{n-1} \times S^2$$

where $s^2 = \sum (x_i - \overline{x})^2 / (n-1)$

$$\therefore E(s^2) = (\frac{n}{n-1}) \times E(S^2) = (\frac{n}{n-1}) \times (\frac{n-1}{n}) \times \sigma^2 = \sigma^2$$

The equation above proves that s^2 is an *unbiased estimator* of σ^2.

According to the estimation, $S^2 = (0.21571)^2 = 0.465308041$ (Refer to Table 22)

$$\therefore s^2 = (29 \times 0.465308041) / 30 \approx 0.045$$

Table 21. Regression results of Debt Ratio (DR) on Current Ratio (CR) for Wal-Mart [Independent variable: X Variable 1 (CR)]

SUMMARY OUTPUT

Regression Statistics	
Multiple R	0.6040742
R Square	0.3649057
Adjusted R Square	0.3422238
Standard Error	0.0217461
Observations	30

ANOVA

	df	*SS*	*MS*	*F*	*Significance F*
Regression	1	0.007607867	0.00761	16.0879	0.000408016
Residual	28	0.01324099	0.00047		
Total	29	0.020848857			

	Coefficients	*Standard Error*	*t Stat*	*P-value*	*Lower 95%*	*Upper 95%*	*Lower 95.0%*	*Upper 95.0%*
Intercept	0.6382243	0.014109025	45.2352	1E-27	0.609323295	0.6671253	0.609323295	0.66712535
X Variable 1	-0.045283	0.011289863	-4.011	0.00041	-0.06840962	-0.022157	-0.06840962	-0.0221572

Thus, it may be stated that 0.045 is the unbiased estimator for population variance σ^2;

- Finally, the Financial Performance Index (FPI) has been formulated as a *Geometric Mean (GM)* of five ratios, i.e., Return on Assets (ROA), Return on Equity (ROE), Cash Flow Adequacy Ratio (CFAR), Debt Ratio (DR), and Net Profit Ratio (NPR) respectively. Formally,

$$FPI = (ROA \times ROE \times CFAR \times DR \times NPR)^{1/5}$$

Table 22. Estimation of Financial Performance Index (FPI) for Wal-Mart (1987 – 2016)

Year	ROA	ROE	CFAR	DR	NPR	FPI
1987	0.11114	0.26627	0.60091	0.58261	0.03779	0.20823
1988	0.12237	0.27825	0.71607	0.56021	0.03935	0.22186
1989	0.1316	0.27826	1.05007	0.52704	0.04053	0.2415
1990	0.13125	0.27131	0.95801	0.51622	0.04169	0.23613
1991	0.11335	0.24063	0.72727	0.52893	0.0396	0.21072
1992	0.10412	0.23004	0.62708	0.54737	0.03664	0.1976
1993	0.09701	0.22777	0.33561	0.57408	0.03596	0.17257
1994	0.08823	0.21696	0.46416	0.59332	0.03464	0.17878
1995	0.08169	0.21067	0.79573	0.61224	0.0325	0.19367
1996	0.07299	0.18569	0.70212	0.60694	0.02927	0.17603
1997	0.07716	0.17827	1.22142	0.56714	0.02914	0.19441
1998	0.07769	0.19056	1.25405	0.5923	0.02989	0.20108
1999	0.08861	0.20983	1.61242	0.57773	0.03219	0.22348
2000	0.07643	0.20814	0.43092	0.63277	0.03259	0.16985
2001	0.08057	0.20084	0.92649	0.59884	0.0329	0.19682
2002	0.07987	0.19005	0.97325	0.57975	0.03063	0.19221
2003	0.0849	0.20436	1.144	0.58455	0.03288	0.20715
2004	0.0859	0.20755	1.31147	0.58614	0.03532	0.21726
2005	0.0854	0.20785	0.98346	0.58913	0.036	0.20591
2006	0.08127	0.21122	0.93733	0.61522	0.03635	0.20475
2007	0.07463	0.18326	0.99503	0.59275	0.03271	0.19243
2008	0.07786	0.19705	0.87685	0.60488	0.03401	0.19428
2009	0.08199	0.20525	1.89481	0.60053	0.0334	0.22971
2010	0.08433	0.1978	1.1023	0.57368	0.03547	0.20635
2011	0.09066	0.23003	1.09565	0.6059	0.03912	0.22219
2012	0.08117	0.20722	1.02174	0.60828	0.0354	0.2059
2013	0.0837	0.20797	1.26469	0.59756	0.03651	0.21692
2014	0.07825	0.19698	0.93372	0.60274	0.03387	0.19661
2015	0.08041	0.19041	0.89708	0.57768	0.03393	0.19321
2016	0.07362	0.17574	1.16872	0.58107	0.0307	0.19328

The first regression analysis revealed the fact that out of 5 independent variables, only one variable, i.e., ROE, was *not* statistically significant at 5 percent level or better. Hence the entire process was iterated by dropping the statistically insignificant variable ROE. The second attempt produced satisfactory regression results with all the coefficients of 4 independent variables showing statistical significance at 5 percent level or better (Insert Tables 25 and 26).

The final regression equation for FPI is given below:

$$FPI = 0.663ROA + 0.043CFAR + 0.113DR + 1.816NPR \tag{28}$$

From equation: (28), it may be clearly inferred that Wal-Mart's financial performance is heavily dependent on two major ratios, viz., NPR and ROA as $\frac{dFPI}{dNPR} = 1.816$, and $\frac{dFPI}{dROA} = 0.663$.

If the aspect of short-term solvency of the business organization is taken into account, then the Debt Ratio (DR) could be expressed as a function of Current Ratio (CR) as follows (Refer to Table 22):

$$DR = 0.64 - 0.045CR \tag{29}$$

By plugging the value of DR in equation: (29), we get:

$$FPI = 0.07232 + 0.663ROA + 0.043CFAR - 0.005085CR + 1.816NPR \tag{30}$$

(Refer to Tables 25 and 26)

Table 23a. Regression of Financial Performance Index (FPI) on Return on Assets (ROA), Return on Equity (ROE), Cash Flow Adequacy Ratio (CFAR), Debt Ratio (DR), Net Profit Ratio (NPR) (First attempt)

Model 1: OLS, using observations 1987-2016 (T = 30) Dependent variable: FPI HAC standard errors, bandwidth 2 (Bartlett kernel)					
	Coefficient	**Std. Error**	**t-Ratio**	**p-Value**	
const	−0.149201	0.108257	−1.378	0.1809	
ROA	1.60552	0.755613	2.125	0.0441	**
ROE	−0.413819	0.321602	−1.287	0.2105	
CFAR	0.0429141	0.00351672	12.20	<0.0001	***
DR	0.328418	0.184549	1.780	0.0878	*
NPR	1.85357	0.251371	7.374	<0.0001	***

Table 23b.

Mean dependent var	0.203364	S.D. dependent var	0.017686
Sum squared resid	0.000245	S.E. of regression	0.003196
R-squared	0.972972	Adjusted R-squared	0.967342
F(5, 24)	457.5513	P-value(F)	5.60e-23
Log-likelihood	133.1526	Akaike criterion	−254.3052
Schwarz criterion	−245.8980	Hannan-Quinn	−251.6157
rho	0.127600	Durbin-Watson	1.725821

Table 24a. Regression of Financial Performance Index (FPI) on Return on Assets (ROA), Cash Flow Adequacy Ratio (CFAR), Debt Ratio (DR), Net Profit Ratio (NPR) (Second attempt)

Model 2: OLS, using observations 1987-2016 (T = 30) Dependent variable: FPI HAC standard errors, bandwidth 2 (Bartlett kernel)					
	Coefficient	**Std. Error**	**t-Ratio**	**p-Value**	
const	−0.0264709	0.0270607	−0.9782	0.3373	
ROA	0.663067	0.0891192	7.440	<0.0001	***
CFAR	0.0430489	0.00374264	11.50	<0.0001	***
DR	0.112967	0.0381270	2.963	0.0066	***
NPR	1.81650	0.249292	7.287	<0.0001	***

Table 24b.

Mean dependent var	0.203364	S.D. dependent var	0.017686
Sum squared resid	0.000255	S.E. of regression	0.003193
R-squared	0.971899	Adjusted R-squared	0.967402
F(4, 25)	359.1335	P-value(F)	1.09e-21
Log-likelihood	132.5682	Akaike criterion	−255.1365
Schwarz criterion	−248.1305	Hannan-Quinn	−252.8952
rho	0.156068	Durbin-Watson	1.684364

Equation: (30) represents the regression equation for FPI with short-term solvency factor in the framework. Although, the coefficient of CR suggests that it has a negligible (negative) impact on FPI for Wal-Mart. The most plausible explanation of this finding is for a financial behemoth like Wal-Mart, short-term solvency is *not* a significant factor. The *second attempt* for regression of FPI (Refer to Table

24) has been performed by *dropping* the *least statistically significant* variable Return on Equity (ROE) as per the final statistical results derived from Table 23.

It should be noted that all the conducted econometrical tests are based on Classical Linear Regression Model (CLRM) (Gujarati, 2003) and executed by Ordinary Least Squares (OLS) method have successfully passed the Granger and Newbold's (1974) *Thumb rule test of Econometric Regression* for verification of spuriousness in regression. The econometrical test results are derived by using Software GRETL v.1.9.4

EMPIRICAL VALIDATION OF THE FINDING IN THE REAL-WORLD SCENARIO

In order to test the efficacy of the multiplier ($\frac{dWC}{dNS}$) in the real word scenario, an empirical study has been done on a former business giant Kodak ® which filed for bankruptcy in 2012, and "exited legacy businesses and sold off its patents before re-emerging as a sharply smaller company in 2013". (Anthony, 2016)

The empirical study based on a regression result for Working Capital (WC) on Net Sales (NS) in case of Kodak ® for the time series study of 10 years (1999 – 2008) provides the following result (Refer to Tables 25 and 26):

Table 25. Documentation of Net Sales (NS) and estimated values of Working Capital (WC) for Kodak (1999 – 2008)

Year	NS	CA	CL	WC
1999	14089	5444	5769	-325
2000	13994	5491	6215	-724
2001	13229	4617	5354	-737
2002	12549	4534	5502	-968
2003	12909	5452	5255	197
2004	13517	5648	4990	658
2005	11395	6096	5489	607
2006	10568	5557	4554	1003
2007	10301	6053	4446	1607
2008	9416	5004	3462	1542

Table 26. Regression results of Working Capital (WC) on Net Sales (NS) for Kodak [Independent variable: X Variable 1 (NS)]

SUMMARY OUTPUT								
Regression Statistics								
Multiple R	0.8077022							
R Square	0.6523828							
Adjusted R Square	0.6089307							
Standard Error	593.20846							
Observations	10							
ANOVA								
	df	*SS*	*MS*	*F*	*Significance F*			
Regression	1	5283307.817	5283308	15.0138	0.004709489			
Residual	8	2815170.183	351896					
Total	9	8098478						
	Coefficients	*Standard Error*	*t Stat*	*P-value*	*Lower 95%*	*Upper 95%*	*Lower 95.0%*	*Upper 95.0%*
Intercept	5907.2546	1462.811417	4.03829	0.00374	2534.005422	9280.504	2534.00542	9280.50378
X Variable 1	-0.460883	0.118944753	-3.8748	0.00471	-0.73517033	-0.186596	-0.73517033	-0.18659615

$$WC = 5907 - 0.46NS \tag{31}$$

From equation: (31), it may be derived that:

$$\frac{dWC}{dNS} = -0.46 < 0$$

The *negativity* condition of the multiplier ($\frac{dWC}{dNS}$) for Kodak proves the 'legitimacy' of the bankruptcy condition as proposed in this article.

EVALUATION OF PERFORMANCE OF WAL-MART IN THE POST-PANDEMIC SCENARIO

An ideal empirical testing of the multiplier $\left(\frac{dWC}{dNS}\right)$ for Wal-Mart for the financial years 2021 and 2022 (Years ending on January 31, 2021 and January 31, 2022 respectively) based on the 'benchmark' year of 2020 (the year of the pandemic) would help us to provide a clear picture on the real-word efficacy of the said multiplier.

For the year ending on January 31, 2021; the change in Net Sales $\left(dNS\right)$ was

$$\left(555233 - 519926\right) = 35307$$

and the change in Working Capital $\left(dWC\right)$ was

$$\left[\left(61806-77790\right)-\left(90067-92645\right)\right]=-13406.$$

Hence $\left(\frac{dWC}{dNS}\right)$ for 2021 was -2.64 (approximately). Similarly, for the year 2022; the value of the multiplier $\left(\frac{dWC}{dNS}\right)$ for Wal-Mart is -3.65 (approximately) contemplating the fact the behemoth's financial strength is withering at a steady pace. In the fiscal 2021, an 1 percent increase in NS facilitated 2.6 percent fall in the WC and in the next fiscal of 2022, 1 percent increase in NS triggered a greater reduction in WC by 3.6 percent. If this trend continues for the forthcoming years, it may not be surprising that even a financial behemoth like Wal-Mart would face the same consequence as other economic powerhouses had faced in the past. The regression equation of WC on NS for Wal-Mart (1987 – 2022) exhibits a *negative* relationship between the two variables as below (Refer to Tables 28 and 29):

$$WC=4752-0.03NS \tag{32}$$

Thus, $\frac{dWC}{dNS}=-0.03<0$. A comparative analysis between the *two* multipliers of Kodak and Wal-Mart respectively, it may be found that the *absolute* value of the multiplier for Kodak is much greater than that of Wal-Mart's. Thus, it may mathematically inferred that in order to sustain its business, Wal-Mart must contain the widening gap of its Working Capital on the negative scale of measurement.

Table 27. Documentation of Net Sales (NS) and estimated values of Working Capital (WC) for Wal-Mart (1987 – 2022)

Year	NS	WC
1987	11909	1013
1988	15959	1161
1989	20649	1565
1990	25811	1868
1991	32602	2425
1992	43887	3571
1993	55484	3444
1994	67344	4708
1995	82494	5365
1996	93627	5877
1997	104859	7036
1998	117958	4892
1999	137634	4370
2000	165013	-1447
2001	191329	-2394
2002	217799	596
2003	244524	-2134
2004	256329	-3419
2005	285222	-4397
2006	308945	-5000
2007	344992	-5166
2008	374307	-10458
2009	401244	-6431
2010	405132	-7511
2011	418952	-6591
2012	443416	-7325
2013	465604	-11878
2014	473076	-8160
2015	482229	-1975
2016	478614	-4380
2017	481317	-9239
2018	495761	-18857
2019	510329	-15580
2020	519926	-15984
2021	555233	-2578
2022	567762	-6039

Table 28. Regression results of Working Capital (WC) on Net Sales (NS) for Wal-Mart

SUMMARY OUTPUT								
Regression Statistics								
Multiple R	0.8210066							
R Square	0.6740519							
Adjusted R Square	0.6644652							
Standard Error	3791.1106							
Observations	36							
ANOVA								
	df	*SS*	*MS*	*F*	*Significance F*			
Regression	1	1010547439	1010547439	70.3111	8.64022E-10			
Residual	34	488665673	14372519.8					
Total	35	1499213112						
	Coefficients	*Standard Error*	*t Stat*	*P-value*	*Lower 95%*	*Upper 95%*	*Lower 95.0%*	*Upper 95.0%*
Intercept	4751.9331	1122.656698	4.23275712	0.00017	2470.420222	7033.44604	2470.420222	7033.446042
X Variable 1	-0.028303	0.003375353	-8.3851705	8.6E-10	-0.035162452	-0.02144337	-0.035162452	-0.02144337

[Independent variable: X Variable 1 (NS)]

LIMITATIONS

The limitations of this study are as follows:

- The major limitation of this study is common to all other research related to the same discipline of financial accounting. The domains related to financial ratios and bankruptcy prediction are still evolving with fresh ideas and concepts. This research paper has laid greater stress on formulation of three separate indices which would mostly help in assessing the financial health / performance of a business organization and it is subject to further scrutiny and analysis; and
- This research is based on a micro perspective; more precisely, on a single financial giant called Wal-Mart and *not* conducted on a macro perspective. However, there is a definite reason for choosing Wal-Mart as the sample organization for study. Since the said company is an economic powerhouse in the corporate sector, hence it may be treated as an 'ideal' benchmark for Strengths and Weaknesses (SW) analysis for other business firms within or outside the same sector (Wal-Mart belongs to Retail and Wholesale sector) of the market. It would be interesting to learn about the results related to replication of the models and indices illustrated in this paper by other researchers in a macroeconomic or industrial perspective.

CONCLUSION

The primary motive of this research work was to formulate two indices to effectively regress the financial soundness / performance of a given business organization. One of the indices, i.e., Altman's Index (AIN) was further modified by means of chain index method in order to include the intermediate years of time-series so that it would be able to provide more robustness in prediction of results and it was named Modified Altman's Index (MAI). The other index was coined as Financial Performance Index (FPI) which was constructed to assess the overall financial performance of a company from a new perspective as it was aimed at addressing two most essential factors related to any firm irrespective of its functioning, viz., financial profitability and solvency. The FPI was formulated with the help of five financial ratios that would specifically address those two factors. The results proved to be satisfactory and formulation of those three indices helped to shed light on other allied issues which are equally important for the pertinent literature. The derivation of the multiplier related to the prediction of bankruptcy for a firm regardless of its functional domain and its validity in the real-world scenario is tested statistically and the final results proved to corroborate the finding. It is expected that the results and findings from this study should be subjected to critical analysis and further exploration in the discipline of financial accounting.

DATA AVAILABILITY STATEMENT

Data available at https://stock.walmart.com/investors/financial-information/annual-reports-and-proxies/default.aspx

Data available at https://investor.kodak.com/search?query=Annual+Reports+Archive

CONFLICT OF INTERESTS STATEMENT

The author has NO interests with / or involvement in any organization or entity with any financial interest (such as honoraria; educational grants; participation in speakers' bureaus; membership, employment, consultancies, stock ownership, or other equity interest; and expert testimony or patent-licensing arrangements), or non-financial interest (such as personal or professional relationships, affiliations, knowledge or beliefs) in the subject matter or materials discussed in this manuscript.

REFERENCES

Altman, E. I. (1968). Financial Ratios, Discriminant Analysis and the Prediction of Corporate Bankruptcy. *The Journal of Finance, 23*(4), 589 – 609. doi:10.1111/j.1540-6261.1968.tb00843.x

Altman, E. I., Iwanicz-Drozdowska, M., Laitinen, E. K., & Suvas, A. (2017). Financial Distress Prediction in an International Context: A Review and Empirical Analysis of Altman's Z-Score Model. *Journal of International Financial Management & Accounting, 28*(2), 131 – 171. doi:10.1111/jifm.12053

Anthony, S. D. (2016, July 15). Kodak's Downfall Wasn't About Technology. *Harvard Business Review*. Retrieved from https://hbr.org/2016/07/kodaks-downfall-wasnt-about-technology

Barnes, P. (1982). Methodological Implications of Non-Normally Distributed Financial Ratios. *Journal of Business Finance & Accounting, 9*(1), 51–62. doi:10.1111/j.1468-5957.1982.tb00972.x

Barnes, P. (1987). The Analysis and Use of Financial Ratios: A Review Article. *Journal of Business Finance & Accounting, 14*(4), 449 – 461. doi:10.1111/j.1468-5957.1987.tb00106.x

Beaver, W. H. (1966). Financial Ratios As Predictors of Failure. *Journal of Accounting Research, 1966*, 71–111. doi:10.2307/2490171

Beaver, W. H., McNichols, M. F., & Rhie, J-W. (2005). Have Financial Statements Become Less Informative? Evidence from the Ability of Financial Ratios to Predict Bankruptcy. *Review of Accounting Studies, 10*(1), 93 – 122. doi:10.1007/s11142-004-6341-9

Bellovary, J. L., Giacomino, D. E., & Akers, M. D. (2007). A Review of Bankruptcy Prediction Studies: 1930 to Present. *Journal of Financial Education*, *33*(Winter), 1–42.

Bird, R. G., & McHugh, A. J. (1977). Financial ratios—An empirical study. *Journal of Business Finance & Accounting, 4*(1), 29 – 46. doi:10.1111/j.1468-5957.1977.tb00159.x

Boritz, J. E., Kennedy, D. B., & Albuquerque, A. (1995). Predicting Corporate Failure Using a Neural Network Approach. *Intelligent Systems in Accounting, Finance, and Management, 4*(2), 95 – 111. doi:10.1002/j.1099-1174.1995.tb00083.x

Campbell, J. Y., Hilscher, J. D., & Szilagyi, J. (2011). Predicting Financial Distress and the Performance of Distressed Stocks. *Journal of Investment Management*, *9*(2), 14–34. http://nrs.harvard.edu/urn-3:HUL.InstRepos:9887619

Campbell, J. Y., Lettau, M., Malkiel, B., & Xu, Y. (2001). Have individual stocks become more volatile? An empirical exploration of idiosyncratic risk. *The Journal of Finance*, *56*(1), 1–43. doi:10.1111/0022-1082.00318

Chava, S., & Jarrow, R. A. (2004). Bankruptcy Prediction with Industry Effects. *Review of Finance*, *8*(4), 537–569. doi:10.1093/rof/8.4.537

Chen, K. H., & Shimerda, T. A. (1981). An Empirical Analysis of Useful Financial Ratios. *Financial Management, 10*(1), 51 – 60. doi:10.2307/3665113

Cindik, Z., & Armutlulu, I. H. (2021). A revision of Altman Z-Score model and a comparative analysis of Turkish companies' financial distress prediction. *National Accounting Review*, *3*(2), 237–255. doi:10.3934/NAR.2021012

Das, N. G. (2008). Statistical Methods (vols. 1-2). *McGraw Hill Education* Private Limited.

du Jardin, P., Veganzones, D., & Séverin, E. (2019). Forecasting Corporate Bankruptcy Using Accrual-Based Models. *Computational Economics, 54*(1), 7 – 43. doi:10.1007/s10614-017-9681-9

Fraser, L. M., & Ormiston, A. (2015). *Understanding Financial Statements* (1st International ed.). Pearson Education Services Private Limited.

Granger, C. W. J., & Newbold, P. (1974). Spurious Regressions in Econometrics. *Journal of Econometrics*, *2*(2), 111–120. doi:10.1016/0304-4076(74)90034-7

Guan, Q. (1993). *Development of optimal network structures for back-propagation trained neural networks* [Ph.D. Dissertation]. Department of Computer Science, University of Nebraska at Lincoln, NE, United States.

Gujarati, D. N. (2003). *Basic Econometrics* (4th ed.). McGraw – Hill, Inc.

Houghton, K. A., & Woodliff, D. R. (1987). Financial Ratios: The Prediction of Corporate 'Success' and Failure. *Journal of Business Finance & Accounting, 14*(4), 537 – 554. doi:10.1111/j.1468-5957.1987.tb00111.x

Jo, H., Han, I., & Lee, H. (1997). Bankruptcy prediction using case-based reasoning, neural networks, and discriminant analysis. *Expert Systems with Applications, 13*(2), 97 – 108. doi:10.1016/S0957-4174(97)00011-0

Johnson, W. B. (1979). The Cross-Sectional Stability of Financial Ratio Patterns. *The Journal of Financial and Quantitative Analysis, 14*(5), 1035 – 1048. doi:10.2307/2330305

Jones, F. (1987). Current techniques in bankruptcy prediction. *Journal of Accounting Literature, 6*, 131–164.

Ko, L., Blocher, E. J., & Lin, P. P. (2001). Prediction of Corporate Financial Distress: An Application of the Composite Rule Induction System. *The International Journal of Digital Accounting Research, 1*(1), 69–85. doi:10.4192/1577-8517-v1_4

Laitinen, E. K. (2018). Financial Reporting: Long-Term Change of Financial Ratios. *American Journal of Industrial and Business Management, 8*(09), 1893–1927. doi:10.4236/ajibm.2018.89128

Lau, H. S., Lau, A. H., & Gribbin, D. W. (1995). On modeling cross sectional distributions of financial ratios. *Journal of Business Finance & Accounting, 22*(4), 521 – 549. doi:10.1111/j.1468-5957.1995.tb00375.x

Lev, B., & Sunder, S. (1979). Methodological issues in the use of financial ratios. *Journal of Accounting and Economics, 1*(3), 187 – 210. doi:10.1016/0165-4101(79)90007-7

Liang, T. P. (1992). A Composite Approach to Inducing Knowledge for Expert Systems Design. *Management Science, 38*(1), 1 – 17. doi:10.1287/mnsc.38.1.1

Lyandres, E., & Zhdanov, A. (2013). Investment opportunities and bankruptcy prediction. *Journal of Financial Markets, 16*(3), 439 – 476. doi:10.1016/j.finmar.2012.10.003

Messier, W. F., & Hansen, J. V. (1988). Inducing Rules for Expert System Development: An Example Using Default and Bankruptcy Data. *Management Science, 34*(12), 1403 – 1415. doi:10.1287/mnsc.34.12.1403

Mohanram, P. S. (2005). Separating Winners from Losers among Low Book-to-Market Stocks using Financial Statement Analysis. *Review of Accounting Studies, 10*(2-3), 133–170. doi:10.100711142-005-1526-4

Mossman, C. E., Bell, G. G., Swartz, L. M., & Turtle, H. (1998). An empirical comparison of bankruptcy models. *The Financial Review, 33*(2), 35 – 54. doi:10.1111/j.1540-6288.1998.tb01367.x

Ohlson, J. (1980). Financial Ratios and the Probabilistic Prediction of Bankruptcy. *Journal of Accounting Research, 18*(1), 109 – 131. doi:10.2307/2490395

Piotroski, J. D. (2000). Value Investing: The Use of Historical Financial Statement Information to Separate Winners from Losers. *Journal of Accounting Research, 38*, 1 – 41. doi:10.2307/2672906

Platt, H. D., Platt, M. B., & Pederson, J. G. (1994). Bankruptcy discrimination with real variables. *Journal of Business Finance & Accounting, 21*(4), 491 – 510. doi:10.1111/j.1468-5957.1994.tb00332.x

Shumway, T. (2001). Forecasting Bankruptcy More Accurately: A Simple Hazard Model. *The Journal of Business, 74*(1), 101 – 124. doi:10.1086/209665

Sloan, R. G. (1996). Do Stock Prices Fully Reflect Information in Accruals and Cash Flows About Future Earnings? *The Accounting Review, 71*(3), 289 – 315.

So, J. C. (1994). The Distribution of Financial Ratios – A Note. *Journal of Accounting, Auditing & Finance*, *9*(2), 215–223. doi:10.1177/0148558X9400900205

Tsukuda, J., & Baba, S. (1994). Predicting Japanese corporate bankruptcy in terms of financial data using neural network. *Computers & Industrial Engineering, 27*(1 – 4), 445 – 448. doi:10.1016/0360-8352(94)90330-1

Walker, M. C., Stowe, J. D., & Moriarty, S. (1979). Decomposition analysis of financial statements. *Journal of Business Finance & Accounting, 6*(2), 173 – 186. doi:10.1111/j.1468-5957.1979.tb01082.x

Watts, R. L. (1977). Corporate Financial Statements: A Product of the Market and Political Processes. *Australian Journal of Management*, *2*(1), 53–75. doi:10.1177/031289627700200104

Whittington, G. (1980). Some basic properties of accounting ratios. *Journal of Business Finance & Accounting, 7*(2), 219 – 231. doi:10.1111/j.1468-5957.1980.tb00738.x

APPENDIX: ACRONYMS

1. SAL: Salaries;
2. TAX: Taxes, other than income;
3. OTH: Other;
4. ACRLIB: Accrued Liabilities (ACRLIB = SAL + TAX + OTH);
5. ACRIT: Accrued Federal and State Income Taxes;
6. CPLD: Current Portion of Long-term Debt (Referred to as Long-term debt due within one year on Balance Sheets of Wal-Mart);
7. LD: Long-term Debt;
8. BVD: Book Value of Debt;
9. MVE: Market Value of Equity;
10. ROA = Return on Assets = Net Income (NI) ¤ Total Assets (TA);
11. ROE = Return on Equity = Net Income (NI) ¤ Total Stockholders' Equity (TE);
12. CFAR = Cash Flow Adequacy Ratio = Cash Flow from Operating Activities (CFOA) ¤ [Capital Expenditures (CE) + Debt Repayments (DRP) + Dividends paid (DIV)];
13. DR = Debt Ratio = Total Liabilities (TL) ¤ Total Assets (TA);
14. NPR = Net Profit Ratio = Net Income (NI) ¤ Net Sales (NS);
15. CR = Current Ratio = Current Assets (CA) ¤ Current Liabilities (CL); and
16. WC = Working Capital = Current Assets (CA) – Current Liabilities (CL).

All definitions are as per Fraser and Ormiston (2015) [**All values in US$ '000**]

Compilation of References

Abid, F., & Mseddi, S. (2010). The Impact of Operating and Financial Leverages and Intrinsic Business Risk on Firm Value. *International Research Journal of Finance and Economics*, *44*(44), 129–142.

Achima, M. V., Marea, C., & Borleab, S. N. (2012). A statistical model of financial risk bankruptcy applied for the Romanian manufacturing industry. *Procedia Economics and Finance*, *3*, 132–137. doi:10.1016/S2212-5671(12)00131-1

Advani, P. S., Reitzel, L. R., Nguyen, T. N., Fisher, F. D., Savoy, E. J., Cuevas, A. G., Wetter, D. W., & McNeil, L. H. (2014). Financial strain and cancer risk behaviors among African Americans. *Cancer Epidemiology, Biomarkers & Prevention*, *23*(6), 967–975. doi:10.1158/1055-9965.EPI-14-0016 PMID:24740200

Agarwal, V., & Taffler, R. (2008). Comparing the performance of market-based and accounting-based bankruptcy prediction models. *Journal of Banking & Finance*, *32*(8), 1541–1551. doi:10.1016/j.jbankfin.2007.07.014

Akçay, Ü. (2018). *Beş Soruda 2018-2019 Ekonomik Krizi* [The 2018-2019 Economic Crisis in Five Questions]. Retrieved from https://www.gazeteduvar.com.tr/yazarlar/2018/12/13/bes-soruda-2018-2019-ekonomik-krizi

Akçay, A., & Bilen, A. (2018). Denetim Kalitesi ve Göstergeleri [Audit Quality and Indicators]. *Yüzüncü Yıl Üniversitesi Sosyal Bilimler Enstitüsü Dergisi*, (40), 227–256.

Akil, C. (2019). *Konkordato Süresinin Alacaklılar Açısından Sonuçları (7101 Sayılı Kanun İle Yapılan Değişikliklere Göre)* [The Consequences of the Concordat Term in Terms of Creditors (According to the Amendments Made with the Law No. 7101 dated 28.02.2018)]. TBB Journal.

Akın, F. (2017). Türk bankacılık sektörünün yapısı ve sorunları [The structure and problems of the Turkish banking sector]. *İş ve Hayat*, *4*(8), 54-73. Retrieved from https://dergipark.org.tr/tr/pub/isvehayat/issue/48947/678738

Aksoy, A., & Tanrıöven, C. (2014). Sermaye piyasası yatırım araçları ve analizi (5th ed.). [Capital market investment instruments and analysis (5th ed.)]. Detay yayıncılık.

Aktaş, R., Doğanay, M., & Yıldız, B. (2003). Financial Failure Prediction: Comparison of Statistical Techniques with the Neural Networks. Ankara University Faculty of Political Sciences Journal, 58(4), 1-24.

Aktaş, R. (1997). *Mali başarısızlık (İşletme riski) tahmin modelleri* [Financial failure (Business risk) forecast models]. Türkiye İş Bankası Kültür Yayınları.

Akyürek, A. (2019). *Konkordato Hukuku* [Concordat Law]. Yetkin Yayınları.

Akyüz, K. C., Yıldırım, İ., Akyüz, İ., & Tugay, T. (2017). 'Borsa İstanbul'da İşlem Gören Kâğıt Ve Kâğıt Ürünleri Sanayi İşletmelerinin Finansal Başarısızlık Düzeylerinin Oran Analizi Ve Diskriminant Analizi Yöntemleri Kullanılarak Ölçülmesi [Measurement of Financial Failure Levels of Paper and Paper Products Industrial Enterprises Traded on Borsa İstanbul by Using Ratio Analysis and Discriminant Analysis Methods]. *Düzce Üniversitesi Orman Fakültesi Ormancılık Dergisi*, *13*(1), 60–74.

Aldana, S. G., & Liljenquist, W. (1998). Validity and reliability of a financial strain survey. *Financial Counseling and Planning*, *9*(2), 11–18.

Alimbekova, G., Kanterbayeva, S., Abdildin, S., Yerzhanova, A., & Kydyrbayeva, S. (2021). Audit as a Tool for Preventing Bankruptcy Risks and Evaluating Development Prospects for Tourism Industry Companies. *Journal of Environmental Management and Tourism*, *12*(6), 1617–1626. doi:10.14505//jemt.12.6(54).17

Altaş, D., & Giray, S. (2005). Mali Başarısızlığın Çok Değişkenli İstatistiksel Yöntemlerle Belirlenmesi: Tekstil Sektörü Örneği [Determination of Financial Failure by Multivariate Statistical Methods: The Case of the Textile Sector]. *Marmara Üniversitesi Sosyal Bilimler Dergisi*, *2*, 13–28.

Altman, E. & Hotchkiss, E. (2006). *Corporate financial distress and bankruptcy*. Wiley. doi:10.1002/9781118267806

Altman, E. I., & Hotchkiss, E. (2006). Corporate financial distress and bankruptcy: Predict and avoid bankruptcy, analyze and invest in distressed debt (3rd ed.). Wiley finance series.

Altman, E. (1968). Financial ratios, discriminant analysis and the prediction of corporate bankruptcy. *The Journal of Finance*, *23*(4), 589–609. doi:10.1111/j.1540-6261.1968.tb00843.x

Altman, E. I., Iwanicz-Drozdowska, M., Laitinen, E. K., & Suvas, A. (2017). 'Financial Distress Prediction in An International Context: A Review and Empirical Analysis of Altman's Z-Score Model. *Journal of International Financial Management & Accounting*, *28*(2), 131–171. doi:10.1111/jifm.12053

Amato, P. R., & Zuo, J. (1992). Rural poverty, urban poverty and psychological well-being. *The Sociological Quarterly*, *33*(2), 229–240. doi:10.1111/j.1533-8525.1992.tb00373.x

Anderloni, L., & Vandone, D. (2008). *Households over-indeptedness in the economic literature*. Universit'a degli Studi di Milano Working Paper, 46,775.

Anthony, S. D. (2016, July 15). Kodak's Downfall Wasn't About Technology. *Harvard Business Review*. Retrieved from https://hbr.org/2016/07/kodaks-downfall-wasnt-about-technology

Antonacopoulou, E. P., & Georgiadou, A. (2021). Leading through social distancing: The future of work, corporations and leadership from home. *Gender, Work and Organization*, *28*(2), 749–767. doi:10.1111/gwao.12533

Apali, İ. (2018). Vergi usul kanunu açisindan konkordato ilani kapsaminda vazgeçilen alacaklarin değerlendirilmesi ve muhasebeleştirilmesi [Evaluation and accounting of abandoned receivables within the scope of concordat announcement in terms of tax procedure law]. *Mali Çözüm Dergisi*, *28*, 211–219.

Archuleta, K. L., Britt, S. L., Tonn, T. J., & Grable, J. E. (2011). Financial satisfaction and financial stressors in marital satisfaction. *Psychological Reports*, *108*(2), 563–576. doi:10.2466/07.21.PR0.108.2.563-576 PMID:21675570

Archuleta, K., Dale, A., & Spann, S. M. (2013). College students and financial distress: Exploring debt, financial satisfaction, and financial anxiety. *Financial Counseling and Planning*, *24*(2), 50–62.

Aslanoğlu, S., Cengiz, S., Dinç, Y., & Dilsiz, M. (2016). Yaratıcı Muhasebe Uygulamalarının Bağımsız Denetim Kalitesi Üzerine Etkisi: BİST'de Bir Uygulama [The Impact of Creative Accounting Practices on Independent Audit Quality: An Application in BIST]. *Muhasebe ve Finansman Dergisi*, (69), 1–24. doi:10.25095/mufad.396655

Aslanoğlu, S., Özalp, A. D., & Özalp, A. R. (2018). Bir Yeniden Yapılandırma Kurumu Olarak Konkordato Başvurusu, Geçici Mühlet Ve Gerekçeleri [Application for the concordat as a restructuring institution, temporary deadline and its justifications]. *Ekonomi İşletme Siyaset ve Uluslararası İlişkiler Dergisi*, (3), 63–68.

Aslund, C., Larm, P., Starrin, B., & Nilsson, K. (2014). The buffering effect of tangible social support on financial stress: Influence on psychological well-being and psychosomatic symptoms in a large sample of the adult general population. *International for Equity in Health*, *13*(1), 2-9. Doi:10.1186/s12939-01400853

Atalay, O. (2007). *Borca Batıklık ve İflasın Ertelenmesi* [Indebtedness and Postponement of Bankruptcy]. Turhan Kitabevi.

Atkinson, A., Mckay, S., Collard, S., & Kempson, E. (2007). Levels of financial capability in the UK. *Public Money & Management*, *27*(1), 29–36. doi:10.1111/j.1467-9302.2007.00552.x

Aydemir, E. (2018). Konkordato ve Yeniden Yapılandırma [Concordat and Restructuring]. Seçkin Yayınları.

Aydın, Ü., & Tuğay, O. (2018). Hileli Finansal Raporlama: Bağımsız Denetçilerin Meslek Etiği ve Hileli Finansal Raporlamaya Bakış Açılarına Yönelik Bir Araştırma [Fraudulent Financial Reporting: A Study of the Professional Ethics of Independent Auditors and Their Perspectives on Fraudulent Financial Reporting]. *Süleyman Demirel Üniversitesi İktisadi ve İdari Bilimler Fakültesi Dergisi*, *23*(1), 279–30.

Azim, A., Hassan, M., & Zakia, A. (2015). Risk Management And Disclosure And Their Impact on Firm Value: The Case of Egypt, International Journal of Business, Accounting, &. *Finance*, *9*(1), 30–43.

Babar, S., Latief, R., Ashraf, S., & Nawaz, S. (2019). Financial stability index for the financial sector of Pakistan. *Economies*, *7*(81), 1–24. doi:10.3390/economies7030081

Bacovia, G. (2011). Analysis models of the bankruptcy risk. *Economy Transdisciplinarity Cognition*, *14*(1), 248–259.

Banerjee, R., & Hofmann, B. (2021). Corporate zombies: Anatomy and life cycle. *BIS Working Papers*, *882*, 1-14.

Banerjee, R., Cornelli, G., & Zakrajsek, E. (2020). The outlook for business bankruptcies. *BIS Working Papers, 30*, 1-6.

Barboza, F., Kimura, H., & Altman, E. (2017). Machine learning models and bankruptcy prediction. *Expert Systems with Applications*, *83*, 405–417. doi:10.1016/j.eswa.2017.04.006

Barışık, S., & Budak, S. (2021). Türkiye'de İşletme İflasları ve Faiz İlişkisi [Business Bankruptcies and Interest Relationship in Turkey]. *Third Sector Social Economic Review*, *56*(4), 2198–2212.

Barnes, P. (1987). The Analysis and Use of Financial Ratios: A Review Article. *Journal of Business Finance & Accounting, 14*(4), 449 – 461. doi:10.1111/j.1468-5957.1987.tb00106.x

Barnes, P. (1982). Methodological Implications of Non-Normally Distributed Financial Ratios. *Journal of Business Finance & Accounting*, *9*(1), 51–62. doi:10.1111/j.1468-5957.1982.tb00972.x

Barry, B. (1975). The Development Organization Structure in the Family Firm. *Journal of General Management*, *3*(1), 42–60. doi:10.1177/030630707500300105

Baş, M., & Çakmak, Z. (2012). Gri İlişkisel Analiz Ve Lojistik Regresyon Analizi İle İşletmelerde Finansal Başarısızlığın Belirlenmesi ve Bir Uygulama [Determination of Financial Failure in Enterprises with Gray Relational Analysis and Logistic Regression Analysis and an Application]. *Anadolu Üniversitesi Sosyal Bilimler Dergisi*, *12*(3), 63–81.

Bayrak, T. (2018). İç Denetim Felsefesi [Internal Audit Philosophy]. *Muhasebe Bilim Dünyası Dergisi, 15*, 977-990.

BDDK. (n.d.). *Aylık Bankacılık Sektörü Verileri* [Monthly Banking Industry Data]. Retrieved from https://www.bddk.org.tr/BultenAylik

Beale, S., & Keddie, P. (2018). *Insolvency and restructuring manual*. Bloomsbury Professional.

Beauchaine, T. P., Ben-David, I., & Bos, M. (2020). ADHD, Financial distress, and suicide in adulthood a population study. *Science Advances*, *6*(40), 1–8. doi:10.1126ciadv.aba1551 PMID:32998893

Beaver, W. H., McNichols, M. F., & Rhie, J-W. (2005). Have Financial Statements Become Less Informative? Evidence from the Ability of Financial Ratios to Predict Bankruptcy. *Review of Accounting Studies, 10*(1), 93 – 122. doi:10.1007/s11142-004-6341-9

Beaver, W. H. (1966). Financial Ratios as Predictors of Failure. *Journal of Accounting Research. Empirical Research in Accounting: Selected Studies*, *4*, 71–111. doi:10.2307/2490171

Bellovary, J. L., Giacomino, D. E., & Akers, M. D. (2007). A Review of Bankruptcy Prediction Studies: 1930 to Present. *Journal of Financial Education*, *33*(Winter), 1–42.

Berkin, N. M. (1972). *İflas Hukuku (4. Baskı b.)* [Bankruptcy Law (4th Edition b.)]. Faculties Printing House.

Berk, J., DeMarzo, P., & Harford, J. (2012). *Fundamentals of Corporate Finance*. Pearson Education.

Bharath, S. T., & Shumway, T. (2004). *Forecasting default with the KMV-Merton model* [Working paper]. University of Michigan.

Bilen, C. İ., & Güler, S. (2019). Konkordato ve Alacakların Akıbeti [Concordat and Fate of Receivables]. *Vergi Dünyası*, *449*, 81–97.

Bird, R. G., & McHugh, A. J. (1977). Financial ratios—An empirical study. *Journal of Business Finance & Accounting*, *4*(1), 29 – 46. doi:10.1111/j.1468-5957.1977.tb00159.x

Biyan, O. (2009). *İflasın Ertelenmesi ve Vergi Hukukuna Etkisi* [Postponement of Bankruptcy and Its Effect on Tax Law]. http://www.ozgurbiyan.com/2009/10/iflasin-ertelenen-ve-vergi-hukuna-etkisi/

Black, F., & Scholes, M. (1973). The pricing of options and corporate liabilities. *Journal of Political Economy*, *6*(3), 637–654. doi:10.1086/260062

Blomgren, J., Maunula, N., & Hiilamo, H. (2016). Over-indeptedness and chronic disease: A linked register-based study of Finnish men and women during 1995-2010. *International Journal of Public Health*, *61*(5), 535–544. doi:10.100700038-015-0778-4 PMID:26733074

Boe, T., Balaj, M., Eikemo, T. A., McNamara, C. L., & Solheim, E. F. (2017). Financial difficulties in childhood and adult depression in Europe. *European Journal of Public Health*, *27*(1, suppl_1), 96–101. doi:10.1093/eurpub/ckw253 PMID:28355649

Bolger, K. E., Patterson, C. J., Thompson, W. W., & Kupersmidt, J. B. (1995). Psychosocial adjustment among children experiencing persistent and ınternittent family economic hardship. *Child Development*, *66*(4), 1107–1129. doi:10.2307/1131802

Boritz, J. E., Kennedy, D. B., & Albuquerque, A. (1995). Predicting Corporate Failure Using a Neural Network Approach. *Intelligent Systems in Accounting, Finance, and Management, 4*(2), 95 – 111. doi:10.1002/j.1099-1174.1995.tb00083.x

Borsa İstanbul DataStore. (n.d.). *Pay Piyasası Verileri* [Equity Market Data]. Retrieved from https://datastore.borsaistanbul.com/

Borsa İstanbul. (2022). *Sürdürülebilirlik Endeksleri.* https://www.borsaistanbul.com/tr/sayfa/165/bist-surdurulebilirlik-endeksleri

Boss, P., Bryant, C., & Mancini, J. A. (2016). *Family stress management: A contextual approach.* Sage Publications. https://books.google.com.tr/books?hl=tr&lr=&id=7U-0DAAAQBAJ&oi=fnd&pg=PP1&dq=Family+stress+management:+a+contextual+approach.+Sage+Publications.&ots=EJgFDQlstp&sig=NARJjhjVFTosUR43aHTzVqdBZo0&redir_esc=y#v=onepage&q=Family%20stress%20management%3A%20a%20contextual%20approach.%20Sage%20Publications.&f=false

Boylu, A. (2014). Tek ebeveynli ailelerde finansal sıkıntı ve fonksiyonlar arasındaki ilişkinin incelenmesi [Examination of the relationship between financial hardship and functions in single-parent families]. *Hacettepe Üniversitesi İktisadi ve İdari Bilimler Fakültesi Dergisi, 32*(1), 55–72. doi:10.17065/huiibf.34906

Bozkurt, C. (2016). Risk, Kurumsal Risk Yönetimi ve İç Denetim. *Denetişim*, (4), 17–30.

Bradley, D. B., & Cowdery, C. (2004). Small business: Causes of bankruptcy. Technical Report, University of Central Arkansas.

Bradley, R. H., & Corwyn, R. (2002). Socioeconomic status and child development. *Annual Review of Psychology, 53*(1), 371–379. doi:10.1146/annurev.psych.53.100901.135233 PMID:11752490

Bragg, S. M. (2002). *Business Ratios and Formulas.* John Wiley and Sons.

Branicki, L. J. (2020). COVID-19, ethics of care and feminist crisis management. *Gender, Work and Organization, 27*(5), 872–883. doi:10.1111/gwao.12491 PMID:32837015

Bray, J. R., (2001). Hardship in Australia: An analysis of financial stress ındicators in the 1998-99 Australian bureau of statistics household expenditure survey. *Macroeconomics: Consumption.*

Brealey, R. A., Myers, S. C., & Marcus, A. J. (2007). *Fundamentals of corporate finance* (5th ed.). McGraw-Hill Irwin.

Breunig, R. & Cobb-Clark, D. (2006). *Understanding the factors associated with financial stress in Australian households.* Australian Social Policy.

Brosent, N. (2018). *Strategische Insolvenzen – Grenzen der Instrumentalisierung des Insolvenzplanverfahrens zur Lösung von Gesellschafterkonflikten* [Strategic insolvencies – limits of the instrumentalisation of the insolvency plan procedure to resolve shareholder conflicts]. Peter Lang.

Bumblauskas, D., Mann, A., Dugan, B., & Rittmer, J. (2020), A Blockchain use case in food distribution: Do you know where your food has been? *International Journal of Information Management, 52.* doi:.2019.09.004 doi:10.1016/j.ijinfomgt

Burnaby, P., & Hass, S. (2009). Ten steps to enterprise-wide risk management. *Corporate Governance, 9*(5), 539–550. doi:10.1108/14720700910998111

Büyükoğlu, B., Buyuran, B., & Ekşi, İ. H. (2022). Ekonomik Özgürlük ve Borçlanma Faiz Oranları Arasındaki İlişkinin Analizi. *Alanya Akademik Bakış, 6*(3), 2667-2682.

Çakır, G. (2023). *The Wells Fargo Scandal: The Ordinary Situations of Capitalism.* Retrived from: https://www.academia.edu/28957463/Wells_Fargo_Skandal%C4%B1_Kapitalizmin_Ola%C4%9Fan_Halleri

Çalışkan, Ş., Karabacak, M., & Meçik, O. (2017). Türkiye Ekonomisinde Eğitim Harcamaları ve Ekonomik Büyüme İlişkisi: Bootstrap Toda-Yamamoto Nedensellik Testi Yaklaşımı [The Relationship Between Education Expenditures and Economic Growth in the Turkish Economy: Bootstrap Toda-Yamamoto Causality Test Approach]. *Kocaeli Üniversitesi Sosyal Bilimler Enstitüsü Dergisi, KOSBED*, *33*(1), 45–56.

Campbell, J. Y., Hilscher, J. D., & Szilagyi, J. (2011). Predicting Financial Distress and the Performance of Distressed Stocks. *Journal of Investment Management*, *9*(2), 14–34. http://nrs.harvard.edu/urn-3:HUL.InstRepos:9887619

Campbell, J. Y., Lettau, M., Malkiel, B., & Xu, Y. (2001). Have individual stocks become more volatile? An empirical exploration of idiosyncratic risk. *The Journal of Finance*, *56*(1), 1–43. doi:10.1111/0022-1082.00318

Can, E. N., & Çetin, C. (2019). COSO ERM 2017 Çerçevesinde Kurumsal Risk Yönetiminde İç Denetimin Rolü [The Role of Internal Audit in Corporate Risk Management in the Framework]. *Akademik Sosyal Araştırmalar Dergisi*, *6*(41), 153–166.

Caro, M. P., Ali, M. S., Vecchio, M., & Giaffreda, R. (2018), Blockchain-based traceability in agri-food supply chain management: A practical implementation. *Proceedings of 2018 IoT Vertical and Topical Summit on Agriculture - Tuscany (IOT Tuscany),* 1–4. doi:10.1109/IOT-TUSCANY.2018.8373021

Carter, D. A., Rogers, D. A., & Simkins, B. J. (2006). Does Hedging Affect Firm Value? Evidence from The US Airline Industry. *Financial Management*, *35*(1), 53–86. doi:10.1111/j.1755-053X.2006.tb00131.x

Casero, C., Panaro, D., & Trucco, S. (2014). A Statistical Analysis of Reliability of Audit Opinions as Bankruptcy Predictors. *Journal of Modern Accounting and Auditing*, *10*(9), 917–931.

Catalano, R., Goldman-Mellor, S., Szxton, K., Margerison-Zilko, C., Subbaraman, M., Lewinn, K., & Anderson, E. (2011). The health effects of economic decline. *Annu Rev. Public Health*, *32*(10). Retrieved May 5, 2022, from https://www.ncbi.nlm.nih.gov/pmc/articles/PMC3855327/

Çavuş, G., & Başar, A. B. (2020). The Role of Cash Flow Information in Forecasting Financial Failure. *The World of Accounting Science, Special Issue of MODAV's 16. International Conference on Accounting*, 292-318. 10.31460/mbdd.647542

Çelik, M. S. (2018). Altman Z-Skor modeli kullanılarak Bist-30 endeksinde yer alan imalat şirketlerinin finansal başarısızlık riskinin tahmin edilmesi [Estimating the risk of financial failure of manufacturing companies included in the Bist-30 index using the Altman Z-Score model]. *ICPESS, 5.*

Çelik, N. (2000). *Tarımda Girdi Kullanımı ve Verimliliğe Etkileri* [Input Use in Agriculture and Its Effects on Productivity]. Devlet Planlama Teşkilatı (DPT). Retrieved from https://www.sbb.gov.tr/wp-content/uploads/2018/11/NebiCelik.pdf

Çelik, M. K. (2010). Bankaların finansal başarısızlıklarının geleneksel ve yeni yöntemlerle öngörüsü [Prediction of banks' financial failures by traditional and new methods]. *Yönetim ve Ekonomi*, *17*(2), 129–143.

Çelik, S., & Akarım, Y. D. (2012). Likidite riski yönetimi: Panel veri analizi ile İMKB bankacılık sektörü üzerine ampirik bir uygulama [Liquidity risk management: An empirical application on the ISE banking sector with panel data analysis]. *Eskişehir Osmangazi Üniversitesi Sosyal Bilimler Dergisi*, *13*(1), 1–17.

Cepec, J. (2021, Sept. 23). Opomnik ob pričakovanju novele ZFPPIPP-H [A reminder of the anticipation of the ZFPPIPP-H novella]. *Pravna praksa.*

Chang, S.E., Chen, Y.C., & Lu, M.F. (2019). Supply chain re-engineering using Blockchain technology: A case of smart contract based tracking process. *Technological Forecasting and Social Change, 144*, 1 – 11. doi: .techfore.2019.03.015 doi:10.1016/j

Charbonneau, M., & Hanse, M. P. (2014). Debt, neolibarislizm and crisis: Interview with maurizio lazzarato on the ındebted condition. *Sociology*, *48*(5), 1039–1047. doi:10.1177/0038038514539207

Chava, S., & Jarrow, R. A. (2004). Bankruptcy Prediction with Industry Effects. *Review of Finance*, *8*(4), 537–569. doi:10.1093/rof/8.4.537

Chen, K. H., & Shimerda, T. A. (1981). An Empirical Analysis of Useful Financial Ratios. *Financial Management, 10*(1), 51 – 60. doi:10.2307/3665113

Chen, S., Goo, Y. J. J., & Shen, Z. D. (2014). A hybrid approach of stepwise regression, logistic regression, support vector machine, and decision tree for forecasting fraudulent financial statements. *The Scientific World Journal*, *9*(16), 1–9. doi:10.1155/2014/968712 PMID:25302338

Choi, L. (2009). Financial stress and its physical effects on individuals and communities. *Community Development Innovation Review*, *3*, 120–122.

Cindik, Z., & Armutlulu, I. H. (2021). A revision of Altman Z-Score model and a comparative analysis of Turkish companies' financial distress prediction. *National Accounting Review*, *3*(2), 237–255. doi:10.3934/NAR.2021012

Çıtak, S. (1999). *Geleneksel risk yönetiminden programlanmış menkul kıymet işlemlerine* [From traditional risk management to scheduled securities transactions]. Dünya yayıncılık.

Çıtak, N., & Güneş, M. A. (2020). Bir Yeniden Yapılandırma Müessesesi Olarak Konkordato ve Bir Üretim İşletmesi Uygulaması [The Concordat as a Restructuring Institution and the Application of a Production Enterprise]. *Finans Ekonomi ve Sosyal Araştırmalar Dergisi*, *5*(3), 501–517.

Çolak, M. S. (2017). *Bilançolara Yeni Bir Bakış: Firmalar İçin Finansal Risk Değerlemesi.* https://tcmbblog.org/wps/wcm/connect/blog/tr/main+menu/analizler/bilancolara_yeni_bir_bakis

Congressional Research Service. (2021, November). *Global Economic Effects of COVID-19.* https://sgp.fas.org/crs/row/R46270.pdf

Coronavirus: How the world of work may change forever. (2020, October 23). *BBC WORKLIFE.* https://www.bbc.com/worklife/article/20201023-coronavirus-how-will-the-pandemic-change-the-way-we-work

Corporate Governance. (2022). Retrieved from: https://www.spl.com.tr/icerik/sinav-calisma-notlari

Coşkun Aslan, M., & Demirkan, S. (2017). *Denetim ve Güvence Hizmetleri* [Audit and Assurance Services]. Muhasebe ve Finansman Dergisi. doi:10.25095/mufad.402669

Coşkun, E., & Özcan, A. (2016). *Finansal Sıkıntı Sürecinde Şirketlerin Etkinlik Düzeylerinin Belirlenmesi (No. 16001)* [Determination of the Effectiveness Levels of Companies in the Process of Financial Hardship (No. 16001)]. WERI-World Economic Research Institute. doi:10.22440/EconWorld.WP.2016.001

Coşkun, E., & Sayılgan, G. (2008). Finansal Sıkıntının Dolaylı Maliyetleri: İMKB'de İşlem Gören Şirketlerde Bir Uygulama [Indirect Costs of Financial Distress: An Application in Companies Traded on the ISE]. *Gazi Üniversitesi İktisadi ve İdari Bilimler Fakültesi Dergisi, 10*(3), 45–66.

Craigh, B. L., & Moores, K. (2006). A 10-Year Longitudinal Investigation of Strategy, Systems and Environment on Innovation in Family Firms. *Family Business Review*, *19*(1), 1–10. doi:10.1111/j.1741-6248.2006.00056.x

Crandall, W. R., Parnell, J. A., & Spillan, J. E. (2014). Crisis management. *Sage (Atlanta, Ga.)*.

Crouhy, M., Galai, D., & Mark, R. (2000). *Risk managemenet: Comprehensive chapters on market credit, and operational risks: Features an integrated VaR framework: Hedging strategies for reducing risk*. McGraw-Hill.

Cui, P., Dixon, J., Guin, U., & Dimase, D. (2019). A Blockchain-based framework for supply chain provenance. *IEEE Access: Practical Innovations, Open Solutions*, *7*, 157113–157125. doi:10.1109/ACCESS.2019.2949951

Çukacı, Y. C. (2019). *Konkordato* [Concordat]. Ekin Yayınları.

Cumhuriyet. (2020). *2019'da 899 şirket konkordato ilan etti* [In 2019, 899 companies declared concordats]. Retrieved from https://www.cumhuriyet.com.tr/haber/2019da-899-sirket-konkordato-ilan-etti-1715448

Curran, E., & Kennedy, S. (2021, November 29). Worst case scenario: Economists analyse how omicron will impact recovery. *Business Standard*. https://www.business-standard.com/article/international/how-covid-variant-omicron-will-impact-global-recovery-economists
-evaluate-121112900293_1.html

Curry, D. S., & Schorer, J. U. (2016). The effects of business insolvency on the duties and liabilities of directors and officers – A comparative analysis with recommendations to promote good decision-making. In T. M. Hajjiri & A. Cohen (Eds.), *Global insolvency and bankruptcy practice for sustainable economic development* (p. 2). Palgrave Macmillan. doi:10.1007/978-1-137-56175-6_5

Darmawan, A., & Supriyanto, J. (2018). The Effect of Financial Ratio on Financial Distress in Predicting Bankruptcy. *Journal of Applied Managerial Accounting*, *2*(1), 110–120. doi:10.30871/jama.v2i1.727

Das, N. G. (2008). Statistical Methods (vols. 1-2). *McGraw Hill Education* Private Limited.

Davis, C. G. & Mantler, J. (2004). *The consequences of financial stress for individuals, families and society*. Carleton University, Centre for Research on Stress, Coping and Well-Being, Ottoawa Canada.

De Vet, J. M., Nigohosyan, D., Ferrer, J. N., Gross, A. K., Kuehl, S., & Flickenschild, M. (2021). Impacts of the COVID-19 Pandemic on EU Industries.European Parliament.

Delafrooz, N., & Paim, L. H. (2013). Role of financial stress on relationship between financial problem and financial wellness among Malaysia workers. *African Journal of Business Management*, *7*(20), 1966–1972.

Demichev, A., & Alexander, K. (2021). Business Process Engineering for Data Storing and Processing in a Collaborative Distributed Environment Based on Provenance Metadata, Smart Contracts and Blockchain Technology. *Journal of Grid Computing*, *19*(3), 2021. doi:10.100710723-021-09544-4

Demir, G. (2019). *İflasın Ertelenmesi ve Konkordato* [Postponement of Bankruptcy and Concordat] [Unpublished Master Thesis]. Işık University Institute of Social Sciences, Istanbul, Turkey.

Demirci, A. (2014). Literatür taraması [Literature review]. In Y. Arı & İ. Kaya (Eds.), Coğrafya araştırma yöntemleri (pp. 73-106). Balıkesir: Coğrafyacılar Derneği Yayınları.

Demir, Ş. (2014). Muhasebe Hataları ve Hileleri ile Bunlara Dair Yaptırımların Yasal Mevzuat Kapsamında Değerlendirilmesi [Evaluation of Accounting Errors and Cheats and Related Sanctions within the Scope of Legal Legislation]. *Muhasebe Bilim Dünyası Dergisi*, *1*, 169–193.

Derici, O., Tüysüz, Z., & Sarı, A. (2007). Kurumsal Risk Yönetimi ve Sayıştay: Uygulaması [Enterprise Risk Management and the Court of Auditors: Its Implementation]. *Sayıştay Dergisi*, *65*, 151–172.

Desai, S., Deng, Q., Wellsandt, S., & Thoben, K. (2020). An Implementation of IoT-Based Product Tracking with Blockchain Integration for a B2B Platform. *Proceedings of the 2020 IEEE International Conference on Engineering, Technology and Innovation (ICE/ITMC)*. 10.1109/ICE/ITMC49519.2020.9198639

Dinh, D. V., Powell, R. J., & Vo, D. H. (2021). Forecasting Corporate Financial Distress in The Southeast Asian Countries: A Market-Based Approach. *Journal of Asian Economics*, *74*, 101293. doi:10.1016/j.asieco.2021.101293

Doğan, N. (2009). İş Etiği ve İşletmelerde Etik Çöküş [Business Ethics and Ethical Collapse in Businesses]. *Sosyal Ekonomik Araştırmalar Dergisi*, *8*(16), 179–200.

Doing Business in 2004. (2004). *Understanding regulation*. The International Bank for Reconstruction and Development / The World Bank.

Donaldson, K., Fonberg, J., Heisz, A., Kaddatz, J., Kaplan, J., Olson, E., & Walker, I. (2021). *The financial resilience and financial well-being of Canadians during the covıd-19 pandemic*. Retrieved May 1, 2022, from https://www150.statcan.gc.ca/n1/en/pub/75f0002m/75f0002m2021008-eng.pdf?st=Bc3GpVCz

Drentea, P. (2000). Age, Debt and anxiety. *Journal of Health and Social Behavior*, *41*(4), 437–450. doi:10.2307/2676296 PMID:11198567

Drentea, P., & Lavrakas, P. J. (2000). Over the limit: The assocation among health, race and debt. *Social Science & Medicine*, *50*(4), 517–529. doi:10.1016/S0277-9536(99)00298-1 PMID:10641804

Dridi, A., El Ghourabi, M., & Limam, M. (2010). On monitoring financial stress index with extreme value theory. *Quantitative Finance*, *12*(3), 329–339. doi:10.1080/14697681003792229

du Jardin, P., Veganzones, D., & Séverin, E. (2019). Forecasting Corporate Bankruptcy Using Accrual-Based Models. *Computational Economics, 54*(1), 7 – 43. doi:10.1007/s10614-017-9681-9

Dubrovski, D. (2006). Insolvenčni postopki kot oblika uspešnega ali neuspešnega razreševanja kriz v podjetjih [Insolvency proceedings as a form of successful or unsuccessful resolution of corporate crises]. *Podjetje in delo, 32*(8), 1795-1829.

Dubrovski, D. (2020). Ali so sodni postopki prisilne poravnave resnično sanacijski postopki [Are compulsory settlement proceedings really remedial proceedings?]. *Podjetje in delo, 46*(2), 294-319.

Dubrovski, D. (2022). *Razsežnosti kriznega managementa* [The dimensions of crisis management]. International School for Social and Business Studies.

Durusoy, R. Y. (2005). *Vazgeçilen Talepler ve Uygulama Örneği* [An Example of Abandoned Claims and Implementation]. https://www.verginet.net/dtt/1/RefikYasarDurusoyYMMAdoptedCreditsAndApplicationIliskinB_9150.aspx

Ege, İ., Topaloğlu, E. E., & Erkol, A. Y. (2017). Fulmer Modeline Dayalı Finansal Başarısızlık İle Finansal Performans İlişkisi: İmalat Sanayi Üzerine Bir Uygulama [The Relationship Between Financial Failure and Financial Performance Based on the Fulmer Model: An Application on the Manufacturing Industry]. *Muhasebe ve Finansman Dergisi*, (74), 119–132. doi:10.25095/mufad.396862

Eiser, J. R., Bostrom, A., Burton, I., Johnston, D. M., McClure, J., Paton, D., Pligt, J. V. D., & White, M. P. (2012). Risk interpretation and action: A conceptual framework for responses to natural hazards. *International Journal of Disaster Risk Reduction*, *1*, 5–16. doi:10.1016/j.ijdrr.2012.05.002

Elitaş, B. L., Doğan, M., & Kevser, M. (2017). Finansal Sıkıntı ve Sahiplik Yapısı Arasındaki İlişki: Borsa İstanbul Üzerine Bir Araştırma. *İşletme Araştırmaları Dergisi, 9*(4), 787-804.

Elmas, B. (2017). Finansal Tablolar Analizi, 3 [Financial Statement Analysis, 3]. Nobel Akademik Yayıncılık Eğitim Danışmanlık.

Embrechts, P., Resnick, S. I., & Samorodnitsky, G. (1999). Extreme value theory as a risk management tool. *North American Actuarial Journal, 3*(2), 30–41. doi:10.1080/10920277.1999.10595797

Emhan, A. (2009). Risk Yönetim Süreci ve Risk Yönetmekte Kullanılan Teknikler [Risk Management Process and Techniques Used to Manage Risk]. *Atatürk Üniversitesi İktisadi ve İdari Bilimler Dergisi, 23*(3), 209–220.

Eroğlu, O. (2018). *Uygulamada Konkordato* [Concordat in practice]. Seçkin Yayıncılık.

Eroğlu, O. (2018). *Uygulamada Konkordato, Seçkin Yayınları, 1* [Concordat in Practice, Distinguished Publications, 1]. Basım.

Ertan, A. S., & Ersan, Ö. (2018). Finansal Başarısızlığı Belirleyen Etkenler: Türkiye İmalat Sektörü Örneği [Factors Determining Financial Failure: The Case of the Turkish Manufacturing Sector]. *Marmara Üniversitesi İktisadi ve İdari Bilimler Dergisi, 40*(2), 181–207.

European Commission. (2016). *Predlog Direktive evropskega parlamenta in sveta o okvirih preventivnega prestrukutiranja, drugi priložnosti ter ukrepih za povečanje učinkovitosti postopkov prestrukturiranja, postopkov v primeru insolventnosti in postopkov za odpust dolgov ter spremembi Direktive 2012/30/EU* [Proposal for a Directive of the European Parliament and of the Council on preventive restructuring frameworks, second chance and measures to increase the efficiency of restructuring, insolvency and discharge procedures and amending Directive 2012/30/EU].

European Environment Agency. (2017). *EEA Report No 10/2017 - Landscapes in transition - An account of 25 years of land cover change in Europe.* Retrieved from https://www.eea.europa.eu/publications/landscapes-in-transition

European Investment Bank. (2021, January). *EIB Investment Report 2020/2021: Building a smart and green Europe in the COVID-19 era.* https://www.eib.org/en/publications/investment-report-2020

Explained: Impact of Omicron variant on global economy. (2021, December 2). *India Today.* https://www.indiatoday.in/business/story/omicron-coronavirus-variant-global-economy-impact-explained-1883353-2021-12-02

Eyüboğlu, S., & Eyüboğlu, K. (2018). Borsa İstanbul Sektör Endeksleri İle Döviz Kurları Arasındaki İlişkilerin İncelenmesi: ARDL Modeli [Investigation of the Relations Between Borsa İstanbul Sector Indices and Exchange Rates: The ARDL Model]. *Ömer Halisdemir Üniversitesi İktisadi ve İdari Bilimler Fakültesi Dergisi, 11*(1), 8-28.

Faulhaber, P., & Landwehr, N. (1996). *Turnaround-management in der praxis.* Campus.

Fay, S., Hurst, E., & White, M. J. (2002). The household bankruptcy decision. *The American Economic Review, 93*(3), 706–718. doi:10.1257/00028280260136327

Fenger, H. (2005). *Insolvenzrecht. Schnell erfasst* [Insolvency law. Quickly captured]. Springer.

Fenton O'Creevy, M., & Furnham, A. (2013). Financial capability, money attitudes and socioeconomic status: Risks for experiencing adverse financial events. *Personality and Individual Differences, 54*(3), 344–349. doi:10.1016/j.paid.2012.09.019

Fenton O'creevy, M., & Furnham, A. (2021). Financial distress and money attitudes. *Journal of Neuroscience, Psychology, and Economics*, *14*(3), 138–148. doi:10.1037/npe0000143

Fernandez, A., Garcia-Alonso, J., Royo- Pastor, C., Garrell-Corbera, I., Rengel-Chica, J., Agudo-Ugena, J., Ramos, A., & Manual Mendive, J. (2015). Effects of the economic crisis and social supoort on health-related quality of life. *The British Journal of General Practice*, *65*(632), e198–e203. doi:10.3399/bjgp15X684025 PMID:25733442

Ferriell, J., & Janger, E. J. (2019). *Understanding bankruptcy*. Carolina Academic Press.

Financial Times. (2008, September 15). *Insolvencies debate rages but there's no silver bullet*. Author.

Fitch, C., Chaplin, R., Trend, C., & Collard, S. (2007). Debt and mental health: The role of psychiatrists. *Advances in Psychiatric Treatment*, *13*(3), 194–202. doi:10.1192/apt.bp.106.002527

Flanagan, R., & Norman, G. (1993). Risk management and construction. Blackwell Science.

Fone, M., & Young, P. C. (2005). *Managing Risks in Public Organisations*. Perpetuity Press.

Fraser, L. M., & Ormiston, A. (2015). *Understanding Financial Statements* (1st International ed.). Pearson Education Services Private Limited.

Freeman, C., Carlson, J., & Sperry, L. (1993). Adlerian marital therapy strategies with middle income couples facing financial stress. *The American Journal of Family Therapy*, *21*(4), 324–332. doi:10.1080/01926189308251003

French, D., & McKillop, D. (2017). The impact of debt and financial stress on health in Northern Irish households. *Journal of European Social Policy*, *27*(5), 458–473. doi:10.1177/0958928717717657

Gathergood, J. (2012). Debt and depression: Casual links and social norm effects. *Economic Journal (London)*, *122*(563), 1094–1114. doi:10.1111/j.1468-0297.2012.02519.x

Geetha, K., Maria Suganthi, L., Vasanthi, K., & Kavitha, B. (2021). Financial stress testing in US banking sector. *Materials Today: Proceedings*, *37*, 2252–2255. doi:10.1016/j.matpr.2020.07.700

Geng, R., Bose, I., & Chen, X. (2015). Prediction of financial distress: An empirical study of listed Chinese companies using data mining. *European Journal of Operational Research*, *241*(1), 236–247. doi:10.1016/j.ejor.2014.08.016

Gercek, A. (2017). *Kamu Alacaklarının Tahsil Hukuku, 5. Baskı* [Collection Law of Public Claims, 5th Edition]. Ekin Publishing and Distribution.

Geršl, A., & Heřmánek, J. (2007). Financial stability indicators: Advantages and disadvantages of their use in the assessment of financial system stability. In CNB Financial Stability Report 2006 (pp. 69-79). Czech National Bank.

Ghosh, P. (2011). Financial Failure: The Case of Hindustan Motors Limited. *Anvesha, 10*(1), 54.

Ghosh, P., Khatun, M., & Tarafdar, P. (2018). Bankruptcy via Learning Volatility: Does it integrate in Financial Institutions? *Asian Economic and Financial Review*, *8*(1), 52–62. doi:10.18488/journal.aefr.2018.81.52.62

Gitman, L. J., & Zutter, C. J. (2015). *Principles of Managerial Finance*. Pearson Education Limited.

Global unemployment to reach 207 million in 2022, says ILO report. (2022, January 21). *India Today*. https://www.indiatoday.in/business/story/global-unemployment-to-reach-207-million-in-2022-says-ilo-report-1902576-2022-0
1-21

Gögül, P. K., & Yaman, D. (n.d.). Hisse Senedi Fiyatına Etki Eden Makroekonomik Faktörlerin İncelenmesi: Simetrik Ve Asimetrik Nedensellik Sınaması (2006-2020 Dönemi) [Investigation of Macroeconomic Factors Affecting Stock Price: Symmetric and Asymmetric Causality Test (2006-2020 Period)]. *Sakarya İktisat Dergisi*, *9*(4), 258–276.

Göğüş, E. H. S. (2012). *Risk Odaklı İç denetimde Risklerin Saptanması ve Değerlendirilmesi* [Determination and Evaluation of Risks in Risk-Oriented Internal Audit]. Türkmen Kitapevi.

Gönen, S. (2017). Risk Raporlamasına İlişkin Kuramsal Yaklaşım [Theoretical Approach to Risk Reporting]. *İnsan ve Toplum Bilimleri Araştırmaları Dergisi, 6*(6), 293-301.

Gonzalez, E. A. (2017). *Predicting Corporate Financial Failure Using Macroeconomic Variables and Accounting Data.* Springer Science and Business Media.

Gonzalez, F. P., & Yun, H. (2013). Risk Management and Firm Value: Evidence from Weather Derivatives. *The Journal of Finance*, *68*(5), 2143–2176. doi:10.1111/jofi.12061

Grable, J., Heo, W., & Rabbani, A. (2015). Financial anxiety, physiological arousal, and planning ıntention. *Journal of Financial Therapy*, *5*(2), 1–18. doi:10.4148/1944-9771.1083

Granger, C. W. J., & Newbold, P. (1974). Spurious Regressions in Econometrics. *Journal of Econometrics*, *2*(2), 111–120. doi:10.1016/0304-4076(74)90034-7

Gratt, L. B. (1987). Risk Analysis or Risk Assessment: A proposal for consistent definitions. Uncertainty in Risk Management. In V. T. Covello, L. B. Lave, A. Moghissi, & V. R. R. Uppuluri (Eds.), *Risk Assessment, Risk Management and Decision Making* (pp. 241–249). Plenum Press.

Griffiths, P. (2005). *Risk- Based Auditing*. Gower Publishing Limited.

Guan, Q. (1993). *Development of optimal network structures for back-propagation trained neural networks* [Ph.D. Dissertation]. Department of Computer Science, University of Nebraska at Lincoln, NE, United States.

Guan, N., Guargilia, A., Moore, P., & Xu, F. (2022). Financial stress and depression in adults: A systematic review. *PLoS One*, *17*(2), e0264041. doi:10.1371/journal.pone.0264041 PMID:35192652

Guégan, D., & Hassani, B. K. (2019). *Risk measurement: from quantitative measures to management decisions*. Springer. doi:10.1007/978-3-030-02680-6

Gujarati, D. N. (2003). *Basic Econometrics* (4th ed.). McGraw – Hill, Inc.

Gümüş, U. T., Şakar, Z., Akkın, G., & Şahin, M. (2017). Finansal Analizde Kullanılan Oranlar ve Firma Değer İlişkisi: BİST'de İşlem Gören Çimento Firmaları Üzerine Bir Analiz [Ratios Used in Financial Analysis and Firm Value Relationship: An Analysis on Cement Companies Traded in BIST]. *Karadeniz Sosyal Bilimler Dergisi, 9*(16), 1–23. Retrieved from https://dergipark.org.tr/en/pub/ksbd/issue/31387/344614

Gürgen, A. R. (2018). Türkiye'nin 2018 krizi: Nereden nereye? [Turkey's 2018 crisis: From where to where?]. *Mülkiye Dergisi*, *42*(3), 449-452. Retrieved from https://dergipark.org.tr/tr/pub/mulkiye/issue/44591/676021

Haberglobal. (2020). *Türkiye'de şimdiye kadar kaç firma konkordato ilan etti?* [How many companies have declared concordats in Turkey so far?]. Retrieved from https://haberglobal.com.tr/ekonomi/turkiye-kac-firma-konkordato-ilan-etti-konkordato-nedir-24979

Halk Yatırım. (2022). *Skor Kart* [Shoes Map]; Retrieved May 27, 2022, from https://analizim.halkyatirim.com.tr/Financial/ScoreCardDetail

Hammoud, O., Tarkanov, I., & Kosmarski, A. (2021). An Architecture for Distributed Electronic Documents Storage in Decentralized Blockchain B2B Applications. *Computers*, *2021*(10), 142. doi:10.3390/computers10110142

Han, C., & Phillips, P. C. (2010). Gmm Estimation For Dynamic Panels With Fixed Effects and Strong Instruments At Unity. *Econometric Theory*, *26*(1), 119–151. doi:10.1017/S026646660909063X

Hanschel, E., & Monnin, P. (2005). Measuring and forecasting stress in the banking sector: evidence from Switzerland. *BIS Work., 22*, 431–449. Retrieved from https://www.researchgate.net/publication/4735258_Measuring_and_forecasting_stress_in_the_banking_sector_Evidence_from_Sw
itzerland/citations

Hasan, H., AlHadhrami, E., AlDhaheri, A., Salah, K., & Jayaraman, R. (2019). Smart contract based approach for efficient shipment management. *Computers & Industrial Engineering*, *136*, 149–159. doi:10.1016/j.cie.2019.07.022

Haw, C., Hawton, K., Gunnel, D., & Platt, S. (2014). Economic recession and suicidal behaviour: Possible mechanisms and ameliorating factors. *The International Journal of Social Psychiatry*, *61*(1), 1–9. doi:10.1177/0020764014536545 PMID:24903684

Head, G. L. (1967). An alternative to defining risk as uncertainty. *The Journal of Risk and Insurance*, *34*(2), 205–214. doi:10.2307/251319

Helfert, E. A. (2000). *Financial Analysis: Tools and Techniques*. McGraw-Hill.

Heo, W., Cho, S. H., & Lee, P. (2020). APR financial stress scale: Development and validation of a multidimensional measurement. *Journal of Financial Therapy*, *11*(1), 1–28. doi:10.4148/1944-9771.1216

Hillegeist, S. & Keating, E. & Cram, D., & Lundstedt, K. (2004). *Assessing the Probability of Bankruptcy*. doi:10.1023/B:RAST.0000013627.90884.b7

Horvathova, J., & Mokrisova, M. (2018). *Risk of Bankruptcy, Its Determinants, and Models*. MDPI. doi:10.3390/risks6040117

Hotchkiss, E. S., Kose, J., Mooradian, R., & Thorburn, K. (2009). *Bankruptcy and the Resolution of Financial Distress. In Handbook of Empirical Corporate Finance*. North Holland.

Houghton, K. A., & Woodliff, D. R. (1987). Financial Ratios: The Prediction of Corporate 'Success' and Failure. *Journal of Business Finance & Accounting, 14*(4), 537 – 554. doi:10.1111/j.1468-5957.1987.tb00111.x

Hull, J. C. (2018). Risk management and financial institutions (5th ed.). Wiley Finance Series.

Hussain, A. H. M. B., Das, S., Chowdhury, M. T. A., Haque, N., Sultana, S., & Ahmed, K. J. (2018). Does financial inclusion increase financial resilience? evidence from Bagladesh. *Development in Practice*, *29*(6), 798–804. doi:10.1080/09614524.2019.1607256

Hwang, R. C., Chung, H., & Ku, J. Y. (2013). Predicting Recurrent Financial Distresses With Autocorrelation Structure: An Empirical Analysis From An Emerging Market. *Journal of Financial Services Research*, *43*(3), 321–341. doi:10.100710693-012-0136-0

IBM. (2018). *The Linux Foundation's Hyperledger Fabric enables confidentiality in blockchain for business*. https://www.ibm.com/blogs/blockchain/2018/04/hyperledger-fabric-enables-confidentiality-in-blockchain-for-business/

İçerli, M. Y., & Akkaya, G. C. (2006). Finansal Açıdan Başarılı Olan İşletmelerle Başarısız Olan İşletmeler Arasında Finansal Oranlar Yardımıyla Farklılıkların Tespiti [Detecting Differences Between Financially Successful Businesses and Failing Businesses with the Help of Financial Ratios]. *Atatürk Üniversitesi İktisadi ve İdari Bilimler Dergisi*, *20*(1), 413–421.

İcra and İflas Kanunu (2018). *Enforcement and Bankruptcy Law No. 2004.* Official Gazette: Law no. 7101, 28/02/2018.

Ilgar, T., & Erdoğdu, G. (2018). Kurumsal Risk Yönetimi Türk Kamu Yönetimine Nasıl Entegre Edilebilir? [How Can Corporate Risk Management Be Integrated into Turkish Public Administration?]. *Denetişim*, *8*, 63–76.

Imeri & Khadraoui, D. (2018). *The security and traceability of shared information in the process of transportation of dangerous goods.* doi:10.1109/NTMS.2018.8328751

IMF. (2020). *World economic outlook. A long and difficult ascent.* Retrieved from https://www.imf.org/en/Publications/WEO/Issues/2020/09/30/world-economic-outlook-october-2020

International Labour Organization. (2020, April). *ILO Monitor: COVID-19 and the world of work. Third edition Updated estimates and analysis.* https://www.ilo.org/wcmsp5/groups/public/---dgreports/---dcomm/documents/briefingnote/wcms_743146.pdf

International Monetary Fund (World Economic Outlook Update). (2022, January). *Rising Caseloads, A Disrupted Recovery, and Higher Inflation.* https://www.imf.org/en/Publications/WEO/Issues/2022/01/25/world-economic-outlook-update-january-2022

Ivanjko, Š. (1997). Kriza podjetja [It's a corporate crisis]. *Podjetje in delo, 23*(6-7), 961-978.

Jacobsen, K., Marshak, A., & Griffith, M. (2009). *Increasing the financial resilience of disaster-affected populations.* Retrieved May 01, 2022, from https://www.semanticscholar.org/paper/Increasing-the-Financial-Resilience-of-Populations-Jacobsen-Marshak/2de16e6ddaba60 a084813199822176cf26ce03da

James, E. H., & Wooten, L. P. (2010). *Leading under pressure.* Routledge.

Jan, C. L. (2021). Financial Information Asymmetry: Using Deep Learning Algorithms to Predict Financial Distress. Symmetry. *Symmetry*, *13*(3), 443. doi:10.3390ym13030443

Jardin, P. D. (2016). A two-stage classification technique for bankruptcy prediction. *European Journal of Operational Research*, *254*(1), 236–252. doi:10.1016/j.ejor.2016.03.008

Jarrow, R. A., & Chatterjea, A. (2019). *An introduction to derivative securities, financial markets, and risk Management* (2nd ed.). World Scientific Publishing. doi:10.1142/y0018

Jenkins, R., Bhugra, D., Bebbington, P., Brugha, T., Farrel, M., Coid, J., Fryers, T., Weich, S., Singleton, N., & Meltzer, H. (2008). Debt, ıncome and mental disorder in the general population. *Psychological Medicine*, *38*(10), 1485–1493. doi:10.1017/S0033291707002516 PMID:18184442

Jo, H., Han, I., & Lee, H. (1997). Bankruptcy prediction using case-based reasoning, neural networks, and discriminant analysis. *Expert Systems with Applications, 13*(2), 97 – 108. doi:10.1016/S0957-4174(97)00011-0

John, M., & Schneider, H. (2022, January 18). Analysis: With Omicron, global economy spots chance to push past COVID. *Reuters.* https://www.reuters.com/markets/europe/with-omicron-global-economy-spots-chance-push-past-covid-2022-01-18/

Johnson, W. B. (1979). The Cross-Sectional Stability of Financial Ratio Patterns. *The Journal of Financial and Quantitative Analysis, 14*(5), 1035 – 1048. doi:10.2307/2330305

Jones, L., Palumbo, D., & Brown, D. (2021, January 24). Coronavirus: How the pandemic has changed the world economy. *BBC News*. https://www.bbc.com/news/business-51706225#:~:text=The%20IMF%20estimates%20that%20the,grow%20in%202020%20was%20China.&text=The%20IMF%20is%2C%20however%2C%20predicting,growth%20of%205.2%25%20in%202021

Jones, F. (1987). Current techniques in bankruptcy prediction. *Journal of Accounting Literature, 6*, 131–164.

Joo, S. (1998). *Personal financial wellness and worker job productivity* [Unpublished doctoral dissertation]. Virginia Polytechnic Institute and State University.

Joo, S., & Grable, J. E. (2004). An exploratory framework of the determinants of financial satisfaction. *Journal of Family and Economic Issues, 25*(1), 25–50. doi:10.1023/B:JEEI.0000016722.37994.9f

Joo, S.-H., Durband, D. B., & Grable, J. (2008). The academic impact of financial stress on college students. *Journal of College Student Retention, 10*(3), 287–305. doi:10.2190/CS.10.3.c

Jourova, V. (2019). Early restructuring and a second chance for entrepreneurs. Fact Sheet. European Commission.

Kahn, J. R., & Pearlin, L. I. (2006). Financial strain over the life course and health among older adults. *Journal of Health and Social Behavior, 47*(1), 17–31. doi:10.1177/002214650604700102 PMID:16583773

Kale, S. (2017). Sorularla konkordato (iflas dışı ve iflas içi adi konkordato) [Concordat with questions (non-bankruptcy and in-bankruptcy ordinary concordat)]. In *Vergi Hukuku Açısından Konkordato Müessesesi ve Sonuçları* [Concordat Institution and Its Consequences in terms of Tax Law]. Vergi Dünyası Dergisi.

Kamuyu Aydınlatma Platformu (KAP). (2022). *KAP Sectors*. Retrieved May 28, 2022, from https://www.kap.org.tr/en/Sektorler

Kanat, E. (2019). Gri İlişkisel Analiz Yöntemiyle Kamu ve Özel Bankaların Performanslarının Karşılaştırılması [Comparison of Performance of Public and Private Banks with Gray Relational Analysis Method]. *Akademik Sosyal Araştırmalar Dergisi, 7*(96), 135–146.

Karaca, H. (2018). *Büyük ve Orta Boy İşletmelerin Sahipleri ve Yöneticilerinin Bağımsız Denetçi Algısı ve Bağımsız Denetimden Beklentilerine Yönelik Bir Araştırma* [A Study on the Independent Auditor Perception and Expectations of Owners and Managers of Large and Medium-sized Enterprises from Independent Auditing]. İnönü Üniversitesi Sosyal Bilimler Enstitüsü, Yüksek Lisans Tezi.

Karadeniz, E., & Öcek, C. (2019). Finansal Başarısızlık Riski Taşıyan İle Taşımayan İşletmelerin Finansal Oranlarının Karşılaştırmalı Analizi: Borsa İstanbul Turizm İşletmelerinde Bir Araştırma [Comparative Analysis of the Financial Ratios of Enterprises with and Not at Risk of Financial Failure: A Study in Borsa İstanbul Tourism Enterprises]. *Seyahat Ve Otel İşletmeciliği Dergisi, 16*(2), 191–206. doi:10.24010oid.600207

Karels, G. V., & Prakash, A. J. (1987). Multivariate Normality and Forecasting of Business Bankruptcy. *Journal of Business Finance & Accounting, 14*(4), 573–593. doi:10.1111/j.1468-5957.1987.tb00113.x

Kassab, M., Destefanis, G., DeFranco, J., & Pranav, P. (2021, May). Blockchain-Engineers Wanted: an Empirical Analysis on Required Skills, Education and Experience. In *2021 IEEE/ACM 4th International Workshop on Emerging Trends in Software Engineering for Blockchain (WETSEB)* (pp. 49-55). IEEE.

Kasser, J. E. (2020). *Systemic and Systematic Risk Management*. CRC Press. doi:10.1201/9780429025389

Kaya, A. (2021). *Borca batıklık sorunlarının çözümünde değerlemenin yeri* [The place of valuation in solving debt indebtedness problems]. https://www.dmflegal.com.tr/yayinlarimiz/borca-batiklik-sorunlarinin-cozumunde-degerlemenin-yeri

Kayacan, M. (2006). *New company agenda in our globalizing world: corporate governance (Publication No: 1)*. Ethical Values Foundation of Turkey.

Kaya, E., & Açdoyuran, B. (2017). Petrol Fiyatları Ve Finansal Sıkıntı Arasındaki İlişki: Türkiye İçin Bir ARDL Yaklaşımı [The Relationship Between Oil Prices and Financial Distress: An ARDL Approach for Turkey]. *Sosyal Ekonomik Araştırmalar Dergisi*, *17*(33), 134–155. doi:10.30976usead.327648

Kempson, E., McKay, S. & Willitts, M. (2004). *Characteristic of families in debt and nature of ındeptedness*. Departmant for Work and Pensions Research Report. No: 211.

Kempson, E., Whiley, C., Caskey, J., & Collard, S. (2000). *In or out? financial exlusion: A literature and research review*. Financial Services Authority.

Keown, A., Martin, J., & Petty, W. (2020). *Foundations of Finance - The logic and Practice of Financial Management* (10th ed.). Pearson Education, Inc.

Khaliq, A., Altarturi, B. H. M., Thaker, H. M. T., Harun, M. Y., & Nahar, N. (2014). Identifying Financial distress firms: A case study of Malaysia's government linked companies (GLC). *International Journal of Economics, Finance and Management*, *3*(3).

Khan, A., Uddin, M., Shaikh, A., Laghari, A., & Rajput, A. (2021). MF-Ledger:Blockchain Hyperledger Sawtooth-Enabled Novel and Secure Multimedia Chain of Custody Forensic Investigation Architecture. *IEEE Access: Practical Innovations, Open Solutions*, *9*, 103637–103650. doi:10.1109/ACCESS.2021.3099037

Kim, J., & Garman, E. T. (2013). Financial stress and absenteeism: An emprically derived model. *JECP Research Journal*, *14*(1), 31–42.

Kim, J., Garman, E. T., & Sorhaindo, B. (2013). Relationships among credit counseling clients' financial wellbeing, financial behaviors, financial stressor events and health. *Financial Counseling and Planning*, *14*(2), 75–87.

Kim, J., Kwon, J., & Anderson, E. A. (2005). Factors related to retirement confidence: Retirement preparation and workplace financial education. *Financial Counseling and Planning*, *16*(2), 77–89.

Kim, W., Kim, T. H., Lee, T.-H., Ju, Y. J., & Park, E.-C. (2016). The effect of childhood and current economic status on depressive symptoms in South Korean ındividuals: A longitudinal study. *International Journal for Equity in Health*, *15*(111), 2–7. doi:10.118612939-016-0402-0 PMID:27430636

Kızılboğa Özaslan, R., & Özşahin Koç, F. (2016). Kurumun Sürdürülebilirliğinde "İtibar Riski" Yönetiminin Yeri ve Önemi. [The Place and Importance of "Reputation Risk" Management in the Sustainability of the Organization]. *Niğde Üniversitesi İİBF Dergisi*, *1*, 273–283.

Kızılboğa, R. (2012). Geleneksel Risk Yönetiminden Kurumsal Risk Yönetim Sistemine Geçiş [Transition from Traditional Risk Management to Enterprise Risk Management System]. *Atatürk Üniversitesi Sosyal Bilimler Enstitüsü Dergisi*, *16*(3), 297–316.

Knecht, T. C. (2006). Steuerung von Zahlungsfähigkeit und Unternehmensliquidität [Management of solvency and corporate liquidity]. In U. Homel, T. C. Knecht, & H. Wohlenberg (Eds.), *Handbuch Unternehmensrestrukturierung*. Dr. T. Gabler/GWV. doi:10.1007/978-3-8349-9149-2_27

Kocamış, T. U. (2019). Konkordato Sürecinde Bağımsız Denetim Raporu GDS 3400- İleriye Yönelik Finansal Bilgilerin İncelenmesi Standardı Açısından Değerlendirme [Independent Audit Report in the Concordat Process GDS 3400- Evaluation in terms of the Standard for the Examination of Prospective Financial Information]. *Turkish Studies - Economics, Finance, Politics, 14*, 1093–1105.

Ko, L., Blocher, E. J., & Lin, P. P. (2001). Prediction of Corporate Financial Distress: An Application of the Composite Rule Induction System. *The International Journal of Digital Accounting Research, 1*(1), 69–85. doi:10.4192/1577-8517-v1_4

Konca, K. N. (2018). Konkordato Uygulamalarına İlişkin Beklentiler ve Riskler [Expectations and Risks for Concordat Implementation]. *Analiz, 263*, 7–18.

Konca, N. K. (2018). *Konkordato uygulamalarına ilişkin beklentiler ve riskler* [Expectations and Risks Regarding Concordat Practices]. SETA Vakfı Yayınları.

Konkordato Talebine Eklenecek Belgeler Hakkında Yönetmelik. https://www.resmigazete.gov.tr/eskiler/2019/01/20190130-2.htm

Koomson, A. Churchill, S. A., & Munyanyi, M. E. (2022). *Gambling and financial stress, social ındicators research.* doi:10.1007/s11205-022-02898-6

Kosminsky, M., Nasciment, M. G., & de Oliveira, G. N. S. (2020). Financial stress and pain, what follows an economic crisis? *Integrative Review. British Journal of Pain, 3*(3), 280–284.

Kovacova, M., & Kliestikova, J. (2017). Modelling bankruptcy prediction models in Slovak companies. *SHS Web of Conferences, 39*. 10.1051hsconf/20173901013

Kübilay, B., & Tunçel, Ö. (2021). The effect of family financial socialization levels on money attitudes of university students. *Süleyman Demirel Üniversitesi Vizyoner Dergisi, 12*(30), 393–416. doi:10.21076/vizyoner.815919

Kücher, A., Mayr, S., Mitter, C., Duller, C., & Feldbauer-Durstmüller, B. (2018). Firm age dynamics and causes of corporate bankruptcy: Age dependent explanations for business failure. *Review of Managerial Science, 14*(3), 633–661. doi:10.100711846-018-0303-2

Küçükbay, F., Uysal, D., & Çırak, A. N. (2021). Covid-19 salgının Dünya ekonomisi üzerindeki etkisinin değerlendirilmesi [Assessment of the impact of the Covid-19 pandemic on the world economy]. *Journal of Aksaray University Faculty of Economics and Administrative Sciences, 13*(4), 15–20. doi:10.52791/aksarayiibd.985481

Küçükoğlu, S. (2021). Covid-19 pandemi sürecinin küresel ekonomik göstergeleri ve Türkiye'de bankacılık ve finans sektörüne etkileri [Global economic indicators of the Covid-19 pandemic process and its effects on the banking and financial sector in Turkey]. *İstanbul Ticaret Üniversitesi Sosyal Bilimler Dergisi, 20*(42), 1269-1291. Doi:10.46928/iticusbe.870711

Kuhle, P., Arroyo, D., & Schuster, E. (2021). Building A blockchain-based decentralized digital asset management system for commercial aircraft leasing. *Computers in Industry, 126*, 103393.

Kumar, P. R., & Ravi, V. (2007). Bankruptcy prediction in banks and firms via statistical and intelligent techniques – A review. *European Journal of Operational Research, 180*(1), 1–28. doi:10.1016/j.ejor.2006.08.043

Kuru, B. (2013). *İcra ve iflâs hukuku: el kitabı* [Enforcement and bankruptcy law: handbook]. Adalet Yayınevi.

Kuşoğlu, M. V. (2018). Konkordato Kapsamındaki Alacak ve Borçların Değerlemesi [Valuation of Receivables and Payables within the Scope of Concordat]. *Vergi Sorunları Dergisi*, (362), 51–58.

Laitinen, E. K. (2018). Financial Reporting: Long-Term Change of Financial Ratios. *American Journal of Industrial and Business Management, 8*(09), 1893–1927. doi:10.4236/ajibm.2018.89128

Lalani, M. (2021). Post COVID 19-Economic Opportunities & Challenges in India: Crisis that led to innovations and the road ahead. *PalArch's Journal of Archaeology of Egypt/Egyptology, 18*(7), 2081-2085.

Lamy, P., & Pedrosa, E. (2020). *Economics: Trade and Connectivity in the Post-COVID-19 World.* Challenges and Opportunities in the Post-COVID-19 World (World Economic Forum). https://www3.weforum.org/docs/WEF_Challenges_and_Opportunities_Post_COVID_19.pdf

Lange, C., & Byrd, M. (1998). The relationship between perceptions of financial distress and feelings of psychological well-being in New Zealand university students. *International Journal of Adolescence and Youth, 7*(3), 193–209. doi:10.1080/02673843.1998.9747824

Lau, H. S., Lau, A. H., & Gribbin, D. W. (1995). On modeling cross sectional distributions of financial ratios. *Journal of Business Finance & Accounting, 22*(4), 521 – 549. doi:10.1111/j.1468-5957.1995.tb00375.x

Leland, H. E., & Pyle, D. H. (1977). Informational Asymmetries, Financial Structure, and Financial Intermediation. *The Journal of Finance, 32*(2), 371. doi:10.2307/2326770

Lenton, P., & Mosley, P. (2008). *Debt and health.* Sheffield Economic Research Paper Series SERP Number: 2008004.

Le, T., Tran, T., Tuan, A., Xuan, S., & Nghia, D. (2022). BloodChain: A Blood Donation Network Managed by Blockchain Technologies. *Network (Bristol, England), 2*(1), 21–35. doi:10.3390/network2010002

Lev, B., & Sunder, S. (1979). Methodological issues in the use of financial ratios. *Journal of Accounting and Economics, 1*(3), 187 – 210. doi:10.1016/0165-4101(79)90007-7

Liang, T. P. (1992). A Composite Approach to Inducing Knowledge for Expert Systems Design. *Management Science, 38*(1), 1 – 17. doi:10.1287/mnsc.38.1.1

Liang, D., Lu, C., Tsai, C., & Shih, G. (2016). Financial ratios and corporate governance indicators in bankruptcy prediction: A comprehensive study. *European Journal of Operational Research, 252*(2), 561–572. doi:10.1016/j.ejor.2016.01.012

Li, D., Wong, W. E., & Guo, J. (2019). A Survey on Blockchain for Enterprise Using Hyperledger Fabric and Composer. *Proceedings of the 2019 6th International Conference on Dependable Systems and Their Applications (DSA)*, 71-80. 10.1109/DSA.2019.00017

Lin, Q. (2018). A Survey of Internal Governance in Family Business. *American Journal of Industrial and Business Management, 8*(4), 1093–1100. doi:10.4236/ajibm.2018.84075

Li, Q., Wu, Y., Ojiako, U., Marshall, A., & Chipulu, M. (2014). Enterprise Risk Management and Firm value within Chine's Insurance Industry. *Acta Commercii, 14*(1), 1–10. doi:10.4102/ac.v14i1.198

Lowitzsch, J. (2007). *The insolvency law of Central and Eastern Europe.* INSOL Europe.

Lubben, S. J. (2011). Financial Institutions in Bankruptcy. *Seattle University Law Review, 34*(1259), 1263.

Lund, C., Breen, A., Flisher, A. J., Kakuma, R., Corrigal, J., Joska, J. A., Swartz, L., & Patel, V. (2010). Poverty and common mental disorders in low and middle income countries: A systematic review. *Social Science & Medicine, 71*(3), 517–528. doi:10.1016/j.socscimed.2010.04.027 PMID:20621748

Lusardi, A., & Tufano, P. (2009). *Debt literacy, financial experiences, and overindebtedness.* National Bureau of Economic Research. Working Paper 14808. doi:10.3386/w14808

Lyandres, E., & Zhdanov, A. (2013). Investment opportunities and bankruptcy prediction. *Journal of Financial Markets, 16*(3), 439 – 476. doi:10.1016/j.finmar.2012.10.003

Lyons, A. C., Kass-Hanna, J., Liu, F., Greenlee, A. J., & Zeng, L. (2020). *Building financial resilience through financial and digital literacy in South Asia and Sub- Saharan Africa*. ADBI Working Paper Series No: 1098. Retrieved May, 01, 2022, from https://www.adb.org/sites/default/files/publication/574821/adbi-wp1098.pdf

Madgavkar, A., White, O., Krishnan, M., Mahajan, D., & Azcue, X. (2020). *COVID-19 and gender equality: Countering the regressive effects*. McKinsey Global Institute.

Mair, S. (2020, March 30). What will the world be like after coronavirus? Four possible futures. *The Conversation*. https://theconversation.com/what-will-the-world-be-like-after-coronavirus-four-possible-futures-134085

Manab, N. A., Hussin, M. R., & Kassim, I. (2010). Enterprise-wide Risk Management Practices: Between Corporate Governance Compliance and Value Creation. International Review of Business Research Papers. *Temmuz.*, *6*(2), 239–252.

Mariano, S. S. G., Izadi, J., & Pratt, M. (2021). Can we predict the likelihood of financial distress in companies from their corporate governance and borrowing? *International Journal of Accounting & Information Management*.

Marin, M. & Montréal, H. (2015). Can financial risk management help prevent bankruptcy? *Journal of Finance and Accountancy*. doi:10.1016/j.jfineco.2004.06.013

Marks, G. N. (2007). *Income powerty, subjective poverty and financial stress*. Australian Government Social Policy Research Paper No: 29. FaHCSIA. doi:10.2139/ssrn.1728587

McCrum, D. (2020). *Wirecard: The timeline*. https://www.ft.com/content/284fb1ad-ddc0-45df-a075-0709b36868db

McLaughlin, K. A., Nandi, A., Keyes, K. M., Uddin, M., Aiello, A. E., Galea, S., & Koenen, K. C. (2011). Home foreclosure and risk of psychiatric morbidity during the recent financial crisis. *Psychological Medicine*, *42*(7), 1441–1448. doi:10.1017/S0033291711002613 PMID:22099861

McNamara, R., Duncan, K., & Kelly, S. (2011, November). Micro and Macro Determinants of Financial Distress. In *15th International Business Research Conference*, Sydney, Australia.

McNeil, A. J., Frey, R., & Embrechts, P. (2005). *Quantitative risk management: concepts, techniques and tools*. Princeton University Press.

Mellahi & Wilkinson. (2004). *Systemic and Systematic Risk Management*. CRC Press.

Mellahi, K., & Wilkinson, A. (2004). Organizational failure: A critique of recent research and a proposed integrative framework. *International Journal of Management Reviews*, *5/6*(1), 21–41. doi:10.1111/j.1460-8545.2004.00095.x

Meltzer, H., Bebbington, P., Brugha, T., Jenkins, R., McManus, S., & Dennis, M. S. (2011). Personal debt and suicidal ideation. *Psychological Medicine*, *41*(4), 771–778. doi:10.1017/S0033291710001261 PMID:20550757

Memiş, M. Ü. (2016). Kurumsal İşletme Yönetiminde Denetimin Önemi [Expectations and Risks for Concordat Implementation]. *Ekonomi Bilimleri Dergisi*, *8*(1), 34–49.

Merkezi Kayıt Istanbul. (2022). *Finansal Oran Hesaplama Kuralları* [Financial Ratio Calculation Rules]. Retrieved from https://www.vap.org.tr/sites/default/files/2022-01/finansal_oran_hesaplama_kurallari_ocak_2022.pdf

Merna, T., & Al-Thani, F. F. (2008). *Corporate risk management* (2nd ed.). John Wiley & Sons.

Merton, R. C. (1974). On the pricing of corporate debt: The risk structure of interest rates. *The Journal of Finance, 29*(2), 449–470. doi:10.2307/2978814

Messier, W. F., & Hansen, J. V. (1988). Inducing Rules for Expert System Development: An Example Using Default and Bankruptcy Data. *Management Science, 34*(12), 1403 – 1415. doi:10.1287/mnsc.34.12.1403

Miller, S. (2008). *The turnaround kid*. HarperCollins.

Min, J. H., & Jeong, C. (2008). A binary classification method for bankruptcy prediction. *Expert Systems with Applications, 36*(3), 5256–5263. doi:10.1016/j.eswa.2008.06.073

Mohamed, M. A. (2021). *Enhancing the traceability of B2B logistic chains using Blockchain, IoT and Deep Learning. Software Engineering*. Institut Polytechnique de Paris.

Mohanram, P. S. (2005). Separating Winners from Losers among Low Book-to-Market Stocks using Financial Statement Analysis. *Review of Accounting Studies, 10*(2-3), 133–170. doi:10.100711142-005-1526-4

Moore, H. (2016). *Business turnaround. How to do it*. Longhirst Publishing.

Morais, B., Peydró, J. L., Roldán-Peña, J., & Ruiz-Ortega, C. (2019). The international bank lending channel of monetary policy rates and QE: Credit supply, reach-for-yield, and real effects. *The Journal of Finance, 74*(1), 55–90. doi:10.1111/jofi.12735

Morni, F., & Masih, M. (2017). *Predicting stress in the banking sector: Malaysian evidence*. MPRA Paper 108445. Retrieved from https://mpra.ub.uni-muenchen.de/id/eprint/108445

Mossman, C. E., Bell, G. G., Swartz, L. M., & Turtle, H. (1998). An empirical comparison of bankruptcy models. *The Financial Review, 33*(2), 35 – 54. doi:10.1111/j.1540-6288.1998.tb01367.x

Mous, L. (2005). *Predicting bankruptcy with discriminant analysis and decision tree using financial ratios*. University Rotterdam.

Mueen, U. (2021). Blockchain Medledger: Hyperledger fabric enabled drug traceability system for counterfeit drugs in pharmaceutical industry. *International Journal of Pharmaceutics, 597*, 120235. doi:10.1016/j.ijpharm.2021.120235 PMID:33549813

Münster, E., Rüger, H., Ochsmann, E., Letzel, S., & Toschke, A. M. (2009). Over-Indebetedness as a marker of socioeconomic status and its association with obesity: A cross- sectional study. *BMC Public Health, 9*(1), 1–6. doi:10.1186/1471-2458-9-286 PMID:19664214

Nadri, K., Ebrahimi, S., & Fadaie, A. (2018). Assessment of financial stability in the banking sector in Iran. *Journal of Monetary Economics, 13*(4), 501–523. https://www.researchgate.net/publication/345733270_Assessment_of_Financial_Stability_in_the_Banking_Sector_in_Iran

Nielsen, D. B. (2010). *Risk Management Reporting and Value Creation in Danish Companies* [Unpublished Master Thesis]. Copenhagen Business School, Finance and Accounting, Denmark.

O' Neill, B., Sorhaindo, B., Prawitz, A., Kim, J., & Garman, E. T. (2006b). Financial distress: Definition, effects and measurement. *Consumer Interest Annual, 52*. Retrieved May, 05, 2022, from https://www.consumerinterests.org/assets/docs/CIA/CIA2006/oneill_financialdistressdefinitioneffectsandmeasurement.pdf

O' Neill, B., Prawitz, A. D., Sorhaindo, B., Kim, J., & Garman, E. Thomas. (2006a). Changes in health, negative financial events, and financial distress/financial well-being for debt management program clients. *Financial Counseling and Planning, 17*(2), 46–63.

O'Neill, B., Sorhaindo, B., Xio, J. J., & Garman, E. T. (2005). Financially distressed consumers: Their financial practices, financial well-being, and health. *Financial Counseling and Planning*, *16*(1), 73–87.

Öcek, C. (2018). *Konaklama İşletmelerinde Finansal Başarısızlık Riskinin Ölçümü: Türkiye ve Avrupa'daki Halka Açık Konaklama İşletmelerinin Karşılaştırmalı Analizi*. Mersin Üniversitesi Sosyal Bilimler Enstitüsü Turizm İşletmeciliği Anabilim Dalı Yüksek Lisans Tezi.

Ochsmann, E. B., Rueger, H., Letzel, S., Drexler, H., & Muenster, E. (2009). Over ındebtedness and ıts association with the prevalence of back pain. *BMC Public Health*, *9*, 451. doi:10.1186/1471-2458-9-451

OECD and Food and Agriculture Organization of the United Nations. (2017). *OECD-FAO Agricultural Outlook 2017-2026* (OECD-FAO Agricultural Outlook). OECD. doi:10.1787/AGR_OUTLOOK-2017-EN

OECD and Food and Agriculture Organization of the United Nations. (2021). *OECD-FAO Agricultural Outlook 2021-2030* (OECD-FAO Agricultural Outlook). OECD. doi:10.1787/19428846-EN

OECD. (2020). *Tourism policy responses to the coronavirus (COVID-19)*. https://read.oecd-ilibrary.org/view/?ref=124_124984-7uf8nm95se&title=Covid-19_Tourism_Policy_Responses

Ohlson, J. A. (1980). Financial Ratios and the Probabilistic Prediction of Bankruptcy. *Journal of Accounting Research*, *18*(1), 109–131. doi:10.2307/2490395

Oksanen, A., Savolainen, L., Sirola, A., & Kaakinen, M. (2018). Problem gambling and psychological distress: A cross-national perpective on the mediating effect of consumer debt and dept problems among emerging adults. *Harm Reduction Journal*, *15*(45), 1–11. doi:10.118612954-018-0251-9

Olson, D. L., Delen, D., & Meng, Y. (2012). Comparative analysis of data minin methods for bankruptcy prediction. *Decision Support Systems*, *52*(2), 464–473. doi:10.1016/j.dss.2011.10.007

Oluwaseyi, O., Islam, A., Zukime, M., Junoh, M., Yusoff, W., & Iqbal, M. M. (2020). Revisiting the Impact of Intrinsic Financial Risks on the Firm Value of Banks in ASEAN-5 Countries: A Panel Data Approach. *Banks and Bank Systems*, *15*(2), 200–213. doi:10.21511/bbs.15(2).2020.18

Organ, İ., & Sevinç, C. (2017). Ticaret Şirketlerinde Ortakların İflas ve İflas Erteleme Döneminde Kamu Alacaklarından Sorumlulukları [Responsibilities of Partners in Trading Companies from Public Receivables during the Bankruptcy and Bankruptcy Postponement Period]. *Gümrük ve Ticaret Dergisi*, (10), 41–48.

Örki, A., Tol, M. A., & Arıkan, N. (2021). 2020 Küresel ekonomik krizi ve kendi kendine yeterli olma konusunda farklı yaklaşımlar: 2020 Ocak – 2020 Mayıs [Different approaches to the 2020 global economic crisis and self-sufficiency: January 2020 – May 2020]. *International Journal of Society Researches, 17*, 3676-3698. Doi:10.26466/opus.776585

Özbilgin, İ. G. (2012). Risk ve risk çeşitleri. *Bilişim dergisi, 145*, 86-93. http://www.bilisimdergisi.org.tr/s145/pdf/86-93.pdf

Özdemir, M. (2018). Konkordatonun muhasebe işlemlerine etkisi [The Effect of Concordat on Accounting Transactions]. *Giresun Üniversitesi İktisadi ve İdari Bilimler Dergisi*, *4*(2), 1–12.

Özden, C., & Gürgen, Y. (2008). Türkiye Ve Avrupa Birliğinde Süt Hayvancılığının Mevcut Durumu İle Avrupa Birliği Üyelik Sürecinin Polonya Hayvancılığına Olan Etkilerinin İncelenmesi [Examination of the Current Status of Dairy Livestock in Turkey and the European Union and the Effects of the European Union Membership Process on Polish Livestock]. *Çukurova Üniversitesi Fen Bilimleri Enstitüsü - Fen Ve Mühendislik Bilimleri Dergisi, 17*(8), 68–78. Retrieved from https://fbe.cu.edu.tr/storage/fbeyedek/makaleler/2008-17-8-8.pdf

Özkazanç-Pan, B., & Pullen, A. (2020). Gendered labour and work, even in pandemic times. *Gender, Work and Organization, 27*(5), 675–676. doi:10.1111/gwao.12516 PMID:32904841

Özşahin Koç, F., & Uzay, Ş. (2015). Risk Raporlaması: Gelişmiş Ülke Uygulamalarından Çıkarılacak Dersler. *Erciyes Üniversitesi İktisadi ve İdari Bilimler Fakültesi Dergisi, 0*(45), 205–230. doi:10.18070/euiibfd.74619

Park, N., Heo, W., Ruiz-Menjivar, J., & Grable, J. E. (2017). Financial hardship, social support, and perceived stress. *Financial Counseling & Planning Education, 28*(2), 322–332.

Patrica, V. (1990). Economic distress and family relations: A review of the eighties. *Journal of Marriage and the Family, 52*(4), 1099–1115.

Pehlivanlı, D. (2014). *Modern İç Denetim* [Modern Internal Auditing]. Beta Yayınları.

Pekcanıtez, H., Atalay, O., & Özekes, M. (2007). *İcra ve İflas Hukuku Temel Bilgiler* [Enforcement and Bankruptcy Law Basics]. Yetkin Yayınları.

Pekcanıtez, H., & Erdönmez, G. (2018). *7101 Sayılı Kanun Çerçevesinde Konkordato* [Concordat within the framework of Law No. 7101]. Vedat Kitapçılık.

Pekcanıtez, H., & Erdönmez, G. (2018). 7101 Sayılı Kanunla Yürürlüğe Giren Konkordato Hükümlerinin Değerlendirilmesi [Evaluation of the Concordat Provisions Enacted by Law No. 7101]. *Bankacılar Dergisi, 105*, 108–156.

Piotroski, J. D. (2000). Value Investing: The Use of Historical Financial Statement Information to Separate Winners from Losers. *Journal of Accounting Research, 38*, 1 – 41. doi:10.2307/2672906

Platt, H. D., Platt, M. B., & Pederson, J. G. (1994). Bankruptcy discrimination with real variables. *Journal of Business Finance & Accounting, 21*(4), 491 – 510. doi:10.1111/j.1468-5957.1994.tb00332.x

Platt, H. D. (1998). *Principles of corporate renewal*. The University of Michigan Press.

Poduska, B. (1992). Money, marriage and Maslow's hierarchy of needs. *The American Behavioral Scientist, 35*(6), 756–770.

Pollack, C., & Lynch, J. (2009). Helath status of people undergoing foreclosure in the Philadelphia region. *American Journal of Public Health, 99*(10), 1833–1839.

Poyraz, E., & Uçma, T. (2006). Türkiye'de Faaliyet Gösteren İhracatçı Sektörlerin Mali Kriz Ortamlarında Finansal Başarısızlıklarının Altman (Z-Score) Modeli Yardımıyla Ölçülmesi [Measurement of Financial Failures of Exporter Sectors Operating in Turkey in Financial Crisis Environments with the Help of Altman (Z-Score) Model]. *Muhasebe ve Finansman Dergisi*, (32).

Prawitz, A. D., Garman, E. T., Sorhaindo, B., O'Neill, B., Kim, J., & Drentea, P. (2006). Incharge financial distress/financial well-being scale: Development, administration, and score interpretation. *Financial Counseling and Planning, 17*(1), 34–50. doi:10.1037/t60365-000

Presidency of the Republic of Turkey. (2021). *Why Invest in Turkish Agro-food Industry?* Retrieved from https://www.invest.gov.tr/tr/library/publications/lists/investpublications/tarim-gida-sektoru-raporu.pdf

Presidency of the Republic of Türkiye. (2022). *Why Invest in Türkiye*. Retrieved from https://www.invest.gov.tr/tr/library/publications/lists/investpublications/neden-turkiyeye-yatirim-yapmali.pdf

PricewaterhouseCoopers (PWC). (2021, December). *Learning from the impacts of COVID-19 and leading the recovery.* https://www.pwc.com/gx/en/issues/crisis-solutions/covid-19.html

Puddu, S. (2013). *Optimal weights and stress banking indexes.* IRENE Working Papers 13-02. IRENE Institute of Economic Research. Retrieved from https://ideas.repec.org/p/irn/wpaper/13-02.html

Purnanandam, A. (2008). Financial Distress and Corporate Risk Management: Theory and Evidence. *Journal of Financial Economics, 87*(3), 706–739. doi:10.1016/j.jfineco.2007.04.003

Rahman, M., Sa, C. L., & Kaium Masud, M. (2021). Predicting Firms' Financial Distress: An Empirical Analysis Using The F-Score Model. *Journal of Risk and Financial Management, 14*(5), 199. doi:10.3390/jrfm14050199

Ramalingam, B., & Prabhu, J. (2020). Innovation, development and COVID-19: Challenges, opportunities and ways forward. *OECD Tackling Coronavirus (COVID-19): Contributing to a Global Effort*, 1-14.

Ramvilas, G., Dhyani, S., Kumar, B., Sinha, N., Raghavan, R., Selvaraj, G., Divakar, N., Anoop, V. K., Shalu, K., Sinha, A., Kulkarni, A., Das, S., & Molur, S. (2021). Insights on COVID-19 impacts, challenges and opportunities for India's biodiversity research: From complexity to building adaptations. *Biological Conservation, 255*, 109003. doi:10.1016/j.biocon.2021.109003 PMID:35125501

Rantakeisu, U., Starrin, B., & Hagquist, C. (1999). Financial hardship and shame: A tentative model to understand the social and health effects of unemployment. *British Journal of Social Work, 29*(6), 877–901.

Reading, R., & Reynolds, S. (2001). Debt, social disadvantage and maternal depression. *Social Science & Medicine, 53*(4), 441–453. doi:10.1016/S0277-9536(00)00347-6

Redıng, K. F., Sobel, P. J., Anderson, U. L., Head, M. J., Ramamoortı, S., Salamasıck, M., & Rıddle, C. (2009). *Internal Auditing: Assurance & Consulting Services* (2nd ed.). The Institute of Internal Auditors Research Foundation.

Restubog, S. L. D., Ocampo, A. C. G., & Wang, L. (2020). Taking control amidst the chaos: Emotion regulation during the COVID-19 pandemic. *Journal of Vocational Behavior, 119*, 103440. doi:10.1016/j.jvb.2020.103440 PMID:32390659

Rezaee, Z. (2005). Causes, consequences, and deterence of financial statement fraud. *Critical Perspectives on Accounting, 16*(3), 277–298. doi:10.1016/S1045-2354(03)00072-8

Roodman, D. (2009). How to do xtabond2: An introduction to difference and system GMM in Stata. *The Stata Journal, 9*(1), 86–136. doi:10.1177/1536867X0900900106

Ross, S. & Westerfield, R. & Jaffe, J. (1999). *Corporate finance.* Irwin.

Ross, S. A., Westerfield, R. W., & Jaffe, J. (2002). *Corporate Finance.* McGraw Hill Irwin.

Roux-Dufort, C. (2003). *Gérer et decider en situation de crise* [Manage and decide in crisis situations]. Dunod.

Rowe, W. D. (1977). *An Anatomy of Risk.* John Wiley.

Rudolph, C. W., & Zacher, H. (2020). COVID-19 and careers: On the futility of generational explanations. *Journal of Vocational Behavior, 119*, 103433. doi:10.1016/j.jvb.2020.103433 PMID:32390654

Ryan, C. (2012). *Responses to financial stress at life transition points.* FaHCSIA Occasional Paper No. 41. doi:10.2139/ssrn.2230176

Saedi, A. & Timimi, B. S. A. (2018). The Relationship Between Financial Failure and Market Value: An Empirical Study Using A Sample of Industrial Firms Listed At Qatar Stock Exchange. *Academy of Accounting and Financial Studies Journal, 22*(5), 1-10.

Sagner, J. (2002). *The Real World of Finance*. John Wiley and Sons.

Saleh, Y. D. (2016). *Crisis management*. Mill City Press.

Salignac, F., Marjolin, A., Reeve, R., & Muir, K. (2019). Conceptualizing and measuring financial resilience: A multi-mensional framework. *Social Indicators Research, 145*(1), 17–38.

Sanchez, A., Sparreboom, P., & Laufer, H. (2021). *Building financial resilience: How financial service providers can help low-ıncome customers to manage risk*. Oxford Policy Management. Retrieved May, 05, 2022, from https://www.opml.co.uk/files/Publications/a0600-savings-at-the-frontier/satf-building-financial-resilience.pdf?noredirect=1

Şanlı, O. (2021). Türkiye'de 1994, 2001 ve 2018-2021 kur krizlerinin yeni nesil kriz teorileri çerçevesinde incelenmesi [Investigation of the 1994, 2001 and 2018-2021 currency crises in Turkey within the framework of new generation crisis theories]. Aydın Faculty of Economics Journal, 6(2), 117-158. Doi:10.53839/aifd.988000

Sari, K. R., Martini, R., Almira, N., Hartati, S., & Husin, F. (2022). Prediction of Bankruptcy Risk Using Financial Distress Analysis. *Golden Ratio of Finance Management, 2*(2), 77–86. doi:10.52970/grfm.v2i2.127

Sarıkale, H., & İlter, B. (2018). Finansal Analiz Sürecindeki Temel Mali Tablo Düzeltmelerinin Oran Analizine Etkisi [The Effect of Key Financial Statement Adjustments in the Financial Analysis Process on Ratio Analysis]. *Afyon Kocatepe Üniversitesi Sosyal Bilimler Dergisi, 20*(1), 165–184.

Saueressig, T. (2021, March 29). The Co-Existence of Challenge and Opportunity for Businesses. *SAP News*. https://news.sap.com/2021/03/co-existence-businesses-challenges-and-opportunities/

Sayılgan, G. (1995). *Finansal risk yönetimi* [Financial risk management]. Ankara Üniversitesi SBF Dergisi.

Scholes, M. S. (2000). Crisis and Risk Management. *The American Economic Review, 90*(2), 17–21. doi:10.1257/aer.90.2.17

Seagon, C. (2004). Grundlagen der insolvenzordnung [Fundamentals of the Insolvency Code]. In A. K. Buth & M. Hermanns (Eds.), *Restrukturierung, sanierung, insolvenz*. Verlag C. H. Beck.

Seidl, A., & Voss, T. (2006). *Die zweite Chance* [The second chance]. Campus Verlag.

Selimoğlu, S., & Orhan, A. (2015). Finansal Başarısızlığın Oran Analizi Ve Diskriminant Analizi Kullanılarak Ölçümlenmesi: BİST'de İşlem Gören Dokuma, Giyim Eşyası Ve Deri İşletmeleri Üzerine Bir Araştırma [Measuring Financial Failure Using Ratio Analysis and Discriminant Analysis: A Study on Weaving, Apparel and Leather Enterprises Traded at BIST]. *Muhasebe ve Finansman Dergisi*, (66), 21–40. doi:10.25095/mufad.396529

Selinšek, L. (2006). Insolvenčna kazniva dejanja. [Insolvency offences]. *Revizor*, (2), 56–68.

Şen, A. F., & Taşdelen, H. (2019). Haberde söylem üretimi: 2018 döviz kuru krizinin haber medyasındaki yansımaları [Discourse production in the news: The reflections of the 2018 exchange rate crisis in the news media]. *Akdeniz Üniversitesi İletişim Fakültesi Dergisi,* (31), 254-275. Doi:10.31123/akil.532292

Sendur, Y., & Doğukanlı, H. (2019). *The Effect of Corporate Governance on Dividend Policy: Theories and Literature*. Gazi Publishing.

Şenol, Z., & Karaca, S. S. (2017). Finansal Risklerin Firma Değeri Üzerine Etkisi: BİST Örneği. *Gazi İktisat ve İşletme Dergisi*, *3*(1), 1–18.

Şenyüz, D., Yüce, M., & Gercek, A. (2019a). *Tax Law (General Provisions)* (10th ed.). Ekin Publishing Distribution.

Şenyüz, D., Yüce, M., & Gercek, A. (2019b). *Turkish Tax System* (16th ed.). Ekin Publishing Distribution.

Sewpersadh, N. S. (2020). K-score categorization of JSE listed sectors under the financial distress continuum theory. *Cogent Economics & Finance*, *8*(1748969), 1–16.

Sezer, S. (2011*). Ticari başarısızlık sonucu ortaya çıkan intihar ve intihar girişimi olaylarının sosyo - ekonomik nedenleri* [Unpublished doctoral thesis]. İstanbul Üniversitesi Sosyal Bilimler Enstitüsü Sosyoloji Anabilim Dalı, İstanbul, Turkey.

Shi, Y. & Li, X. (2019). 1354 An overview of bankruptcy prediction models for corporate firms: A systematic literature review. *Intangible Capital, 15*(2), 114-127.

Shin, K. S., Lee, T. S., & Kim, H. J. (2005). An application of support vector machines in bankruptcy prediction model. *Expert Systems with Applications*, *28*(1), 127–135. doi:10.1016/j.eswa.2004.08.009

Shumway, T. (2001). Forecasting Bankruptcy More Accurately: A Simple Hazard Model. *The Journal of Business, 74*(1), 101 – 124. doi:10.1086/209665

Sloan, R. G. (1996). Do Stock Prices Fully Reflect Information in Accruals and Cash Flows About Future Earnings? *The Accounting Review, 71*(3), 289 – 315.

Smithson, H. (2016). Role of insolvency practitioners in restructuring and bankruptcy in the UK. In T. M. Hajjiri & A. Cohen (Eds.), *Global insolvency and bankruptcy practice for sustainable economic development* (Vol. 2). Palgrave Macmillan. doi:10.1007/978-1-137-56175-6_2

Society of Practitioners of Insolvency. (1996). *Company insolvency in the United Kingdom*. Jardine Insolvency Insurance.

So, J. C. (1994). The Distribution of Financial Ratios – A Note. *Journal of Accounting, Auditing & Finance*, *9*(2), 215–223. doi:10.1177/0148558X9400900205

Sönmez, F. (2015). Kredi skorunun belirlenmesinde yapay sinir ağları ve karar ağaçlarının kullanımı bir model önerisi [The use of artificial neural networks and decision trees to determine the credit score is a model proposal]. *Anadolu Bil Meslek Yüksekokulu Dergisi*, *37*, 1–22.

Sorgun, C. & Türk, M. (2008). Aile Şirketlerinde Yönetim Sorunları: Adana İlinde Bir Araştırma [Management Problems in Family Companies: A Study in Adana Province]. *Çukurova Üniversitesi İktisadi ve İdari Bilimler Fakültesi Dergisi, 12*(1), 56-72.

Sözcü. (2020). *2019 yılında 900'e yakın şirket konkordato ilan etti!* [In 2019, nearly 900 companies declared concordats!]. Retrieved from https://www.sozcu.com.tr/2020/ekonomi/2019-yilinda-900e-yakin-sirket-konkordato-ilan-etti-5578534/

Spurk, D., & Straub, C. (2020). Flexible employment relationships and careers in times of the COVID-19 pandemic. *Journal of Vocational Behavior*, *119*, 103435. doi:10.1016/j.jvb.2020.103435 PMID:32382161

Sturgeon, J. A., Arewasikporn, A., Okun, M. A., Davis, M. C., Ong, A. D., & Zautra, A. J. (2016). The psychological context of financial stress: Implications for ınflammation and *psychological health. Psychosomatic Medicine*, *78*(2), 134–143.

Sun, L. (2007). A Re-Evaluation of Auditors' Opinions Versus Statistical Models in Bankruptcy Prediction. *Review of Quantitative Finance and Accounting*, (28), 55–78.

Tanriver, S. (1993). *Trustee in composition.* Yetkin Publishing House.

Tapiero, C. (2004). *Risk and financial management: Mathematical and computational methods.* John Wiley & Sons. doi:10.1002/0470020369

Taylor, M. (2011). Measuring financial capability and ıts determinants using survey data. *Social Indicators Research, 102*, 297–314. doi:10.100711205-010-9681-9

TCMB. (2022). *Oran Formülleri.* Retrieved June 9, 2022, from https://www3.tcmb.gov.tr/sektor/dosyalar/menu/ratios_tr.pdf

Tedeshi, R. G., & Calhoun, L. G. (2004). Posttraumatic growth: Conceptual foundations and emprical evidence. *Psychological Inquiry, 15*, 1–18.

Tekin, B. (2021). Finansal Başarısızlık Ve Hisse Senedi Fiyatı İlişkisi: Xutek Endeksinde Panel Eşbütünleşme Ve Nedensellik Analizleri [The Relationship Between Financial Failure and Stock Price: Panel Cointegration and Causality Analysis in Xutek Index]. *Finans Ekonomi ve Sosyal Araştırmalar Dergisi, 6*(4), 780–790.

The Economist. (2002, March 23). Fear of failure. *The Economist,* 15.

The Economist. (2009, January 3). European bankruptcy law. *The Economist,* 45-46.

The World Bank. (2020, June). *The Global Economic Outlook During the COVID-19 Pandemic: A Changed World.* https://www.worldbank.org/en/news/feature/2020/06/08/the-global-economic-outlook-during-the-covid-19-pandemic-a-changed-world

Thornhill, S., & Amit, R. (2003). Bankruptcy, firm age, and the resource-based view. *Organization Science, 14*(5), 497–509. doi:10.1287/orsc.14.5.497.16761

Tinoco, M. H., & Wilson, N. (2013). Financial Distress and Bankruptcy Prediction among Listed Companies Using Accounting, Market and Macroeconomic Variables. *International Review of Financial Analysis, 30*, 394–419. doi:10.1016/j.irfa.2013.02.013

TOBB. (2013). *Türkiye Tarım Sektörü Raporu* [Turkey Agricultural Sector Report]. TOBB.

Toda, H. Y., & Yamamoto, T. (1995). Statistical Inference in Vector Autoregressions with Possibly Integrated Processes. *Journal of Econometrics, 66*(1-2), 225–250. doi:10.1016/0304-4076(94)01616-8

Tong, Y. (2021). Predicting Predictions of failure and financial distress: A study on Portuguese high and medium-high technology small and midsized enterprise. Foundation of International Studies, 9.

Topaloğlu, E. E. (2018). Finansal Riskler ile Firma Değeri Arasındaki İlişkinin Belirlenmesi: Borsa İstanbul Firmaları Üzerine Bir Uygulama. *Mehmet Akif Ersoy Üniversitesi İktisadi ve İdari Bilimler Fakültesi Dergisi, 5*(2), 288–301.

Toroslu, M. V. (2019). *Hukuksal ve Finansal Açıdan Konkordato* [Concordat from a Legal and Financial Perspective]. Adalet Yayınevi.

Tsai, C. F., Hsu, Y. F., & Yen, D. C. (2014). A comparative study of classifier ensembles for bankruptcy prediction. *Applied Soft Computing, 24*, 977–984. doi:10.1016/j.asoc.2014.08.047

Tsukuda, J., & Baba, S. (1994). Predicting Japanese corporate bankruptcy in terms of financial data using neural network. *Computers & Industrial Engineering, 27*(1 – 4), 445 – 448. doi:10.1016/0360-8352(94)90330-1

Tsuruta, D., Marea, C., & Xu, P. (2007). *Debt Structure and Bankruptcy of Financially Distressed Small Businesses.* RIETI Discussion Paper Series (No:07-E -032 pp.1).

Tunçsiper, B., & Köroğlu, Ö. (2006). Enflasyonun Otomotiv Sektöründeki İşletmeler Üzerindeki Etkisi: Balıkesir İli Örneği [The Impact of Inflation on Enterprises in the Automotive Sector: The Case of Balıkesir Province]. *Balıkesir Üniversitesi Sosyal Bilimler Enstitüsü Dergisi*, *9*(15), 43–65.

Turaboğlu, T. T., & Timur, E. (2018). İşletmelerde Kârlılığı Etkileyen Faktörler: BİST Kurumsal Yönetim Endeksindeki Firmalara İlişkin Bir Uygulama [Factors Affecting Profitability in Enterprises: An Application for Companies in the BIST Corporate Governance Index]. *Bulletin of Economic Theory and Analysis*, *3*(2), 135–157.

Turunen, E., & Hiilamo, H. (2014). Health effects of ındebtedness: A systematic review. *BMC Public Health*, *14*(1), 489. doi:10.1186/1471-2458-14-489

Uğur, S. (2011). *Finansal Risk Yönetiminin Firma Değeri Üzerine Etkileri (Yayımlanmış Doktora Tezi)*. İstanbul Üniversitesi Sosyal Bilimler Enstitüsü.

United Nations. (2022, January). *COVID-19 variants, rising debt, threaten global economic growth: World Bank*. https://news.un.org/en/story/2022/01/1109702

Ural, K. (2020). *İflas Tahmin Yöntemlerinin Karşılaştırılması: Borsa İstanbul Üretim Şirketlerinde Uygulama*. Yaşar Üniversitesi Sosyal Bilimler Enstitüsü İşletme Anabilim Dalı Doktora Tezi.

Uyar, T. (2018). Yeni Konkordato Hukukumuzun Temel İlkeleri [Basic Principles of Our New Concordat Law]. *İstanbul Barosu Dergisi*. 4,15-102.

Uyar, T. (2019). *Yeni Konkordato Hukukumuzun Temel İlkeleri* [Basic Principles of Our New Concordat Law]. Türkiye Barolar Birliği Yayınları.

Uzay, Ş. (2017). *Bağımsız Denetimin İşletmenin Sürekliliğine Katkısı, Kamu Gözetimi Kurumu, Muhasebe ve Denetim Sempozyumu* [The Contribution of Independent Auditing to the Continuity of the Enterprise, Public Oversight Authority, Accounting and Auditing Symposium]. İktisadi Gelişmede Muhasebe ve Denetimin Önemi, İstanbul, Turkey.

Uzay, Ş. (2019). İflasın Ertelenmesi Kurumunun Türkiye Uygulamasının Değerlendirilmesi [Evaluation of the Turkish Practice of the Bankruptcy Postponement Institution]. *Uluslararası İktisadi ve İdari İncelemeler Dergisi*, *23*, 169–178.

Uzel, Ö. (2018). *İflas ertelemenin yürürlükten kaldırılması ve konkordato süreci*. http://www.uzeldanismanlik.com/iflas-ertelemenin-yururlukten-kaldirilmasi-ve-konkordato-sureci/

Uzun, E. (2005). İşletmelerde Finansal Başarısızlığın Teorik Olarak İrdelenmesi [Theoretical Investigation of Financial Failure in Business]. *Muhasebe ve Finansman Dergisi*, (27), 158–168.

Uzun, E. (2005). İşletmelerde finansal başarısızlığın teorik olarak irdelenmesi. *Muhasebe ve Finansman Dergisi*, (27), 158–168.

Van, M.V.,, & Şehribanoğlu, S. (2021). Analysis of Factors Which Affect Financial Failure and Bankruptcy with Generalized Ordered Logit Model. *International Journal of Management Economics and Business*, *17*(1), 63. doi:10.17130/ijmeb.803957

Virgós, M., & Garcimartín, F. (2004). *The European insolvency regulation: law and practice*. Kluwer Law International.

Viseu, J., Leal, R., Neves de Jesus, S., Pinto, P., Pechorro, P., & Greenglass, E. (2018). Relationship between economic stress factors and stress, anxiety, and depression: Moderating role of social supoort. *Psychiatry Research*, *268*, 102–107. doi:10.1016/j.psychres.2018.07.008

Vovchenko, N. G., Andreeva, A. V., Orobinskiy, A. S., & Filippov, Y. M. (2017). Competitive Advantages of Financial Transactions on the Basis of the Blockchain Technology in Digital Economy. *European Research Studies*, *20*(3B), 193–212.

Waldron, J. (2020, November 4). Challenges and Opportunities for Startups in the Time of COVID-19. *metasfresh*. https://metasfresh.com/en/2020/11/04/challenges-and-opportunities-for-startups-in-the-time-of-covid-19/

Walker, M. C., Stowe, J. D., & Moriarty, S. (1979). Decomposition analysis of financial statements. *Journal of Business Finance & Accounting, 6*(2), 173 – 186. doi:10.1111/j.1468-5957.1979.tb01082.x

Walker, E. W., & Baughn, W. H. (1961). *Financial Planning and Policy*. Harper-Row.

Walker, P. L., Shenkir, W. G., & Barton, T. L. (2002). *Enterprise Risk Management: Pulling it all Together*. The Institute of Internal Auditors Research Foundation.

Wang, J., Yang, J., Iverson, B., & Kluende, R. (2020). *Bankruptcy and the COVID-19*. Harvard Business School. (Working Paper 21-041)

Wang, L., Zhang, S., Tsai, C., & He, G. (2011). Financial Failure Analysis Based on Both Financial and Non-financial Indicators with Financial Materilas. *Applied Mechanics and Materials*, *63-64*, 1009–1012. doi:10.4028/www.scientific.net/AMM.63-64.1009

Warth, J., Beckmann, N., Puth, M. T., Tillmann, J., Porz, J., Zier, U., Weckbecker, K., Weltermann, B., & Münster, E. (2020). Association between over-ındebtedness and antidepressant use: Across-sectional analysis. *Plos One. Public Library of Science*, *15*(7), 1–11.

Watts, R. L. (1977). Corporate Financial Statements: A Product of the Market and Political Processes. *Australian Journal of Management*, *2*(1), 53–75. doi:10.1177/031289627700200104

Wen, Q., Gao, Y., Chen, Z., & Wu, D. (2019). A Blockchain-based data sharing scheme in the supply chain by iiot. *2019 IEEE International Conference on Industrial Cyber Physical Systems (ICPS 2019)*, 695–700. doi: 10.1109/ICPHYS.2019.8780161

Westerkamp, M., Victor, F., & Küpper, A. (2018). Blockchain-based supply chain traceability: Token recipes model manufacturing processes. *2018 IEEE International Conference on Internet of Things (iThings) and IEEE Green Computing and Communications (GreenCom) and IEEE Cyber, Physical and Social Computing (CPSCom) and IEEE Smart Data (SmartData)*, 1595–1602.

White, M. J. (2020). The treatment of secured credit in bankruptcy: A unified model. In B. E. Adler (Ed.), *Research handbook on corporate bankruptcy law* (pp. 210–236). Edward Elgar. doi:10.4337/9781781007884.00017

Whiting, D. G., Hansen, J. V., Mcdonald, J. B., Albrecht, C., Steve, W., & Albrecht, W. S. (2012). Machıne Learnıng Methods For Detectıng Patterns Of Management Fraud. *Computational Intelligence*, *28*(4), 505–527. doi:10.1111/j.1467-8640.2012.00425.x

Whittington, G. (1980). Some basic properties of accounting ratios. *Journal of Business Finance & Accounting, 7*(2), 219 – 231. doi:10.1111/j.1468-5957.1980.tb00738.x

Widome, R., Joseph, A. M., Hammett, P., Ryn, M. V., Nelson, D. B., Nyman, J. A., & Fu, S. S. (2015). Associations between smoking behaviors and financial stress among low-ıncome smokers. *Preventive Medicine Reports*, *2*, 911–915. doi:10.1016/j.pmedr.2015.10.011

Wieczorek-Kosmala, M., Błach, J., & Trzesiok, J. (2018). Analysis of Bankruptcy Threat for Risk Management Purposes: A Model Approach. *International Journal of Financial Studies*, *6*(98), 1–17. doi:10.3390/ijfs6040098

Wood, P. R. (2013). Principles of international insolvency. In I. F. Fletcher (Ed.), *A special collection celebrating 21 years.* INSOL International & John Wiley & Sons. https://thismatter.com/money/credit/bankruptcy/chapter-conversion.htm

Worthington, A.C. (2006). Debt as a source of financial stress in Australian households. *International Journal of Consumer Studies*, *30*(1), 2-15. Doi: .1470-6431.2005.00420.x doi:10.1111/j

Wrosch, C., Heckhausen, J., & Lachman, M. E. (2000). Primary and secondary control strategies for managing health and financial stress across adulthood. *Psychology and Aging*, *15*(3), 387–399.

Wuth, A., & Cismaru, M. (2021). A conceptual and operational review of the negative financial health terminology and constructs. *International Business Research*, *14*(4), 1–16.

XBRL International. (2022). *An Introduction to XBRL.* Retrieved May 29, 2022, from https://www.xbrl.org/the-standard/what/an-introduction-to-xbrl/

Yakymchuk, I. P., Olkhovetskyi, S. M., Beyz, A. M., & Martseniuk, M. O. (2021). Experiencing and overcoming financial stress in married couples: A study in covıd 19 pandemic era. *Amazonia Investiga*, *10*(42), 124–140. doi:10.34069/AI/2021.42.06.12

Yarız, A. (2012). *Bankacılıkta Risk Yönetimi Risk Matrisi Uygulaması* [Risk Management Risk Matrix Application in Banking]. Nobel Akademik Yayıncılık.

Yavuz, M. (2018). Konkordato Talebi Üzerine Mahkemece Verilen Mühlet Kararlarının Amme Alacaklarına Etkisi [The Effect of the Decision of the Court on the Concordat Request on Public Claims]. *Vergi Sorunları Dergisi*, (362), 92–98.

Yavuz, M. (2019). Son Düzenlemeler Işığında Konkordato Talep Eden Şirketlerce Mahkemeye Sunulması Gereken Belgeler [Documents to be Submitted to the Court by Companies Requesting Concordat in the Light of Recent Regulations]. *Mali Çözüm.*, *153*, 239–248.

Yenilmez, F., & Erdem, M. S. (2018). Türkiye ve Avrupa Birliği'nde Ekonomik Büyüme İle Enerji Tüketimi Arasındaki İlişki: Toda-Yamamoto Nedensellik Testi [The Relationship Between Economic Growth and Energy Consumption in Turkey and the European Union: Toda-Yamamoto Causality Test]. *Eskişehir Osmangazi Üniversitesi Sosyal Bilimler Dergisi*, *19*(1), 71–95. doi:10.17494/ogusbd.457078

Yenisu, E. (2019). Finansal Tabloların Oran Analizi İle İncelenmesi: ADESE Örneği [Finansal Tabloların Oran Analizi İle İncelenmesi: ADESE Örneği]. *Aksaray Üniversitesi Sosyal Bilimler Enstitüsü Dergisi, 3*(1), 19–45. doi:10.38122/ased.537634

Yıldız, B., & Demireli, E. (2019). Nakit Yönetimini Etkileyen Değişkenler Üzerine BİST Perakende Sektöründe Panel Veri Analizi [Panel Data Analysis in BIST Retail Sector on Variables Affecting Cash Management]. *Hitit Üniversitesi Sosyal Bilimler Enstitüsü Dergisi*, *12*(2), 416–429. doi:10.17218/hititsosbil.589396

Yokuş, T., & Ay, A. (2020). Kur krizleri ve Türkiye: 2006-2018 dönemi [Exchange Crises and Turkey: 2006-2018 period]. *Journal of Management and Economies Research*, *18*(1), 295–316. doi:10.11611/yead.608003

Yong, J. (2020). An intelligent Blockchain-based,system for safe vaccine supply and supervision. *International Journal of Information Management*, 52.

Yousaf, M., & Bris, P. (2021). Assessment of bankruptcy risks in Czech companies using regression analysis. *Problems and Perspectives in Management*, *19*(3), 45–53. doi:10.21511/ppm.19(3).2021.05

Yürük, M. F., & Ekşi, İ. H. (2019). Yapay Zekâ Yöntemleri ile İşletmelerin Finansal Başarısızlığının Tahmin Edilmesi: BIST İmalat Sektörü Uygulaması [Estimating the Financial Failure of Enterprises with Artificial Intelligence Methods: BIST Manufacturing Sector Application]. *Mukaddime*, *10*(1), 393–422.

Zacher, H., & Rudolph, C. W. (2021). Individual differences and changes in subjective wellbeing during the early stages of the COVID-19 pandemic. *The American Psychologist*, *76*(1), 50–62. doi:10.1037/amp0000702 PMID:32700938

Zhang, X., Sun, P., Xu, J., Wang, X., Yu, J., Zhao, Z., & Dong, Y. (2020). Blockchain-Based Safety Management System for the Grain Supply Chain. *IEEE Access: Practical Innovations, Open Solutions*, *8*, 36398–36410.

Zhou, L. (2013). Performance of corporate bankruptcy prediction models on imbalanced dataset: The effect of sampling methods. *Knowledge-Based Systems*, *41*, 16–25. doi:10.1016/j.knosys.2012.12.007

About the Contributors

Fahri Özsungur graduated from Ataturk University Faculty of Law, Çağ University Department of Private Law- Master of Laws- LL.M., Hacettepe University Department of Family and Consumer Sciences PhD., Aksaray University Department of Business Ph.D., Anadolu University Department of Private Law- Doctor of Law (student). He serves as a Higher Degrees by Research (HDR) Examiner /Ph.D. Examiner for the University of New England. He is a Eurostars Technical Expert (EUREKA Secretariat). He is the head of the Department of Social Work and Counseling of Mersin University Vocational School of Social Sciences. He is affiliated with Adana Science and Technology University, Rotary International, Osmaniye Korkut Ata University, Çağ University, WEGATE- European Gateway for Women's Entrepreneurship, and Canadian Institute for International Law Expertise (CIFILE). He has more than 120 works (Books, chapters, articles, etc.). He is the editor of 24 Journals (2 SSCI/SCI/SCI-Expanded), and the reviewer of 450 Journals (15 SSCI/SCI/SCI-Expanded,40 ESCI).

* * *

Pınar Avcı is a lecturer at School of Marmara Ereglisi Vocational in Tekirdag Namik Kemal University, Tekirdag, Turkey. She teaches capital market, firm value, financial management and accounting and finance. She received the B.S. degree in Business Trakya University, 2007, M.S. degree in Business, Trakya University, 2012, and PhD degree in Accounting- Finance, Gazi University, 2019. She has 12 years of teaching experience at university level. Her main research interests are financial market and institutions, capital market, firm value, financial management, financial economics and panel data.

Abdullah Cevdet Bayhan graduated from Bilkent University, Business Administration Department. He received his master's degree from Galatasaray University and his PhD degree from Marmara University. He is working in Borsa İstanbul. He has experience over 14 years in capital markets.

Sihan Chen is an independent researcher. Her research interests include Chinese economy, FinTech and supply chain management.

Jeya Mala D. has a Ph.D. in Software Engineering with Specialization on Software Testing and is Senior Associate Professor in School of Computer Science and Engineering (SCOPE), VIT - Chennai. She had been in the industry for about 4 years. She has a profound teaching and research experience of more than 24 years. Her research interests include Artificial Intelligence, Software Engineering, Cloud Security and Blockchain. She has published a book on "Object Oriented Analysis and Design using

UML" for Tata McGraw Hill Publishers and also published 2 edited books for IGI Global, USA and 1 course book. She has published more than 60 papers in SCI, SCIE and Scopus indexed journals and conference. As a researcher, she has completed a sponsored research project funded by UGC under Major Research Project scheme. Her dissertation has been listed as one of the best Ph.D. thesis in the CSIR – Indian Science Abstracts. She is a life member of Computer Society of India and an invited member of ACEEE. She forms the reviewer board in Journals like IEEE Transactions on Software Engineering, Elsevier – Information Sciences, Springer, World Scientific, International Journal of Metaheuristics, etc.

Gizay Daver has successfully defended his doctoral thesis entitled "Turkish Banking Sector Performance Analysis After the 2001 Crisis" and has earned the right to use the title of Doctor in Banking and Finance. He is actively involved in various institutions and organizations such as the Ministry of Justice, the Expertise Department, and the Banks Association of Turkey. He works towards establishing a healthier and more transparent financial system, and participates in various volunteer activities to prepare future generations for their careers in finance and banking. He is a member of the Global Association of Risk Professionals and holds Capital Markets Board of Turkey's licenses for derivative instruments and level 3 capital market activities. With over ten years of teaching experience, he is a highly qualified educator in the field. In 2022, he began studying computer programming at Istanbul University, Turkey, as he believes that the future of finance lies in the digital realm.

Drago Dubrovski took his doctorate degree in Economics, from the Business Faculty in Maribor (Slovenia), field International Business. He is a part-time Associate Professor at International School for Social and Business Studies Celje and managing director in a private management consulting company, which focuses on restructuring projects and crisis management. He worked also as sales manager in international industrial company and was also a crisis manager in several Slovenian companies. He is verified expert of Slovene Economists' Association and judicial expert; he is a member of several Supervisory Boards and has a licence for managing insolvency proceedings. His research interests are in crisis management and corporate renewal, strategic alliances, mergers and acquisitions, and international business. He gives regular lectures at several Slovene faculties. He is author of 8 books and 80 articles from the above-mentioned fields.

Cihan KAYACIK was born in 1992 in Zonguldak, Türkiye. He is an Lecturer at Zonguldak Bülent Ecevit University. He graduated from Çanakkale Onsekiz Mart University, Department of Finance. He completed his master's degree in finance from Zonguldak Bülent Ecevit University. He has researches in public finance.

Bilgehan Kübilay completed her undergraduate education at Karadeniz Technical University, Faculty of Economics and Administrative Sciences, Department of Labor Economics and Industrial Relations, her master's degree in Business Administration at Zonguldak Bülent Ecevit University, and her doctorate at Muğla Sıtkı Koçman University, Department of Business Administration. She has CMB Derivatives and CMB Advanced Licenses. She received Human Resources certificate from Middle East Technical University. She has private sector experience in the Financial Market. She has a book called Finansta Psikosoyal Boyut: Yatırım Psikolojisi ve Sosyolojik Faktörler Üzerine Bir İnceleme. (Psychosocial Dimension in Finance: A Study on Investment Psychology and Sociological Factors). She works mainly in Behavioral Finance. She still works as the Deputy Director of the Bulent Ecevit University School of Applied Sciences and continues her academic studies.

Priya N. is currently working in Jain University, Bangalore, Karnataka and completed her undergraduate in Mepcoschlenk Engineering College, Madurai Kamaraj University and did master degree in Kalasalingam University, Tamil Nadu. She is currently pursuing her Ph.D in Bharath Institute of Higher Education and Research, Chennai, Tamilnadu, India. She has about 9 years of teaching experience Her area of interest are cloud computing, big data analytics, network security and blockchain. She published research papers on blockchain and cyber security domain.

Emrah ÖGET was burn in 1990 in Kastamonu, Türkiye. He is an Lecturer Dr. at Zonguldak Bülent Ecevit University. He completed his undergraduate, graduate and doctoral studies in the field of business administration at Bolu Abant İzzet Baysal University. He has researches in finance.

Ramalakshmi Prabha is a research scholar and is doing her research works in Software Project Management, Software Testing, AI and data analytics.

Debasish Roy is currently a PhD Research Scholar in Marketing Management at Sikkim University, Gangtok, India with backgrounds in Postgraduate Diploma in Transportation and Logistics Management from Indian Institute of Social Welfare and Business Management (IISWBM) - India's one of the premier Business Schools, and Bachelor of Science (Honors) in Economics from University of Calcutta. His works in the fields of Business and Economics had been published in different international journals and reference books.

Yeşim Şendur graduated from the Department of Business, Faculty of Economics and Administrative Sciences, Anadolu University in 2005. In 2019, she completed her Ph.D. in the field of Finance by submitting the thesis entitled "The Effect of Corporate Governance on Dividend Policy: An Empirical Analysis at BIST" to the Department of Business, Graduate School of Social Sciences, Çukurova University. She still works as an assistant professor at International Trade and Business Department, İzmir Katip Çelebi University. She is interested in subjects including forex markets, theory of corporate governance, dividend policy, digitalization in finance, and crowdfunding.

Sevgi Sümerli Sarıgül was born in 1977 in Kayseri. She is an assistant professor at Kayseri University Technical Sciences of Vocational School. Dr. Sümerli Sarıgül completed her university education in Kayseri, Erciyes University, Faculty of Economics and Administrative Sciences, Department of Business Administration and completed master's degree in Gazi University foreign trade program and doctorate in Erciyes University Social Sciences Institute Accounting and Finance Department. Her research interests are accounting, finance, performance, strategic management approaches, sustainable development, financial development, and foreign trade. She has publications in national and international peer-reviewed journals. She has so far published more than 40 research articles in national and international referenced publications. She took part in many organizational committees such as USVES (International Social Sciences and Educational Sciences Symposium), ISBES (International Sustainable Business and Economic Strategies Congress), and CEO (Communication, Economy, Organization and Social Sciences Congress). She received her Associate Professor degree in 2022.

Poshan (Sam) Yu is a Lecturer in Accounting and Finance in the International Cooperative Education Program of Soochow University (China). He is also an External Professor of FinTech and Finance at SKEMA Business School (China), a Visiting Professor at Krirk University (Thailand) and a Visiting Researcher at the Australian Studies Centre of Shanghai University (China). Sam leads FasterCapital (Dubai, UAE) as a Regional Partner (China) and serves as a Startup Mentor for AIC RAISE (Coimbatore, India). His research interests include financial technology, regulatory technology, public-private partnerships, mergers and acquisitions, private equity, venture capital, start-ups, intellectual property, art finance, and China's "One Belt One Road" policy.

Index

T

U

V

Z

www.ingramcontent.com/pod-product-compliance
Lightning Source LLC
LaVergne TN
LVHW060424300926
849162LV00006B/1521